THE VILLAGE EFFECT

Susan Pinker is a developmental psychologist, journalist, and author whose first book, *The Sexual Paradox*, won the American Psychological Association's most prestigious literary prize, the William James Book Award, and was published in seventeen countries. A national columnist, lecturer, and broadcaster whose work has garnered many writing awards, Pinker's ideas have been featured in *The Times*, the *Guardian*, *The Economist*, the *Globe and Mail*, the *New York Times*, *The Atlantic*, the *Financial Times*, *Der Spiegel*, and *O, The Oprah Magazine*, among other publications. She lives in Montreal.

'Good peers help make centenarians' *New York Times*

'Drawing on scores of psychological and sociological studies, Pinker suggests that living as our ancestors did, steeped in face-to-face contact and physical proximity, is the key to health, while loneliness is less an exalted existential state than a public health risk. Smart readers will take the book out to a park to enjoy in the company of others.' *Boston Globe*

'A terrific book . . . Susan Pinker makes a hardheaded case for a softhearted virtue. Read this book. Then talk about it – in person! – with a friend.' Daniel H. Pink, *New York Times* bestselling author of *Drive* and *To Sell Is Human*

'Pinker, a psychologist, and deft synthesizer of theories, anecdotes, evidence and trends, uses the relatively new field of social neuroscience and her own original research to convincingly explain why face-to-face contact is now more important than ever. Hers is not a tedious rant against Internet culture – it's a more measured look at why socia ivity can't quite satis

'For those who look forward to life with cool robots, think again. Pinker shows us that crucial personal interactions are essential to true human feelings. *The Village Effect* is brilliant and compelling.' Michael Gazzaniga, professor of psychology, director of the SAGE Center for the Study of Mind at the University of California, Santa Barbara

'Intimate, face-to-face contact with partners, family, and friends is an ancient and deep human need. How do group-living primates like us make the transition to an online world in the evolutionary blink of an eye? Can they? Pinker shows how this is happening. And – even more important – she shows us how this should happen with a valuable prescription based on the best science. Pinker writes with authority and verve, and she offers an integrated treatment of online and offline interactions. She sketches our modern digital interactions on the ancient parchment of our minds.' Nicholas Christakis, author and psychologist, Human Nature Lab, Yale University

'Susan Pinker's *The Village Effect* is a bold, intelligent foray into what social isolation does to each of us in an age of technology. She offers keen insights into how social engagement enhances romance, parenting, career, family and friendship. Most impressively, Susan Pinker explores how gender and invisible social forces play into our daily lives.' Susan Shapiro Barash, author of *The Nine Phases of Marriage* and *Toxic Friends*

From the reviews of THE SEXUAL PARADOX

'*The Sexual Paradox* has forced me to have a rethink – and a radical one at that. In her intelligent, thoughtful and profoundly important work, Pinker takes us through the facts. . . Pinker's book should mark a watershed.' Rosie Boycott, *Daily Mail*

'Susan Pinker's wide-ranging look at the nature of the sexes is a highly readable and welcome contribution to this perennial debate.' Professor Simon Baron-Cohen

'At last, common sense. . . This highly readable book on a familiar theme succeeds where others do not, with its potent combination of scientific research, interviews and astute observation. It is a large contribution to an important debate.' Tony Little, *Financial Times*

'Raises intriguing questions. . . To me, this book comes as a relief.' Camilla Cavendish, *The Times*

'Defying taboos, Pinker, a psychologist and columnist for the *Globe & Mail*, presents a compelling case for a biological explanation of why men and women make different career choices.' *Publishers Weekly*

'Fascinating, insightful and deeply captivating. Every thinking man and woman should read this book.' Louann Brizendine, M.D., author of *The Female Brain*

'Pinker crafts a biologically based and sure-to-be-controversial examination of sex differences between "fragile men" and gifted women who opt out of successful careers. A valuable demonstration of how discounting biology during the last 40 years has done a disservice, especially to men.' *Kirkus Reviews*

'In this marvelous book, Susan Pinker presents a fascinating analysis of "the gender gap," introducing a continuous flow of exciting ideas and new insights into old problems and controversies. It's a pleasure to read a book that is so informative and entertaining about a complex topic that is rarely examined, as it is here, from all points of view.' Ron Melzack, E.P. Taylor Professor Emeritus, in the Department of Psychology, McGill University

'All these many years of running a business, I thought I was an anomaly. Susan Pinker's work has grounded my intuitions in reality: a woman's success is going to knock the spiritual stuffing right out of her if she tries to come at it from traditional angles. Instead she must invent a workplace that not only provides food for the table but gives social and emotional meaning to her life. Susan Pinker helps you understand that it's not you that's crazy, it's the system.' Margot Franssen, social activist and co-founder of The Body Shop Canada

'Susan Pinker's *The Sexual Paradox* is meticulously researched, brilliantly argued and thoroughly persuasive. It moves the debate over sex differences to a new level of sophistication.' Christina Hoff Sommers, author of *Who Stole Feminism?* and *The War Against Boys*

'Presented with flair, sensitivity, and determination, Pinker's penetrating conclusions shed important new light on how gender differences affect every strata of contemporary existence.' *Booklist*

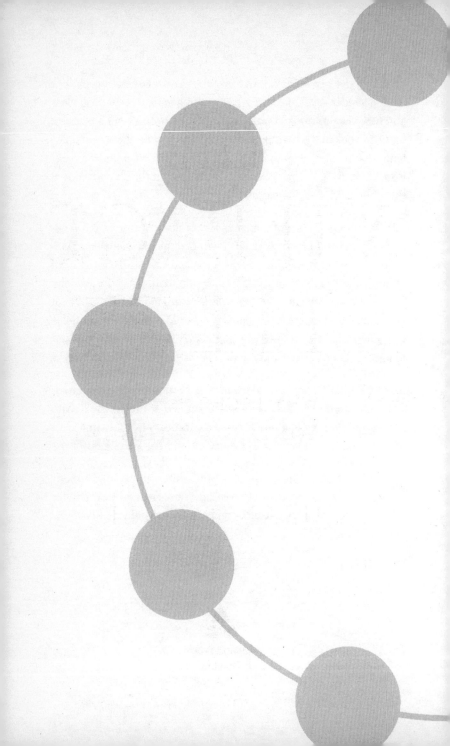

THE
VILLAGE
EFFECT

WHY FACE-TO-FACE
CONTACT MATTERS

SUSAN PINKER

Atlantic Books
London

First published in the United States in 2014 by Random House Canada, a division of Random House of Canada Limited, a Penguin Random House Company.

First published in Great Britain in 2015 by Atlantic Books, an imprint of Atlantic Books Ltd.

This paperback edition first published in Great Britain in 2015 by Atlantic Books.

10 9 8 7 6 5 4 3 2 1

A CIP catalogue record for this book is available from the British Library.

E-book ISBN: 978 1 78239 0 183
Paperback ISBN: 978 1 84887 8 594

Text design by Terri Nimmo
Printed and bound in Great Britain by Clays Ltd, St Ives plc

Atlantic Books
An Imprint of Atlantic Books Ltd
Ormond House
26–27 Boswell Street
London
WC1N 3JZ
www.atlantic-books.co.uk

To my parents,
Roslyn and Harry Pinker

You cannot live for yourselves. A thousand fibres connect you with your fellow-men; and along those fibres, as along sympathetic threads, run your actions as causes, and return to you as effects.

—REVEREND HENRY MELVILL, 1856

CONTENTS

People Who Need People

O ne June day in 2009, a rock musician named John McColgan was told that he needed a new kidney and he needed it fast. Every day in the United States, twelve people died waiting for a kidney, and when John's name was added to the kidney transplant waiting list, the list was 86,218 names long. At the time he was living in Canada, though, where the list included only 2,941 people.[1] Still, he took the news badly.

John is a drummer, an energetic, sinewy man with a smoothly shaved head. Though he had been diagnosed with progressive kidney disease when he was in his mid-twenties, he'd had few symptoms and until that moment hadn't spent much time worrying about his health. At forty-eight he was often on the basketball court with men a decade younger, and he liked nothing better than to shoot a few hoops with his seventeen-year-old son. John skateboarded around town in summer, snowboarded in winter, and did pushups and crunches every day on the floor of his living room, not to mention all the drumming, a workout in itself. Before turning thirty he had played with Linda Ronstadt and Kate and Anna McGarrigle, and a short time later he backed up Big Mama Thornton and opened for superstars such as James Brown and Stevie Ray Vaughan. Still, when money was scarce, he wasn't above digging irrigation ditches and working renovation jobs. John's gas tank was often empty, his rent overdue. But his exuberance onstage and his lightheartedness offstage gave him the eternal charm of a schoolboy; he always got by with a little help from his friends.

John was rich in one important way: he had amassed a committed circle of friends, most of whom knew each other and regularly crossed paths—a feature of the most powerful and effective social networks. A large bank balance wouldn't have helped him much in this situation in any case, as it's illegal to buy or sell organs for transplantation everywhere in the world except Iran and Singapore.[2] And in the current crisis, family couldn't help him—his father had died at fifty of polycystic kidney disease, a genetic disorder he'd passed on to John, and his mother had died a few years earlier of cancer. After months of dialysis, John realized he couldn't simply wait for his turn for a new kidney. He had to go looking for one.

By the time I met up with John less than eighteen months later, the transplant ordeal was behind him. I'd known him for at least twenty years and the change in him was stark. He seemed frail; the buzzed hair around the back of his bare skull was as short as a day's growth of beard, and his skin looked transparent in what little light filtered in through the high, grimy windows of the Montreal café where we met. He told me that four people he knew had offered to give him a kidney.

The first was his ex-wife, Amy. But her drug addiction had savaged her health along with their marriage. Though she had recently kicked the habit, her organs had paid the price. His wife's sister had also offered, but John decided that would just be too complicated. (When I asked Jessie, a mother of three small children and a professional dancer, why she would take this huge risk, she was taken aback. "Well, you know John. Everyone loves him. Why *wouldn't* I give him my kidney?")

Then a longtime friend, Kate, walked up to John at a gallery opening and blurted out that she wanted to help. She told me later that as soon as she offered her kidney, she felt scared. She then called the transplant nurse to ask what would be the worst thing that could happen if she went ahead. The nurse told her that one person in three thousand dies during the operation, and that the surgeon might accidentally knick her spleen. "Then I thought, *I'm not going to die. That's just not going to happen to me.*"

Still, the testing was grueling, and it didn't stop even after they found that her blood type and tissues were compatible with John's. "During that year I went back more than five times. I gave sixteen vials of blood. They took various cells to test my compatibility. Then they tested my health. They did ultrasounds and CAT scans. I had a mammogram, which found a cyst, so they did a biopsy. Then I did a twenty-four-hour urine test, twice."

She also underwent a long interview during which the transplant team examined her motives. "I could tell they were suspicious because I wasn't family." As powerful anti-rejection drugs had been available for a decade, it was now less important for the donor and recipient to be related. Still, medical professionals needed to know: Why on earth would someone volunteer to go through this?

It turned out that Kate was ready for the surgery before John was, so in the end the timing didn't work out; she couldn't be John's donor. The kidney John ultimately received was a gift from his longtime friend Fred, with whom he had listened to Hendrix and Zappa as a teenager, two fifteen-year-olds trying out guitar riffs in Fred's basement. Thirty years later they saw each other perhaps once or twice a year. Still, when John needed a kidney, Fred came forward.

The probability that a person not biologically related to you will offer you a kidney is very small—about three in a thousand. The chances of two people doing so are infinitesimal.[3] Then there is John, who received four serious offers. By virtue of his strong relationships, groomed over decades, John beat the odds—and the disease that had killed his father.

John's story is an unusually concrete example of how strong social bonds can prolong our lives. In the following pages I'll show how those of us who invest in meaningful personal relationships with lots of real social contact are more robust and have better physiological defenses than those who are solitary or who engage with the world largely online. Digital networks and screen media have the power to make the world seem much smaller. But when it comes to certain life-changing transformations, they're no match for face-to-face.

Face-to-face interaction does not just spur selfless acts like those of John's friends, it also affects how well we learn to read, how quickly we fight off infection, and ultimately how long we live. So how exactly does that happen?

Less than 0.01 percent of the Western world's population needs a new kidney.[4] But every one of us needs a tight knot of friends and family in our corner, and not just when the chips are down. If we don't interact regularly with people face-to-face, the odds are we won't live as long, remember information as well, or be as happy as we could have been. What do I mean by regularly? When my son was small and went to his first violin lesson, he asked his music teacher, an impish man from Belgrade, if the rumor was true: did he really have to practice every day? Crouching down to Eric's level and putting a slender hand to his chin, Dragan considered the question. "Not every day. Just every day you eat."

Social contact is like that. It's a biological drive. So I learned after spending three years delving into a fairly new field—social neuroscience. The field didn't exist when I trained as a psychologist, back when brain scans were as rare and expensive as private jets.[5] But by the early 1990s brain imaging had become more accessible, with hulking fMRI machines proliferating in windowless rooms in most large hospitals and universities. Research psychologists started to use them, along with demographic and biochemical tools, to track the science underpinning human relationships, and vice versa—to spy on the way our relationships transform our bodies, including our hormonal and neural circuits. I was hooked. In the meantime, though the social parts of our brains had become easier to observe, the meaning of the phrase *social network* had morphed. Instead of referring to all the people you know and your messy mutual relationships, it had come to mean the way our machines are connected. And I noticed a surefire reaction among those who inquired about my book: they immediately assumed that I was writing about Facebook and Twitter.

Conflating computer-driven networks with face-to-face contact reflects a social trend. Indeed, recent books on social interaction typically blend the two. Even the venerable Bureau of Labor Statistics American Time Use Survey, which tracks how many hours a day Americans spend on activities like personal care (9.6) or eating and drinking (1.2), lumps online and face-to-face activities together. It codes buying in-season cantaloupes at a farm stand and arranging for escort ser-

vices on Craigslist the same way— as shopping. Sitting alone in a room for hours losing track of time while playing a MMORPG (a massively multiplayer online role-playing game such as World of Warcraft), falls in the same category as one of my favorite childhood activities: playing gin rummy with my grandfather.[6]

My grandfather and I (age five) play cards while my grandmother looks on.

So, do we register digital simulacra the way we react to people who are right in front of us, in the here-and-now? If not, what does social neuroscience tell us we're missing? Now that Americans spend a total of 520 billion minutes a day online—and the residents of most other countries spend proportionally the same—what stories do our face-to-face relationships tell?[7]

This book is about the kind of social contact we need to thrive. While researching my previous book, *The Sexual Paradox*, I discovered that women's tendency to put a premium on their social connections is one of the main reasons they live longer. This fact prompted an *aha!* moment in me. I realized that pastimes we had long written off as frivolous time-wasters—such as chatting with friends on the porch or over a meal—serve important biological functions. That's likely why we've evolved to find them irresistible. Research shows that playing cards once a week or meeting friends every Wednesday night at Starbucks adds as many years to our lives as taking beta blockers or quitting a pack-a-day smoking habit. *How does that work?* I wondered. Whatever the secret substance or process is, learning about it felt like rubbernecking at a restaurant when the server goes by with a steaming plate of something wonderful. *I want what they're having*, I said to myself.

But what was that, exactly? To find out, I began with the question of longevity, sparked by stumbling across the fact that several remote Sardinian villages are the only places in the world where men live nearly as long as women. Everywhere else there is a gender gap in lifespan of about five to seven years. Though the longevity gap has been shrinking a bit, it's substantial and nearly universal. These Italian mountain villages are also home to an astonishingly high number of centenarians of both sexes: proportionally, six times as many hundred-plus-year-olds as in any modern city (in some of the villages the ratio is ten to one). Why so many Sardinians born at the beginning of the twentieth century are still alive today is the story I tell in Chapter 2. As you will see, there's no magic elixir. But one essential piece of the puzzle, I discovered, has to do with the epoxy-like social bonds of village life.

I could have called this book *Face-to-Face*, and I nearly did. Instead I chose *The Village Effect* because it evokes a feeling of belonging. It's a metaphor, of course. You don't need to experience a health crisis like John McColgan's or live in a remote Italian village to feel surrounded by a tight circle of people in whom you've invested serious time and affection over the years—and who have returned that attention. You can create the effect with the people you know, right where you live. This book is about the long-term impact of those face-to-face interactions. Even if these connections are now buttressed by electronic communication, I will show how physiological immunity, enhanced learning, and the restorative power of mutual trust derive from face-to-face contact with the people in your intimate circle. This "village effect" not only helps you live longer, it makes you want to.

THE SCIENCE

The universal hunger to connect and belong explains much of human behavior from birth until death. Our very survival depends on it. In *A Short History of Nearly Everything*, Bill Bryson put it this way: "Not one of your pertinent ancestors was squashed, devoured, starved, stranded, stuck fast, untimely wounded, or otherwise deflected from its life's quest of delivering a tiny charge of genetic material to the right partner at the right moment in order to perpetuate the only possible sequence of hereditary combinations that could result—eventually, astoundingly, and all too briefly—in you."[8] If that happened and you're reading this now, you can thank the powerful nature of our social bonds.

Yet our recent understanding of what drives health and happiness has centered on the concrete: food, earning power, exercise, drugs. We've discovered, for example, that cigarettes, salt, animal fat, and being fat shorten our lives, while antibiotics, physical activity, and the right diet prolong it. Now new findings tell us that our relationships—the people we know and care about—are just as critical to our survival. And not just any kind of social contact, mind you, but the kind that takes place in real time, face-to-face. Beginning from the first moments of life and at every age and stage, close contact with other people—and especially with women—affects how we think, whom we trust, and where we invest our money. Our social ties influence our sense of satisfaction with life, our cognitive skills, and how resistant we are to infections and chronic disease.[9] While information about diet, exercise, and new classes of drugs has created the life-changing breakthroughs of past decades, new evidence shows that social bonds are equally transformative.

Interacting with others exerts such fundamental changes in us that it is hard to deny that we have evolved for face-to-face social contact. University of Chicago psychologist John Cacioppo and his colleagues, as well as British researchers Catherine and Alex Haslam, have found that people with active social lives recover faster after an illness than those who are solitary—MRIs show greater tissue repair. Dozens of recent studies demonstrate how close social contact affects our physiological resilience, that is, how briskly our bodies bounce back after a trauma. A 2006 University of California study of three thousand women with breast cancer found that those with a large network of friends were *four times* as likely to survive as women with sparser social connections. And in 2007 the first study was published that revealed one of the hidden mechanisms linking social interaction to recovery in humans: Steve Cole and his team at UCLA discovered that social contact switches on and off the genes that regulate our immune response to cancer and the rate of tumor growth.[10]

It's not just a North American phenomenon. When the habits of nearly seventeen thousand utility workers in France were monitored throughout the nineties, researchers discovered that their degree of social involvement was a good way of predicting who would still be alive by the end of the decade. Chance interactions, our weak networks of far-flung friends and colleagues, and the hours we spend with those intimately tied to us may seem ephemeral, but they have a concrete impact on our brains and psyches. For example, if you're surrounded by a tightly connected circle of friends who regularly gather to eat and share gossip, you'll not only have fun but you're also likely to live an average of fifteen years longer than a loner. One study of almost three thousand Americans found that people with close friendships are far less likely to die young, and in 2004 a Swedish epidemiologist discovered the lowest rate of dementia in people with extensive social networks. Fifty-year-old men with active friendships are less likely to have heart attacks than more solitary men, while people who have had a stroke are better protected from grave complications by a tight, supportive social network than they are by medication.[11]

Despite this powerful evidence, our habits are becoming more solitary. Since the late eighties, when social isolation was first earmarked as a risk for early death in a landmark article in *Science*, more and more people say that they feel isolated and lonely, according to population surveys in the United States, Europe, and Australia. Exactly how much friendlessness has increased and why this is happening has caused academic tussling and fierce public debate. Some say we're more connected now than ever—mostly due to the Internet—and some say we're less connected—mostly due to the Internet. Both views are correct.

LONELINESS

Running through the stories you'll encounter in this book is the question of quantity versus quality in relationships. Why is this question important? Studies show that we are now connected to a larger and more diverse circle of people, but between 12 and 23 percent of Americans say they have nobody to talk to (in 1985 that figure was 8 percent). And we're not talking about solitary pensioners spending their days alone on park benches, scattering breadcrumbs to the pigeons. The middle-aged are the loneliest group of all in the United States. A third of those between the ages of forty-five and forty-nine say they have no one to confide in. In the United Kingdom it's young adults between the ages of eighteen and thirty-four who feel the loneliest.[12] If that fact weren't sobering enough, people in Britain take note: a nationally representative survey commissioned by the UK Mental Health Foundation in 2010 found that a quarter of Britons of all ages feel emotionally unconnected to others, and a third do not feel connected to the wider community.[13]

The Harvard sociologist Robert Putnam sounded the first alarm about increasing civic apathy in 2000, in *Bowling Alone*, a book said to have launched a thousand debates about whether Americans are becoming disengaged from their communities.[14] Whether or not fewer bridge clubs and bowling leagues are apt signs of declining social involvement, one thing is certain: Americans don't have a monopoly on loneliness. In the European Union, loneliness varies by country, but it's safe to say that, at around 34 percent, the rates of intense anomie felt by adults living in the former Soviet republics—including Ukraine, Russia, Hungary, Poland, Slovakia, Romania, Bulgaria, and Latvia—are through the roof.[15]

That's yet another reason why I'm grateful my grandparents fled that part of the world for Canada. Here in my home country, at least 80 percent of people over sixty-five say they frequently see family and friends, volunteer, or go to concerts and sports events (probably hockey).[16] I'm not sure if the 19 percent who say they feel lonely don't get out that much, but the data tell us that the quality of their interactions is more important than the quantity. The same principle holds for Americans, which is a mighty good thing, as their "villages" are shrinking. When researchers from the General Social Survey sat down with thousands of people of all ages and asked, "Who are the people with whom you discussed important matters over the last six months?" they discovered that the number of Americans' quality connections had taken a dive in the past two decades. In 1985, Americans had an average of three confidants. In 2004 they had less than two, including members of their families. In short, they have fewer people they can lean on. "There are lots of people we have relationships with," says Matthew Brashears, a sociology professor at Cornell and one of the authors of this study. "But this question picks up ties to people that are particularly strong—people we can go to if we're in trouble, who could give you a substantial loan, who would help you. They're important key people, so the number tends to be small."

What Hurricanes Sandy, Katrina, and Haiyan, as well as the Chicago and Paris heat waves, taught us is that surviving is often a matter of who cares enough to check up on you. Who will come by to offer you a lift, some groceries, or a place to stay if you need it? Research shows that those people most at risk of dying have no one nearby to ask for help.[17] So I was shocked that most Americans say they have fewer than two people they can depend on. When I said as much to the even-keeled and soft-spoken Brashears, he demurred. "Maybe there's a decline in the people you are close to, but our larger networks haven't declined."

"You mean our online networks?" I asked.

He answered with a qualified yes. "We haven't figured out how to measure our relationship to the Internet yet. But people may be having fewer important discussions face-to-face if they're having discussions online." The gist, according to Brashears, seems to be that we don't have fewer people to talk to in the broad sense. But a significant slice of the social interactions that would have taken place in person a few decades ago are now getting "siphoned off by Facebook." As Tolstoy put it in *War and Peace*, we are connecting to a crowd—"a numberless multitude of people, of whom no one was close, no one was distant."[18]

Of course, talking to fewer people about what matters and feeling lonely are not the same thing. Loneliness is the *feeling* of being bereft, deprived of intimacy, of hungering for companionship, as opposed to the physical state of being alone. Many of us crave being left to our own devices, as Susan Cain and Anthony Storr rightly point out in their books *Quiet* and *Solitude*.[19] But loneliness is not about that sacred block of uninterrupted time that we need to think and work. It's a distressing physiological state. The evidence tells us that about a third of us now feel lonely, sometimes acutely. "Research on loneliness, conducted mostly in Western countries, has shown that any given time, twenty to forty percent of older adults report feeling lonely, and from five to seven percent report feeling intense or persistent loneliness," write John Cacioppo and his colleagues at the University of Chicago.[20] While I was writing this book, three women—one in her thirties, another in her fifties, and the third in her sixties—told me that living alone was fine during the week, while they were busy with work. But weekends were miserable. "I cry every Saturday," Veronica, thirty-seven, said when I met her in the locker room at the gym. "The loneliness is unbearable."

Feeling lonely is as painful as being wildly hungry or thirsty. This makes sense, says Cacioppo, if human brains evolved at a time when social cohesion meant survival while social isolation meant starvation, predation, and certain death. If our big brains evolved to interact, loneliness would be an early warning system—a built-in alarm that sent a biological signal to members who had somehow become separated from the group. Like physical pain or hunger, loneliness effectively says, *Hey, you! If you don't find your people (or they don't find you), you're a goner.*

If intimate face-to-face contact is protective—girding our cardio-vascular and immunological systems and even raising our lifetime IQ levels—loneliness has the opposite effect. Feeling lonely exaggerates the inflammation and reactivity to stress that are linked to heart disease while interfering with our ability to retain facts and solve problems, according to work by the British epidemiologist Andrew Steptoe.[21] Loneliness is particularly risky for women. In one huge population study of middle-aged Japanese citizens, women who rarely had the chance to spend time with their relatives had the highest risk of dying.[22] Women are also more likely to be affected by their friends' feelings of loneliness, as feelings spread more easily within their social networks.[23] But other studies show that lack of intimacy is an equal-opportunity stalker. John Cacioppo and his colleagues have found that loneliness drives up the cortisol and blood pressure levels that damage the internal organs in both sexes, and at all ages and stages of adult life.[24]

Whether we're college students or retirees, the data are telling us that chronic loneliness is less an exalted existential state than a public health risk. Yet there is a glib insouciance about loneliness in popular culture. Headlines such as "Get Over Your Loner Phobia" and "Eat to the Tweet" suggest that it's now dorky to admit that if you live alone you might be lonely, or to imagine that other people might feel that way.[25] In their book *Networked*, Lee Rainie of the Pew Internet Project and Barry Wellman, a Canadian sociologist who is the doyen of electronic social networks, mock the "Eleanor Rigby" lyric *All the lonely people, where do they all come from?* Skeptical that screen time could be contributing to loneliness, they call it a trap to assume that "internet encounters contain less social information and communication that might cause relationships to atrophy." We have a strong sense of the people we meet up with online, and the medium is not the message, they write, adding this odd postscript: "People rarely interact with strangers over the internet."[26]

Yet there is an undeniable fact: due to the convenience and power of the Internet, many of us now live, shop, go to school, and work alone. With classes now posted online and the proliferation of MOOCs (massive open online courses), many college students don't bother to leave their rooms. Just as the sidewalk vanished in much of American urban planning in the mid twentieth century, when the car became the dominant form of transportation, the post office, newsstand, bookstore, and video store—all places where we crossed paths just a few years ago—are becoming obsolete. True, there are lots of online conversations and apps that connect people, and cafés are more common on street corners than supermarkets. In effect the Internet has allowed us to be more choosy about whom we meet, at least in person. Instead of bumping into neighbors or distant friends spontaneously, *we* are in control. Some research shows that our networked devices make us less solipsistic, more involved in the world outside ourselves. "Internet use does not pull people away from public places, but rather is associated with frequent visits to places such as parks, cafes, and restaurants," write Wellman and Rainie.[27] But as the *Boston Globe* columnist, Ellen Goodman, reminds us, "Go into Starbucks and a third of the customers are having coffee dates with their laptops."[28]

Not that there's anything wrong with that. But it can hardly be viewed as an intimate connection. Still, talking to our friends and loved ones by landline, mobile phone, or Skype is the next best thing to being there, as Ma Bell presciently put it. I'm certainly a convert. We recently Skyped the son of a close neighborhood friend into our Passover seder. He was serving in the military at the time, but we set a place at the table for the "Ethan" laptop. Another friend who used to live across the street joined us at Chinese New Year celebrations via her father's iPad, which was passed around from guest to guest like a wedding videographer's microphone so everyone could greet her.

Indeed, there's a long history of women in my family using the telephone to keep their social ties alive. At the end of every workday my grandmother picked up the receiver of her black rotary model to check up on the health and happiness of her female friends, who despite the intimacy of their conversations she addressed formally as Mrs. Dubow, Mrs. Silver, Mrs. Cooper, Mrs. Tartar, and Mrs. Teitelbaum. During her years at home with small children, my mother's fully extended nine-foot long kitchen phone cord kept her attached—in more ways than one—to her social circle. Now it's my turn. If I can't see my friends and loved ones in person, I use a combination of cordless, cellphone, email, text, and

Skype to keep up with my social network, which, graphed out, looks something like this:

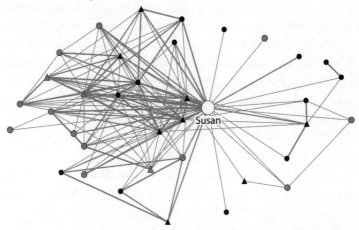

My sociogram: The circles are female, the triangles are male, and the black dots indicate people profiled in this book. The thickness of the line shows the strength of the connection.

A Pew Internet study confirms that cellphone users have larger personal networks—12 percent larger, to be precise—than the small fraction of people who shun them.[29] But in a different set of studies, the same group of scientists showed that avid users of social networking sites have more diverse electronic networks but know fewer of their neighbors and are less integrated into their local communities than those who rarely use social media.[30] "A man must be clothed with society, or we shall feel a certain bareness and poverty," Emerson wrote in 1857. True, that was a long time ago, but are we really that different?

The power and immediacy of electronic media have persuaded us that the different ways of "clothing ourselves" in social contact are interchangeable. In the coming pages I'll show that the latest evidence upends this idea. Electronic media can sway voters and topple newspapers, but when it comes to human cognition and health, they're no match for the face-to-face.

The "come-hither" aspect of electronic media has pulled the wool over our eyes, convincing us that different ways of making contact are the same as being there, and leading us to believe that our networks are expanding. In fact, even if our electronic networks are larger, the size of our face-to-face social networks has stayed roughly the same, while the number of people we feel close to is shrinking. Given that the only person many Americans say they can trust is their spouse, it turns out that many of us are just one person away from having no one at all.

Of course, there are paradoxes. The longer you live—which is usually a good thing—the more likely that your spouse, partner, and close friends will predecease you, leaving you on your own. Unless you're resourceful and have groomed your networks over a lifetime, solitary living can mean forgoing face-to-face contact on a day-to-day basis. Claude Fischer, a Berkeley sociologist who has been studying social networks and urban life for three decades, points out that "living alone is largely what Americans do," and that the widowed and divorced are largely responsible for the boom in people living alone.[31] While a quarter of American men over seventy-five now live alone, fully half of all women that age do, many of them having divorced or outlived their spouses. In Britain the number of people living alone has doubled since the early 1970s; in 2010, sales of single-serving cookware increased by 140 percent, according to the *Daily Mail*, which reported that "frying pans small enough for just one egg, plates for one slice of toast, and one-cup teapots are now some of the fastest selling items in cookware." Where large casseroles were the must-have items of the latter half of the twentieth century, the article notes that "even woks have been downsized for the single market." Given that 80 percent of British citizens over eighty-five live alone, those whipping up one-egg omelets are very likely to be seniors.[32]

These are extraordinary statistics, and they can be understood in a couple of ways. The good news is that in North America, Japan, and Europe, people, especially women, are living longer than ever and the majority can now afford to live alone, if that's what they choose. But the other part of the story is that they might live even longer if they had the right company. In a study of nearly seven thousand older people in Finland, epidemiologists found that one of the most powerful predictors of loneliness was living alone; when they followed up four years later, the lonely folks—no matter their state of health to begin with—were 31 percent more likely to have died in the meantime than people who felt intimately connected.[33] In a huge study of 11,500 middle-aged Japanese citizens led by Tokyo epidemiologist Motoki Iwasaki, urban women who rarely had the chance to interact face-to-face with their relatives had the highest risk of dying.[34] The researchers followed all of the women between the ages of forty and sixty-nine who lived in Gunma Prefecture; these women were hardly the oldest, nor were they the poorest. Yet their resilience was fatefully affected by their opportunities for face-to-face contact.

In the following pages I'll address some crucial questions about human relationships in a digital age. How important is face-to-face interaction as children develop new skills, when adults fall in love, when they negotiate business deals, and as they age?[35] How did humans evolve such finely tuned barometers of trust and betrayal, and do these mechanisms still work if you're not face-to-face with your partner? Why are women's social networks tighter than men's, and what does this mean for their health and the health of others? For example, Tom Valente, at the University of Southern California, among others, has shown that smoking, drinking, and drug use among adolescents spreads (and may be reversed) via popular kids who act as hubs of influence through overlapping cliques.[36] Without deploying adolescents' social networks, expensive public health programs are likely to fail, even if Twitter and Facebook are used to spread the message.

This research is telling us that proximity matters. Sixty years ago Jean-Paul Sartre wrote, "Hell is other people." In the following pages, you'll see that he was wrong.

1

Swimming Through
the School
of Hard Knocks

How Social Bonds Rejig
the Outcome of Chronic Disease

When Sylvie La Fontaine was diagnosed with breast cancer in April 1999, she had just competed with her team in the Canadian Masters national swimming championships. Five foot ten, with rectangular tortoiseshell glasses and pixie-cut hair, Sylvie favored snug wraparound tops she sewed herself, worn over leggings and boots; she hardly looked the part of a grandmother of three. A real estate agent and interior designer, she was the de facto hub of several intense face-to-face social networks, including her swim team. Its president for seven years by that time, she fielded a multitude of personal and training questions from its 150 members, including but not limited to their health issues, reproductive concerns and sports injuries, marital flare-ups and child-rearing doubts, thoughts on the pool's water quality and the coach's latest endurance workout. She was even a shoulder to cry on when a member's beloved pet had to be put down. She sustained this role with bemused equanimity until a teammate blasted her—and not for the first time—about some insignificant mishap at a competition. The attack penetrated her usual defenses and really stung. Given her recent cancer diagnosis, Sylvie wondered whether she should pull back from the team in order to conserve her emotional resources.

But she found that it wasn't that simple for her to withdraw. Not only did people keep seeking her out for advice, Sylvie couldn't resist getting involved when there was work to be done. Along with being swim team president, she was also president of a rural home-owners association that had recently planted sixty thousand trees to naturalize communally owned farmland (she had planted fifteen thousand of them herself). She unwittingly drew confidences from people she barely knew—which puzzled her, as she tended to keep her own counsel. I was just one of what seemed like several hundred swim buddies, colleagues, and neighbors who considered Sylvie a friend. And that was just her middle social layer: she had many closer friends too.

Sylvie and her husband had formed strong bonds with several navy couples while he was enlisted and their kids were young. Closer still were three couples she had met through the swim team; they now dined and traveled together whenever they got the chance. When Gary, one of these close swim friends, found out he had colon cancer, the same week Sylvie received her diagnosis, she competed alongside him at the national championships, then threw herself into his care, organizing tag teams to drive him to the hospital and helping to coordinate his treatment regimen. Supporting Gary as he fought his six-month survival estimate became her most pressing project. "I wasn't sick. He was," she flatly retorted when I asked why she talked about Gary when I asked about her own health. (Gary outlived his initial prognosis by three and half years.) "I didn't really need anything at the time. Breast cancer is not something that hurts, you know. It's very mental."

Not everyone would agree with this assessment. What's indisputable is that despite her vow to withdraw, Sylvie continued to be deeply immersed in several face-to-face social networks that involved taking care of other people. Though cancer did prompt

her to give up her leadership
roles for a while, she still swam
with the team, entertained
family and friends, and took
care of people in her circle
she thought needed her help.
Few see looking after others
as therapeutic for the person
who does the caretaking, or
consider community involvement as therapeutic as drugs.

*The swim team in 1999: Sylvie, third
from the right, top row; Gary, third
from the right, bottom row.*

Yet there is mounting evidence that a rich network of face-to-face
relationships creates a biological force field against disease.

WHAT IS SOCIAL CONTACT, REALLY?

As is true of many women, Sylvie's social connections were so
deftly woven into the fabric of her daily life that she didn't see them
as remarkable. Yet even if she was blind to the benefits, her social
entanglements would stand her in good stead as she faced down
her own cancer. That's a handy side benefit of social interaction.
Unlike a placebo, which requires you to believe you are receiving
medical attention, face-to-face social bonds bolster our immune
responses by stealth. No needles pierce the skin. Nothing gets swallowed, inserted, or inhaled. Outside Latin cultures, most social
contact doesn't even involve the laying on of hands. So how does
social contact exert its effects?

To begin with, the right kind of social contact (hostility doesn't
work) instructs the body to secrete more endogenous opiates, which
act as local painkillers, and fewer hormones such as adrenaline,
noradrenaline, and corticosteroids—the body's often destructive
answer to immediate stressors—which can wage an ongoing war
on our tissues and our physical resilience. More and more proof is
emerging that in many cases, full social lives can slow down, if not

halt, an existing cancer's progress.[1] How a complex, interwoven social life can bolster survival in the face of a grave illness is the story I'll tell in this chapter. I'm not referring here to the number of Facebook friends or Twitter followers you've accumulated simply by clicking "invite" or "accept," but to something more concrete.

Think of social contact as having three prongs or arms of support. One is a route to timely information that's uniquely valuable to you. In the case of breast cancer, these are the friends and family—and the people they know—who refer you to surgeons and oncologists with good track records, to clinical trials and experimental drugs, and to reliable facts while you sojourn in the disorienting land of chronic illness. When Sylvie was diagnosed, she asked a swim buddy who was a medical researcher for the name of a good surgeon. Seven years later, when a suspicious mass was found in my right breast, I asked Sylvie if she could help and she passed that name on to me. I was three connections away from information critical to my health, and her word-of-mouth testimonial damped down my anxiety as I considered my next step. (As you read on, you'll see that the number three keeps resurfacing as I describe how information and trends get transmitted within social groups.)

Lifts to the doctor's office, sitting with the patient while there, babysitting, and preparing meals comprise that second arm of social support: material assistance. One husband I read about in the *New York Times* perfected the "ask" when coordinating crucial social support for his wife, Alexandra Bloom, a forty-one-year-old psychologist and mother of their four-year-old twins. Describing himself as highly organized, Tom Nishioka swung into action when his wife learned she had breast cancer:

> Within days, Mr. Nishioka and three friends designed a website for people to sign up to help them. It's hard to ask people things like, "Who's comfortable sitting through chemo with you, or who likes to cook?" said Dr. Bloom. Ten team captains signed up to organize

researching oncologists and health-insurance options, making home-cooked meals, shopping for groceries, going on doctor visits, taking the girls to and from school, and tidying up the apartment each day. More than 150 friends signed on. Three are honorary grandmas, Dr. Bloom said. "Each of them visits once a week. They read books to the girls, they bring the girls their favorite foods, like string cheese, strawberries and blueberries. They see their role as spoiling them."[2]

This extraordinary couple recognized that their face-to-face social networks were a critical factor in Dr. Bloom's recovery. The Internet was a part of their communication plan, to be sure. Their friends signed up to help on a dedicated website. But when it came to pitching in, the members of their village had to show up; they had to be there, *in person*. And of course, providing food, rides, and other favors is not all that close friends and family have to offer. They also encourage you to eat, to take your medication, to see the doctor—and perhaps come along to ask probing questions while you're there.

Along with this concrete support is the mood- and health-bolstering effect of having loved ones nearby—the third arm of support.[3] Perhaps this is why people without such social buttressing are more than twice as likely to die prematurely than those with active face-to-face social lives. In fact, neglecting to keep in close contact with people who are important to you is at least as dangerous to your health as a pack-a-day cigarette habit, hypertension, or obesity.[4] And while the first benefit of social contact I described—access to timely information—has been beautifully streamlined by Google searches, the last two benefits—concrete and emotional support—work most powerfully if those people are near enough to see, hear, and touch you.

SOCIAL CONTACT AND THE SHAPE-SHIFTING DISEASE

Proving the link between social contact and cancer survival is not just complex from a scientific point of view, it's also controversial.

On the complex side, your genes, history of pregnancy and child-birth (or childlessness), hormone levels, menopause, hormone replacement therapy and its timing, diet, exercise, alcohol and cigarette habits, radiation exposure, where you live and the nature of the social and work life you lead there are just some of the factors that combine to create the toxic brew that causes cancer cells to proliferate . . . or not. The sheer number of causes and the way they shift and interact over time make for a seemingly impenetrable tangle. To add to the mess, cancer seems to be not one disease but several hundred that share a common process—that of unchecked hegemonic growth—one reason why the oncologist and author Siddhartha Mukherjee refers to cancer in his book, *The Emperor of All Maladies*, as "a shape-shifting disease of colossal diversity."[5] Still, when researchers attempt to isolate each of these factors and hold them constant, the link between consistent social contact and breast cancer survival remains.

But what does this mean exactly? Social contact can be a grab bag of connections. There's the intimate encouragement and support offered by your life partner or best friend, the day-to-day contact with colleagues, neighbors or teammates; the loose affili-ations to people you meet in your professional networks or at church. Compare these types of contact to what you experience when you meet strangers in a cancer support group or on Facebook. Though evidence tells us that social connections are as protective as regular exercise—those with the most face-to-face connections have a two-and-a-half-year survival advantage over those with the same disease who are isolated—not all types of social contact are created equal.

Some cancers are the body's terrorists: they're rare, swift, and indiscriminate killers. In contrast, breast cancer's growth patterns are usually lazier.[6] Given its longer horizon, the vast numbers of people affected, and the political will (and the research budgets that follow suit), breast cancer survival rates are a good way to examine whether social bonds can slow or halt the march of this disease. And as of the 1990s, multiple studies have shown that women with breast cancer who feel supported by caring friends and family—and who actively seek out such social contact—have a more favorable response to the disease and ultimately a better prognosis. More than any other factor, a woman's network of active social contacts and her perception of social support predict her blood levels of lymphocytes and natural killer cells, both of which eradicate cancer cells.[7] Though she is just one case, this was certainly true of Sylvie. She thinks of herself as an introvert. But she surrounded herself with people who mattered, and as a result she not only felt supported but survived.

The question is how. Two types of studies do a good job of connecting the dots between our social bonds and our health. The first are demographic sweeps that probe the social lives of thousands of people at a time and then follow them into the future—as they get older and start to fall apart. The scientists at the helm of these studies, neck-deep in data for decades, draw lines between the number and types of get-togethers with friends, colleagues, kids, cousins, and fellow parishioners penciled in on their calendars and what kind of health problems hit these people, and when.

In the seventies, Harvard epidemiologist Lisa Berkman was the first to conduct population studies that made the link between our social lives and our "best by" dates. She lived in northern California at the time, and her study of every single Alameda County resident (a total of 6,928) showed that, among other surprising findings, the women who were socially isolated had an elevated risk of dying of cancer, and isolated men who already had cancer were more likely to die prematurely.[8]

The sheer volume of participants in studies like Berkman's makes certain links indisputable. We know that the connection between social involvement and robust physical and mental health is no fluke, and that the benefits of regular social contact are at least as powerful as regular exercise and a healthy diet. But the downside of such large-scale population studies is that, though they prove that two factors are connected, they can't tell us which one comes first. Do people with lots of friends and family live longer because their active social lives protect them from cardiovascular events and cancer? Or are the type of people who seek out lots of interaction with friends, children, parents, cousins, neighbors, and colleagues simply the type of folks who are also biologically destined to live long, healthy lives, come what may? If people who are less healthy in general have a hard time developing and maintaining connections with other people, then it may not be their social isolation that's at the heart of the matter, but their poor health.

The way to solve this chicken-and-egg dilemma is to randomly assign people to one of two groups. In the first they are surrounded by solicitous buddies and loving kin, and in the second they live a monastic life. Meanwhile, everything else stays the same. They start out healthy and cancer free; they have similar genetic, life-style, and health backgrounds; they're the same sex and age; and they're similarly privileged, deprived, or addicted in the food, drink, and comfort departments. Then you watch what happens as time passes. Does social contact affect the growth of cancerous tumors?

We can't try this sort of experiment with human beings, of course. Even if it were possible, it's not ethical to deprive people of social contact just to see what might go wrong.[9] But you can try it with rats, which despite their serious image problem share almost all the genes linked to human diseases and like us, are also highly social animals.[10] When research psychologist Martha McClintock, her oncologist collaborator Suzanne Conzen, and their colleagues tried isolating red-eyed albino rats bred for research purposes, the team made a remarkable discovery. Socially isolated female lab rats developed eighty-four times as many breast cancer tumors as female rats who lived in groups. Eighty-four times! Published at the end of 2009, their study drily relates this extraordinary finding: "Isolation increased the number of discrete tumor masses by 135%. Among isolates, tumors were more widespread, developing in three if not all four mammary quadrants." The researchers go on to report that 50 percent of the isolated female rats developed malignant breast cancer, while the incidence among their group-housed mates was only 15 percent. Compared to the party animals, the solitary females' tumors were not only more numerous but bigger. Clearly, if you're a female mammal, having little contact with a close circle of family members and friends not only causes psychic pain in the short term but increases your risk of developing breast tumors in the long term.[11]

Social isolation not only increased the number and size of breast tumors, it also exaggerated the animals' biological stress responses. In another experiment, McClintock and Conzen isolated a group of female lab rats for three months right after birth. Then the researchers put them in a cage liberally sprinkled with fox urine, a signal that a predator was lurking nearby. In response, the social isolates secreted ten times more corticosteroids (hormones released from the adrenal gland when mammals are stressed out) than a control group of female rats raised in social groups. This exaggerated biological response changed their behavior, making the rats less willing to explore their environment. It also had epigenetic effects, altering the way genes were expressed in their mammary glands.

If you're a rat, the scent of fox urine is unnerving. If you're a human, you're likely to be stressed out by something else, such as public speaking, being bullied by your boss, or missing the last train to Clarksville. Whatever makes you sweat, Martha McClintock's research tells us that as mammals we need stable social contact at the beginning of life in order to cope with stress later on. Being denied secure, steadfast relationships predisposes us to overblown biological reactions to stress, which by disrupting the gene pathways that suppress tumor growth, add to our existing risk factors for breast cancer.[12]

This suite of experiments also reveals how critical early social contact is to our ability to handle stress as we age. It also suggests one

A *socially isolated female rat (left) compared to one raised in a group.*

reason why children placed in orphanages as infants—where they're usually deprived of regular contact with parental figures—often experience enormous developmental challenges, even when they're adopted by stable families later on.

LONELINESS KILLS

Now that I've shown how a lack of social contact can cause tumors in rats, let's return to those population sweeps I mentioned earlier to see what these findings might mean for humans. One such study, led by Californian public health researcher Candyce Kroenke and her colleagues, followed about three thousand nurses who had recently been diagnosed with invasive breast cancer who had also filled out a detailed questionnaire about their social lives. A team of epidemiologists then followed their progress for the next twelve years. Knowing how many friends and family members these nurses hung out with *before* they received a breast cancer diagnosis (as opposed to after, when a cancer patient may suddenly face boosted contact with social workers, medical staff, and hospital volunteers), the researchers then asked these pivotal questions: Was there any difference between the health of the nurses who were deeply immersed in their social lives and those with sparser social connections? And did nurses with lots of friends live any longer than those who were more solitary?

The answer is yes, and yes. By the time the study ended, four times as many solitary women had died of breast cancer than had women with active social lives. The survivors were more likely to be women like Sylvie. They weren't necessarily extroverts, but they were surrounded by people they saw week in and week out. (In fact, there is evidence that introverts have a greater mortality risk from cancer, and even an increased susceptibility to catching colds.)[13]

The type of contact varied, ranging from the ropelike bonds between intimate friends and family members to the weaker threads that tied them to colleagues and neighbors. The critical factor? The women who survived the longest weren't lonely. And while the more face-to-face contact the women had, the rosier their breast cancer prognosis, they needed just a few close friends to protect them from premature death.

Interestingly, though women with big families lived longer than those with small families, when it comes to living a long life after cancer, friends were the most protective social bond of all.[14] Socially isolated women were 66 percent more likely to die of breast cancer than women who had at least ten friends they could count on. Those friends not only helped by providing information and concrete assistance, they also provided that neuroendocrine flush that comes with spending time with people you like and who care about you. And that means spending time *with* them, hearing the sounds of their voices and perhaps being touched. A hug, a squeeze on the arm, or a pat on the back lowers one's physiological stress responses, which in turn helps the body fight infection and inflammation. Being there in person is key.

Of course, electronic communities help people stay in touch who are separated by geography or who have rare or virulent forms of a disease. The Internet has an astonishing capacity to aggregate like-minded people, and is a rich source of information that can help them feel more proactive about their illness. Indeed, online forays can radically alter many cancer patients' lives.[15] But unless joining an online community is just a first step—one that allows people to meet and form meaningful relationships—there is no decent scientific evidence showing that online activity can transform our health prospects the way face-to-face social networks can.[16]

That's because social isolation kills. Behind the scenes, one of the effects of loneliness is that it can alter our genetic response to disease. In other words, chronic loneliness—the subjective experience of feeling isolated and alone for long periods—alters the expression of genes in every cell of your body. As incredible as it sounds, feeling isolated creates a "lonely" fingerprint on every cell. That genomic fingerprint, or identifying stamp, confuses the body's usual reactions to disease and stress, instructing some cells to turn on the fireworks of inflammation while instructing other cells to turn off the body's usual immune defenses. Under normal circumstances these processes would protect cells from being damaged by disease. But feeling lonely for long periods throws a monkey wrench into the complex genetic code we've developed as a social species, making us more vulnerable by switching off antibodies that would protect us from viruses and infection, and bamboozling leukocytes (white blood cells) so they can't attack their targets.[17]

Interestingly, individuals differ in the amount and type of social contact they need to avoid feeling lonely. John Cacioppo has discovered that the subjective state of loneliness—and its power to erode our natural resilience—is very much like other biological appetites, like the need for sleep, food, and sex. How often we need to be in close contact with our friends and family in order to stay healthy and happy varies from person to person, and has a powerful genetic component.[18] We can inherit the destructive capacity for loneliness from our parents. Given that it runs in families, it seems to be a feature of their family histories people should know, much the way you'd want to know whether hypertension or kidney disease is in your family background. Just as different plant varieties need different amounts of water to survive and thrive, introverts need less social contact while extroverts need more. But everyone needs a certain amount of meaningful face-to-face contact in order to maintain their own unique social metabolism.

Still, even if face-to-face contact can help protect us from maladies ranging from the common cold to cancer, there is no evidence that people bring cancer on themselves, nor that the right type of thinking or mood can prevent it. The idea that you can control your own health with the right attitude has been promoted in New Age books, in popular magazines, and on talk shows, and the vast majority of people believe it.[19] But it's a pernicious untruth. Not only does the idea have no scientific basis, it shifts blame for the disease onto the victims and away from the biochemical mechanisms that are still, for the most part, maddeningly beyond their control.

LET'S GET METAPHYSICAL

One of the studies that tried to show that you can control the direction of breast cancer with your thoughts and feelings (but failed to prove the connection) drew my attention because the "Let's Get Physical" pop star and breast cancer survivor Olivia Newton-John funded it. The study worked this way: More than seven hundred young Australian women diagnosed with non-metastatic breast cancer filled out detailed questionnaires about their anxiety levels, their adjustment to their cancer diagnosis, and the extent to which they suppressed or expressed their feelings about it. Then the women's health was tracked for eight years.

What did they find? There was no connection between mood and breast cancer outcomes. Teaching women with breast cancer to think positively and proactively about their illness doesn't cure them. The coaching does make them feel less anxious and depressed—which is valuable and important in its own right—but it doesn't help them live any longer.[20] The thinking at the end of the twentieth century was that healing the mind would heal the body—and many preliminary studies suggested that psychotherapy might extend cancer patients' survival. But none of the more rigorous studies that followed have shown that to be true.[21] Psychotherapy can relieve emotional distress, but it can't extend your lifespan.[22] Chemotherapy and radiation can improve your lifespan, but they certainly can't relieve your distress. Only your friends can do both.

STRESS, CANCER, AND ELIZABETH EDWARDS

This raises what I'll call the Elizabeth Edwards question—one of the touchier aspects of the social-support-affects-cancer-survival idea. While I was researching this chapter, Elizabeth Edwards, the estranged wife of former presidential hopeful John Edwards, died of breast cancer at sixty-one. Her death shook up cancer survivors who had long seen her as a model of tenacity or, as one *New York Times* reporter put it, "the cancer patient who would not be defined by her disease."[23] Edwards had written candidly about tragedy and resilience in two memoirs that described how she faced her son's accidental death at sixteen and what it was like to live in the political spotlight while fighting chronic illness. Controversially, she had stepped up her campaign schedule instead of pruning her commitments when, in 2006, it was discovered that her cancer was spreading.

The day before Edwards died, in early December 2010, her family announced that her cancer was no longer treatable. She posted the following statement on her Facebook wall: "I have been sustained throughout my life by three saving graces—my family, my friends, and a faith in the power of resilience and hope. The days of our lives, for all of us, are numbered. We know that." Within minutes the airwaves and blogosphere were awash with tributes, but also with suggestions that marital stress and lack of support had triggered her metastatic breast cancer.[24] This question had surfaced before, in light of lurid revelations of her husband's infidelity in the run-up to his 2008 campaign for the Democratic nomination. Though the cancer had metastasized to her bones and was considered untreatable in 2006, had his subsequent affair relaunched his wife's cancer, just when she seemed to be getting the better of it?

We will never know. But Elizabeth Edwards's three public struggles—first with her son's tragic death, then with breast cancer, and finally with her husband's infidelity—seemed to support the widespread belief that stress causes cancer. One study about women's attitudes shows that nearly half the women who have had breast cancer attribute their diagnosis to hard times in their lives: a separation or a divorce, a death in the family, workplace stresses, financial struggles—or all of the above. And 87 percent chalk up their remission to their efforts to think positively and reduce stress.[25] My swim-team friend Sylvie had linked the arrival of her cancer to "stress I was unable to control," and her mother's and grandmother's experiences with breast cancer to sudden stressful events in their lives (as opposed to, say, a breast cancer gene).[26]

But does facing hardship or thinking negative thoughts really cause cancer? And does maintaining a sunny disposition while trying to lead a stress-free life prevent it? The answer to both questions is no. There is no good scientific evidence that stress causes cancer, even though studies have repeatedly tried to establish the connection.

Many of these studies asked people to look in the rearview mirror to identify stressful events that could be linked to the onset of their cancer. But human memory is highly selective. We're more likely to remember dramatic events that give a narrative arc to our life stories rather than think that our flame will be blown out due to some random cell mutation (scientific jargon for "shit happens"). The Stanford biologist and renowned stress researcher Robert Sapolsky doubts the stress-causes-cancer connection, noting that "someone with a cancer diagnosis is more likely to remember stressful events than someone with a bunion."[27] Other problems with these studies include using very small samples and neglecting to control for a whole host of other factors that could be affecting women's cancer outcomes, such as whether they smoke, drink too much or are overweight, the stage of their disease, and how old they are at the time they are diagnosed (the longer you live, the more likely it is you'll get cancer, because that's what happens when other disasters haven't killed you first). Whether people faced adversity before their cancer diagnosis or are possessed with a fighting spirit thereafter are red herrings. Most adults, in good health or ill, have faced some hard knocks.[28] Still, when confronting cancer, most of us look back on our own life stories to try to answer the "Why me?" question. Our minds don't seem built to comprehend multiple factors and statistical probabilities; our minds are built to look for the ping-pong of cause and effect.[29]

In 1986 a Danish cancer researcher named Marianne Ewertz studied the marital histories of 1,800 women with breast cancer and compared their situations to 1,800 healthy women of the same age. She discovered that a long marriage or a short-lived one, the recent death of a husband or a long-ago loss, a separation or a divorce—none had an impact on the women's cancer risk.[30] There's even some evidence—as counterintuitive as it sounds—that stress helps to *protect* you from breast cancer, by impairing your ability to synthesize estrogen (reduced levels of estrogen can suppress the growth of some types of tumors).[31] In a study that would give anyone pause, almost seven thousand women from Copenhagen were asked about their baseline stress levels and then were followed for the next ten to twelve years. The women with the highest levels of stress had a 40 percent *lower* chance of being diagnosed with breast cancer.[32]

There are also many natural experiments showing that extreme stress might well kill your spirit but it does not cause cancer. People who were imprisoned and tortured in concentration camps or the Soviet gulag, for example, or parents of children who died of cancer—all acutely traumatic events—don't have a higher incidence of cancer than people who did not live through these harrowing experiences.[33] Nor is there a higher rate of cancer among almost twenty thousand Danish parents who have had a child diagnosed with schizophrenia—one of the most stressful events to ever strike a family. In short, social contact can stall the progress of breast cancer. But the stress of losing that support doesn't bring it on.

THE FEMALE EFFECT

When I interviewed Sylvie for this book, she was skeptical about the connection between social contact and her recovery. Her brisk guide to cancer survival? "First they cut you, then they poison you, and then they burn you. Then it's all over and your hair grows back."

When describing her experience, she downplayed her fears and turned up the volume on how she went about solving the concrete problems related to her diagnosis: how she chose her treatment regimen, found the right medical expertise, and engineered the environment she needed to focus on recovery. In every situation Sylvie had deployed her social networks during a period of crisis, but she seemed oblivious—as most of us are—to the way her face-to-face social connections helped her. "I was reading about it, I called my doctor friends, I got together with them, and I got all this information from people I knew," she told me.

I asked who had helped her the most. "Friends," she replied, without so much as a pause. "I called my good friend Mona, who lives in another city and is married to an oncologist. I then talked to her husband for three hours, even though we weren't really friends as two couples. She was my friend when I lived in that city, so her husband helped me. And I had Celeste. Celeste helped because she's totally organized and very businesslike, and she's a nurse and has been in this medical world forever. And she said okay, you're going to this doctor, because she's the best surgeon in town, and you're going to do this and you're going to do that. So I got all this information from all these people. Then I went *tut-tut-tut*, like this." Here Sylvie pointed her index finger as if it were a gun and shot down the problems she'd faced after her diagnosis.

I asked about her husband, an affable family man who seemed close to her and to the kids. So far he hadn't figured in her description of the battle plan. She paused, looking at me with concern over the dark frames of her glasses. "David didn't know what to do, and my sons didn't really know what to do either," she said. "They were in the same boat as I was. But my friends, they really helped me, because they're women and they're close in that way, you know? Celeste was excellent with information, and Dominique, well, she helped me by coming to sit with me when I went to the hospital for treatment. Then she drove me to my cottage afterwards so I could rest. She especially likes the country, so we'd hop in the car, drive up to the cottage, and stay over. We'd have a meal together and the next day she'd be gone."

Sylvie didn't know about Marianne Ewertz's study showing that marriage isn't that critical to the onset or remission of breast cancer; indeed, being married is more essential to a sick man's ability to pull through than it is to a sick woman's.[34] Powerful sex differences

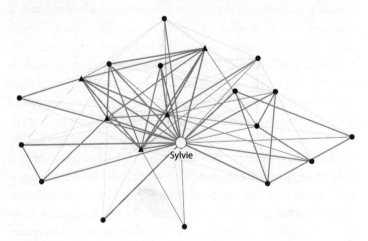

Sylvie La Fontaine's sociogram.

emerge in people's responses to cancer. To begin with, there is evidence that the cancers most common in women (breast and uterine cancers) are hormone related and constitute one set of diseases, while the cancers most common in men comprise a different set, with distinct triggers as well as different responses.[35] And unlike most men with their guy friends, most women reach out to their female friends and relatives to share the emotional burden of the illness, as did Sylvie. The intimacy of these interactions is what counts most in warding off loneliness and fear.[36]

The other side of that coin, though, is that women's negative social interactions have a more corrosive effect on their health. Studies show that compared to men, women experience bad relationships as more physiologically disruptive and show higher levels of urinary cortisol, among other neuroendocrine markers of distress, when things break down.[37] It's as if their intimate relationships—good or bad—take center stage. Men's relationships, except with a spouse, are more likely to play bit parts.

In Sylvie's case the lion's share of the information and social support she received traveled along her network of female friends, a trend I'll call the female effect. Reaching out to other women releases oxytocin, a neuropeptide that has both analgesic and euphoric effects. This hormone, secreted during orgasm, childbirth, breastfeeding, cuddling, and nurturing, not only offers pain relief and an immediate jolt of pleasure, it also reinforces your commitment to people in your inner circle. Oxytocin creates a feedback loop that rewards both the women who reach out to others at times of crisis and those who receive help.[38] Shelley Taylor, the UCLA psychology researcher who pioneered some of the research in this area, calls this the "tend-and-befriend" phenomenon. You need not be aware of the role of biology in fueling the tend-and-befriend process: how oxytocin surges through your bloodstream, damping down pain and inflammation, making you feel good in the here and now, and ultimately increasing your chance of survival. But, like Sylvie, most women intuitively know that other women in their circle offer valuable support, both the instrumental kind that comes with the exchange of information and the ineffable kind of emotional support that takes place when women share confidences.

THE POWER OF WEAK BONDS

Are we to believe, then, that friends are more important than family when facing a chronic illness? Sylvie's experience reveals two important rules about the movement of crucial information through our social networks. First, it's our weaker connections who are often most influential when we need something concrete—a new job, a new doctor, a new apartment. Such important bits of information usually come our way through people we're only loosely connected to, a principle proved many times since Stanford sociologist Mark Granovetter first proposed his idea about "the strength of weak ties" in the early 1970s.[39] The reason we're most likely to find a great surgeon, our dream job, or Ms. or Mr. Right through a friend or a colleague's spouse, or a spouse's colleague is that we already share so much of what we know with our family and close friends. Our backgrounds, networks, and interests are similar, so our sources of gossip overlap. Weak ties offer bridges to novel information. Our acquaintances know things our family members and best friends don't, and they are often connected to different cliques of people whose stock of contacts and information would never reach you if you didn't have that person in common.

In *My Own Country*, his moving memoir of his clinical education working in Tennessee during the AIDS epidemic, the Stanford-based infectious disease specialist and novelist Abraham Verghese describes how he, along with other physicians trained in India, first made inroads into the American medical system by virtue of the power of weak bonds:

By the time I completed medical school in India and returned state-side, a few of my seniors from my medical school in India had begun internships at county hospitals across America. Through them and through their friends and their friends' friends, an employment network extended across the country. With a few phone calls, I could establish for any city which hospital to apply to, which hospital to not bother with because they never took foreign graduates, and which hospital took foreign graduates for the first year, used them for scut work, but never promoted them to the second year—the infamous "pyramid" residencies. And the network invariably provided me with the name of someone to stay with.

A few pages later he describes how weak bonds can act as an invisible hand that brings far-flung people with similar backgrounds together in places as unlikely as a town in the Smoky Mountains of eastern Tennessee:

The effect of having so many foreign doctors in one area was at times comical. I had once tried to reach Dr. Patel, a cardiologist, to see a tough old lady in the ER whose heart failure was not yielding to my diuretics and cardiotonics. I called his house and his wife told me he was at "Urology Patel's" house, and when I called there I learned he and "Pulmonary Patel" had gone to "Gastroenterology Patel's" house. Gastroenterology Patel's teenage daughter, a first generation Indian American, told me in a perfect Appalachian accent that she "reckoned they're over at the Mehtas' playing rummy," which they were.[40]

If Verghese were white and from Boston instead of from Addis Ababa, his splendid achievements might seem diminished by the suggestion that he simply tapped into an old boys' network. But he and the medical Patels had intuitively done what successful immigrants do: make the most of their weak bonds.

Whether it's how to be a good doctor or how to find one, we're more likely to discover redemptive solutions to concrete problems through people we see only occasionally or who are friends of friends of friends. This loosely linked network is what largely powered the roaring Silicon Valley engine in its early days, according to Granovetter, who has written extensively about how individual social networks alter business or cultural horizons on a grand scale. On a smaller scale, I realized that Sylvie's life, as well as my own, had been transformed by our weak bonds.

For instance, I had long wanted to spend most of my time writing. It took a chance encounter with a health writer I knew only slightly to help me make the jump from working as a clinical psychologist who occasionally wrote for newspapers to working as a writer who occasionally practiced psychology.[41] In this way I was like 84 percent of the several thousand Quebec government managers who found their positions through weak social connections. Even though the provincial government tried to formalize hiring practices in the late seventies, hoping to make access to a highly sought-after civil service job less a matter of who you know than what you know, the sociologist Simon Langlois discovered that almost half (42.7 percent) the employees had found their jobs through personal contacts. Interestingly, the more educated the employees, the more likely that weak social ties had led them to their jobs.

The opposite was true for Quebec's blue-collar workers. Whereas 84 percent of professionals, managers, and administrative staff found their positions through acquaintances, only 19 percent of blue-collar workers had. It was their *strong* ties—to close friends and family members— had that made the difference, a finding that's been replicated many times since, from the shanty towns of Mexico City to American families living in poverty. "Poor people rely more on strong ties than do others," Granovetter writes.[42] Though your needs may be great, having to depend on strong

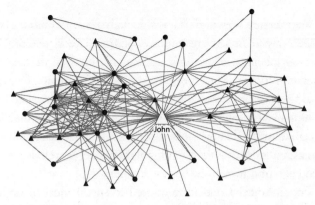

John's sociogram illustrates a larger social circle with many weak ties.

networks of close friends and immediate family means that you have less information about new opportunities. Granovetter believes that the poor's exclusive dependency on strong bonds is why poverty can be self-perpetuating.

A provocative corollary to the weak-versus-strong bond rule is that most girls and women prefer intimate, one-to-one relationships with a tight group of close family and friends, whereas most boys and men go long and wide, sustaining many more weak relationships in larger social networks—such as big teams, multinational corporations, or the military—while investing much less in each one.[43] Roy Baumeister, an American social psychologist, puts it bluntly: "The female style builds a few strong, close social bonds. The male style builds many weaker ones. Do you want a loving marriage with strong family ties? Then you need the female style. Do you want a work group, like a ship's crew or a hunting group or a soccer team? Then the male style will work better."[44] Each style

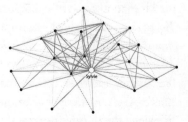

Sylvie's sociogram shows a smaller network comprised primarily of close female relationships.

requires tradeoffs, he explains, and though most of us want to excel at both, if we're honest, we're usually better at one of the two.

Using the logic of weak ties, it might seem that the ultimate weak connection—that between far-flung Facebook friends—would be the most influential of all. And it's true that these weak cyber contacts might be just the ticket if you're looking for something concrete, like a new job, a restaurant recommendation, or a quick hookup for Saturday night. But if your needs are existential—if you're trying to recover from a frightening, debilitating illness, for example—cyber connections are no replacement for the face-to-face. One reason may be that live interaction sparks far greater activity in the brain regions linked to social cognition and reward (the anterior cingulate cortex, ventral striatum, and amygdala), according to the first fMRI study to compare the brain's responses to face-to-face interactions with canned, prerecorded ones. Rebecca Saxe, the MIT neuroscientist who led this study, explained that it shows why it feels good to be together with someone in the same room, paying attention to exactly the same thing at the same time.[45]

But does it follow that interactions that lack that in-person, dynamic social element make you feel bad? Well, sort of. There is evidence that turning to the Internet for social connection may stir up feelings of isolation. One study in the early 2000s showed that New York women with non-invasive breast cancer who used their computers as a research tool reported feeling more socially supported than women who didn't use the web. However, using their laptops to seek medical information was one thing. But the more time these women spent on the Internet, the lonelier they felt.[46] This finding has surfaced in several studies and has been called the "Internet paradox," because the web is supposed to connect us, right?[47] Well, that depends on what you need. If it's information, that's one thing. If it's the reassurance of a hug or of sharing a private joke in real time, that's another.

When American cancer researchers Paula Klemm and Thomas

Hardie compared face-to-face with online cancer support groups, they found that the groups were statistically similar except for one thing: the participants' moods. Most (92 percent) of the participants in the electronic groups were depressed, while none of the participants in the face-to-face groups were.[48] It could be that people who already feel low are attracted to online rather than in-person groups. But it could also be that people who spend more time on the Internet—even in cancer support groups—spend less time hanging out with their family and friends.

This proved to be the case in a large Stanford time-diary study that was published in 2002. People who spent more than five hours a week of their personal time online had less face-to-face contact with their strong ties. The authors of the study, inventor and social scientist Norman Nie, along with several Stanford colleagues, were clear: "For every personal e-mail message sent or received there is almost a 1 minute drop in the amount of time spent with family. With a mean of 13 personal emails sent and received, that amounts to about 13 minutes less of family time a day, or about 1.5 hours a week. . . . The more time spent on the internet, the less time spent with friends, family, and colleagues."[49] This is just common sense, but it's been hotly debated. Most of us send dozens, if not hundreds, of emails and texts a day. Whatever the benefits, that's mostly time spent alone.

Later in the book we'll encounter this phenomenon again in the guise of "Facebook depression," that bilious stew of envy and anomie that engulfs people who click through online signs of their friends' achievements in the mistaken belief that such voyeurism is a form of social glue. It's not. While networked technologies can do many wonderful things, they can't make an ill person feel cherished and less existentially alone. Only the people who are near and dear to her can do that. As we shall see, proximity matters.

It Takes a Village to Raise a Centenarian

Longevity as a Team Sport

A ny visitor to an Italian town soon finds herself standing in the central square, surrounded by its standard architectural features: an imposing church on one side, a municipal building on the other, and a fountain in the middle. The town's roads radiate from that square and the cafés set into the buildings along its perimeter are perfect places to put down the guidebook and admire the surroundings. To say that Italian town squares are built on a human scale is a platitude; the square's primary function has always been to assemble its residents at a de facto crossroads.

A couple of millennia before Facebook, the square was the one-stop gathering place for gossip, shopping, and spiritual guidance, a magnet for social interaction, public and private. The government offices and the private chapels located on the square were where the region's power brokers held their tête-à-têtes. Deals were also made on the square, and in the streets and alleys leading off it; betrothals, marriages, and of course funerals happened there too.

In the Sardinian village of Villagrande Strisaili, which is built on a steep hillside in the central Gennargentu Mountains, the bars, bakeries, and grocery stores surrounding the hulking eighteenth-century church are pitched at a sharp incline—I felt my exploration of the town in my hamstrings. The doors to the shops are a short flight of stairs up or down from the pavement and as I made my way around the streets near the square, popping in and out of little stores as I shopped for a small gift to offer my dinner hosts one evening, I was unaware that people were watching me intently from windows and doorways. I was new to a place that doesn't get many visitors.

As I crossed the square, I met the gaze of a tall, black-clad woman in her late seventies. After a perfunctory greeting she asked me who I was and what I was doing there. Only when I named my hosts for that evening—my Sardinian interpreter, Delia, and her family—did the shutters on her eyes lift. She knew Delia, and Angela, Delia's mother, not to mention Angela's mother, aunt, and great-aunt. Having established where I belonged—however temporarily—in the town's social order, she finally offered, *"La posso aiutare? Figlia di chi sei?"* (Can I help you? Who are your parents?)[1]

It was October 2008, and I was visiting this remote region of Sardinia with my twenty-four-year-old daughter on a research trip we were combining with a mother-and-daughter adventure. Eva had graduated from university and was between jobs, while I had just finished *The Sexual Paradox*, about the science of unexpected sex differences. One of the most intriguing of those paradoxes, I'd discovered, is a biological fragility among males that is nearly universal. Almost everywhere in the world, men die an average of five to seven years before women do, leaving nations of widows to populate their town squares, supermarkets, and seniors' homes.[2] The residents of the rugged hilltop villages of central Sardinia are the world's only exceptions to this rule. Almost everywhere else, including on the Italian mainland, there are six female centenarians for every male.[3] Elsewhere, most men don't make it to eighty, but once Sardinian men in this region have lived through their dangerous, risk-taking adolescent and young adult years, they tend to live as long as their wives and sisters—well into their nineties and even beyond.

And there was another local mystery. Despite living hardscrabble lives as shepherds, farmers, and laborers in a rugged, inhospitable environment, Sardinians who were born and live in Villagrande and the surrounding villages are outlasting their fellow citizens in Europe and North America by as many as two or three decades. The huge number of centenarians in this part of Sardinia is intriguing, not only because they're already living decades longer than the rest of us, but because so many of them remain active, working well into their eighties and nineties and living in their own homes, usually with people they've known their whole lives (most of them women, as it happens). Currently, ten times as many men in Villagrande live past the age of one hundred as men who live elsewhere. While the rest of us slather on sunscreen, down fistfuls of vitamins, sweat it out with hot yoga, and practice mindfulness meditation, the residents of Villagrande are the ones who are living to tell the tale.[4] These Sardinian hilltop villages comprise one of the world's exceptional "Blue Zones"—a handful of mountainous regions where more people live to the age of one hundred (and beyond) than anywhere else.[5] I wanted to know why.

Sardinia is Italy's second largest island, after Sicily, and sits smack dab in the middle of the Mediterranean, with Corsica to the north and North Africa to the south. It has nearly the landmass of Switzerland but less than a quarter of its population. Just a million and a half people live in the towns dotting its rugged shoreline and the pastoral mountain villages in the Ogliastra region, the epicenter of the Blue Zone. Centuries of invaders and regular attacks from North African pirates drove residents away from the coast and inland, beyond the rugged Gennargentu mountain range, which formed a natural barrier against invasion (as well as coastal malaria). This geographic isolation forcibly created the area's tightly bonded families and communities—that's the upside. The downside is that always having to defend your boundaries created a longstanding mistrust of strangers, aptly illustrated by the local saying *"Furat chie benit dae su mare"*: those who come from the sea come to steal.

During the twentieth century, though, the threat was more likely to come from within. Warring factions among neighboring villages gave this area a Wild West reputation. Even then these hilltop villages were "as remote from one another as the stars," as the Sardinian novelist Salvatore Satta wrote. My guidebook informed me that the area boasted one of the island's worst reputations for vendettas, banditry, and violence.[6] In recent decades, though, things have calmed down. Now the area is better known for its breathtaking panoramas, political murals, and black-shawled older women than for deadly multigenerational grudges. Still, before Eva and I left for the interior, we thought it best to get the lay of the land. We decided to fly into Alghero, a Moorish-looking seaside town with an airport and a university, on the western side of the island. The plan was to meet one of the two experts who had discovered the phenomenon of Sardinian super-longevity, a local physician and biomedical researcher named Giovanni Pes.

Sporting a generous moustache and a short gray beard, Dr. Pes wore the mid-career academic's uniform of polo shirt, khakis, and rimless glasses, and like most Sardinian men, he is compactly built. Known to everyone as Gianni, he is as warm and personable as he is erudite. The evening we arrived, he met us in the lobby of our small hotel in Alghero, bringing along a young graduate student, Francesco Tolu, and a geneticist colleague, Paolo Francalacci. Gianni had arranged for our interpreter and accommodations in the Blue Zone, and the day we met he handed me a blue plastic folder packed with local information and maps. But most important, he immediately included us in his lively circle of close friends, family, and colleagues. This feeling of inclusion turned out to be a crucial piece of the longevity puzzle. For better or for worse, no one is left alone here for long.

SARDINIA'S MYSTERIOUS MALE METHUSELAHS

Though belonging is key, extreme longevity also runs in families here, Gianni told us. As a family doctor he had examined at least two hundred Sardinian centenarians. He went on to investigate their family and medical histories and whatever genetic information he could collect, along with details about their diet, physical activity levels, and cognitive states. While Gianni was responsible for first identifying the local clinical phenomenon of super-longevity, a Belgian demographer named Michel Poulain helped him validate the data. Municipal records in hand, the two men went from village to village in and outside the Blue Zone, interviewing and examining the centenarians, along with any living family members, to make sure the municipal records jibed with reality. "By the end of 2001 I had visited, alone or with Michel, about 261 municipalities out of a total 377 in Sardinia," Gianni told me.

As I found out that evening in Alghero, Gianni had a personal stake in the longevity question. "I am the nephew of the very rare Sardinian man who reached the record age of 110. Up to now I can find only four people in Sardinia who have reached that age, and one of these four lucky persons is my great-uncle. So that stimulated my curiosity to know the secret of an exceptionally long life." (By the time this book went to press, the number of Sardinians who had lived to 110 had doubled; there are now eight).

Gianni's curiosity is matched only by his hospitality. Taking a day off from the lab, he and his wife, Sandra, her brother, Peppuccio, and Francesco, Gianni's graduate student, drove in a convoy to lead me from Alghero to Sardinia's Blue Zone. Eva and I brought up the rear in our battered rented Smart car. The extraordinary social support network that allows its seniors to live well beyond their "best by" date could well be tied to how hard it has always been to get to these villages. There's an ocean to cross, then miles and miles of *macchia*, or pastured scrubland. Finally, barricaded behind a forbidding mountain range, the villages of the Blue Zone rise into view.

The ancestors of the roughly 3,500 people currently living in and around Villagrande have inhabited this spot since the Bronze Age. While driving to the Blue Zone we saw hundreds of *nuraghi*, which are mysterious conical stone structures. No one knows whether they were used as houses, temples, or observation towers, but they still stand in farmers' fields and on hills all over the Sardinian countryside, architectural testaments to the Nuragic people who lived here at least four thousand years ago. Inside the *nuraghi*, buried in rubble, archaeologists have found dozens of Smurf-like statuettes called *bronzetti*. These tiny statues clue us in to the community's social cohesion even then. Looking like Bronze Age Happy Meal toys, three-inch-tall women cradle small children and lift their hands in cheerful greeting, while male warriors sport fearsome shields and quizzical grins on their faces. The social environment was clearly convivial, even if the physical surroundings were as inhospitable then as they are now. Outside the cozy hilltop villages, this is still a remote, windswept place, a landscape almost as empty of human settlement as the moon.

The small subsection of the Sardinian population that now lives here became genetically isolated somewhere between five thousand and ten thousand years ago. And while the small genetic pool that resulted from this isolation made diseases such as thalassemia and familial multiple sclerosis much more common, it also meant that powerful feelings of reciprocal altruism reverberate throughout these villages. People treat their neighbors and friends like

Ancient bronzetti from Sardinia.

family because . . . well, most of them are. Called kin selection by evolutionary psychologists (and nepotism by everyone else), keeping close tabs on members of the community—even taking risks and making personal sacrifices on their behalf—became a normal feature of life in these small towns. Helping people was a way of helping your own genes survive, though no one is explicitly aware of that. Residents simply expect that when they need help they'll get it, and at some point they'll return the favor. Yogi Berra summed up the concept nicely: "Always go to other people's funerals. Otherwise they won't come to yours."

That's how reciprocal altruism can be fostered by kin selection in such small, isolated groups of people. Given how tight the Blue Zone Sardinians are, how committed to watching out for each other, this longevity-promoting social cohesion may have been selected for over many centuries of geographic and genetic isolation.[7] In the here and now, the act of helping other people releases feel-good neuropeptides and endorphins—that's the positive side. On the negative side, those folks who don't take constant, solicitous care of older family members, neighbors, and friends are shunned. Even as a visitor I felt the chilly breeze of censure when, after interviewing a 102-year-old charmer named Zio Giuseppe, his 72-year-old son Nino learned that my mother, who was around his own age, had come home ten days earlier from a hospital stay. She was in Canada and I was here? Disapproval cast a shadow over his handsome face. How could that be?

Gianni had told me that a team of Italian geneticists had recently discovered certain polymorphisms—distinct clusters of DNA sequences—that are ten times more common among the male centenarians in this part of Sardinia than in a comparison group of younger Italian men from elsewhere on the island. This finding confirms oral histories told in Villagrande. The older residents describe having descended from just a few founding families, and they regard their town's genealogy as a sacred trust. To be precise, they're likely the descendents of two founding *mothers*, as the mitochondrial DNA hosting these genetic variations can be inherited only from mothers, not fathers.[8]

It's tantalizing to consider that there may be clusters of longevity-promoting genes that are primarily transmitted through the maternal line but influence men's lifespans exclusively—an interesting gloss on the female effect. If that's true, then women are skewing extreme longevity in Sardinia in more ways than one. They're passing on their genes—in this case a particular haplogroup of mitochondrial DNA that promotes health across the male lifespan—and they're also offering the TLC and companionship that allow their elders, husbands, and children to benefit from the protective village effect.

When it comes to the lineage for longevity, it may be a one-sided contribution. As the Y chromosome markers (paternally inherited polymorphisms) in male Sardinian centenarians don't differ that much from those of younger Sardinian men, or from western European men in general, it's hard to argue that genes on their own tell the whole story of male longevity in the Blue Zone. A study of nearly three thousand Danish twins born at the turn of the twentieth century found that genes answer 25 percent of the longevity question, at most.[9] So it's interesting to consider how the social habits particular to this place—very likely transmitted through its mothers and grandmothers—have transformed the already propitious genetic hand the community has been dealt.

BECAUSE THEY LOVE ME

A life as long as Teresa Cabiddu's might be a blessing or a curse. The elegant white-haired centenarian was born in 1912 and has lived in the same house for seventy-five years.[10] The morning we visited her, a light rain was falling in Villagrande and the surrounding mountains were obscured by fog. Squeezed between two larger, recently built houses, Zia Teresa's place seemed doll-like in its dimensions. It was constructed in the typical Sardinian village style: dark, wood-framed windows with shutters, sandstone-colored walls, and a red tiled roof. The paving stones were slick that day, and as we shook out our umbrellas and bent our heads under the low door frame to enter the kitchen, I was struck by the Hans Christian Andersen–like setting. As if drawn by a child with a checklist of life's necessities, the room was small but complete: round wooden table with four ladder-back chairs, a fireplace, narrow gas stove and fridge flanking the sink, a small couch next to the fireplace, a glass china cabinet, and a plate of cookies on the counter, freshly baked in anticipation of our visit.

Zia Teresa was sitting on the pink loveseat by the hearth with her neighbor Marietta Monni, at eighty-two nearly twenty years her junior. The two women were dressed identically, in black sweaters and knitted black shawls. Black skirts and pastel-colored floral aprons covered their expansive laps, Teresa's pale blue, Marietta's sage green. Both were knockouts: high cheekbones, white hair tightly wrapped into a knot at the nape of the neck, and lively black eyes. Though Teresa's forehead showed a few freckles—souvenirs of a life of work in the fields—both women's faces were remarkably devoid of the crepey folds and creases common in the elderly. The room smelled pleasantly of wood smoke and cookies. The contrast to the antiseptic pall of institutional living, the fate of the oldest old in most industrialized nations, couldn't have been greater.

Though the house hardly seemed large enough, it had once accommodated a family with six children, one of whom, Angela, around fifty, was seated on a kitchen chair facing me. She had recently moved back in with her mother to look after her. Including her friend Marietta, my daughter, the interpreter, and me, we were six in that tiny kitchen, all talking about Zia Teresa's exceptionally long life. There was no escaping the fact that getting older in central Sardinia is an intensely communal affair. Every centenarian we met was surrounded by a tight web of kith and kin.

It's not as if I didn't want to meet the centenarians' families and neighbors. But I viewed the centenarians as individuals, with unique stories to tell, and wanted them to tell them uninterrupted. The people around them, though, considered them to be communal property and were fiercely protective of their "treasures"—the word one woman used to describe her 102-year-old uncle. Feeling isolated was simply not possible for these centenarians. As the Sardinian demographer Luisa Salaris put it at an international conference on longevity, "All centenarians live at their children's house and have frequent contact with other relatives, including grandchildren and great-grandchildren, with whom they love to natter." Nattering with whoever happens to be hanging around is how one ages in central Sardinia.[11]

One of the first things Zia Teresa told me about herself was that she left school after the third grade and her graduation gift was a hoe. She was born in Arzana, a village about eighteen kilometers south of Villagrande, and she "tilled the wheat, set the potatoes in the garden, made the bread" from the time she left school until she married at the age of twenty-five, after which the farm work, cooking, and family responsibilities only intensified. As a young wife, a typical day meant waking in the dark at two a.m., then walking to the family fields near Nuoro ("a thirty-kilometer trip each way!" daughter Angela interjected). As soon as she was able, Teresa's eldest, Giulia, stayed home from school to look after the younger children.

When I asked if her field work and domestic life in Villagrande were lonely jobs for a young woman from a different village, Zia Teresa shook her head no. "I helped the neighbors and my neighbors helped me. Still now, on Saturdays and Sundays, we all make bread together—*su pani pistoccu*," she said, referring in Sardinian to the parchment-like flatbread typical of the region. Angela added, "We still do it—me, my sister, my mother, and my sister-in-law— every Saturday and every Sunday." The conversation progressed to the making of *culurgiones*, the local specialty: pasta purses, about the size of a child's fist, filled with ricotta, potato, and mint, each one filled and crimped by hand. On the loveseat, the two older ladies demonstrated by rhythmically squeezing their thumbs and forefingers together; clearly a light touch was needed to create the right seal. "We make them for the entire family—three or four hundred at a time—and then we give them to everyone," said Angela. The *culurgiones* are boiled for a few minutes and then eaten smothered in homemade tomato sauce.

For a moment I felt jealous. Not just because Zia Teresa's now adult children had learned the secrets of Italian country cooking well before Marcella Hazan and Mario Batali taught the rest of us. But because this type of take-it-for-granted social bonding, which seems to be a key feature of the scientific recipe for a long, healthy life, seemed so effortless here.

Sardinian centenarian Teresa Cabiddu demonstrating how to make culorgiones.

Still, Teresa had spent seven decades, sixteen hours a day, doing back-breaking work, which held no appeal for me at all, even if that was one piece of the Sardinian longevity puzzle. Long treks by foot over steep inclines and hours of vigorous farm work are still features of daily life for most of the residents there. Even food deprivation—common in the region during and after both world wars—can add years to one's life, some experts say. Though the impact of caloric restriction on longevity is controversial, famine (for a limited period, anyway) has been known to slow down or suspend age-related cell death.[12] Recent research by cognitive neuroscientist Lisa Barnes has shown that going hungry as a child predicts a slower rate of cognitive decline in old age. By following more than six thousand older Americans as they aged, she and her team discovered that her subjects were a third less likely to suffer from serious memory loss or dementia if they reported not having had enough to eat as children.[13] Zia Teresa, who lived through the deprivation caused by two world wars, may have benefited from brief periods of caloric restriction during the first half of her life.

None of that sounded like a lot of fun to me, least of all consecrating one's oldest daughter to a life of domestic slavery at the age of eight. At twenty-four, my daughter was planning for a future that revolved less around the confection of homemade pasta pockets than on a decade more of schooling, probably far from home. My husband and I wanted our children to make independent decisions, even if that meant moving thousands of miles away from us—an idea we didn't exactly relish.[14] And in North America we are not unusual; fostering independence is the goal of most parents. But generational separation is not universal. In Sardinian villages, children tend to build their adult lives near their extended families. Zia Teresa had spent her morning with two of her daughters, Gabriella and Bruna, and with her neighbor Marietta. The three women had come by to keep her company while Angela was out of the house, working her morning shift at the local bakery.

During our visit, we learned that Zia Teresa had been a headstrong child and that she'd loved to sing as a young woman. We learned the name of the man who played the accordion several decades earlier so everyone else could dance, and how he repaired it with flour and water when it broke. We learned about her favorite dish (minestrone) and her least favorite (pizza), and her nickname for another centenarian in town (Crabittu). We learned that her short- and long-term memory worked fluidly: she could recount the names and dates of birth and death of her parents and the seven siblings who'd predeceased her, all in their late eighties and nineties. She knew my interpreter's complex family history once she'd greeted Delia with *"Figlia di chi sei?"* Zia Teresa at one hundred was what she had been her entire life: a gregarious woman with many friends, relations, and neighbors, all of whom popped in regularly to visit and chat, all the while bolstering her importance in their lives, and her place in the community.

To properly "age in place" as Teresa has, you don't need to live in a literal village but near a group of like-minded people who create the intimacy of one. Research by Harvard professors Subu Subramanian, Felix Elwert, and Nicholas Christakis shows that widows (and widowers) live longer if they choose to live in neighborhoods filled with other widows. Never mind how well off the community is or how healthy its residents are to begin with; when it comes to living longer, the age and marital status of one's neighbors holds more sway. The global phenomenon of widowed people dying soon after they've lost a spouse—called *the widowhood effect*—is attenuated when someone who is grieving is surrounded by lots of other widowed people, especially if they're women.

Yet another example of the female effect, it probably works this way: if you feel unbearably lonely because your spouse has died, nearby female friends with the same life experience are more likely to know how it feels and to step in to fill the companionship gap, as Marietta did with Zia Teresa. To weather the inevitable indignities of advancing age, geographic proximity to close friends and confidantes is what really matters, according to research by Teresa Seeman and Lisa Berkman.[15] Indeed, what the data tell us is that the elderly, and especially widowed people, live longer in places such as Villagrande or Boca Raton—where there are lots of residents of the same age with the same concerns—than they would if they lived among Brooklynites pushing baby strollers and riding fixed-gear bikes.[16]

Zia Teresa reminded me of my grandmother, who at eighty, as we bent our heads over my Russian homework, told me that she might look like an old woman to other people, but she continued to see the world through the eyes of her younger self. Teresa was able to tap into her younger persona by virtue of living so close to relatives and friends who had known her for decades, in the place where she had raised her six children. Those children lived there too, or in towns nearby. Instead of communicating electronically, they came by in person to gossip, bring food, or press her into service for the weekly baking. There were no strangers in Zia Teresa's social network, no nurse's aides paid to visit or support groups with others who shared the same ailments.

Remarkably, our bodies know the difference between real social support offered by people we know and the contrived version. "The source of support matters," Brigham Young health psychologist Julianne Holt-Lunstad told me. "Not all relationships are equal. When you introduce social support, there may not be any real relationship there." As anyone in a failing or hostile relationship knows, interaction with the wrong person can make matters worse. In one well-designed study, led by McGill nursing professor Nancy Frasure-Smith, cardiac nurses repeatedly called and visited about a thousand psychologically vulnerable men who'd recently had heart attacks. Unfortunately, these calls and visits from strangers had no impact at all on the men's survival. And in a subsequent study, the nurses' visits actually doubled the likelihood that high-risk women with heart disease would die within the year.[17] How could this be? The study's authors speculate that cardiac care had improved men's survival rates so dramatically in the 1980s that it would have been hard for the nurses' support visits to boost them further. But the higher number of women's deaths after the nurses' so-called supportive phone calls and visits could mean only one thing: with friends like these, who needs enemies? Shallow bonds may be good for many things, but improving one's chances of surviving after a heart attack doesn't seem to be one of them.

When I asked Zia Teresa how it was that she has lived so long, her neighbor Marietta answered for her. "Because it's God's will!"

But Zia Teresa lightly slapped Marietta's knee to shut her up. "No, it's because they love me," she said softly.

"Well, I am going to the church to thank God for that," said Marietta.

"Okay. Pray for us all, then," retorted Teresa with a smirk, "and don't let the priest kiss you while you're there."

THE FOUNTAIN OF YOUTH

Zia Teresa's unusually long life would be but an amiable detour in my story if it did not illustrate several powerful scientific findings. As we've seen in the previous chapter, social contact can help keep individuals alive when they happen to get sick. But where we live and the social life we lead there can also keep us healthy, creating pockets of longevity—or dare I use that twee word *wellness*—tied to a specific place.[18] When Gianni Pes and Michel Poulain first presented their Sardinian Blue Zone data, they expected other scientists to greet their findings with skepticism, if not derision. After all, discovering a longevity hotspot is nothing new. Strange practices and obscure places where people supposedly live longer than elsewhere have surfaced at regular intervals since at least the biblical period, when Methuselah supposedly lived to the age of 969. A millennium later, people thought eating the meat of poisonous snakes would add decades to their lives. In the nineteenth century a neurologist, Charles-Édouard Brown-Séquard, injected himself with an extract from ram's testes, declaring that it would add years to his life. Meanwhile, Serge Voronoff, a Russian physician, tried an extract of chimpanzee testes instead, and thought it a far superior product.[19] Needless to say, none of those practices panned out.

More recently, in the 1970s, several longevity hotspots surfaced, including the Caucasus in the former Soviet Union (where the local Abkhasian people supposedly live longer because they drink kefir instead of water), the Hunza Valley in Pakistan, various

Japanese islands, and an Ecuadorean village called Vilcabamba. Tales of men fathering children at the age of 160 (yes, yogurt is that good for you!) were rampant. Unfortunately, when researchers delved deeper into the phenomena of 160-year-olds who swilled kefir (or was it vodka?) first thing in the morning, then swam across frigid fjords and had indefatigable libidos, they discovered that record-keeping in many of those places was unreliable, to say the least.[20] Residents' extravagant claims about themselves or their family members often couldn't be confirmed. There is an aspirational, if not a public relations aspect to exaggerating one's age. After all, if peasants on the Russian steppes lived to the age of 150, how bad could life really be under Soviet-style communism?

Other so-called longevity Shangri-Las reflected different, dire realities. In Japan, which ranks among the countries with the highest median age (that is, the greatest number of people who survive the longest), a significant proportion of its oldest citizens had simply gone missing. Most of them were men who'd moved to the big cities looking for work during Japan's economic boom years. Finding industrial jobs, these men worked obsessively long hours for decades, never building any social networks in their urban locales. They died miserable deaths, anonymous and alone. With no record of what had happened to them, their previous home municipalities assumed they were still alive and crowed about their growing cadre of centenarians.

At 111, Sogen Kato was supposedly Tokyo's oldest man. His mummified corpse was discovered by officials who arrived at his home in the summer of 2010, hoping to congratulate the gentleman on his birthday. Instead they found his skeletal remains lying on a bed, wearing underwear and pajamas and covered with a blanket. Kato had died thirty-two years earlier, at the age of seventy-nine. His family told police that Kato had confined himself in his room more than thirty years before to become a living Buddha. They had been cashing his pension checks ever since. Such grisly discoveries put the Japanese longevity record in question and prompted some national soul-searching. The country's social services tried to track down the rest of its so-called centenarians and could not find 234,354 of them.[21] If any confirmation was needed that proximity to friends and family who care about you is essential to survival, this was it.

WHAT IS IT ABOUT PLACE?

Sardinia, however, is no mystical Shangri-La. The residents aren't blessed with extraordinarily long lives because they drink the local red wine or eat plum tomatoes from their gardens. While the resveratrol in the regional wine matters some, ongoing face-to-face social contact with people who know and care about them matters more than any of the molecules on their plates or swirling around in their wineglasses.[22]

In fact, two places in the United States where people live unusually long lives are places where people don't drink any alcohol at all. Loma Linda is a modern city of twenty-two thousand in San Bernardino County, just east of Los Angeles. Downwind from L.A.'s smog clouds and right beside a Lockheed-Martin plant that has long been leaching perchlorate—a chemical by-product of rocket fuel—into the town's groundwater, the Loma Linda area boasts rates of perchlorate in its drinking water that are eighty-three times higher than the limits recommended by California's Department of Health. It also has the worst ozone pollution in the nation, according to the American Lung Association. Yet Loma Linda's residents live an average of six years longer than other Americans, in large part due to the social bonds among the Seventh-day Adventists who live there. Their support systems and diet, combined with a state-of-the-art medical center, mean that the residents live longer there than they do in neighboring towns.

And, as in the mountains of Sardinia, the culture of the place is beginning to close the mortality gap between men and women.

The average thirty-year-old Adventist man from Loma Linda lives 7.3 years longer than male citizens elsewhere in the United States; the average Adventist woman lives an average of 4.4 years longer than other American women (and women already have a six-year head start).[23] David Snowdon is an epidemiologist from southern California who pioneered some of the basic research linking the lifestyle of the Loma Linda Adventists to their reduced rates of chronic disease. He realized early on that longevity is less about a place than about who lives there and how they interact.

After he'd studied the Adventists of Loma Linda, Snowdon chose to shine his statistical searchlight on Catholic nuns. He and his research team followed 678 members of the School Sisters of Notre Dame for fifteen years, from 1986 to 2001. The nuns, all between 75 and 106, were living in convents in the American heartland: Wisconsin and Minnesota. Snowdon and his colleagues mined the minutiae of their childhoods for data and tracked their cognitive abilities and eventual decline. As the environment of these nuns was fairly consistent and there were several siblings among them, Snowdon tried to tease apart the relative influence of genes and early experience on their lifespans and lucidity as they aged. Most of the nuns bequeathed their brains to his lab, and Snowdon was able to make some astonishing connections between early experience and the neural tangles of Alzheimer's disease. For our purposes, though, one of his most important discoveries was that once these nuns reached the age of sixty-five, their risk of dying in any given year was 25 percent lower than it was for other American women their age. Why would these nuns, whose diets were high in animal fat and who exercised very little, live significantly longer than average American women?

In his book about the nun study, Snowdon concludes that, alongside their "deep spirituality," the real reason these women lived so much longer was their powerful sense of belonging.

For more than fifteen years now, I have witnessed how the School
Sisters of Notre Dame benefit from their ever-present network of
support and love. The community not only stimulates their minds,
celebrates their accomplishments, and shares their aspirations, but
also encourages their silences, intimately understands their defeats,
and nurtures them when their bodies fail them. How many of us
are held so securely throughout life?[24]

THE VILLAGE EFFECT

Clearly, it is not only what individuals do on their own steam that
matters. Where they live is crucial, and not just because some neighborhoods are posher. Sociologists dub our connections to friends,
neighbors, and co-workers "social capital," which is the knowledge
and mutual trust captured in our relationships. Unlike the tally of
one's Facebook friends, social capital is hardly noticeable to outsiders. Still, it brings real benefits. One evening in 2006, my mother
and I were visiting my father in the hospital, where he had just been
admitted for treatment of lymphoma. On our way out, we bumped
into the mother of one of my son's elementary school classmates.
Ruth was a nurse on the ward, and after we exchanged greetings, she
offered to check in on my father during her overnight shift. If something concerned her she would phone me during the night, she
promised, tucking my phone number into the pocket of her nurse's
smock. This interaction took just a few seconds, but in an environment where medical errors cause more than 100,000 deaths a year,
it could well have saved my father's life. Happily, he survived his
lymphoma, in no small measure due to a lifetime of social capital.

Surprisingly, face-to-face social capital in a neighborhood can
predict who lives and who dies even more powerfully than whether
the area is rich or poor. In 2003, when several Harvard epidemiologists put nearly 350 Chicago neighborhoods under the microscope,
they discovered that social capital—as measured by reciprocity, trust,

and civic participation—was linked to a community's death rates. The higher the levels of social capital, the lower its mortality rates, and not just from violent crime but from heart disease too.[25] Clearly the *place* makes a difference to your health: some locales foster more trusting relationships.

But places can also foster hostility toward outsiders. In tightly knit villages such as Villagrande, the powerful sense of cohesion is counterbalanced by an equally powerful distrust of outsiders— including hostility toward residents of neighboring towns, say, two valleys over. Having spent the equivalent of two years in the 1990s researching daily life in Villagrande, McGill University anthropologist Philip Carl Salzman concluded that the Sardinians living in adjacent towns were always seen as "rivals and potential enemies." Having trusted only themselves for centuries, even the arrival of local police stations in the nineties was seen as a form of meddling. The response, Salzman writes, was "social isolation of members of the Carabinieri [police officers] and the frequent and repeated shooting and bombings of Carabinieri stations, cars and homes, and even individuals, at least one of which happens every day."[26] Describing a similarly insular mining town in Ukraine, Russian-born American Keith Gessen writes that "when you leave the house in Donetsk, you bring a knife, in case you run into someone you know."[27] Just because you know him doesn't mean that you're from the same town, or that you trust him.

BEING THERE

Most of us wouldn't choose to live as cloistered nuns or Sardinian villagers, even if their lifestyles do confer an extra decade or two. But it's worth considering the social nature of these places for a moment. How do they compare to what happens in mainstream societies as people age? In the United States, Canada, and the United Kingdom, for example, life is closer to the vision of American comedian George Burns, who quipped that "happiness is having a large, loving, caring, close-knit family . . . in another city." There are advantages to this vision, of course. One of them is that geographic distance safeguards the much-vaunted value of independence at every stage of adult life and promotes a type of personal freedom that is so emblematic of the American dream. When Alex Perchov, the comic antihero of Jonathan Safran Foer's novel *Everything Is Illuminated*, strives to leave Ukraine for the United States, he's trying to escape Soviet-era privations and provincialism, to be sure, but also his mother, who tells him, "One day you will do things for me that you hate. That is what it means to be family."[28]

The no-strings-attached Western ideal creates gaps in intimacy that, despite the miracle of Skype, are not being bridged by technology. In the United States, more than sixty-two million people—equal to the entire population of the United Kingdom—say they are socially isolated and unhappy about it. More than half of them (thirty-two million) live alone, the highest proportion in the nation's history. Indeed, the rate of Americans living alone has been rising every decade since the early twentieth century. Whereas 1 percent of the American population lived alone in 1920, over 10 percent did in 2010, according to American census data, which tracks an increase in solo living of more than 300 percent in the past forty years. Many of those living solo are divorced and widowed seniors. While a quarter of American men over seventy-five now live alone, fully half of all women that age do, many of them having outlived their spouses.[29]

This is not just an American phenomenon. In Britain, a third of all adults now live alone, and a record number of Canadians, especially those over sixty-five, are now on their own too.[30] The uptick of solitary living means that in Canada, the United States, and every European Union country, greater swaths of the population are waking, eating, and sleeping without in-the-flesh human contact. And while living alone doesn't necessarily mean that you're lonely, it does mean that, like it or not, you have less physical proximity to other human beings whom you care about and who have an interest in your survival—fewer impromptu conversations, fewer shared puns and jokes, and, of course, less physical contact.[31] Just as people who are married have more sex than single people (proximity counts for something, after all), people who are solitary are deprived of the daily pats, hugs, and eye contact that primates have been communicating with for at least sixty million years.[32]

Reading people's feelings and intentions from their faces and showing trust by touching them are crucial interactions that we humans and all group-living mammals crave. When Helen Boardman, a centenarian from Illinois, was interviewed by a Chicago public radio producer about the prerequisites for living a long, long life, she zeroed in on companionship and physical closeness. For her, this meant continuing to make new friends as she lost old ones, even falling in love again at age ninety. She married the man in question a few years later, telling the producer, "I enjoy having his arms around me, just as much as I did when I was twenty. You never get tired of that. And you miss it when you don't have it."[33]

Could it be that close physical contact with romantic partners, friends, and children fosters the physical resilience that helped keep Helen Boardman and Teresa Cabiddu alive for more than a hundred years? This is not as farfetched as it sounds. Oxytocin and vasopressin, two neuropeptides that are secreted into the bloodstream when we form and maintain meaningful relationships, help damp down stress and heal wounds. A number of animal experiments show that oxytocin boosts immunity and recovery, and as we saw in the previous chapter, evidence is emerging that this rule holds for humans too.

THE TERMITES

In 1921 a controversial California psychologist, Lewis Terman, began following the life trajectories of 1,528 eleven-year-olds born near San Francisco and Los Angeles, who were soon dubbed "the Termites." He and subsequent researchers tracked their lives from late childhood until death. Born around 1910, they intrigued me because their birthdates roughly matched those of the Sardinian centenarians I'd studied. Far fewer of the Termites lived to the age of one hundred than the Blue Zone Sardinians (0.3 percent of the Termites lived to that age, compared to more than 4 percent of the Sardinians).[34] Still, the lessons drawn from their life stories echo the Sardinian picture.

Since he was mainly interested in top classroom performers, Terman didn't survey typical Americans. Instead, he chose to study exceptionally bright kids. More than two-thirds of his research sample were middle-class WASPs—one reason why his work has been controversial.[35] He tested their IQs and followed their school progress closely. But he and a tag team of successors also shone the spotlight on the kids' family backgrounds, their physical and mental health as they grew up, their stress levels, and ultimately their sex and marital lives, career choices, and political and religious beliefs. The researchers kept up this intrusive level of inquiry for the next eighty-odd years, accumulating a treasure trove of correlations (the project is still going, having been handed off to the next generation of researchers). Not all of what was revealed was pretty, bringing to mind Ralph Waldo Emerson's aphorism "Sorrow makes us all children again—destroys all differences of intellect." Slightly fewer of these bright students survived to the age of one hundred than other Americans born in 1910, and the ones who did were more likely to be women.[36]

Still, in this teeming mountain of data, Terman's first concern was giftedness, and he was able to show that these talented kids didn't conform to the stereotype of the era: the super-smart kid as the neurotic, bespectacled, antisocial nerd. In fact, his subjects were as healthy and sociable as their peers. This wasn't the only myth shattered by the Termites. In their 2011 book *The Longevity Project*, University of California psychologists Howard Friedman and Leslie Martin use the Termites' life stories to destroy some of our most cherished old wives' tales about what it takes to live a long, long time. They summarized some of their findings as follows:

- Worrying is bad for your health. Myth!
- Thinking happy thoughts reduces stress and leads to a long life. Myth!
- Take it easy and don't work so hard and you will stay healthier. Myth!
- Retire as soon as you can and play more golf to stay healthy and live longer. Myth!
- The good die early and the bad die late. Myth!

So what *does* promote health and longevity, according to Friedman and Martin? Conscientiousness and hard work, combined with a large, active network of family, friends, and community ties—people whom you help and who help you. If you want to live a long, healthy life, worrying and working hard won't kill you.[37] But doing it alone just might.

HISTORY OF AN IDEA
As long ago as 1979, Lisa Berkman and Leonard Syme, epidemiologists in Berkeley, California, discovered that a community's social bonds accurately predicted its mortality rates. By analyzing the results of a standard survey they devised, they could tell someone's fortune based on how many times the person purposely met up with other people face-to-face. Among the nearly seven thousand residents from Alameda County who participated in the study, the people most likely to survive to old age were those with solid face-to-face relationships: they were married, they got together frequently with friends and family, they belonged to a religious group, or they had a regular social commitment such as choir practice, a hiking group, or a bridge club.[38] Each of these factors individually predicted mortality, independently of how healthy, well-to-do, or

physically fit these Californians were. Interestingly, the protective effect of one social bond could pinch-hit for another. If you weren't happily married but had lots of close buddies, your prognosis might still be good. And if you were happily married but didn't see your friends all that much, that close relationship with your spouse could also protect you. The life-threatening risks surfaced in people who were disconnected on multiple fronts—people who were lonely.

Fast-forward thirty-one years to 2010, when Julianne Holt-Lunstad, a psychologist at Brigham Young University in Utah, along with two colleagues, examined 148 longitudinal studies about relationships and mortality—which was like summarizing the diaries of about 309,000 people over seven and a half years. That's a lot of data, and when the researchers crunched it all, they were astonished to learn that those who were integrated into their communities had half the risk of dying over the course of the seven years as those who led more solitary lives. Similar to Berkman and Syme's first study, those who experienced various kinds of social contact increased their odds of survival— not just by a little, but by 91 percent, nearly doubling their odds of dodging the ultimate bullet for a long while. It wasn't simply a question of living alone, or being married or single. What was important was being a part of a community in more ways than one—not just by being happily married, not only by belonging to clubs and groups, but by being involved in several of these activities and relationships at the same time. That feeling of belonging had to come from interacting with people you really know, in what the researchers called "naturally occurring" social relationships. The longevity-inducing contact didn't come from support groups, hired minions, or non-human sources, whether digital devices, a higher power, or pets.[39] Among those 309,000 subjects, a person who sustained different kinds of relationships was more likely to live a long life than one who had lost a lot of weight, had flu shots, quit smoking, or breathed unpolluted air.

What Reduces Your Chances of Dying the Most?

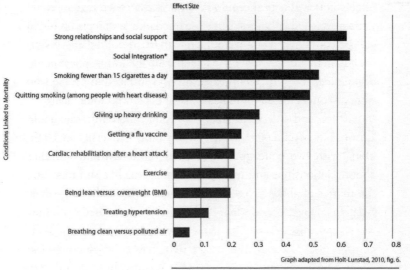

Graph adapted from Holt-Lunstad, 2010, fig. 6.

* social integration refers to social involvement on multiple levels

What reduces your odds of dying most? According to an analysis of existing research, social interaction.

Let's return to inland Sardinia for a moment, and Dr. Gianni Pes. As I mentioned, longevity runs in his own family. His great-uncle was born in 1893, the year the diesel engine was invented, and died in 2004, the year Facebook was founded; he had lived for 110 years and 125 days. Gianni also had a grandmother who died at ninety-three and a paternal uncle who died in 2011 at the age of ninety-seven. And though Gianni is well-versed in the conditions that foster an exceptionally long life in a Blue Zone, including the genetic isolation, the mountainous terrain, and the dietary factors, he also stresses the importance of the constant face-to-face contact that is so central to Sardinian village life. "Everybody is in close contact with other members of the community. My great-uncle was no exception. He used to visit friends and relatives and was fond of going hunting on Sundays until he was ninety-eight years of age. And if I remember correctly, he was able to shoot a wild boar at that age."

Gianni's own father made his social rounds at the age of 105 by walking the countryside paths he'd walked his whole life. When

that was no longer possible, he lived with one of his daughters and everyone came to him. "The old and the oldest old are very protected. They are considered the symbol or strength of the family," added Gianni.

Just as they looked after their parents, adults in the community expect that as they become frail, they too will be cared for.

Pasquale Frasconi, 110, walking with his great-nephew, Dr. Gianni Pes.

But there is also the sense that a person who has reached the age of ninety or a hundred deserves respect and is entitled to be listened to. Both kinds of support are freely offered. Even though he is an academic of international renown, Gianni still lives within a hundred kilometers of his birthplace and found time to visit and discuss politics with his 105-year-old uncle. For him, such ongoing social contact is obvious. No matter how well-educated or far-flung, Sardinians treat close contact with aging family members as a moral imperative.

Though there is a powerful "female effect"—women are more likely to look after their aging relatives in their own homes than men—I wondered how working people of either sex sustained this level of commitment. "Of course we have to balance our careers with family life," Gianni told me when I asked. "But as a Sardinian, I never forget to visit my mother. She lives seventy kilometers from me, but every week, on Sunday, I go to visit her. She is eighty-seven now but is mentally fantastic. I talk to her about my work at the university and she always gives me a lot of interesting advice. You know, sometimes in the academic world there are conflicts. And I talk openly with hcr about these problems and she is able to tell me, for example, 'You should be less conflictual with the people who criticize your work, or in the way you're dealing with the university.' I recognize her ability and her competence in dealing with these types of problems." He clearly viewed a close relationship between adult children and their aging parents as a Sardinian trait. More interesting to me, though, was that he was describing true reciprocity. Caring for increasingly fragile seniors was more than a duty.

EVERYBODY DOES IT

The afternoon that I met Giovanni Corrias, a 102-year-old bachelor from Villagrande, he was sitting in a wooden rocking chair surrounded by younger women. Maria Corrias, the sixty-five-year-old niece who had lived with him for the past twenty-three years, was there. Also his twenty-five-year-old grandniece, Sarah, and the visitors: Eva, Delia (my interpreter), and me. We were drinking espresso from thimble-like cups in Maria and Giovanni's immaculate living room when the doorbell rang. His sister-in-law had come to drop off some produce. That made six of us. If he thought all this female company unusual, he didn't let on.

Zio Giovanni's white shirt and gray trousers were carefully pressed. Under a woolen cap, his black eyes were alert; his sober, slightly hostile manner put the lie to the notion that you need to think positive thoughts to live a long life. When I asked him why he thought he'd lived so long, he shot back, "Why would I die?"

Maria: "He doesn't like that question. Ask him a different one."

So what's the secret of a long life, Zio? I asked. Is it a lifetime of hill walking? Family time? Playing the *sullitu* (the Sardinian flute) or drinking the local red wine?

"Eh, beh. I like wine—maybe little too much," he replied. Then a pause. He cast a dark look in my direction and tipped his chin up angrily, suddenly erupting: "Nobody has to know my secrets!"

The real secret lies as much in his genes as in the culture of his village. Zio Giovanni was lucky to have been born in a place where female family members refer to him as *il tesoro* and find it a *gioia* to live with him and offer him love, companionship, and a large dose of respect. I asked Maria, his sixty-five-year-old niece, if it really is a joy to mind an irascible shut-in. To make sure he doesn't fall. To prepare and purée his favorite foods. To bathe him every morning while he sits on a special waterproof chair in the shower. To carefully pat him dry and then soothe his easily abraded 102-year-old skin with expensive creams, a different one for each part of his body. Or is it a duty?

"No, no! It's a pleasure for me," his niece insisted. "You don't understand. He is my heritage. The seniors of this village are my heritage. I do it with love."

I persist with another question. So does living this way really make you happy?

"*Certo!* It's difficult and it's a great sacrifice, but I do it with pleasure. When I was young, he helped me a lot. Now I'm grateful. And our jewel is still here!"

I turn to her niece, Sarah, a dark-haired young beauty with cell-phone in hand. "Well? Are you going to do this for your elderly parents, aunts, and uncles too?"

"*Certo.* Of course I will," she replied. "You have to find time to do it. Everybody does it."

Whether Sarah's generation will provide the TLC that her relatives require to live to one hundred is anyone's guess. But when your spouse and your friends—and even your children—have died, people decades younger who call you *il tesoro* can make a world of difference.

But what if you don't happen to live in an isolated mountaintop village?

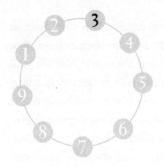

A Thousand Invisible Threads

Face-to-Face Contact and Social Contagion

Out of seven billion people in the world, six billion think religion helps them live a long, meaningful life—and science tells us they're onto something. People who practice a religion are happier, healthier, and live longer than atheists, according to a mountain of empirical evidence.[1] One seven-year study of ninety thousand women from across the United States found that those who attended religious services at least once a week were 20 percent less likely to die. Another study, of three thousand older women, found that religious practice forestalls cognitive decline.[2] And even if there's a sex difference—there are more long-living female believers around the world than male—the health benefits of religious practice accrue to men too. Most psychologists agree that the protective effects of religion are primarily social, due not so much to the redemptive power of prayer as to the fact that religions help bring human beings together in one place. Rabbi Marc Gellman of the US cable show *God Squad* agrees, and told the following story to American journalist Zev Chafetz. "The writer Harry Golden once asked his father, who was an atheist, why he went to services every Saturday. The old man told him, 'My friend Garfinkle goes to talk to God, and I go to talk to Garfinkle.'"[3]

If Golden's father and Garfinkle had lived in the same village, they might not have needed the structured weekly gathering that religions provides. In fact, belonging to a religious group *is* a lot like living in a village. On the one hand, your behavior is on display: people watch your every move. But on the other hand, people also know when you need help and are more likely to provide it.

These acts of altruism are contagious and they bind the community. One of my academic heroes, the down-to-earth American sociologist Arlie Russell Hochschild, considered her childhood summers spent on the family's farm in Turner, Maine (population 5,734), as a series of pointless chores at first. Weeding her aunt's cornfield and stacking roof shingles just didn't do it for the ten-year-old. At the time she didn't perceive what is implicit in village life: long-term bonds are forged through a casual exchange of home-baked goods, babysitting, borrowed tools, shared expertise, and spur-of-the-moment visits. "People didn't give practical help just to get things done; they got things done, in part, to affirm their bonds," she writes. "Part of such bonds expressed love of one another's company, but they also represented an unspoken pact: 'I'm on call for you in your hour of need and you are for me.' Villagers might quarrel, gossip, get bored, and leave. But living there, they paid a moral tax to the community in this readiness to 'just do.'"[4]

Religious people are more likely to pay that tax, surveys tell us. They volunteer more time to community service, offer more spare change to homeless people they pass on the street, and donate more money to organized charity and more blood to blood banks than secular folks do.[5] Compared to atheists, their altruism is amplified if, right before they're asked to pitch in, they're somehow reminded of God (or of some supernatural "watcher"), which erases their anonymity, according to experiments by Canadian psychologists Ara Norenzayan and Azim Shariff.[6] Earlier research in the United Kingdom had shown that people were three times more likely to pay for their cup of tea when a picture of human eyes (as opposed to a still life) was posted in an "honor system" office kitchen, and were more likely to give to charity when they sensed that someone was watching them.[7] It's as if there's a little sensor in our brains that picks up cues about how to behave in a group environment. Even bonobos, one of our closest primate ancestors, will open a trapdoor in order to share their food with strangers as long as there's a little social interaction first, according to research by Duke University primatologists Jingzhi Tan and Brian Hare. Animals that wouldn't interact with the potential "donor" bonobos were out of luck.[8] Could it be that altruism evolved and is more likely to catch on when there's no chance of anonymity? That's what the evidence suggests. Anyone who's been the target of online trolls knows that anonymity can provide cover for pretty nasty behavior. But the sense that you're being observed in the here and now seems to make people more civil.

Whether prompted by empathy, guilt, the wrath of God, the promise of rewards in the world to come, or the fact that the neighbors are watching from behind their lace curtains, there is clearly a religious—and village—impetus to pay it forward. Such mutual aid was adaptive, meaning that in the evolutionary past, religious adherents were more likely than non-practitioners to make it to adulthood and to have children who survived long enough to produce children of their own. Norenzayan and Shariff speculate that by the time human settlements got so large that people couldn't see the whites of each other's eyes, reminders of God or an omniscient supernatural power may have curtailed bad behavior, while increasing trust, loyalty, and generosity toward others within the group, ultimately making social groups more cohesive and impervious to outside threats.[9]

But there's something else too. Praying, chanting, singing, swaying, and rocking all together in the same room feel good; such coordinated social rituals are often the main event at religious gatherings. When I asked my friend Judy, a secular Jew, why she attended synagogue, she told me that the rituals provided "a sense of community without talking." They also prompt the release of serotonin, a neurotransmitter that regulates mood and digestion and plays a role in wound healing. Neurotransmitters released during such activities are why evolutionary anthropologist Lionel Tiger calls religious practice "brain-soothing."[10] They're also infectious. If you've ever attended a religious service where you're prompted to stand, sit, bow, kneel, sing, or clap in unison, you'll know how viscerally persuasive it feels to be one of many—and how difficult it is to resist. Doing the wave at an arena or saluting the flag prompts similar feelings of unity.

If doing things together in the same room makes us feel like we're being watched over and looked after and induces a sense of mutual trust, where does this shared influence begin?

EMOTIONAL CONTAGION

Genuine social contact can effectively rewire our brains and nudge us toward life-altering decisions. It turns out that it can also transmit deep-seated feelings such as joy, hostility, or shame, as well as thoughts and intentions. While language adds a layer of richness and clarity to our intentions, it's not always required to get the message across. A glance lasting about twenty milliseconds is all I need to read whether my daughter is anxious or elated, and that brief glimpse helps me predict what is likely to happen next. I am her mother, after all, as well as a psychologist, but I can't take much credit, given that monkeys can do this too.

In a classic experiment from the 1960s (which would never get past university research ethics committees today), University of Pittsburgh psychologist Robert E. Miller showed how attuned rhesus monkeys are to the expression of emotion in each other's faces. He and his colleagues put two rhesus monkeys in separate rooms, connected by a window. The monkey in one room was taught to associate a clicking sound with an impending electric shock. The monkey in the other room couldn't hear the warning clicks, but he could see his buddy's facial expression. During the short pause between click and shock, the observer monkey could disable the mechanism by pressing a lever, though his only clue as to what was coming was the anxious look on the face of his buddy. The researchers showed that the observer monkey very quickly learned to press the lever before they both got zapped. "Apparently, the monkey with the lever had no trouble reading the face of the one who could hear the warning," writes primatologist Frans de Waal in *The Age of Empathy*, adding that "the monkey was better at reading the other's expressions than the scientists."[11]

EMOTIONAL CONTAGION STARTS WITH MIMICRY

It's not terribly surprising that members of the same species are better able to read signs of impending danger in each other's facial expressions and body language than other species that—if they could grasp their prey's signals—might anticipate their next move and eat them for dinner. Animals that evolved the ability to read and act on subtle in-group cues would have stood a better chance of surviving and passing on their genes than those who were immune to such social signals. And on the predators' side, any animal that could accurately decode another species' movements and messages would have an advantage.

Despite a large frontal cortex that grants us outsized powers of imagination, reasoning, and communication, we are still largely at a disadvantage when it comes to understanding the instant messaging that goes on between members of other species. On a trip to Uganda in the summer of 2010, I observed several adolescent male wild chimps lolling near me in the shade of a tree in Kibale Park. One in particular drew my attention. He spent about twenty minutes scratching his armpits and crotch with his long, delicate fingers, not bothered at all by my presence. Then, without warning, an older male popped up about twenty yards away and started banging excitedly on a tree trunk. At the sound, about a dozen other chimps materialized out of nowhere, and all of them—including my slacker—were suddenly galvanized into action. Within minutes a critical mass of males was hooting and banging on tree trunks in some crazy syncopated rhythm. The feverish cacophony electrified the damp forest air.

Then, at some invisible signal (or at least invisible to me), they all galloped off excitedly after their leader into the pines.

It's easy to anthropomorphize or to see other animals as our poor cousins, Commodore 64s to our iPads. Both assumptions are wrong. The idea that nonhuman animals are always less sophisticated than humans

Adolescent male chimp in Kibale Forest National Park.

has been eclipsed by the past few decades of research on animals' complex social lives, from apes to elephants, from spotted hyenas to ants. Referring to the baroque social signaling that guides the division of labor and sharing of resources in ant societies, the Harvard biologist E. O. Wilson once quipped that Karl Marx was right; he just applied his theory to the wrong species.

According to Wilson and his co-author, Bert Hölldobler, in their 2009 book *The Superorganism*, there is no master plan in the brain of an ant, no blueprint of honeybee social order in the mind of the queen bee. Insects don't reason. Nor do they plan—or follow others' plans—for the future. "Instead, colony life is the product of self-organization," in which each individual automatically follows specific behavioral algorithms based on environmental cues. For example, depending on how much nectar it's found and how much help it has already recruited, a foraging honeybee flies back to the hive and communicates a status update by waggling figure eights on the walls. These torso wags map the exact location of a food source in relation to the sun, as well as its precise distance from the hive. If there are not enough bees outside the hive to exploit the find, the forager bee adds flourishes such as grabbing a hive mate from above and shaking him all over. Not enough workers in-house to process the flood of incoming nectar? The bee will tremble while moving through the hive "with forelegs held aloft like Saint Vitus dancers," write the entomologists. Signaling bees can also embellish a work order with rhythmic buzzing, more dynamic dance moves, and squirts of scent.

If that level of specificity—including an ability to remember where the flower with the sweetest nectar is in a row of identical-looking perennial beds—can exist in a brain the size of a pinhead, then it can't be thinking about what symbols to communicate to its mates, any more than a motorist thinks about how she'll drive home from work. She may be turning at the right intersections, dutifully stopping at stop signs and red lights, all the while access-ing her mental road map, but, according to Wilson and Höldobler, she is "pondering neither the trip nor the operation of the auto-mobile."[12] Like honeybees, humans respond to immediate bio-chemical and geographic cues that, despite being invisible, sway how they "decide" what they'll do next.

MONKEY SEE, MONKEY DO: MIRROR NEURONS AND MIMICRY

That kind of automatic response is at the heart of the superorganism—an organic phenomenon created by dozens, if not hundreds, of leaderless individuals somehow acting in concert—whether in a beehive or the New York Stock Exchange. A similar lack of self-reflection characterizes one of the building blocks of human empa-thy: the mirror neuron system.

In the late eighties, mirror neurons were discovered by two Italian neurophysiologists, Giacomo Rizzolati and Vittorio Gallese. They were investigating how the neural circuits of the pre-motor cortex register what happens before you execute a simple action, such as reaching for something you want to eat. If a tasty morsel— say, a piece of dark chocolate—was sitting on your desk within arm's length and you finally decided to reach for it, which of the brain's hundred billion neurons would become excited and light up right before you extended your arm? To answer that question, the scientists implanted electrodes in the pre-motor cortices of macaques so they could see which neural area became activated when the monkeys prepared to grab something.[13] Then their most remarkable finding surfaced, completely by accident.

The day it happened, one of the electrode-implanted macaques was sitting on a chair in Gallese's lab watching the scientist move around. When Gallese reached for something, he suddenly heard an explosive crackling on the computer connected to the monkey's brain. "It signalled a discharge from the pertinent cell in area F5," recalled a colleague, Marco Iacoboni. "The monkey was just sitting quietly, not intending to grasp anything, yet this neuron affiliated with the grasping action had fired nonetheless." Other colleagues in the lab were able to provoke a similar reaction in the area of the brain specialized for grasping, lifting, or tearing things. Simply picking up a peanut or an ice cream cone elicited the same excited response in the monkey's pre-motor cortex, even though the animal was just sitting there, watching the experimenters.[14]

The discovery of mirror neurons—motor cells that fire when *someone else* moves—added a new twist to the idea of passive observation. Here, then, was the neural hardware underlying all sorts of unconscious contagion, from the way people reflexively flinch when they see that someone is about to get smacked, to the way a tennis player's arm tenses when he watches another athlete prepare his swing. Mirror neurons aren't helping you *imagine* how it feels; they're literally putting you through the paces.

This mirroring happens even when you're watching the action on a screen—or, rather, broadcast on your goggles—as Iacoboni discovered when he collaborated with an adman to test people's neural reactions to Super Bowl commercials. When Iacoboni and his team projected the ads while subjects were in the scanner, their mirror neuron systems became activated. It was not so much the actors' gestures that elicited a response, Iacoboni suggests, but the degree to which a test subject identified with the particular actor on the screen.[15]

Though the automatic nature of mirror neurons doesn't account for more shaded forms of empathy, such as feeling someone's psychological pain, the discovery of mirror neurons went a long way toward explaining many of our everyday experiences. People unconsciously use a more halting rhythm of speech when they're chatting with someone who stutters, and adjust their posture to mirror the stance of the person they're talking to. In a face-to-face conversation, when one person crosses his arms, usually the other follows suit. And as anyone in a lecture or symphony audience knows, yawning, scratching, and coughing are also contagious.[16] Some studies have even shown greater electrical activity in parts of the body of a person directly observing an action performed by someone else: the lips of a person listening to someone stutter showed greater electrical activity than the lips of someone who couldn't hear the stutter, even though the observer's lips weren't moving; people watching an arm-wrestling tournament had increased electrical activity in their biceps even though they weren't wrestling themselves.[17]

Not only that, but when people are interacting face-to-face, unconscious mimicry elicits emotions that grease the wheels of social interaction. Studies by MIT's Sandy Pentland and his team have shown that the more people mirror each other in conversation, the more they say they trust each other. To measure how synchronized people were, the researchers used a sensor they'd designed called a sociometer, which is the size of an iPhone and is worn around the neck like a conference nametag. The device measures the back-and-forth nonverbal interaction within groups, such as reciprocal smiling and head nods. Pentland and his colleague Jared Curhan used the sociometer to show that the more verbal mimicry there was between a manager and a boss in the first five minutes of salary negotiations, the more satisfied the two felt about the discussion, and the more generous the negotiated package. Unconscious mimicry—including quick vocal blips such as "Okay?" "Okay!"— was associated with a 20 to 30 percent increase in salary and benefits for the new hire.[18] Restaurant wait staff also benefit from social mimicry. You're likely to tip a waiter an average of 140 percent more if he repeats your food order verbatim than if he just paraphrases what you want.[19] This type of unconscious imitation hints at how much our "thinking" hinges on face-to-face contact.

ANIMAL SYNCHRONY

My son Eric, a keen birdwatcher, once described seeing a single sandpiper on a Cape Cod beach abruptly look up. The whole flock followed suit within milliseconds. Like a mob of tiny tourists staring at a Manhattan skyscraper, they all tipped up their heads because one did it first. Then the flock mysteriously rose into the air and fell again as one unit, responding to some silent signal of alarm that only one of them had seen.[20] Such synchrony is familiar to snorkelers, who can spook thousands of fish with a tiny tip of a flipper, and to those who herd mammals, which, whether munching on grass or trading stocks, often act in concert. The singing of blue whales off Half Moon Bay, south of San Francisco, for example, coalesces into a single frequency of sixteen hertz, according to physicist Roger Bland. After analyzing 4,300 recordings, Bland observed that the whales are "like a choir singing together, mutually tuning in to the same frequency."[21]

Meanwhile, the footfalls of people crossing a bridge at the same time can become so coordinated as to collapse the structure. This almost happened on June 10, 2000, when London's elegant Millennium Bridge started swinging precariously as soon

as it was opened to the public. Designed to allow London pedestrians to traverse the Thames between the Tate Modern and St.
Paul's Cathedral, the bridge's arcing steel balustrades, resembling
a giant spider's filaments, are the epitome of sturdy modern
design. The supports are not only graceful, they don't sag as
much as other suspension bridges. Yet, as journalist John Cassidy
reported in the *New Yorker*,

> Within minutes of the official opening, the footway started to sway
> alarmingly, forcing some of the pedestrians to cling to the side rails.
> Some reported feeling seasick. The authorities shut the bridge,
> claiming that too many people were using it. The next day, the
> bridge reopened with strict limits on the number of pedestrians,
> but it began to sway dangerously once again. Two days after it had
> opened, with the source of the wobble still a mystery, the bridge
> was closed for an indefinite period.

The reason for the wobble, the engineers discovered, was that
too many people had "caught" the rhythm of their neighbors' gait.
When everyone was moving in lockstep, the bridge started to move
in synchrony. "Once the footway starts swaying, however subtly,
more and more pedestrians adjust their gait to get comfortable,
stepping to and fro in synch. As a positive-feedback loop develops
between the bridge's swing and the pedestrian's stride, the sideways
forces can increase dramatically and the bridge can lurch violently," Cassidy wrote. The same goes for the financial markets, he
added, referring to the work of the Princeton economist Hyun
Song Shin. "Where previously there were diverse views, now there
is unanimity: everybody's moving in lockstep."[22] Whether it's birds
flying, whales singing, chimps banging, or bridges swaying, there
is an infectious aspect to each individual's behavior that makes the
whole more than the sum of its parts.

INVISIBLE SIGNALS

Close physical proximity is crucial to emotional contagion. Good fiction writers know this, making observations about one character's loopy stride, or the ammoniac scent of dread of another's plaid shirt that pull the unsuspecting reader right into a scene. In *Annie John*, Jamaica Kincaid's coming-of-age novel set on the island of Antigua, her young protagonist's tight synchrony with her new-found best friend tells us all we need to know about an adolescent's heady first experiments in intimacy. Like teenagers everywhere, the two girls do the same thing at the same time in the same way, yet attribute their matchiness to karma:

> Gwen and I were soon inseparable. If you saw one, you saw the other. For me, each day began as I waited for Gwen to come by and fetch me for school. . . . When finally she reached me, she would look up and we would both smile and say softly, 'hi.' We'd set off for school side by side, our feet in step, not touching but feeling as if we were joined at the shoulder, hip and ankle, not to mention the heart.[23]

Kincaid might have added the uterus while she was at it. In the late 1960s, when the American experimental psychologist, Martha McClintock, was an undergraduate at an all-girls college in suburban Massachusetts, she noticed that as she and her Wellesley roommates began to spend more and more time together, their menstrual periods became synchronized. When she mentioned it to several male scientists who were discussing a similar phenomenon in caged female mice, her frank observation prompted ridicule. "Don't you know? Women do that, too," she remembers telling the skeptics at a summer workshop at the Jackson Labs in Maine. Three years later, in 1971, twenty-three-year-old McClintock showed them. In a pioneering article published in *Nature*, titled "Menstrual Synchrony and Suppression," McClintock showed how increased social interaction among 135 female roommates and close friends prompted their menstrual cycles to overlap. The synchrony of the young women's periods hinged not only on time spent together but on the intimacy of the relationship—close friends had greater synchrony than roommates who were just roommates. McClintock hypothesized that the catalyst was pheromones: airborne microscopic, odorless chemical signals about our emotional states that can shift the behavior of people who are close to us.

Today menstrual synchrony is called the McClintock Effect, and it has been found in women living in college dormitories (single-sex and co-ed), on kibbutzim, in cohabiting mothers and daughters, in lesbian couples, in commune and co-op residents, and among nurses and female office workers.[24] Menstrual synchrony is not universal, and scientists are still debating how it works. Still, even if the mechanisms underlying face-to-face contagion remain obscure, the McClintock Effect tells us that details about our emotional or reproductive status can be communicated to others—without our permission, and without their awareness.

If you're wondering why anyone would care about this phenomenon, consider this bizarre research finding. Geoffrey Miller, an evolutionary psychologist at the University of New Mexico, managed to persuade eighteen lap dancers in Albuquerque to participate in a study designed to track their earnings against their menstrual cycles. This wasn't a huge sample but the dancers worked long hours, so Miller and his two colleagues were able to map 5,300 lap dances over two months' time. The experimenters had never met the performers, who were given ID numbers to preserve their anonymity and a confidential mailbox where they could drop off their completed questionnaires. When the researchers mapped where a dancer was in her cycle against her earnings per five-hour shift, they discovered an intriguing pattern. The male patrons unwittingly selected ovulating women more often than they chose women who were menstruating. The ovulating women also seemed to be earning bigger tips per dance. In the fertile phase of their cycles, the dancers earned $354 per five-hour shift, or $70 per hour. Menstruating women earned $185 per shift, or $35 per hour, exactly half that amount. (Meanwhile, between the two phases of their cycles, the women earned $264.)[25]

Where our primate relatives advertise their fertility with colorful genital swellings, human primates have evolved to be somewhat more subtle. But we communicate this information nonetheless, with invisible signals that can have a transformative effect on our friends, not to mention our pocketbooks. Powerful women such as IMF head Christine Lagarde, Hillary Clinton, and Michelle Obama understand the importance of their appearance when meeting people face-to-face. And it's not just women who benefit from appearances. Research shows that, on average, tall men earn more than their shorter colleagues, and women on the lookout for male companions prefer those who are expensively dressed.[26] Like it or not, we broadcast a range of signals—such as hormonal fluctuations, behavioral synchrony, and other "in-person" indicators—that require us to be in the same room with another person for the message to hit home. And the stakes can be high, altering not only the contents of our pocketbooks but also our plans for the future.

PREGNANCY IS CATCHY

When a young Montreal couple, whom I'll call Diane and Bob, considered starting a family, they told me they didn't think it was anyone's business but their own. Like any young couple, they were a world unto themselves, wrapped up in each other, everyone else on the outside. Or so they thought. But when Bob heard that his older sister's first baby had just been born, he dropped everything and bought a plane ticket. He wanted to meet this baby.

At thirty-one, Bob was five years younger than his sister. His wife, Diane, had only recently graduated from university, and while they had been thinking about having kids, they were wondering whether it was really the right time. "There were some things

I wanted to make sure we had in life before we had our first kid. I'd been saying to Diane, 'Let's wait, let's think about it,'" Bob told me as we drank tea in his sunny kitchen in the Mile End neighborhood of Montreal.

The day his niece was born, Bob held her against his chest, and she fell asleep there for over an hour. "That was so nice," he recalled, eyes focused on the middle distance. "I remember that as soon as the baby woke up I called Diane, saying—"

At this point the more reserved Diane jumped in to finish his sentence, "—'I want one!'" Six months later, Diane was pregnant with their first child, now a lively, curly-haired little girl named Jessica.

This conversation would be no more than a sentimental anecdote if it didn't illustrate a surprising finding. Fertility is contagious between siblings, according to research by Columbia University economist Ilyana Kuziemko. And the contagion isn't between just any two siblings—it starts with a sister's pregnancy. It's as if she transmits her fertility to her siblings, especially after her first child is born. At that point the likelihood that one of her brothers or sisters will decide to start a family within the next two years jumps by 30 percent. And the contagion goes in only one direction. "The most striking finding is that fertility rises dramatically for both men and women after their *sister* has a child—yet the birth of a child to a brother appears to have no effect on an individual's fertility," Kuziemko writes.[27]

How do siblings "catch" pregnancy from each other? Kuziemko suggests that the prospect of having a baby becomes more appealing after a sister has one. She's suddenly in a position to pass on timely childcare and medical information, not to mention hand-me-downs and the skinny on the best preschools. This makes sense, given that the contagion effect is strongest for siblings who live near each other. There are also other incentives to ensure that an extended family's babies are clustered by age. Social scientists call these subtle influences "network externalities," which is just a fancy way of saying that the fun and benefit of doing things together outweighs doing them alone.

Could something other than social contagion be at the root of the sibling baby boomlet that follows a sister's first child? Siblings who are two years apart in age might naturally space their children the same way, for instance, so that the pattern mimics the domino effect. Or perhaps sibs explicitly plan to have children in close succession, thus creating a little soccer team for their extended families. When I raised these possibilities, Kuziemko said no, having babies really is contagious. "The sibling effects are *in addition* to any coincidental correlations in the fertility patterns of individual siblings," she told me. Adult siblings are significantly more likely to have a baby, increasing their family size, as a reaction to their sister having a baby. The effect isn't immediate. Most childless siblings take time to absorb the information, often only deciding to have a baby themselves after connecting with a niece or nephew face-to-face—or chest-to-chest—then thinking it over for a few months. By that time, many of them want one for themselves.

WHETHER YOU WANT ONE OR NOT

Among teenagers, pregnancy can be particularly contagious. In September 2008, in the middle of the election campaign, US vice-presidential candidate Sarah Palin's seventeen-year-old daughter Bristol announced that she was pregnant. Far from outrage, the ensuing avalanche of support from evangelical Christians revealed that many of them didn't seem to find a pregnant high-school student all that unusual. Like tattoos, once emblems of biker gangs and prison culture, teenage pregnancy had become so common in the community as to become respectable. Keeping the baby was regarded as a sign of moral fiber. "Like so many other American families who are in the same situation, I think it's great that she instilled in her daughter the values to have the child and not sneak off someplace and have an abortion," a Louisiana delegate told a reporter at the Republican convention. Writing in the *New Yorker* later that fall, Margaret Talbot quoted Marlys Popma, head of evangelical outreach for John McCain's campaign, expressing a similar sentiment. "There hasn't been one evangelical family that hasn't gone through some sort of situation," said Ms. Popma.[28] Even Bristol Palin added her two cents: "Everyone should be abstinent, but it's not realistic at all. . . . Sex is just more and more accepted now among kids my age."

While 75 percent of evangelical teenagers say they believe that there should be no sex before marriage (compared to 50 percent of other Protestants and 25 percent of Jews), their convictions and their behavior collide. According to a huge US government survey of adolescents, even though three-quarters of them oppose premarital sex, teens from evangelical and conservative Christian families have an earlier sexual debut, are more sexually active, and are less likely to use contraception than teenagers from nearly every other religious group in America.[29]

This disconnect has subtle social roots. As Mark Regnerus, a sociologist at the University of Texas, points out in his book on teenage sex and religion, *Forbidden Fruit*, abstinence pledgers— a trend among evangelical Protestant teens—are unlikely to use contraception the first few times they have sex. "More often than not they will have experienced first sex without planning to do so, and lack of planning usually means lack of contraception. For such youth to introduce contraception into their own sexual activity would require a drastic change of script," he writes. As virginity is a big deal and they're not supposed to be thinking about sex before marriage, "sex eventually 'happens' to most evangelical youths, despite their best intentions." That's one reason why their STD infection and pregnancy rates trump those of other American teens.[30] The no-sex-before-marriage rule, combined with an aversion to talking about sex, contraception, and abortion, creates a knowledge vacuum. Then, as more and more teens become pregnant, what was initially taboo gradually becomes acceptable, if not contagious, within the group—even if its members don't want it to.

So which teenagers are able to resist the pressure to have unprotected sex early on? The ones who are deeply embedded in tightly woven face-to-face social networks, according to Regnerus. Those teenagers with close relationships to friends and family (who also have close relationships with each other) are more likely to get the social support they need to delay sex until they're ready. As Margaret Talbot writes, "close-knit families make a difference. Teenagers who live with both biological parents are more likely to be virgins than those who do not. And adolescents who say that their families understand them, pay attention to their concerns, and have fun with them are more likely to delay intercourse, regardless of religiosity."[31]

BEING THERE

As we've seen, the process of social contagion begins with mimicry: sensing what other people are doing in real time and unconsciously doing it too. Like the chimps who "aped" their tree-signaling buddies, you have to be in close proximity for synchrony to happen. Online networks can mobilize people's votes and political protests can spread via Twitter and Facebook, as was the case during the astounding transformations of the Arab Spring and the Occupy movement. But even if the images and invitations to participate were transmitted electronically, the protests happened face-to-face. Anyone who saw the mobs, the tent cities, and the riot police knows that the expression "You had to be there" still holds. The tweets, digital photos, and messages inflamed people, invoking them to join in. But if the political activity had only taken place in the virtual world, those protest movements would have been emasculated.

The same is true for other types of behavioral contagion. Being there in person means you're more likely to be so deeply affected by someone's emotional state that you'll do something about it. And the closer your relationship to someone, the more infectious his happiness—and also his frustration and despair. Which is to say that not all social contagion is for the good. Nowhere is this more evident than when neurological symptoms spread from person to person within tightly knit social groups. When several close friends who have been in face-to-face contact with each other come down with mysterious symptoms—tics, fainting, nervous laughter, dizziness, headaches, nausea—that have no clear physiological causes, emotional contagion is usually the culprit.

Sometimes such events can seem almost comical. In January 1962, when three teenage girls near Lake Victoria, Tanzania, started laughing uncontrollably, it wasn't taken very seriously. But within months their mirthless laughter had ignited an epidemic of giggling, spread via face-to-face contact with other students throughout the Lake Victoria district. Ultimately 217 teenagers were affected, most of them girls. Their infectious laughter closed down four schools in three different villages. "The epidemic was no laughing matter," the social scientists James Fowler and Nicholas Christakis write in their book, *Connected*. Like other cases of mass hysteria, this one provoked paranoia about environmental toxins. But lab tests, medical exams, and environmental assays found nothing suspicious in the lake, the groundwater, the school, or the girls' bodies.[32]

In October 2011, a seventeen-year-old cheerleader named Katie Krautwurst, from a small town in western New York, woke up with a violent facial tic; her muscle spasms were out of control. Katie was still being plagued by tics when her best friend, Thera Sanchez, captain of the girls' cheerleading squad, woke from a nap stuttering and unable to keep her arms and head from jerking spasmodically. Throughout their ordeal, the two friends remained close. "They spoke in shorthand and overlapping sentences," Susan Dominus wrote in the *New York Times*, noting this comment from Thera: "Katie told me that she wouldn't wish tics on anyone, but if it had to be someone, she was glad she was going through it with her best friend." Two weeks later, another friend from the same high school, Lydia Parker, started humming and swinging her arms uncontrollably, once unintentionally bashing her face with her cellphone. By January 2012, eighteen students from a single small-town New England high school, seventeen of them girls, were twitching, humming, and jerking their limbs.

With understandable dismay, the members of this working-class community saw their teenagers' strange behavior attract national attention. *Dr. Drew* and the *Today Show* featured live footage of the bruised faces of the flailing girls, whose symptoms worsened with all the media coverage. The frightened parents turned to concrete villains—environmental contamination from a now defunct Jell-O factory, or from natural gas wells near the school. But the real culprits turned out to be more subtle. In this formerly prosperous but now struggling community, most of the biological fathers were absent. An unusual number of families were headed by single mothers—more than the national average—and these mothers worked long hours, often leaving younger siblings in the teens' care.

There were other stresses, too. Suffering from a painful chronic illness, Katie's mother had yet another operation in a series of surgeries the week before her daughter's tics appeared. Thera had epilepsy. Lydia's father had been abusive. As with other epidemics of psychogenic illness, there was no evidence of environmental contamination or viral illness. Yet the girls were neither faking nor malingering. Instead, through a kind of instinctive empathy built through common experience and unconscious synchrony, they were expressing as a group what none of them was able to voice on her own.

Psychologists call such behavior "conversion disorder"—the involuntary conversion of psychological symptoms into physical ones—or the Victorian-sounding "mass hysteria."[33] While witch hunts, and worse, were the most common responses to mass hysteria in the seventeenth century, recently social scientists are more likely to see these epidemics as one way in which tightly bonded groups transmit common feelings of anxiety and stress among their members. Like a flock of geese rising into the air at the sound of the first gunshot, panic can hit a group of closely connected people, binding their behavior together in alarming ways. It's the village effect gone wild.

Who's Coming to Dinner?

Food, Drink, and Social Bonds

In the first two chapters we saw how face-to-face social contact prompts some of the good things in life, such as health, happiness, and longevity. In the previous chapter it was a mixed bag; if gait, teen pregnancy, and tics can be contagious, then social contact is not always a force for good. The latest evidence on that score is as intriguing as it is controversial. In 2007, two academics living on opposite American coasts, physician and social scientist Nicholas Christakis, in Boston, and political scientist James Fowler, in San Diego, published a study in the *New England Journal of Medicine* that rocked the research world. Already interested in the social transmission of longevity (Christakis) and of political leanings (Fowler), they happened on a rich source of data: the Framingham Heart Study, which had been tracking the health status and habits of all the residents of a Boston suburb since the late 1940s. Intended to be an investigation of cardiovascular health, the study had gone on so long that the grandchildren of the original subjects were now taking part, providing priceless data about the genetic blueprint of the disease.

But what was most valuable to Fowler and Christakis was that each research subject had named one social contact. If, in the future, the study's organizers needed to track a subject down, that person would be the one to call. The nomination had to be a good indicator of social intimacy, Christakis and Fowler thought. Already armed with knowledge about their subjects' spouses and family members, they realized they could plumb how people's social networks had evolved over several decades and draw parallels to any changes in their health. Obesity, smoking, alcoholism, depression, and happiness were just some of the behaviors and traits they thought might be socially transmissible.

How did Christakis and Fowler get hooked on this idea of contagion in the first place? Both men were deeply curious about the way trends spread through human networks. They were lucky in happening on the Framingham data. They also spent many hours on Skype talking to each other and to other colleagues. Plus . . . did I mention that a matchmaker was involved? Christakis, a scholarly George Clooney lookalike, was introduced to the sunny, boyish Fowler by the latter's doctoral supervisor. The supervisor didn't know what to do with Fowler's thesis on how social networks influenced political beliefs. When he heard Christakis give a talk about how social networks were implicated in the widowhood effect (when husbands die soon after their wives do), he put the two researchers together. At least a dozen scientific articles and a book later, they are still collaborating, and have been referred to as the Batman and Robin of social science.

As the Framingham data set predated popular use of the Internet, there were no wireless networks, Facebook friends, texts, or tweets to track. But the data did include 5,124 offspring of the original Framingham subjects, who had been assessed every four years, from 1971 to 2003. Like the residents of Villagrande, many of them were connected to one another in multiple ways—as relatives, friends, neighbors, and colleagues. To investigate the impact of their relationships, Christakis and Fowler plumbed the nature of their overlapping social contacts, which added up to 12,067 subjects with 38,600 ties linking them together. It wasn't just the size of a small town, it *was* a small town. Most of these people had been

checking in with their doctors for decades, getting weighed and
measured and reporting on what they ate and drank, on the status
of their marriage, and their moods—all the while providing the
name of that one important Framingham-based social contact (the
nominated person had to live in Framingham), even switching that
person for someone else as relationships changed.

It was a new approach to an old idea. When John Donne wrote,
"No man is an island" in the early 1600s, the field of social neuroscience didn't exist. Nor had scientists come up with a way to
measure the effect of human bonds 230 years later, when Reverend
Henry Melvill wrote the lines I've used as the epigraph for this
book: "A thousand fibres connect you with your fellow-men." One
hundred and fifty years later, the researchers hoped those fibers
could be made visible.

With a little help from a few Intel processors, not to mention a
legion of research assistants entering and analyzing data, the contents of dozens of dusty file boxes confirmed the researchers'
hunches: behaviors related to health and happiness can sweep
through populations the way epidemics do. Over time, health

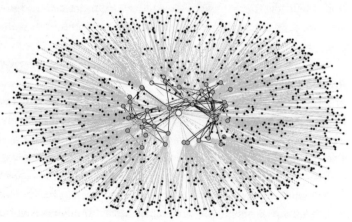

*John McColgan's second-degree sociogram, which includes his friends, as
well as the friends of his friends.*

problems such as obesity and alcoholism seemed to travel from person to person within identifiable cliques. In other words, becoming dangerously overweight could be contagious within real social networks, much the way a bad cold gets passed along with the bean salad at a potluck supper.

Here, then, was a paradox. On the one hand, socializing with friends can help you fight off loneliness and chronic illness. But on the other, close relationships, especially to certain people, can trash your self-control, making you fatter than you would have been if you'd been left to your own devices.

ARE YOUR FRIENDS MAKING YOU FAT?

Christakis and Fowler's findings came as a surprise to experts who thought that unbridled appetites, supersized portions, "fat genes," and sedentary habits were the main causes of our ballooning midriffs. By 2012 two-thirds of Americans were overweight and a third of them were obese—73 million adults and 13 million kids— as were a quarter of all Canadian and British citizens. Apparently this wasn't just because there was a fast-food joint on every corner and not enough time, money, or motivation to exercise and prepare healthy meals. According to this new research, it was also because obesity is contagious. If your best friend or sister, or even your best friend's sister packed on the pounds, you'd be more likely to put on weight too.[1]

In the United States, a nation preoccupied with its obesity epidemic, Christakis and Fowler's finding made public health officials sit up and take notice. It also piqued the interest of the press. A front page *New York Times* article was headlined "Are Your Friends Making You Fat?" and Oprah's production team and the *Colbert Report* came calling. The attention was karmic, given that Fowler was the one who had put some scientific meat on the bones of the rumored "Colbert Bump"—the surge in popularity that followed a politician's appearance on the show.[2]

Even more surprising than the idea that you can catch obesity from your best friend is the suggestion that it can move from one person to another and then to another within a social network, even if the first and third links in the chain never meet. The researchers came to this conclusion after comparing the Framingham data to a computer simulation of random relationships. In the Framingham sample, not only did obesity appear in clusters, serious weight gain seemed to move from contact to contact, petering out after three social links. As Christakis and Fowler point out in *Connected*, "The average obese person was more likely to have friends, friends of friends, and friends of friends of friends who were obese than would be expected due to chance alone," suggesting, as they put it, "your friends' friends can make you fat."

After learning about obesity contagion, I couldn't help but wonder: with friends like these, who needs enemies? And there was something else, too. As we saw in the previous chapter, the more intimate our connection to someone, the greater their influence on us. So how can we be influenced by someone we've never met?

First, as the researchers themselves note, friends are fairly likely to enjoy the same foods and have the same habits—that's why they're friends! So a friend of yours might like someone you've never met but who shares your interests and appetites. So it might not just be contagion at work but the effect of birds of a feather flocking together. Moreover, a participant in the Framingham Heart Study would likely have named a friend who was similar to her as her primary contact. Each person would resemble the person they'd nominated. Then, as these similar people started to have children, stopped jogging, or approached middle age—or all those things happened at once—their waistlines would expand, if not exactly at the very same time, then in a hiccuppy but still connected sort of way.

Indeed, in 2011 Fowler and Christakis, along with Jaime Settler, demonstrated how friends self-segregate at the genetic level. We're drawn to people with whom we share matching clusters of nucleotides.[3] So, whatever our friends are doing, whether it's drinking pitchers of beer or eating artisanal cheeses, we're more likely to be doing it too, not only because monkey-see, monkey-do, but because we gravitate toward people who have the same cravings. Catching obesity from friends of friends could be more a matter of shared characteristics than social contagion, though friends who are in close proximity would certainly copy and influence each other too, amplifying the effect.

The researchers knew, of course, that social networks aren't the only reason for the obesity epidemic. Still, when Christakis and Fowler created a computer animation of the spread of obesity, they expected to see it expand outwards in a predictable way—the way an epidemic spreads from Patient Zero or, as they put it, the way "a pebble is dropped in a still pool of water, and a concentric circle of waves moves away from it." Instead they saw something messier.

> There seemed to be chaotic weight gain all over the place. And we realized that the proper analogy was not a single pebble dropped in a pool, but rather a whole handful of rocks thrown in over a wide area, creating a choppy surface, obscuring the impact of a single pebble and its waves. Sure obesity can spread, but it is not spreading from just one spot, and social contacts are not the only stimulus for weight gain. People take up eating, stop exercising, get divorced, lose a loved one, stop smoking or start drinking, and each one of these changes can form the epicenter of another tiny obesity epidemic, like the thousands of overlapping earthquakes that shake our tectonic plates every year.[4]

Clearly there was more than one thing going on at once. Aside from social contagion and homophily, there could be other causes of weight gain among friends, such as a new McDonald's in the neighborhood (or in my case, a great ice cream shop), catalysts for eating that might have little to do with social influences. The researchers tested for this by seeing if the direction of the esteem one person had for another predicted the direction of contagion. If two people named each other as their closest contact, then one person's weight gain should affect the other's equally. But if I nominated my friend Rosie as my one person to contact and she nominated someone else, Rosie's weight gain should affect my waistline more than my waistline would affect hers. And that's what Fowler and Christakis found: the contagion was lopsided. Susan (who had nominated Rosie as her one important contact) would be 57 percent more likely to pack on the pounds if Rosie became a little broad in the beam first. But if Rosie had not nominated Susan in return, Rosie would be only 13 percent more likely to put on weight if Susan did. Christakis and Fowler attribute the difference between these two numbers to social contagion.

This conclusion is controversial, and statisticians and health economists have since disputed whether the difference between these numbers is meaningful.[5] Still, Christakis and Fowler's ability to anticipate how obesity might spread via social ties within a single town is ingenious. And given what we know about mimicry, I think that they are right. Putting on weight *can* be infectious—as long as people have face-to-face contact, and especially if they're tightly linked by an emotional bond.

But I doubt that there is a mysterious iCloud effect that causes people to sync their eating, drinking, or moods without genuine interaction. And this body of research rests on a single nomination—the name of that one Framingham resident who would know your whereabouts if the researchers couldn't find you for a follow-up visit. But is that person always a close friend? When I was first reading these social network studies, I asked my husband, who was reading in his favorite chair across from me in the living room, whom I should call if I couldn't reach him on his BlackBerry about an upcoming doctor's appointment. "Carole," he answered, naming his highly competent administrative assistant. He looked up at me briefly over his stack of documents and added, "She has access to my agenda."

Even if we don't know why exactly, friends are indeed power-fully swayed by each other's eating habits. Sarah-Jeanne Salvy, a psychologist at the University of Buffalo, has shown that we match our eating to what our friends are consuming, eating more when we're face-to-face with people in our circle and less when we're eating alone or with strangers.[6] This rings true to me. When I travel for work and eat alone, I eat the minimum, getting the job done in fifteen minutes. But if I'm lucky enough to be dining with friends, as I was when I attended a conference in Heidelberg a few years ago, then I'm happy to consume three courses over three hours in a candlelit restaurant—venison consommé with dump-lings, herb-roasted free-range chicken with buttered greens and potatoes, and a goblet of red wine or two, followed by a confection made with pralines, crème anglaise, and meringue—at least 3,500 calories, all of which went down with no trouble at all, accompa-nied as it was by jokes, gossip, and stories. My four svelte compan-ions ate those three courses too. Why do we eat more when we're with friends or family than when we're alone?

THE ROOTS OF COMMUNAL EATING

In 2008, the twelve-thousand-year-old remains of a middle-aged woman were unearthed from a burial site in a cave in the Galilee hills, along with the fossilized bones of seventy tortoises, three wild oxen, several mountain gazelles, two martens, an eagle, a wild boar, and a leopard. Our Mesolithic ancestors held big parties, apparently. On this occasion, archeologists surmise that they bar-becued about 660 pounds of meat so that approximately thirty-five people could pay their respects to a recently deceased Natufian

woman—not excessive, I suppose, when it came to honoring someone they think was an important shaman. She certainly had status:
she was buried with her skull resting on one tortoise shell and her
pelvis elevated by half a dozen others.[7]

But another reason this woman was mourned with a lavish
feast is that eating together is a form of social glue, according to
Natalie Munro and Leore Grosman, the two archeologists who
investigated the burial site. The transition from a nomadic hunter-
gatherer existence to life in settled communities meant that these
mourners were living cheek by jowl with large numbers of people
for the first time in human history. In other words, they now had
neighbors. Anyone who has had to ask the folks next door to turn
down their thumping hip hop or to curb their beloved cocker-
doodle knows what that means. The inevitable interpersonal fric-
tion created by population density was eased by big communal
parties; sharing food helped such ragtag bands cohere. Indeed,
when people share food, they're more likely to feel that they are
part of a group and to compromise to resolve a conflict.[8] Who
knew that the business lunch began in a dry Middle Eastern
wadi where the area's disparate residents gathered to gnaw on
barbecued gazelle ribs? There may also have been pilaf on offer,
made from the local barley they were just starting to cultivate, and
a few dogs hanging around the fire—the first pets in history—
begging for scraps.

Hunter-gatherers settling down where they could grow grain,
instead of wandering around chasing wild herds, gave birth to village life about ten thousand years ago, and this settling down is
what allowed our forebears to let the good times roll. Neil
MacGregor, director of the British Museum, describes it as "a time
of newly domesticated animals, powerful gods, dangerous weather,
good sex and even better food."[9]

But how did the villagers figure out who belonged?

INSIDERS AND OUTCASTS

In-groups and out-groups are such common features of human—and primate—societies that most of us have felt the pain of social ostracism at some point in our lives. Even if we've only experienced it in small doses, social isolation provokes a unique type of anxiety that distorts our ability to think clearly and to see events with any optimism, according to John Cacioppo and William Patrick in their book *Loneliness*. The roots of social pain are biological. Our ancestors wouldn't have survived predators or privation for very long if they hadn't belonged to an inclusive group. Living in a community is so essential to survival that an early warning system evolved that rings biochemical alarm bells when we're ostracized. We experience these warnings as acute anxiety, which—like other metabolic warnings such as extreme hunger, thirst, or pain—essentially communicates the following message: *fix this or you're finished.*[10]

Enforcing the boundaries between in-groups and out-groups is the dark side of forming social bonds. When the leaders of Nazi Germany compelled twenty million people—German Jewish citizens stripped of their civil status, and deportees from nearly every country in Europe—to perform forced manual labor during the Third Reich, they wanted to ensure that they would be ostracized from mainstream German society. This wasn't a given, despite the National Socialists' racist propaganda campaign. One reason was that the forced laborers were assigned to work on family farms, in local businesses, and in factories under the supervision of ordinary citizens, whose feelings of empathy might have been aroused by the fate of their onetime neighbors and colleagues. How could empathy be avoided? One way was to forbid "Aryans" from sharing meals with the forced laborers. If anyone might be tempted to include them in the fabric of daily life in wartime Germany, the Third Reich created new social norms, publicized on posters, on the radio, and in daily newspapers. A cartoon called "Figure of the

"*Figure of the Week,*" *Amstettner Anzeiger, April 18, 1943.*

Week," published on April 18, 1943, in the *Amstettner Anzeiger,* illustrates how forced laborers were to be excluded from what was called the "community of the table."[11]

"Like the herd animals we are, we sniff warily at the strange one among us," wrote anthropologist Loren Eiseley, hinting at how natural it feels to form a tight circle of family and friends and wall off others, especially in times of unease or uncertainty about scarce resources.[12] Forcing people to eat or drink separately has long been used in traditional societies to humiliate and punish. Among the Pirahã Indians of Brazil, for example, the punishment for violating a social norm "begins with excluding someone from food-sharing for a day, then for several days, then making the person live some distance away in the forest, deprived of normal trade and social exchanges. The most severe Piraha sanction is complete ostracism," writes Jared Diamond in *The World Until Yesterday.*[13] But until the Rwandan genocide, Nazi Germany was in a class of its own in its ability to manipulate the desire to belong to an identifiable group and transform it into xenophobia and a murderous hunt for scapegoats. If our Mesolithic ancestors held big feasts to help their fledgling communities cohere, racist movements do the opposite: they use food to exclude.

Even in democratic societies it's not hard to find examples of the ways our feelings about sharing food are exploited. In the American South, for example, Jim Crow laws ensured that restaurants and drinking fountains were segregated for nearly a century. "By 1915, black and white textile workers in South Carolina could not use the same water bucket, pails, cups, dippers or glasses," writes Isabel Wilkerson in *The Warmth of Other Suns*.[14] Interestingly, racial seg-regation began to disintegrate when black students staged sit-ins at lunch counters in 1960. To this day, high-school students are highly territorial about who sits at which cafeteria table, and prisoners in solitary confinement eat alone, their meals pushed through a slot in a locked door.

ALONE AND WITHOUT PURPOSE

Long used in many traditional societies as the gravest form of pun-ishment, social ostracism, recent research has shown, disrupts the ability to think rationally. Isolating someone effectively disables some aspects of cognitive functioning. And younger people are far more affected than older ones.[15] That's one reason why adolescents who are ostracized at school are in danger of committing suicide. They experience the exclusion viscerally. If no one comes to their aid, their physical and psychological distress can preempt all ratio-nal thought. Three days before I wrote this section, a fifteen-year-old girl living in the Gaspé region of Quebec killed herself because she had been forcibly excluded from her social group: classmates bullied and isolated her while she was at school and taunted her on Facebook when she got home. Marjorie Raymond left a note for her mother saying, "Mom, I'm sorry for what I did. You are the best mom in the world," suggesting a close bond that, tragically, couldn't protect her from the impact of isolation from her peers.

Marjorie's death was the fourth in a series of social ostracism and bullying–related suicides in Canadian teens between the ages of eleven and fifteen in less than a year, and it was followed by a subse-quent tragedy. Amanda Todd, a tenth-grade student from British Columbia, hanged herself after being cyberbullied by a stranger who posted lurid photos and comments to her classmates each time she tried to make a fresh start in a new school. These terrible deaths prompted a public outcry in Canada for school expulsions and legal

sanctions for adolescents who cyberbully, isolate, or otherwise torment their classmates. Meanwhile, suicides of children who have
been bullied in the United States and elsewhere have led to criminal
charges and recent changes in school and public policy.[16]

Torment is not too strong a word. Writing about the impact of
solitary confinement in US prisons, physician Atul Gawande quotes
John McCain, the former Republican presidential candidate who
spent two of his five years in a Vietnamese POW camp in a tiny
isolation cell, cut off from all human contact. "It crushes your spirit
and weakens your resistance more effectively than any other form
of mistreatment," Gawande writes. "And this comes from a man
who was beaten regularly; denied adequate medical treatment for
two broken arms, a broken leg, and chronic dysentery; and tortured
to the point of having an arm broken again." Gawande goes on to
describe a study of nearly 150 US naval aviators who returned from
imprisonment in Vietnam: they reported that social isolation was as
agonizing as any abuse they had suffered.

But what happened to them *was* physical. "EEG studies going
back to the nineteen-sixties have shown diffuse slowing of brain
waves in prisoners after a week or more of solitary confinement,"
writes Gawande. Some prisoners whose only social contact was a
food tray shoved through a slot became catatonic or developed
autistic features, such as rocking or "stimming" (self-stimulating).
Others regressed, throwing their food or playing with their feces.
Still others had panic attacks or became extraordinarily aggressive.
These symptoms suggest neurological damage. Neuroimaging
studies confirm that ostracism creates the same level of activity in
the anterior cingulate cortex and the anterior insula as does physical distress; the neural signs of social pain look a lot like the signals
created by physical pain.[17] Even months after they were released,
MRIs of prisoners of war in the former Yugoslavia showed the gravest
neurological damage in those prisoners who had been locked in
solitary confinement. "Without sustained social interaction, the

human brain may become as impaired as one that has incurred a traumatic head injury," Gawande concludes.[18]

THE FEMALE EFFECT

If isolation damages our neural networks, social eating does the opposite: it links the physiological hit of needed calories, as well as the aromas and flavors of food, with the visceral reassurance of belonging. "Show me another pleasure like dinner which comes every day and lasts an hour," wrote Charles Maurice de Talleyrand. An eighteenth-century French diplomat who was a bishop, advisor to Napoleon, inveterate womanizer (he took his first mistress as a seminary student and had affairs with influential women ever after), and a famously committed gourmet, Talleyrand knew that by preparing food and deciding who gets to eat it, women play a persuasive role in deciding who is part of the in-group and who stays on the outside looking in.

Consider the modern dinner party. In three out of four families, a woman's assessment of her social relationships determines who's invited and the quantity and quality of the food that will be served.[19] This accounting may be a legacy of our primate forebears. Female Japanese macaques, for instance, allow others to eat from their food stash according to a savvy calculus. The more closely she is related to another macaque, the more the dominant female "shares," which in the primate world means turning a blind eye to others snagging food you could easily keep for yourself, according to anthropologist Bernard Chapais. In one experiment, Chapais and a doctoral student discovered that the length of time a female macaque tolerated others snacking from her stash of raisins depended on how closely they were related. The most generous were mothers toward their daughters. Then came grandmothers with granddaughters, then pairs of sisters, and in last place, aunt–niece pairs. A niece's opportunities for "co-feeding" from her aunt's portion ranked with non-kin, meaning not very high.

There may be no culture that doesn't share food, but the way it's shared is hardly a free-for-all, and female relationships often provide important clues as to who gets to eat what. Not only macaques but also mother–daughter and sister–sister rhesus monkey and baboon pairs play favorites when it comes to sharing food. This indicates that many nonhuman female primates can make fine-grained social distinctions and, like us, exercise their discriminatory powers when it comes to deciding who's coming to dinner.[20]

I'm no Martha Stewart. But as someone who enjoys preparing elaborate meals for family and friends, I agree with anthropologist Sarah Hrdy, who thinks that the impulse to share food is hard-wired. I get pleasure from watching my family and friends enjoy an autumn meal of curried squash soup, roast marinated lamb with cauliflower, and crispy potatoes, followed by a salad of bitter greens and julienned Jerusalem artichokes (last week's menu). I like to think it's because I have an unusually generous spirit. But the more likely reason is that the human brain—and particularly the female brain—evolved in the context of mothers investing in their off-springs' survival via hefty donations of their own calories, whether through nursing or by offering a portion of their own food stash. Such behavior developed alongside the acute mind-reading and social skills that allow mothers to suss out their preverbal babies' needs. And the mothers are lavishly rewarded with infusions of oxytocin, the feel-good neuropeptide that promotes incipient social behavior and also rewards it after the fact—providing the pleasurable double whammy that makes us want to do it again and again.[21]

And while women have long known intuitively that *voluntarily* offering up food often makes them feel good, recent brain imaging studies show that the neural mechanisms activated by the act of sharing are precisely the ones that register other kinds of social pleasure. Put a woman in the scanner and ask her to share while interacting with a real human being, and those reward areas of her brain light up. But the neural correlates of sharing don't respond the same way if her partner is virtual.[22]

As I mentioned earlier, the reward areas I'm referring to also register social pain. Ask someone in an fMRI scanner to play a game with two other people who then proceed to exclude her, and those brain regions go wild (and the more left out the volunteer feels, the greater the neural activity). But tell her that a computer glitch interfered with the other players' ability to include her—suggesting there's no human agent involved—and those areas stay quiet.[23] People, and women especially, are exquisitely wired to assess the social cues they get from real human interaction.

Despite the common assumption that all social networks are interchangeable, different types of social signals don't have the same impact. As miraculous as Skype is, interacting with a pixelated version of my daughter eating a bowl of noodle soup at her desk in Brussels doesn't elicit the same visceral pleasure in either of us as preparing and eating it together. Such shared experiences prompt us to perceive others as physiologically similar to ourselves, British cognitive neuroscientist Manos Tsakiris has shown. A mother–daughter pair may already look alike, of course. But doing things together synchronously—like eating that bowl of soup together in the same room—makes us think that we resemble each other even more than we do, blurring our identities further.[24]

LIFE IS A BOWL OF DORITOS

Interestingly, women, who are on average more sensitive to social cues than men, are also much more likely to match the amount of food they eat to how much a companion is eating.[25] If two people are faced with snacks and one or both of them are women, they'll unconsciously coordinate their snacking. Men exhibit no such synchrony. When it comes to sharing a bowl of Doritos, you might say that it's each man for himself.[26] And the more overweight the person—especially if she's young and female—the

more her peers influence her waistline. In a study by the economist Justin Trogdon and his colleagues, teenage girls were much
more susceptible to "catching" their friends' weight increases
than were teenage boys.[27]

Given the mechanics of social transmission, it seems you have
to be there to "get the music." Emotional synchrony—not to mention the synchrony of one's daily schedule—can play a strong role
in weight gain and weight loss. Unwittingly, my friend Florence
Velly demonstrated how physical proximity to friends can affect
one's waistline. Soon after she moved from France onto my street
in 2009, Florence and I happened to meet in a nearby park while
she was walking her dog. It was an early morning in spring.
Sparkling with dew, the grass was alive with squirrels. As our paths
crossed there was flash of recognition, though we had never met.
When I stopped to give her dog a friendly pat, we discovered that
not only were we neighbors but she had just begun to swim with
my team three times a week (along with Sylvie, whom you met in

Chapter 1, and Lou, whom I will
introduce in Chapter 8). Florence
and I started walking her dog
together in Montreal's Mount
Royal Park every Thursday morning. Her pace was brisk. Her black
lab, Talia, eagerly bounded uphill
no matter how icy it was, and we
followed behind, chatting amiably.
After several consecutive Thursdays,
I noticed that a couple of pounds
had dropped off.

*From left, swim team members
Christine Cardinal, Florence
Velly, and the author, in clothes
designed by Florence's brother.*

That was a good thing, as Florence's
brother was a dress designer in Paris,
and he soon sent her a box of samples.
Several teammates gathered in

Florence's living room to try on the slinky silk jersey dresses in eye-popping prints. To watch my athletic teammates slide those brilliantly colored sheaths over their heads was to know that French fashion is one thing and French fries are another. Sadly, Florence's return to France two years later ended our casual get-togethers and Thursday walks, and I really missed her. Her departure registered on my scale too: those lost pounds reappeared. While she was my neighbor and a member of my "village," her proximity had affected me. I not only enjoyed her company, I exercised more often and felt a subtle pressure to meet her aesthetic standard. Those influences evaporated when she was no longer close by.

FAMILIES AND GETTING FAT

Given the role of proximity, not to mention shared genetic predispositions, it makes sense that siblings also influence each other's weight. Nicholas Christakis and James Fowler discovered that if one brother in the Framingham study became obese, then, controlling for other factors, his brother's chances of putting on weight increased by 40 percent. The siblings probably viewed each other's creeping weight gain as a normal part of aging, providing another explanation for obesity contagion. If most everyone in your tight circle of friends, family, or co-workers has started going out regularly for margaritas and nachos and acquires love handles in the process, your standards for what a normal waist size looks like might change.

At this point you won't be surprised to learn that sibling contagion is more intense among women. If a sister in Framingham got fat, her sister's chances of subsequently packing on the pounds increased by whopping 67 percent, nearly 30 percent more than the impact between brothers. Husbands' and wives' weights rose in tandem, though wives affected their husbands' waistlines more than the reverse (and given that this effect persisted up to three degrees of separation, it wasn't just about who was doing the shopping and cooking). Here was the female effect again, showing that within intimate networks, women are more likely to transmit behavior change than are men.[28]

The implication of such connectedness is clear. If close friends and family are influenced by the biscotti or bowls of frozen yogurt you scarf late at night—if *they* are what *you* eat—then your daily habits are not only public, they could have a life-and-death impact on those who feel closest to you.

THE KIDS ARE ALL RIGHT?
THAT DEPENDS ON DINNER

When Lord Byron wrote in *Don Juan* that "since Eve ate apples, much depends on dinner," he probably meant sex, not his kids' grade point averages. Yet research shows that skill in reading, writing, and arithmetic, academic standing in high school, scores on college entrance tests and much more besides, are linked to sitting down to family dinner. The more meals you eat with your child, the larger the child's vocabulary and the higher his or her grades, an effect that is exaggerated in girls. From toddlerhood continuing through the ornery teen and then young adult years, studies consistently show that family meals are a handy predictor of a kid's vocabulary, reading scores, and academic achievement, not to mention whether or not he or she will get derailed by sex, drugs, binging and purging, depression, or suicidal thoughts.[29] Even boys who carry a particular gene variant that predicts violent behavior seem protected by regularly sitting down to eat with their families, one 2008 study shows. "If people with the gene have a parent who has regular meals with them, then the risk is gone," Guang Guo, the American sociologist who led the study, explained.[30] Not bad for a ten-thousand-year-old custom. What is striking is that it doesn't matter what you eat. Consuming organic broccoli is not what makes kids smarter.

Why does eating regularly with their families make young kids better readers and writers, and adolescents happier and healthier, with loftier SAT scores and lower rates of drug and alcohol use compared to teenagers who graze on their own or eat in front of a screen? Family income is important, though it doesn't tell the whole story. While there's no disputing that parents with ample incomes can give their kids more opportunities—including more time with parents and often better schools—there are also many well-off kids with overworked professional parents, 24/7 nannies, and a plasma display in every room who are not eating that many meals with their families. Roughly a third of middle-school kids rarely eat with their parents, a phenomenon that's familiar to me after twenty years of clinical psychology practice. Sometimes the parents just can't. Social historian Stephanie Coontz points out that almost 15 percent of married couples have a joint workweek of more than a hundred hours, which doesn't leave a lot of time for meal preparation and chatting.[31] One successful couple I saw in my clinic felt so ill at ease as parents that when they returned from work at the end of the day, they'd circle the block until they were sure their nanny had already tucked the kids into bed and it was safe to drive into the garage.

There is some evidence that the ritual of family meals provides ballast for a family in times of stress, reinforcing a sense of belonging, especially during transitions.[32] *If times are tough, at least we have this*, is the feeling. But more importantly, sharing meals is an intimate act, an expression of the closeness of our family bonds. It's also a way for kids and parents to check in daily and connect. If the kitchen is not just a place to scarf down calories but an arena for sharing stories, confidences, lessons learned, and gossip, then families who talk and eat together might have children who are psychologically healthier and who do better in school than families who don't, right?

That's what researchers are finding. Banter—and specifically banter about the child's experiences—is what links family meals in childhood to boosted achievement later on, according to Harvard psychologist Catherine Snow and her colleagues. It's no surprise that Snow, who was one of the first researchers to document the peculiar way mothers everywhere talk to their babies (those high-pitched, singsong Q-and-A sessions we call "motherese"), would be interested in parents' other conversational quirks. Snow and her collaborators thought families with academically successful children might demonstrate certain social habits that are less common in other families, notwithstanding differences in ethnic background or income. If they could unearth these behavioral "tics," they might be able to teach the tricks to other parents, they thought.

The researchers expected that children who were exposed to complex table talk with adults might develop better language skills, which would then enable them to become better readers. And those who were better readers would do better in school. To test these ideas, the researchers started tracking about sixty low- and middle-income Boston families from the time their children were three, observing and recording their behavior every year. They caught up with them ten to fourteen years later, when the kids were finishing high school and getting ready to apply to college (well, at least some of them). The researchers had given tape recorders to the families at the outset and asked them to put them on the table when it was time to eat. They ended up with 160 recorded mealtime conversations. While some of the families treated the recorded meals as showtime, asking their little tikes to stand on a chair and chant their ABCs, other parents just turned on the recorder and got on with the business of dinner. The resulting taped conversations, like this one between a mother and her three-year-old son Tommy, show that table talk between adults and their preschoolers can be as existential as it is instructional:

MOTHER: There aren't a real lot of wild animals around here.
TOMMY: No, but if we see a whole bunch um I would have
            waked up. And when I waked up they will still be there.
MOTHER: Think so?

TOMMY: Mmhm. Because I see them when I'm asleep, when I was asleep. I, my dreams . . .

MOTHER: Yeah. When you're asleep sometimes your dreams are very real. But it's just your imagination working while the rest of you sleeps.

TOMMY: Mommy, Mommy? My dreams did come true.

MOTHER: No.

TOMMY: It did.

MOTHER: It did? What was your dream about?

TOMMY: It was a monster, and I was . . . with his tongue. Mom, his, his whole . . . and he dropped me on my neck.

MOTHER: You think the monster grabbed you on your head but that didn't come true. No monster really grabbed you on your neck.

TOMMY: It did come true.

MOTHER: It did? When?

TOMMY: A long time ago.

MOTHER: Yeah?

TOMMY: And it jabbed me in the eye.

MOTHER: No, honey, it didn't come true.

TOMMY: Mmhm.

MOTHER: You know I would never let any monsters get you. Besides what did I tell you about monsters?

TOMMY: What?

MOTHER: They're only make-believe and they only live in movies because somebody with a wonderful imagination makes up monsters. And all other sort of special effects to make the really scary monsters. You know, like how you watch Michael Jackson? And they show him putting his makeup on for "Thriller"? That's just because somebody had a great imagination.

TOMMY: Mmhm.

MOTHER: But no there's no such things as monsters.[33]

This vivid exchange includes storytelling (the dream), new information (the mother's explanation), maternal TLC, counterfactuals (imagining what would happen if Tommy faced a hypothetical monster), as well as turn-taking and sophisticated vocabulary. According to Snow and Beals, this type of back-and-forth during a meal serves to move a child's language and literacy skills onward and upward—at least compared to the type of exchanges typical of other families. Many parents talked to their children only when giving them orders. *Sit up straight. Use your napkin. Chew with your mouth closed.* Or they didn't talk to them at all at mealtime because meals were silent, serious affairs. Or because there were no mealtimes.

For most of these families, mealtime meant sitting together for anywhere between two and forty-seven minutes. The average was about twenty minutes. Most often it was the mother who sat with the children. Fathers were present for only a third of the dinners, and "even when present contributed relatively little to the conversations," write the researchers. So here the female effect is by default, though as we shall see, mothers exert extraordinary influence even when both parents are present. One meal consisted of two children eating cereal alone in front of the TV, while another meal was a recording of a mother and son baking cornbread. As there were only the two of them at home, there was no point to real dinners, the mother explained to the researchers.

That's understandable, but it's also a pity. Family meals trump almost every other activity—including reading books and playing with toys—when it comes to jumpstarting a child's vocabulary, according to a 2001 study.[34] More recently, in an astounding naturalistic experiment called the Human Speechome Project, MIT computer scientist Deb Roy and his wife, Northeastern University psycholinguist Rupal Patel, installed eleven omnidirectional fish-eye cameras and fourteen high-performance microphones in the ceilings of their suburban Boston bungalow a few months before their first child was born. They have since recorded more than 250,000 hours of audio and video—nearly every waking moment of their son's first three years. The point was to capture the uniquely social aspect of human language acquisition right where most babies learn to talk—at home. It will likely take decades to parse the two gigabytes of data recorded every day the pilot project was running. But a preliminary peek shows that there are social hotspots where much of the action happens. These hotspots are also where most of the baby's "word births" take place, according to Roy, and one of the hottest of those spots is the kitchen.[35]

A parent's banter with her toddler over the mashed potatoes turns out to be a pretty good predictor of that child's vocabulary level a few years later, notwithstanding how high the child's IQ might be, how educated the parents are, or how much they earn.[36] Though Roy has found a strong link between how often a parent says a word and how early the child utters it, it's not just about the number of words the child produces.[37] Face-to-face conversations can prompt empathy too, through reading people's facial expressions and engaging in back-and-forth dialogue about "counterfactuals," which developmental psychologist Alison Gopnik defines as thinking about "what might have happened, but didn't—the woulda-coulda-shouldas of life."[38]

It might be mind-numbingly boring to play out a hypothetical scenario involving fictional monsters over and over and over again with a toddler. But parents need to consider this: "By the time they are two or three, children quite characteristically spend much of their waking hours in a world of imaginary creatures, possible universes, and assumed identities," Gopnik writes in *The Philosophical Baby*. Imagining these what-if worlds and understanding how the real one works are more tightly connected than you think, she asserts, providing mountains of evidence from her Berkeley lab. Apparently, if they are to develop enhanced vocabulary and communication skills, kids need unstructured social time when they're not being drilled on number concepts with the help of Brainy Baby videos. There is even evidence that babies who spend time in front of such instructional DVDs have significantly *lower* vocabulary levels compared to babies who interact with people.[39] If developing empathy hinges on maintaining close contact—"the kind of contact that lets us actually see the grief or joy on someone's face," as Gopnik puts it—then shooting the breeze at mealtime with your small fry trumps Baby Einstein any day of the week.[40]

TEENS, FOOD, AND MORE FEMALE EFFECTS

We know now that children get more out of a family meal than nutrition. An enriched vocabulary is one benefit. Another is empathy: the capacity to imagine the thoughts and feelings of another person. The ability to get out of our heads and into someone else's is built into our species, though some of us are better at this than others. Along with the genes and prenatal hormones that foster this ability, getting lots of practice reading other people's facial expressions during family meals is like spring training for ball players; the kitchen table is the ideal spot to practice and make corrections before they're really put to the test in the outside world.

Still, one of the most surprising findings about regular family meals is their capacity to transform teenagers, particularly teenage girls. One 2008 study surveyed eight hundred Minnesota teenagers about their eating habits when they were twelve and their substance use five years later (other factors, such as financial status, were held constant). The results showed that twelve-year-old girls who regularly ate with their families at the beginning of middle school had half the odds of other kids their age of drinking, smoking, and regularly using marijuana when they were seventeen.[41] The meals seemed to work as a protective umbrella for the girls, though not for the boys. And this wasn't an isolated finding. Another study, published the same year, of more than 2,500 adolescent boys and girls surveyed over a five-year span, revealed that girls who regularly ate family meals were less likely to develop eating disorders years later.[42] (Given that so few boys develop eating disorders in the first place, family meals are not particularly predictive on that score.)

Not only are women more sensitive to their friends' and sisters' food habits than men, but at an early age they're also more affected by the transformative power of social meals. The researchers explain this peculiar finding as follows: "Females may be more attuned to subtle emotional support offered during family meals, resulting in a more profound protective effect for females than for males."[43] A few years earlier, this same research group had looked into the lives of almost five thousand American teens and found that a third of them rarely, if ever, ate meals with their families. Compared to those who did eat with their families, the girls who didn't were almost twice as likely to attempt suicide. And that finding surfaced after the researchers accounted for the protective effect of having a close-knit family. The less often these teenagers—boys and girls—ate with their families, the higher their odds of getting low grades, becoming depressed, smoking cigarettes, using drugs, and thinking about or attempting suicide.[44]

But why? Clearly something transformative is happening at the dinner table, though we don't know exactly what. Almost all the studies about food and social relationships are correlations: they document the way two separate phenomena are yoked together, but they don't plumb the reasons.[45] Do kids who regularly eat meals with their parents and siblings turn out to be clean-livers—more psychologically stable and academically more successful—because parental support is part of what goes on at the dinner table? Or is it more about the children? Perhaps the types of kids who eat regularly with their parents are better conversationalists to begin with, or less angry at the world. If a parent is working spirit-draining hours just to keep the fridge full or to pay into the kids' college fund, he or she might not be keen to eat dinner every weeknight with a sullen pot-head who sees school as a waste of time. "If they can't stand each other, they won't eat together," is how my son Carl put it. "Sharing food is all about the absence of conflict."

Peace in the valley can lead to communal dinners, that's true. Or a shared feast can jumpstart a feeling of cooperation, as was suspected of the Natufian funeral barbecue—or its modern equivalent, block parties intended to instill solidarity among neighbors.[46] The only real way to answer this chicken-and-egg question is to randomly assign children at birth to different types of meals—with family, with friends, with both, or alone—and then watch what happens to them as they grow. That can't happen, of course. One of the best alternatives is a longitudinal study, which asks lots of questions about people's habits and then tracks what happens to them over time (as we've seen in the Framingham study, as well as the nurses study on breast cancer).

One recent such study, led by University of Minnesota's Ann Meier and Cornell's Kelly Musick, tracked eighteen thousand American adolescents. After ruling out other causes, they found that face-to-face interaction is what's protective about family dinners, not shared meals per se. Eating together is simply a focused— often the only—way many parents connect with their kids; the more engaged and less embattled the parenting, the stronger the connection between eating together and reduced rates of depression, delinquency, and substance abuse later.[47]

Looking at food habits in particular, the American psychologist and eating disorder expert Debra Franko and her colleagues followed nearly 2,400 girls between the ages of nine and nineteen. They found that more frequent family meals in the first three years of the study neatly predicted greater family cohesion and more salubrious personal habits in years seven and eight. So, when it comes to all these positive outcomes, in many ways family meals *do* come first. Specifically, girls who said they "never or almost never" ate with their parents from the ages of nine to eleven (about 10 percent of the sample) were more likely than other kids to

become teenagers who were stressed-out smokers with weird attitudes toward food. Social contact around the dinner table seemed
to promote family cohesion and "problem-focused coping," the
authors write, which probably reduced the girls' risky antics later.[48]

I'm not suggesting that children need sit-down dinners with their
families every night of the week, complete with lively mealtime
banter, in order to avoid turning into anorexic dropouts or insensitive
brutes. That would be preposterous, especially as different cultures
feature different styles of table talk. For example, Catherine Snow
and Oslo psychologist Vibeke Grover Aukrust matched Norwegian
and American families with preschoolers of the same age and compared their mealtime conversations. The researchers discovered that
Americans relate half as many stories at mealtimes as Norwegians
do, but they explain things twice as often. And when they do, they
like it to be dramatic. (*Norwegian preschooler*: Nils wore a green
sweater to preschool today. *American preschooler*: Johnny threw up
today and it was orange.)[49] What's common to both statements is
that they invite parents to respond—to throw the ball back to the
child, who will likely toss it back again, keeping the volley going.

That's why I am suggesting that shared meals offer a head start
for picking up the subtleties of language and social interaction.
They also help us feel that we belong somewhere.

THE CHANGE THAT CHANGES OTHERS

As a newspaper columnist I've watched book sections and venerable broadsheets come and go (actually, mostly go), but among the
survivors there is one change that's here to stay: weekly columns on
dieting by dieters. I saw it first in my local paper, where a news-
room administrator attempting to lose weight was asked to write
her "diary of a fat girl" in a column called "Shaping Up." Then
came one called "How I Lost It" in one of the national papers. The
section's editors asked readers to write in with their weight-loss
stories, which it published along with before-and-after photos. The

point is to inspire others. But does reading about strangers' experiences really spur people to change their own behavior?

There's no evidence that it does, though it would certainly be a handy solution to a health problem that affects three-quarters of North America. Just about the only commercial approach to weight loss that works is Weight Watchers, which exploits the powerful social features of eating. Studies that randomly assign overweight people to various programs show that none can compete with Weight Watchers' record of sustained moderate weight loss.[50] The critical factor seems to be that Weight Watchers requires members not just to keep track of every ingested morsel but to attend weekly meetings. There they get weighed, and for every few pounds they've shed since the previous meeting, they receive applause and, at certain milestones, even a token gift.

I signed on to Weight Watchers in March 2011, along with three companions, to see how it worked. "I think the social support is huge. If you look around, everyone's in twos and threes," said one of my friends at the meeting, who maintains a "svelting" thread on a writers' email list to help cheer on fellow dieters and "hold each other accountable." This type of vocabulary makes sense in 12-step-like programs such as Weight Watchers. After all, these movements began with the assumption that overindulgence is a moral failure that requires, as Dr. Franklin Nathaniel Daniel Buchman, one of AA's missionary founders put it, "confession as a prerequisite to change," not to mention a social responsibility to experience a "change that must change others."[51] Overbearing zealots though they were, these self-control missionaries were right about one thing. When it comes to changing human habits around consumption, social pressure—especially from people you admire—works.

THE REAL GOD OF 12-STEP

In January 2009, the *New York Times Magazine* ran a profile of Dr. Drew Pinsky, an addictions specialist and the star of the reality TV shows *Sober House* and *Celebrity Rehab with Dr. Drew*. Pinsky's decision to pursue addiction medicine as a career—his "burning bush moment," as he called it—came while he was a medical resident providing care to recovering alcoholics and addicts at a Pasadena hospital. "I watched these people—these young people— go from dying to better than they ever knew they could be. And I was like, 'Whoa.' In medicine you go from dying to chronically ill. You don't go from dying to better than you ever knew you could be. That just doesn't happen," he said.

Pinsky soon evolved into the camera-ready therapist who could challenge, on air, the hidden demons of celebrity substance abusers like Rodney King and Heidi Fleiss, which earned him their public gratitude and the moniker "the God of 12-step." The title is a reference to the first therapeutic group to exploit peer support to help people exert self-control: Alcoholics Anonymous. In a profile in the *New York Times*, Chris Norris points out how Pinsky connects through non-verbal cues:

> I was struck by Pinsky's disarming conversation style, which involved frequent nods, appreciative laughs, affect mirroring and gentle knee pats—all of which had me sharing intimate details about my childhood before we reached the Hollywood border. Apparently, this comes with the territory. "We affect each other," Pinsky said of his relationship with addicts. "You're telling people, I'm here with you, having your feelings, sharing them, understanding them, appreciating them."[52]

That basic human contact—so crucial to addicts' and alcoholics' ability to kick their habits, according to Pinsky—was also one of the catalysts that started them drinking or doing drugs in the first place. As anyone who has watched *The Wire* knows, ghetto kids use and Baltimore cops drink, in large part because all their friends do. It takes outsized self-control to resist peer pressure. Make that iron-clad discipline when one's entire social network has taken on a bad habit, whether it's downing three drinks before dinner, sniffing glue at recess, or toking up at noon. Your mother may have warned you about the dangers of hanging out with the wrong crowd, and it turns out your mother was right: research confirms that as your friends change, so do your ideas about what's acceptable, whether it's what you're eating, drinking, smoking, or putting up your nose.[53]

Those who drink too much could be drowning their sorrows or mirroring their friends. If it's the latter, they're simply playing bit parts in the "human superorganism," as Fowler and Christakis call it. Social contagion spurs boozing and smoking much the way it transmits obesity. If we are wired to communicate our feelings and proclivities through language and nonverbal signals alike (think of menstrual synchrony, or the fertility contagion described in the previous chapter), then the same mechanisms can also promote bad habits.

On that score, Niels Rosenquist, a Harvard-based psychiatrist, mined the Framingham data to show that the alcohol a person downs a day is tied to how much his or her friends drink. They found that if someone's buddy drinks a glass or two of wine a day, then he or she is 50 percent more likely to do the same, compared to what their drinking habits would be if they were suddenly parachuted into some random, computer-generated social network. Being surrounded by "heavy drinkers" (oddly, the study defines "heavy" as one or more drinks a day for women, two or more for men) increased people's reported alcohol consumption by 70 percent. Conversely, being surrounded by abstainers halved it. Again, women played a much more powerful role in swaying people's drinking habits than did men, whether it was to drink more or to drink less.[54]

The scientists didn't observe the drinking itself, but what people said they were drinking. Still, how much you admit you drink is also colored by your peers. In some social circles drinking is shameful, while in others it's a point of pride. "A bum who ain't drunk by midnight ain't trying," was what Toots Shor, owner of the eponymous

New York watering hole told patrons like Frank Sinatra and Ernest Hemingway in the 1950s.[55] Booze and bonhomie are still considered inseparable, so it's not surprising that what people say they drink is fairly accurate.

And as with obesity, the social effect diminishes with each step away from the personal connection. If a close friend of yours drinks heavily, he or she increases your alcohol consumption by 50 percent, the consumption of a friend of hers by 35 percent, and of a friend of a friend of a friend by 8 percent. Like secondhand smoke, the effect dissipates; after three degrees of separation, your influence on friends and family is no different from that of any stranger.

WOMEN AND BOOZE

Interestingly, the female effect shows up yet again with alcohol. Given that men's social lives are often so closely linked to drinking, one might expect that contagion would work best within male social circles. But the Framingham data show that female contacts are far more influential in the spread—or censure—of boozing. Whether subtly or overtly, it seems that women's influence on men's consumption is a powerful vector of change.

The female effect in Rosenquist's study was subtle, if not invisible, before statistical analysis. But during Prohibition women openly exploited their influence. In *Last Call*, Daniel Okrent's lively history of Prohibition, we learn that female suffragettes such as Carry Nation, Susan B. Anthony, and Elizabeth Cady Stanton cut their political teeth in the temperance movement. Susan B. Anthony's first public speech was on the dangers of alcohol, but "none quite hated it with Carry Nation's vigor or attacked it with her rapturous glee," writes Okrent, who describes Nation as "six feet tall, with the biceps of a stevedore, the face of a prison warden, and the persistence of a toothache." Saloon owners and committed drinkers in the Midwest had to face Nation and her weapons of choice: a hatchet and her self-published newspaper, *The Smasher's Mail*. By the turn of the twentieth century, female activists had helped reduce the vast quantities of alcohol consumed daily by most Americans and were well on their way to making drinking illegal.

I had known that women had slowed the rivers of booze during the years of Prohibition (1920–33), but until I read Okrent's book I hadn't known that women played a key role in opening the beer taps again. A different group of women, this time more likely to sport pearls than hatchets, helped turn public opinion away from what they considered the unconstitutional meddling in the private lives of Americans. In 1930 the *Washington Post* reported the female anti-prohibitionists' appearance at a Senate hearing on the front page: "Women whose names stand out prominently in the social register . . . outnumbered the men in the room four to one. These were grandmothers, matrons and debutantes, all pledged to a war on prohibition." And after they had presented their case, "there was every evidence that the bill was dead."[56]

It would not be the last time that two groups of passionately committed women knocked heads over what people should eat and drink. At around the time women were arguing about men's boozing, the debate about what *babies* should drink was heating up. And it wasn't just ideologically committed women who had strong opinions. Factions in science, politics, medicine, and business were at war about what infants should be fed—which was really a war about how they should be raised. The stakes were considered so high that, 150 years after the debate started, the shouting match has only become more shrill.

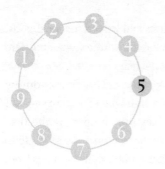

5

Baby Chemistry

How Social Contact
Transforms Infants' Brains

William was almost two months old when we first met. With two babies under the age of two, life was hectic for his parents, Bob and Diane (who, as I described in Chapter 3, first caught the pregnancy bug from Bob's sister). Thankfully, Bob's mother lived upstairs. She had been ready to sell her duplex in a gentrified part of Montreal's Mile End neighborhood when Bob and Diane decided to buy in. Now the young family lived downstairs and the grandmother upstairs, much the way most of the area's immigrant families had lived for more than a hundred years. Being under the same roof as her mother-in-law was more than an economic choice for Diane. "I've always thought that the way to stay close to your family is to stay physically near them. Some people would think that it's insane. But I've always wanted to bring my people close to me. Elizabeth's a wonderful mother-in-law. If she's home, we usually eat together, though that wasn't part of the plan at the beginning."

I wasn't the only dinner guest that night. Diane's father, Dennis, was visiting from his home in the suburbs. Shortly after I walked into the aqua-tiled kitchen, he propped the cranky baby's padded bottom on the kitchen table, his beefy hands encircling William's torso. William's downy head began to jiggle alarmingly as his grandfather started pumping him up and down on the edge of the table. "Bouncy, bouncy, baby! Bouncy, bouncy, baby!"

William immediately stopped crying and leveled his face with his grandfather's. His slate-gray eyes were wide open now. He dropped his lower jaw with the rising pitch and volume of that last *ba-by!* then stuck out his small pink tongue and fixed his gaze on his grandfather's eyes, shifting slightly from what he had been staring at a second earlier: the older man's cavernous open mouth, his huge tongue and white teeth. This floor show was so absorbing that William forgot he had been demanding to be fed.

Soon enough, Diane scooped William off the teak table and sat down. She tucked him into the crook of her elbow, deftly positioning his head under the folds of her sweater. Frantic sucking sounds ensued, then slowed, the baby's back rising and falling rhythmically. Suddenly it was quieter. Those of us who'd been talking loudly automatically adjusted our volume to the tenor of William's nursing, just as five minutes earlier he'd adjusted his level of alertness to ours.

This is the mammalian pas de deux, honed over tens of millions of years of evolution. Breastfeeding is the infant's slow food movement. It's antithetical to a fast-paced lifestyle and it can interfere with a woman's earnings—precisely because it's a slow process that requires the mother to be with her baby six to ten times a day, and to be fairly immobile, too. There's longstanding evidence that the physical contact and unhurried pace of breastfeeding releases a steady stream of oxytocin into both the mother's and baby's bloodstreams, the infusion dulling pain and promoting mutual trust. As a side benefit, the neuropeptide also enables mother and baby to sit still.[1] Clearly, oxytocin greases the wheels of attachment in ways that can't be mimicked by technology.

Yet even though it seems set up to promote social bonding, less than 40 percent of American mothers are still breastfeeding their infants by time they are William's age (two months old). That number falls to 27 percent by the time babies are four months old, just when they'd be able to hold themselves upright enough while nursing to palm the breast with one hand and twiddle their mother's ear with the other. Though the World Health Organization recommends a diet of only breast milk until a baby is six months old, by that time a mere 14 percent of American mothers are still nursing their babies.[2] The other 86 percent are either working full-time or they find the demands of a nursing infant intrusive. As American journalist Hanna Rosin observed, "It was not the vacuum that was keeping me and my 21st-century sisters down, but another sucking sound."[3]

Does it really make any difference whether a baby is fed from the breast or from a bottle? As a child born the year the Russians launched Sputnik into space, when the zeitgeist was all about using science to race against time, I wasn't breastfed and I can't say I feel deprived. Still, in the coming pages I'll present some of the latest evidence from developmental neuroscience that shows that face-to-face (if not skin-to-skin) contact tunes up the circuitry of the newly formed human brain, which until at least the age of eight is still a work in progress. This chapter is not so much about breast-feeding as it is about how a baby's intimate bonds transform her neural networks. Human infants are hardwired to make lasting social connections. And not with just anyone.

THE MOUTHS OF BABES

The capacity to comfort a hungry infant with your breast is a singular pleasure. Some women describe it as orgasmic. Perhaps that's one reason why the fervor of breastfeeding advocates rivals that of Carrie Nation, the prohibition activist we met in the previous chapter. When an article in the *British Medical Journal* suggested that an exclusively breastfed baby over four months of age is more prone to allergies and anemia than a baby who drinks breast milk but eats other foods too, a British breastfeeding advocacy group labeled the article "backward" and accused the researchers of being shills for the baby-food industry.[4] Passions run high when it comes to breast-feeding: you either endorse the practice absolutely or you're a sell-out. And along with such ideological rifts, there's a class divide.

When Hanna Rosin mentioned that she was considering switching her one-month-old from the breast to formula, she was shunned by the other educated upper-crust mothers in her Brooklyn playground. "Circles were redrawn such that I ended up in the class of mom who, in a pinch, might feed her baby mashed-up Chicken McNuggets," she wrote.[5]

Social class notwithstanding, in the United States, where there is no guarantee of paid maternity leave and new mothers get a token four weeks off with their babies (only Lesotho, Liberia, Swaziland, and Papua New Guinea are as stingy), working women of all stripes find themselves switching to the bottle before their little one can hold up his head and smile: at about five weeks of age. In Canada, where parents get an average of nine months of maternity leave, more mothers breastfeed than in the U.S., but half of them have given it up by the time their babies are three months old. Meanwhile, breastfeeding rates among British mothers—who get twenty weeks of paid leave—are even lower than Americans'. The downward trend in the industrialized nations is unmistakable.[6] By the time babies are a few months old, two-thirds to three-quarters of mothers in Western democracies are either pumping out their breast milk and dating the baggies with a Sharpie before tossing them in the freezer, or they're mixing up formula.

This wholesale switch to formula gives public health authorities the heebie-jeebies. Scholars have linked breastfeeding to reduced rates of diarrhea, meningitis, urinary tract infections, sudden infant death syndrome, necrotizing enterocolitis, ear infections, and respiratory tract infections. If all that weren't incentive enough, several good studies show that exclusive breastfeeding during the baby's first six months is associated with boosted intelligence, fewer behavior problems in childhood, and eventually, upward social mobility.[7]

Still, there's a basic confusion about terms. Governments and women's groups are "purblind, unwilling to eye whether it's his mother, or her milk that matters more to a baby," the Harvard historian Jill Lepore noted in a 2009 *New Yorker* article.[8] As far as the Centers for Disease Control in Atlanta is concerned, it's not about bonding but about the chemical composition of the milk. "It doesn't matter if it is coming straight from the breast or being pumped into a bottle," the CDC's Karen Hunter wrote me in an email. "If the baby is getting breast milk, they are getting breast-fed." Oxytocin and intimacy don't enter into the equation. If Sarah Palin can tout her family values by telling *People* magazine that she often had to "put down the BlackBerries and pick up the breast pump," the inference is clear. Once you give birth, a baby's routine feeding and maintenance is no big deal. An electric pump and a bottle can do the job just as well as the mother can.

Well, not quite. Breastfeeding the old-fashioned way does seem to make most babies healthier and smarter, regardless of social class. One landmark study of Belarusian mothers and babies—the largest randomized trial of breastfeeding mothers ever conducted—assigned more than seventeen thousand mothers and babies from thirty-one maternity clinics to either a breastfeeding promotion group or a control group (one that offered postnatal care but no breastfeeding education or advice). The twenty-strong team of international researchers who conducted this study found that the increased rate of early breastfeeding in the experimental group led to fewer digestive and skin ailments in the babies in the short term, and also to a boosted verbal IQ score in the long term, when these children were tested six years later.[9]

Presumably every parent wants clever children, and an average increase of 7.5 IQ points is nothing to sneeze at. So impressed were they with the data showing enhanced health and intelligence in breastfed babies that officials at the World Health Organization based its international breastfeeding strategy on a meta-analysis of these studies. This leads us to an uncomfortable question. If the majority of women in the West are giving up the practice before their infants can hold up their heads, what are they missing?

I asked this question of Michael Kramer, the McGill-based pediatric epidemiologist who is the Belarusian study's lead author. I also wanted to know what he thought was making the breastfed babies smarter. "I like to think it's the social contact," he said while chatting with me in the waning light of a late December afternoon. A wiry man in his early sixties, Kramer had dropped by my office on his way home from a Friday afternoon squash game. He looked scrubbed and relaxed—not at all like the driven young scientist I remembered from thirty years earlier. We had been members of the same hospital-based research group then, he as an epidemiologist, I as a newly minted child psychologist.

"It could even be something as simple as the fact that breastfeeding takes longer," he said. "And the mothers are talking to their babies and stimulating them, smiling at them, singing to them all that time. When you're breastfeeding, you spend more time talking to the baby face-to-face, and we did find greater increases in verbal IQ compared to nonverbal IQ."

Do babies who drink pumped and bottled breast milk show the same effects? He couldn't answer that question definitively but confided that, as bottle-feeding is a more efficient delivery system, bottle-fed babies are likely spending less face time with their mothers. Besides, all the women in his Belarus study who breastfed did so the traditional way, he told me—no pumping, no bottles. "I can tell you that there are no good data showing that the omega-3 fatty acids in breast milk lead to higher IQs. The bottom line is, we don't know if it's the greater time spent, the social interaction, or the physical contact."[10]

To be sure, breast milk contains lots of biochemical compounds that have the power to change behavior, including prolactin, cortisol, and oxytocin. But the psychological benefits of nursing seem to have less to do with breast milk as a magic elixir and more to do with how much time is spent engaging the baby in affectionate repartee. If that's the case, all the programmable breast pumps, legally mandated "pump breaks," pumping rooms, and human milk banks in the world won't have the same effect on the baby's brain as breastfeeding. Just as reducing road accidents has more to do with what the driver is doing at the wheel than with the gasoline he or she pours into the tank, much of the protective halo of breast-feeding may well come down to the neural boost parents and babies give each other when their faces are eight inches apart.

SOCIAL CONTACT AND THE BRAINS OF BABES

Unable to feed themselves or run away from a threat, to survive parental neglect or predators, human babies come into the world with innate social skills that create immediate chemistry with the adults around them. They turn their heads to fix a wide-eyed gaze on an adult's face, calm their crying when they hear their mother's voice, tightly grasp an adult's finger, or rest a tiny hand on the breast that feeds them. From the first hours of life, new-borns can also mimic an exaggerated look of surprise, or the pursed lips or protruding tongue they see in someone else, psychologist Andrew Meltzoff has found.[11] These young babies, some just a few days old, are hardwired to connect face-to-face, and adults are similarly pro-grammed to respond with alacrity to their crying, gazing, and cooing. This is an engrossing social duet, not a soliloquy.[12]

In fact, mothers' voices exert a special effect on their children. More than thirty years ago, European cognitive psychologist Jacques Mehler discovered that one-month-old

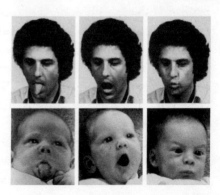

In the 1970s Andrew Meltzoff—shown here—and Keith Moore discovered that newborns imitate facial expressions.

infants got excited and sucked more vigorously when they heard their mother's voice. These babies did not respond in the same way when they heard a stranger talking, or if their mother's voice lacked its usual cadence.[13]

There's other evidence that humans are born ready to respond to their own parents'— and especially their mother's—smell, voice, and touch. Within twenty-four hours of birth, for example, the language circuitry in a newborn's brain comes alive at the sound of its mother's voice, according to a 2011 experiment led by University of Montreal neuroscientist Maryse Lassonde. Compared to what happened when a female stranger's voice was played, a brief snatch of the mother's voice provoked a dramatic neural response in the tiny subjects. "This proves for the first time that the mother's voice is special to babies," said Lassonde, whose newborn granddaughter was among the test subjects. "When the mother spoke, the scans very clearly show reactions in the left-hemisphere of the brain, and particularly the language processing and motor skills circuit. Conversely, when the stranger spoke, the right-hemisphere [associated with voice recognition] reacted."[14] Even hours after birth, babies need their parents to engage with them as conversation partners.[15] Though we don't yet know whether a father's voice exerts the same effect as a mother's, we know that neither a stranger's voice nor an image on a screen wields the same power.[16]

Clearly babies come into the world with their brains prepared to interact. Not only do they respond to their parents, babies are exquisitely wired to pick up little signs that their parents are attuned to them. When adults sit face-to-face with babies and imitate exactly what they're doing (much the way a good spouse or therapist mirrors your tone of voice and posture to show that she's paying attention), the baby looks at the parent longer and smiles more. "The baby brain lights up at this!" Andrew Meltzoff explained, describing his recent EEG studies of infants. Taking this finding one step further, Meltzoff and his colleagues Joni Saby and Peter

Marshall have found mirror-neuron-like structures in the baby's brain that become activated when he or she watches an adult execute a specific action.

"You know Penfield's famous homunculus body maps that show the 'body in the brain' with exaggerated hands, lips, and feet? We discovered the beginning of a baby-sized homunculus in the brain of the infant," Meltzoff wrote in an email. "Penfield would have loved it. Remarkably, when the baby sees the adult use her hand, the baby's own hand area lights up; when the baby sees the adult use her foot to bring something about, the baby's own foot area lights up. There is a very primitive body scheme in a baby's brain that acts like an invisible bungee cord connecting them to their moms. This mapping from the baby's body to the mom's supports early nonverbal feelings of attachment, connectedness, and belonging. Babies look at moms and see themselves."[17]

TOO MUCH MOTHER LOVE

The idea that babies need a steady diet of parental contact and affection is fairly novel as child-rearing approaches go. For more than a century, from the Victorian era until the late 1950s, bringing up baby in the Western world was a rather chilly affair. Chastened by the spread of infectious childhood diseases and browbeaten by early child-rearing pioneers (including a number of influential pediatricians, as well as the behaviorist John B. Watson), parents were instructed not to comfort, cuddle, or play with their babies, but to maintain a certain reserve, lest they spoil them with too much love.

I remember my grandmother visiting a few weeks after my first child was born. Small at birth, Eva cried incessantly during her first few weeks, and I responded by nursing her on demand, cuddling, rocking, and walking her in an attempt to calm her. This shocked my usually affectionate grandmother. Allowing babies to exhaust themselves by crying "exercises their lungs," she informed me, and rocking or nursing unhappy babies spoils them (I later learned that she had acquired this parenting advice from the women's magazines of her day). Doling out boiled cow's milk in precise amounts from sterilized glass bottles, on a fixed schedule, fit this approach better than breastfeeding did, to be sure. And physical contact? That was a no-no. As Deborah Blum writes in her marvelous book *Love at Goon Park*, "John Watson's instructions were clear: Don't pick them up when they cry; don't hold them for pleasure. Pat them on the head when they do well. Shake their hands; okay, kiss them on the foreheads, but only on big occasions. After a while, 'you'll be utterly ashamed of the mawkish, sentimental way you've been handling your child,' Watson wrote."[8]

Given this sanctioning of parental *froideur*, it should come as no surprise that Watson's own mother was a Bible-thumping prohibitionist. For both mother and son, it seems, pleasure was something to be avoided. They were hardly alone. At the beginning of the twentieth century, the desire for a disciplined approach to children became a national obsession, so much so that the American government got into the act, recruiting Columbia pediatrician Dr. Luther Holt to write a federally endorsed child-rearing manual, *The Care and Feeding of Children: A Catechism for the Use of Mothers and Children's Nurses*. His book was in such demand that fifteen editions were printed between 1894 and 1935. But this so-called scientific approach to raising children was actually anti-science. At a time when evidence of stepwise stages of cognitive development was emerging, the manual viewed children as flawed mini-adults, little homunculi who needed a rigorous training program from the moment they were born. To foster immediate independence, Holt was firmly opposed to the "vicious practice of rocking a child in a cradle, picking him up when he cried, or handling him too often." He also frowned on hugging older children.[19] For two-thirds of the twentieth century the parental zeitgeist was to deny babies and children any physical or emotional comfort. To make them grow up. Fast.

Fast-forward a hundred years, and scientific opinion has made a complete about-face. Infants are no longer seen as miniature adults with incredibly bad table manners. Nurses no longer take them from their mothers right after birth and place them in "isolettes" in antiseptic neonatal nurseries designed to protect newborns from germs and the corrupting effect of human contact (This was still the practice at university-affiliated hospitals when my first child was born, in the mid 1980s.) Upon discharge from the hospital, new mothers aren't handed their swaddled newborn along with cases of free infant formula in beautifully pebbled four-ounce bottles. Instead, they're urged by lactation consultants to breastfeed, come what may. Fathers are no longer confined to the waiting room but are now expected to be present at the birth and to interact meaningfully with their children ever after.

Until recently, pediatricians were considered experts who diagnosed, immunized, and prescribed from the remote and comfortable remove of their offices. Now, directives from the American Academy of Pediatrics (issued in 2012) state that if pediatricians sense that something is amiss, they must also intervene in the child's social world. New evidence from the fields of neuroscience and epigenetics shows that without the protective effect of healthy relationships, other stresses—such as addicted or warring parents, and even "inappropriate electronic media, or fragmented social networks"—can have lasting effects on the developing brain. According to the report, an indifferent or abusive parent, or even a screen habitually substituted for social contact, can alter the young child's brain circuitry and lead to school failure or heart disease. The *New York Times* op-ed writer Nicholas Kristof paraphrased the academy's findings this way: "Affection seems to defuse toxic stress—keep those hugs and lullabies coming! Stress emerges when a child senses persistent threats but no protector."[20]

If there is little active, affectionate parental engagement, it's now up to the pediatrician to help the child find that protector.

This is a far cry from the expert advice of pioneering pediatrician Dr. Holt, who a hundred years earlier had advised parents that "infants should be kissed, if at all, upon the cheek or forehead, but the less even of this, the better."[21]

KANGAROO CARE

Being advised to hold your naked newborn against your bare chest would have shocked the pants off the Victorians. Touching infants is now permissible, thank goodness, not only because it is one of life's pleasures but because skin-to-skin contact has been found to be a homegrown analgesic for babies, as well as a stimulant for growth. In what is called "kangaroo care," a baby wearing nothing but a diaper is held right up against the parent's skin, preferably nestled between the mother's breasts. The pair are then wrapped in a blanket. After just one minute of this total embrace, researchers have discovered that babies who have been subjected to a painful medical procedure—such as having their heel lanced for blood samples—feel half as much pain as babies who undergo the same procedure and are then placed in incubators.[22] Not just any bare chest has that effect, mind you. Premature babies who were tested this way felt less pain when held by their mothers than by their fathers, according to Celeste Johnston, the lead researcher and a nursing professor at McGill University.[23]

But if the mother is unavailable, the father is a good stand-in. One Swedish study found that full-term infants who'd been delivered by C-section and who were held by their fathers in a skin-to-skin embrace cried less and slept more than those in bassinets.[24] The evidence for holding newborns is so strong that some hospitals are starting to use professional "baby cuddlers"—trained snugglers who step into the breach when a parent can't be there. Hugging and rocking have been shown to be particularly soothing to fragile babies. When a baby-cuddling program was introduced in a Pennsylvania hospital in 2009, for example, babies going through drug withdrawal were strong enough to leave the hospital an average of four days earlier.[25] Being cuddled, especially skin-to-skin, helps the baby gain weight faster, breathe more regularly, and regulate its own body temperature.[26] It's no wonder that the American anthropologists Sarah Hrdy and Kristen Hawkes have suggested that the human species could never have evolved its big, social brain and long lifespan without the assistance of grandmothers and other "alloparents," who would have helped feed, protect, and hold babies close. Without her "village," a mother alone wouldn't have been enough.[27]

Cuddling skin-to-skin with her infant tweaks the mother's physiological responses too. Her stress levels dip (as measured by the cortisol in her saliva), her mood lifts, and her heart rate stabilizes. Her milk production increases, which is one reason why her baby is quicker to put on much needed weight than a baby in an incubator.[28] If the baby is born too early and is placed in the neonatal intensive care unit right after birth—an anxiety-provoking experience for all concerned—kangaroo care in the hospital can also solidify the new relationship between a mother and her baby.

What made the biggest impression on me when reading this research was that holding their fragile babies in this skin-to-skin embrace reduced signs of postpartum depression in new mothers. The mothers in the kangaroo care group touched and looked at their babies more and their babies were more likely to return their gaze. Their synchrony became a fact through physical contact. And that early synchrony had a positive influence on the child's motor and verbal skills months later.[29]

PARENTS' BRAINS GET A BOOST

If proof were needed that social and physical contact can build neural networks in children, this was it. And the baby's brain isn't the only beneficiary; adults can also generate new neurons from close contact with their newborns. In the 1990s, studies showed that a mother rat's interaction with her young pups improved her learning and memory, and in the first decade of the 2000s, neuroscientists wondered whether that might be true of human mothers too. Now evidence is growing that supports that hunch.[30] One study by researchers at Yale and Bar Ilan Universities shows that interacting with her new baby substantially increases the gray matter in a woman's prefrontal cortex (the planning and problem-solving areas of the brain), the parietal lobes (the navigational portions), and the midbrain, including those areas linked to memory, emotion, reward, and coordinated movement.[31]

An infant's scent seems to flip certain neural switches in the parents. The mother's sense of smell gets completely rewired during pregnancy, so that the scent of her own infant becomes incredibly alluring. In the meantime, though, because the olfactory infrastructure is being overhauled, other wonderful aromas may smell disgusting. When I was pregnant, the scent of freshly ground coffee, which ordinarily makes me swoon, made my stomach roil. Neuroscientists think that the redo of the pregnant mother's olfactory system is what drives her mysterious food cravings and aversions. Not only does her sense of smell get revamped but a prospective mother's hypothalamus gets a tune-up, ensuring that the right hormone cocktail is released so that she feels *truly excellent* when close to her baby. During pregnancy, the volume of gray matter in her midbrain, parietal lobes, and prefrontal cortex ramps up too, so that after the baby is born the mother nearly always perceives her child in a positive light.[32]

Though mothers have a head start, thanks to their enhanced oxytocin pathways, new fathers are not left out of the neural renovation plans, at least in studies involving animals. Right after his pups are born, new brain cells sprout in the male mouse's olfactory bulb—but only if he sticks around. If he skips town, the neural boost to his sense of smell just doesn't happen. As a result, he is unlikely to recognize and remember the sounds and smells of his own baby, a prerequisite for mice as well as for men.

Without close proximity to his infant, a father's brain cells may take a hit, according to the work of two neuroscientists, Gloria Mak and Samuel Weiss. Though they work with mice, not humans, they've discovered that for any neural changes to take place in the fathers' brains, they have to be in close physical proximity to their offspring; simply seeing their babies isn't enough. When the neuroscientists allowed the dads to nuzzle their pups, the fathers' brains formed new networks. But when the new fathers could only sniff them through a mesh screen, nothing happened. Neurogenesis depended on real interaction.[33]

THE CUTE EFFECT

This contact-driven brain boost is no accident. Human babies have evolved over ten thousand generations to draw out solicitous care and feelings of intense pleasure in the adults around them, especially those who share their genes. Their oversized heads, rounded foreheads, huge eyes, button noses, rosebud mouths, and sweet scent make them irresistible to almost anyone with a pulse. Like all mammals, they're cutest when they're the most dependent. In 1950 the German ethologist Konrad Lorenz wrote that the appearance of immature animals creates an "innate releasing mechanism" on contact that switches on an adult's interest, affection, and nurturing.

Primatologist Robert Sapolsky calls this response the Cute Effect. When we see small babies, our usual defenses often melt away. Even when we see baby rats and mice, we engage in admiring high-pitched baby talk, which would sound ridiculous if not for the fact that everyone, everywhere, does it (in Japan, this predictable reaction to cute things even has a name: *kawaii*). Mammalian biology primes us to feel excited, tenderly protective, and even acquisitive (as in *I want one of those*) when we see these universal cuteness signals—a state of arousal exploited by the designers of

Hello Kitty, Bambi, Pokemon, and even Alessi, the Italian designer of kitchen "cutensils."

Walt Disney had the Cute Effect in mind when his animators transformed the long-snouted, sadistic Mickey Mouse of *Steamboat Willie* (1928) into a harmless munchkin in his 1953 film *The Simple Things*, according to the late Harvard biologist Stephen Jay Gould. Where Steamboat Willie plays an absurdist "Turkey in the Straw" on sentient instruments—he cranks a goat's tail, tweaks a pig's nipples, plays a cow's teeth like a piano, and uses her udder as bagpipes—twenty-five years later, right after Lorenz's paper was published, the newly cute Mickey "cannot even subdue a squirting clam."[34] In creating a helpless, toddler-like Mickey (complete with a huge head, eyes, and ears, and sagging trousers to metaphorically accommodate a diaper), Disney was banking that our protective impulses would be tweaked, even if Mickey is a rodent.

If cuteness turns on tender feelings in all of us, it's because we're biologically prepared to react that way. In fact, several recent experiments show that the Cute Effect doesn't just alter our feelings, it improves certain abilities too. If they saw pictures of cute baby animals first, people were then much more careful when carrying out a fine motor task (they had to use tweezers to pick up tiny objects from tight spaces). Pictures of adult animals had no such effect. Several Japanese scientists took this idea one step further. Having replicated the tweezer study, they found that looking at cute baby animals also enhanced speed, perception, and performance on a test that had nothing to do with taking care of something. Seeing something cute helped people focus, and thus improved their performance.[35] With these results in mind, the authors of the study suggest that babies—or pictures of babies—be used to improve our performance behind the wheel, at the office, or anywhere narrow focus is required. Imagine on-site infant contact rooms in the workplace, explicitly designed to enhance productivity—a questionable idea, to say the least.

Strategically deploying the Cute Effect is not unique to humans. Infants are so attractive to adult primates that male Barbary macaques in the wild hold and cuddle infant macaques as a way of bonding with other males in the troop. "When a Barbary macaque male encounters another male with an infant, a bizarre ritual takes place," according to German ethologist Julia Fischer. "The males sit together, embrace each other, then they hold up the infant and nuzzle it. Their teeth chatter and lips smack while making low frequency grumbling noises." When Fischer and her colleagues did a social network analysis, mapping out who was interacting with whom in the troop, they discovered that the males who carried newborn infants had significantly stronger relationships with other males, compared to males who were more likely to carry around, say, pieces of wood. Carrying these newborn infants was not merely a status symbol, it was a type of social glue. The baby helped these males start conversations with other members of their troop and drew them closer together.[36]

In three species of New World monkeys—marmosets, squirrel monkeys, and spider monkeys—the number of infants who survive can be predicted by how many non-paternal males carry the infants around.[37] This may be a matter of new mothers exploiting their male social ties for protection. When their babies get slightly older, though, it is the mother's female friends that count. Over decades of studying baboons in the Okavango Delta in Botswana and in Amboseli National Park in Kenya, Joan Silk and her fellow primatologists discovered that female baboons with the strongest bonds with other females—not just with their female relatives but also with female "friends"—were the most likely to have offspring who survived into adulthood.[38]

THE ONE-TWO PUNCH OF ADVERSITY

In *The Sexual Paradox*, I explored why lovingly looking after their babies ignites the reward centers in mothers' brains, in the

process making the mothers smarter. Mothers who deploy problem-solving skills in order to feed and protect their babies are
more likely to have offspring who survive—at least long enough
to pass on this astute solicitousness to their own offspring. It's a
Darwinian thing. Whatever parents do to increase their children's chances also launches the genes promoting that selfsame
behavior into the future. That's how face-to-face contact between
mother and baby has become a hidden cognitive self-improve-
ment program for both parties. But what happens if bad luck
throws a monkey wrench into the works? What happens if war,
illness, or deprivation gets between mother and baby? Does a
parent's hard life affect the traits they pass on to their children?
The answer to that question is a qualified yes.

One of the displays in Antwerp's quaint Maagdenhuis Museum is
a model of a discreet wooden drawer that was installed in the
stately building's masonry wall when it was a Catholic girls' orphanage and *vondelingenhuis*, or "foundling house." In the 1500s needy
mothers would deposit their baby girls, usually dressed in their best
outfits, in this street-side hatch under cover of night. Lowering the
wooden hatch automatically sounded a bell inside the building.
Within minutes the orphanage staff would have pulled open the
baby drawer on the other side of the wall. The baby would then
live there as she grew from infancy to toddlerhood and into childhood and adolescence, fed daily with warm gruel served in little
white and blue faience bowls and taught by the nuns to read,
embroider, and do housework.

The Maagdenhuis and the vondelingenhuis next door were just
two of hundreds of religious buildings featuring such drawers or
"foundling wheels," often made out of half a beer barrel. The
wheels had been decreed by Pope Innocent III in the twelfth century so that desperate (read unwed) mothers could leave their
babies in the care of the Church instead of drowning them in the

Tiber. By the beginning of the thirteenth century, there was even a foundling wheel in the Vatican.

These babies were rarely unwanted. At the Maagdenhuis, a mother's intention to reclaim her child was signaled by a token she would leave with the baby: the jagged half of a playing card or picture of a saint that had been torn in two. If the mother returned with her matching half she would be reunited with her child, no matter how much time had elapsed. In one of the most forlorn exhibits I have ever seen, several dozen unclaimed playing-card halves are displayed in the museum, now sandwiched between ATMs and tchotchke boutiques on an upscale street in downtown Antwerp.

More than five hundred years later, foundling drawers have made a comeback. Between the years 2000 and 2010, modern foundling wheels—now called baby hatches, angel cradles, or Moses baskets—have

Torn foundling token at the Maagdenhuis Museum, Antwerp, Belgium.

resurfaced in Italy, France, Germany, Hungary, Austria, Poland, Switzerland, Japan, Slovakia, the Czech Republic, South Africa, Canada, the Philippines, India, and Pakistan. There is even one in Antwerp, though strictly speaking it's illegal in Belgium to abandon a child. Still, as they did in the twelfth century, frightened or desperate mothers in poor neighborhoods can leave their babies in contraptions that look like library drop-off bins. These days, pulling open the stainless steel drawer reveals a

Plexiglas bassinette, equipped with a heated mattress and a source of oxygen. The baby's weight on the mattress triggers an alarm that rings in the hospital's neonatal unit. The baby is retrieved, cared for, and, if unclaimed after several months, placed in foster care.

The common assumption is that these abandoned babies will thrive once caring adults step into the breach. Frankly, any outcome is preferable to starting life in a dumpster. But here's something to consider: if early interaction between a parent and his or her baby can switch on and off genes linked to that baby's future, unless the staff who took them in were affectionate and emotionally engaged with their charges, their care might not have been enough to trigger the healthy development of these infants. According to evidence from the nascent field of epigenetics, clusters of genes activated by the parents' behaviour early on help determine how well a child fares later— how likely he or she will be able to manage stress, for example, or to become a problem drinker or drug user. A parent's early face-to-face interaction with an infant may well determine whether a genetic predisposition to psychological disorders will skew his life journey or be silenced. Even the child's lifespan, and that of his future children and grandchildren, can be influenced by the impact of early parenting on his genome. The give-and-take of face-to-face interaction in infancy affects how a child's genetic programming will play out.

Randy Jirtle is a Duke University biologist who has demonstrated that cloned mice with exactly the same genome can develop fur coats of dramatically different colors, depending on what their mothers or their grandmothers ate before they were born. Even before they were conceived, their ancestors' behavior mattered. We used to think that identical twins had exactly the same foundational material—the same eye color, the same height, even the same sense of humor and IQ scores. Yet according to work such as Jirtle's, we now know why identical twins might not develop the same physical and psychological traits. Despite sharing the same genome, diverging personal histories might produce diverging characteristics.

Sitting on top of the genome, the epigenome (the Greek prefix *epi* means "on") transforms the way DNA is expressed without changing anything about the DNA itself. Traditional evolutionary mechanisms are slow. It would take many generations for a mutation that was perfectly adapted to global warming to thrive, for example. But epigenetic transformation is fast, allowing the genome to "respond to the environment without having to change its hardware," Jirtle explains. If we think of the genome as the computer's hardware, then "epigenetics is the software. It's just so darn beautiful if you think about it."[39]

It *is* beautiful, if only because we now have a way to understand how something as simple as holding an infant against your chest can transform the baby's developing synapses. This close contact provides the baby with clues about whether it's a safe and predictable world. But if something goes wrong and adversity interferes with the parent–child pas de deux, that rupture in human contact communicates to the vulnerable infant that its system should be on high alert. Epigenetics translates environmental threats into chemical signals that activate—or silence—the gene clusters that govern the baby's metabolism and endocrine systems. These gene clusters tell the baby how to apportion its available calories or how to prepare itself to face danger. In other words, parenting influences how a baby's genes are expressed. If that doesn't make new parents more anxious than they already are, consider this: there's evidence that a baby's early warning systems are triggered in utero, based on chemical signals secreted by a stressed-out mom. And that pregnant mother's brushes with anxiety or adversity can be passed on to the next generation.

THE DUTCH HUNGER WINTER

The Dutch Hunger Winter, from November 1944 to May 1945, occurred when a German food embargo combined with a particularly harsh winter. The disastrous result was that thirty thousand people starved to death in less than six months. The Dutch women who were pregnant at the time (and who survived) gave birth to unusually small babies. That wasn't a big surprise. What was shocking was that the fetuses' experiences of deprivation in utero—especially if the mothers faced famine during the first two trimesters of the pregnancy—led to high rates of diabetes, cardiovascular disease, and cancer when these babies, who are now in their sixties, grew up. Not only that, the children and even the grandchildren of women who had been exposed to famine in utero shared their mothers' and grandmothers' high-risk profile. They had very small babies themselves, with endocrine systems preset to secrete gobs of stress hormones. In other words, they inherited the effect of their grandmothers' privations and could pass them on to their own offspring. These epigenetic effects could still be detected six decades after the famine.[40] The fetuses' hunger had stamped food insecurity onto their genes.

When it comes to deprivation, generational effects are also gender effects. Feast and famine patterns in northern Sweden from the 1800s, discerned by studying meticulously kept community health records, show that a grandmother's diet could predict how long her granddaughters lived. Meanwhile, a grandfather's prenatal or childhood brushes with food scarcity predicted the lifespan of his grandsons. If, after a shortage, food suddenly became plentiful and Grandpa could gorge to his heart's content (especially during middle childhood, a slow growth period), his sons and grandsons were at much higher risk of dying of diabetes and heart disease. Perversely, lack of food during other chapters of the grandfather's life conferred some protection from stress-related diseases on his heirs.[41] This was true of the Sardinian centenarians we met in

Chapter 2. Along with their ancestors, they experienced well-timed lean periods that, combined with the lifelong TLC offered by their friends and family, allowed them to live long enough to blow out more than a hundred birthday candles.

WHAT'S LOVE GOT TO DO WITH IT?

The McGill University neuroscientist Michael Meaney was gesticulating in front of a PowerPoint slide at an international psychology conference in Toronto. The slide showed mother rats nursing several tiny purplish pups. Meaney pointed out how some of the dams were hunched over as they nursed their babies, rounding their backs to create a space for the little ones to latch on and move freely underneath. Other dams weren't hunched. They remained flat-backed, their teeny-weeny violet-tinged pups hanging off their teats. Still other rat mothers were lying on top of their nursing babies, nearly suffocating them. Not all rat mothers are created equal, Meaney explained. By attentively watching mother rats and their pups during the first week of life, he and his research team also noticed that some mothers licked and groomed their newborns a lot, others less or not at all. The mothers that licked and groomed the most were the same ones who arched their bodies to accommodate the nursing pups.

As it happened, these more attentive dams ended up with pups that were better able to face the stresses of adult life. Solicitous nurturing during the first days and weeks of life meant fewer stress-related hormones circulating in the pups' bloodstreams when they faced a scary event. They startled less easily. They were also more open to eating new foods. They were more adventurous in new terrain. They could navigate mazes and recognize objects better than pups of low-licking moms. And their enhanced memory and spatial skills were matched by synaptic changes in the hippocampus, an area of the brain specialized for memory. If the pups were female, their early experience with responsive, attentive mothers seemed to make them more responsive mothers themselves.[42]

Rather than turning them into wimps, maternal TLC increased the pups' resilience. What's more, such responsive maternal care was transmitted to the next generation. When pups born of low-licking mothers were fostered by high-licking dams, they acted more like their adoptive mothers than their biological ones. Being on the receiving end of solicitous mothering in the first weeks of life transformed their responses to stress.

Like the descendants of the women who lived through the Dutch hunger winter, the offsprings' DNA itself wasn't changed by early experience. But the chemical coating surrounding their DNA was, and that altered layer determined how their genetic code would play out. According to Meaney's research, subtle differences in maternal behavior could permanently change the way a baby's genes are expressed. And that baby could pass on these environmentally tweaked traits to subsequent generations.

Though this research profoundly shifted the way many psychologists thought about child development, we've long known that nurturing-related brain changes are not limited to rodents. In the late 1950s, American research psychologist Harry Harlow separated rhesus monkeys from their mothers at birth and watched what happened when they were raised by their peers or with wire models he called surrogates. The surrogates were hollow metal forms that he had fitted with milk-filled baby bottles. They provided nourishment and a frame to cling to, but nothing else. Harlow soon discovered that without the affectionate give-and-take of early maternal contact, the monkeys couldn't learn how to play or to interact in a normal way. They just sat there, engaging in repetitive, self-stimulating behaviors. As Deborah Blum writes in *Love at Goon Park*, instead of playing with other monkeys and trying new experiences on for size, the surrogate-raised infants clung to the bars of their cages for hours and shrieked at passersby. "Others mauled themselves, biting their arms, ripping out fur."[43]

More recently, studies by a former student of Harlow's, Stephen Suomi, and his colleagues at the National Institute of Child Health, have shown that infant monkeys deprived of solicitous maternal care become impulsive and aggressive adults. Suomi and the team separated infant rhesus monkeys from their mothers and raised them with their peers; they had social contact but not motherly love. Nearly all of the monkeys who'd been separated from their mothers within the first six months of their lives exhibited weirdly exaggerated responses to stress as adults, including elevated levels of cortisol in their bloodstream and marked differences in the proteins that regulate neural cell growth and survival.[44] When given the opportunity, these monkeys downed large quantities of alcohol—especially if they were male.[45]

Could a major disruption in face-to-face care be the catalyst that helps turn on the genes related to certain psychological disorders, such as attention and anxiety disorders, major depression, and alcoholism? If so, inheriting the genes for a disorder would mean you'd received the raw materials, but you'd need a double whammy of adversity to switch on the problem. Scientists called this the "two-hit" model. The first hit would be the loss of engaged parenting in infancy. The second hit would come much later, when these babies were older.

Digital Natives

Does Steady Exposure to
Electronic Devices Affect Children's
Language Development, Academic Progress,
and Happiness?

6

Her name was Claudia Aristy and she may well have been
headed for a life of inner-city poverty had she not found herself in Bellevue Hospital's adolescent parenting group in New York.
It was 1996; Aristy was just sixteen and she had recently arrived
from the Dominican Republic. During a previous visit to New York
she had fallen in love with a thirty-year-old man and become pregnant. "So I had come back to New York to live with my baby's
father," Aristy told me as we chatted in Bellevue's pediatric day
clinic. "And my grandmother decided Bellevue was a safe place
where I could get good medical care."

A home-care worker who knew her way around the city, Claudia's
grandmother took the subway to the clinic with her granddaughter
the first time. After that, Claudia was on her own. She admits now
that she had a tough time. "Being in a different country and having
to learn to navigate a different culture, a different language, and
being far away from your family when you're pregnant and you're
going through so many emotions—it's really difficult," she said. "And
I was starting to wonder, what's going to happen? Am I going to be a
good parent? You want to show and prove to the world that even
though you are pregnant and everybody considers it such a big mistake, that you're going to be okay, you're going to be a good mom."

Now thirty-two, Claudia is employed as a bilingual parent educator by one of the hospital's longstanding outreach programs that target New York's low-income families. Claudia *had* faced difficulties. But, buttressed by the social support provided by Bellevue, she had made it past them; her son, Alejandro, was a thriving, guitar-playing teenager. Now her job is to connect with other parents to show them what it takes so that their kids will be able to make it too.

Banking on the deep trust most parents have in their kids' doctors, in the late eighties a few pediatricians at Boston City Hospital asked themselves the following question: what would happen if pediatricians prescribed face-to-face interaction and a daily diet of reading to children with the same gravitas they applied to medical issues? The reasoning was that if some children lived in highly verbal, print-rich home environments while others did not, then promoting reading and giving out free books might help level the playing field a little. It would certainly do no harm. And it would be cheaper than previous early childhood stimulation programs.[1] By incorporating books into vulnerable kids' regular medical checkups there would be built-in continuity as the child grew. Besides, which doctor wouldn't enjoy sharing the books they had read to their own children?

The group, which included pediatricians Robert Needlman, Barry Zuckerman, and Alan Mendelsohn, decided to test the idea empirically. They started by putting developmentally appropriate books into the hands of low-income parents at each child's medical checkup, targeting clinics with a high number of vulnerable families. Along with encouraging parents to read to their children, the hope was that a growing collection of books at home might help narrow the gap between the five-year-olds who walked into kindergarten ready to learn to read, and the more than one-third who did not. It was a simple idea that took off. By the time I visited the program at Bellevue on a balmy February day in 2012, there were twenty-eight thousand medical professionals, thousands of parent educators like Claudia Aristy, and innumerable volunteers working in more than five thousand pediatric clinics all over the United States. Together they had handed out 6.5 million new books to millions of preschoolers.

By all accounts the program is a success. A dozen peer-reviewed articles in medical journals show that parents in the program read to their children ten times as often as other parents did. And reading to their children boosted the kids' language skills. One long-running study found that children in Reach Out and Read understood language at a level that was eight points higher on standardized tests than that of similar kids who weren't in the program. They were more advanced in their spoken language, too.[2] Another study showed that explicitly teaching parents of two- and three-year-olds how to read to them interactively significantly improved the children's language skills.[3] Impressive on their own, these gains also augured well for the children's later school progress. And that was the point. Concerned about the evidence that certain types of parent–child interactions were less common in low-income homes and that TV and other screens had often replaced face-to-face banter between parent and child, these doctors had come up with a plan they hoped would help change that trajectory.

Their idea was prescient. A study of more than two thousand children published by the Kaiser Family Foundation in 2010 found that media use had increased dramatically since they started monitoring it in the late nineties; most children now devote well over seven and a half hours a day to TV, video games, and social networking sites. Most striking was a class-related digital divide. Children whose parents did not have a college degree were spending ninety minutes more a day with various media than children from more educated families. Black and Hispanic children spent nearly four and a half hours more a day on TV and computer games than white children. There was no proof that screens were the cause, but children who were heavy media users were getting lower grades in school.[4]

Dr. Perri Klass, a pediatrician, author, and NYU professor, has been associated with Reach Out and Read since its inception and is now the program's medical director. When I met her in the clinic that day, I discovered that Reach Out and Read is an ethical commitment for her as well as a professional one. "When I think about children growing up in homes without books, I have the same visceral reaction as I have when I think of children in homes without milk or food or heat: It cannot be, it must not be. It stunts them and deprives them before they've had a fair chance," Klass writes on her website. When we sat down to chat in one of Bellevue's few vacant examining rooms, one of the first questions I asked her was about digital technology. Books seemed so, well, quaint, compared to the recent zeal for tablets, apps, and educational software. A recent article in the *New York Times Magazine* was typical in its enthusiasm: it suggested that underperforming third-grade children from a working-class Chicago suburb had boosted their intelligence simply by playing a computer game for fifteen minutes a day; the game required them to remember the location of a black cat in a haunted house.[5] I asked whether she thought that handing a parent a copy of *Goodnight Moon* could trump this sort of thing.

Klass paused, considering, then said, "I don't want to dismiss touch screens and e-books, because they're going to be important in some families. And I can tell you stories of ways that videos have been used that are wonderful. But as far as we know, nothing replaces face time—the parent–child interaction—when it comes to language, cognitive, and socio-emotional development. And with reading aloud, they're all in there together. When you take a child on your lap and use dialogic reading—asking 'Where's the baby? Where's the baby's nose?'—a lot is happening around language. But something is also going on about social and emotional development, and something is going on around written language. The book is promoting this interaction. And as kids get older they're learning about sequencing of words in print, on the page, and all of that is happening in a pleasurable, safe place, often sitting on the parent's lap. There's an awful lot that goes on with the book. And most parents grasp that. If you tell a room of parents, 'Think about holding your baby on your lap and reading to him,' parents tear up."

Still, even though Reach Out and Read was getting results, it was hard to know exactly what was doing the trick. After interviewing Klass, I watched how it all unfolded for parents at Bellevue. First, a bilingual parent educator, in this case Claudia Aristy, greeted parents and kids in the waiting room, encouraging the parents to talk to their babies and toddlers and to engage them in banter and play. Dressed in gold sling-back heels and a zebra-print skirt that swung jauntily when she walked, Aristy was hardly able to finish a sentence before she stopped to hug, pat, squeeze, or greet—in rapid-fire Spanish—one of the toddlers who crossed her path. Weaving her way through the packed, sun-filled waiting area, she warmly greeted each of the children and the nearly sixty young parents by name, while in the background the clinic receptionist bellowed out patients' names, the phones rang incessantly, and the hospital PA system blared.

A handful of trained volunteers sat on gym mats reading aloud and chatting with any children who happened by, trying to draw them in. The point was to model what interactive reading looked like and to show these stressed-out parents that their kids could really be engaged by books. After their names were called and the family finally got to the examining room, the doctor offered a book to the child sitting on his or her parent's lap. The books were used as distractions from the physician's prodding, but also as diagnostic tools that could tell the doctor something about the child's development. Could she hold a book upright? Bring it to her mouth? Point to the baby on the page? Count the ducklings? The pediatrician shared that knowledge with the parents, then showed them how books could be used to tell stories (a print-shy parent was encouraged to use the pictures to make up her own stories). At the end of the exam, the pediatrician exchanged the drooled-on board book the child had been handling for a new one to take home, often in the child's native language.

Later, Claudia walked me over to where the new books were stored, in a low metal cabinet hidden in an alcove. As I kneeled down to peer in, I inadvertently blocked a young doctor who was reaching in to pull out a book in Mandarin for a toddler. I recognized favorites from my own kids' childhoods, and Claudia pointed out books in Spanish, Portuguese, Bengali, Haitian Creole, and Vietnamese, all neatly sorted by language and age level, from board books for six-month-olds to simple stories that some preschoolers could sound out on their own. By the time a child turned five and was ready to enter kindergarten, he or she would have had a number of checkups at Bellevue, gotten to know the pediatrician and Claudia (or Jenilda, the other parent educator), been read to by volunteers in the waiting room dozens of times, and would have a library she could call her own.

"With minimal intervention we're having a big impact," Alan Mendelsohn told me the day I visited the hospital. A professor of developmental pediatrics and one of the lead researchers evaluating Bellevue's parent-training programs, Mendelsohn said that the average six-month-old baby seen at the clinic watches two hours of television a day. Programs such as Reach Out and one its offshoots, the Video Interaction Project (which films parents at home with their children and coaches them via watching video playbacks together), help parents interact with their children instead of sitting them down in front of a screen. Kids whose families participated in either program ended up watching fewer hours of TV, a decline that was matched by an increase in IQ. In fact, a twenty-year follow-up study found that the participants started school with language skills that were six months ahead of their peers.[6]

These are encouraging results, and I stopped by Mendelsohn's office to ask him a bit more. Dressed in a striped shirt and an animal-print tie, Mendelsohn had squeezed in a few minutes for me between a meeting and a class he had to teach that afternoon. "What's really cool about Reach Out and Read is that it's based on health care. All children receive health care in their first five years because they need vaccinations to go to school," he said, leaning back in his chair and playing with his tie. "So this is a platform where you can reach everybody. And three million of the children in Reach Out and Read across the country are low-income children, which represents 20 to 30 percent of all low-income children in the States."

"Now, if you ask parents what their concerns are, the main thing parents want to talk about when they come to these visits is their child's development and behavior," he continued. "Whether they're low-income, low-education, low-literacy, or the other extreme, all parents want the exact same things for their children. They want them to stay in school and succeed. They want their children to become professionals, to be doctors." Here he laughed ruefully. "Of course, that's what you'd say to a doctor who just asked what they wanted their children to be. Still, they want their children to be successful." But they don't always have the tools they need, especially in the early stages. "In the late nineties we did home visits around New York City as part of a study. And we found that every single family, almost without exception, if they had nothing else in their homes, they had a TV and a VCR." These parents want their children to start school ready to succeed, he told me, but they don't realize that technology isn't the answer.

Most of the kids at the Bellevue clinic are native Spanish speakers whose parents are Hispanic immigrants, some of them as young as Claudia Aristy was when she first showed up at the hospital, pregnant at sixteen. If the clinic waiting room was any indication, many of these parents believe that gadgets are part of the American dream.

Nearly every one of them was preoccupied by a smartphone, lost in his or her own silent screen world. Meanwhile their babies and toddlers were being ignored, some of them transfixed by their own screens. That is, until Claudia planted herself in their sightlines.

SIXTEEN AND PREGNANT

If Claudia had been the average teenage mother, persuading herself that she and her baby would enjoy a rosy future would have been an exercise in self-delusion. In the United States, which has the highest rate of teenage mothers in the developed world, more than 360,000 girls between the ages of fifteen and nineteen have babies every year. That's more than a thousand a day. The rate has dropped over the past twenty years, but it is still nine times what it is in other industrialized countries.[7]

Only half of these girls end up graduating from high school (compared to 90 percent of their non-pregnant peers). And compared to the children of mothers in their twenties or thirties, the children of teen moms are more likely to be born prematurely or underweight; receive inadequate medical care; be neglected or abused; become dropouts, juvenile delinquents, or teenage parents themselves; live in poverty as adults; suffer from poor health and unemployment; or land up in jail than any other American group. This sad litany is hard to square with Claudia's upbeat personality. Demographically, she knows she fits the stereotype, even if she sidestepped the dire outcomes.

I once teased my mother that she too fit the stereotype. I'd just returned from an academic conference on high-risk mothers and I listed the risk factors for her, counting them off on my fingers. She became pregnant as a teenager and was just twenty when her first child, my brother Steve, was born. Like many of her generation, she was also a smoker and a coffee drinker, and her first child was a boy—of the two sexes, far more vulnerable to developmental problems. She was not amused. Her stony response was a reminder that people are not a laundry list of predisposing factors. They're individuals. My mother is exceptional now and was surely exceptional then, even if she did conform to her era's expectations that women should marry and have children before they were twenty. Now this is considered risky behavior; then it was normal. Norms and developmental risks morph with each generation.

Even if it's politically incorrect to point this out, Hispanic and black girls make up barely a third of American teenage girls yet give birth to 60 percent of all babies born to adolescents in the U.S.[8] In Britain it's a similar story: its teenage birthrates are the highest in the European Union, matching those of the former Soviet republics.[9] Reflecting on this fact, British economist Marco Francesconi wrote that adolescent motherhood in the U.K. "is not just a symptom, but a *cause* of socioeconomic disadvantages that are transmitted across generations," because having a baby when you're barely an adult can generate lasting consequences. Like the epigenetic mechanisms we encountered in the previous chapter, deprivation gets handed off from mother to child. The associations between teenage pregnancy and iffy outcomes are hard to ignore. The children of British teenagers are far less educated, for example, and are twice as likely to be poor as the children of older mothers. Like their American counterparts, they are highly likely to become teenage mothers themselves.[10]

If that legacy weren't onerous enough, in the United States young Hispanic immigrant mothers interact less with their babies and toddlers than American-born mothers do, Claudia told me. "To have a conversation with a baby doesn't feel natural to everyone," she said quietly. Whereas middle-class families often engage their young children in Socratic-type discussions, especially around the dinner table, that interaction is less likely to go on in Latino families, especially among new immigrants, she continued. "In a lot of these families it's not the custom to ask children to express themselves. You just don't challenge authority."

Compare that reality to the other extreme. In a parenting blog, *Huffington Post* writer Lisa Belkin describes having been so hell-bent on using sophisticated language with her toddlers that her three-year-old explained "that he wasn't responsible for making his brother cry because 'he provoked-ed me, Mommy.'" Research shows that using simplified speech promotes language development and bonding between mother and child, as Belkin notes. "Yet I came to feel like an idiot babbling inanely at my kids, particularly in public, when the English language was filled with evocative and descriptive words."[11]

For the moment, let's put aside the debate about the value of motherese and consider which child will be more voluble at circle time when the kindergarten teacher asks a volunteer to describe the shape of the clouds that day. Is it the child whose parents don't expect him to use up any airtime? Or is it the child whose parents view him as an active participant in family life before his infant eyes can focus? And here's another thought: Studies show that most parents in the U.S., Canada, the U.K., and the rest of the EU are not that concerned about how much screen time their kids are getting. Fewer than one in three American children say their parents limit TV watching or playing video games. The parents of British children—who spend an average of six hours a day in front of such screens—"felt that they had things about right," summarized Lydia Plowman, the lead British researcher of a long-term study of media use.[12] In families where the culture is to leave kids to their own devices (literally), what role do hours of screen time play in a child's psychological development, school progress, or even happiness?

SCREENS AND SOCIAL CLASS

Before I even get to the screens, consider how skill gaps are widened by social class. In *The Social Animal*, David Brooks describes some of the ways that child-rearing styles among lower-class families differ from the engaged, debate- and tutorial-driven parenting of the professional classes. In lower-class homes "there tends to be a much starker boundary between the adult world and the children's world," Brooks writes. "Parents tend to think that the cares of adulthood will come soon enough and that children should be left alone to organize their own playtime." This hands-off approach means children spend less time interacting with adults and more time in front of the screen. For school-aged children, the average is over eight hours a day, more time than most adults spend at a full-time job.[13]

The class divide begins early. Babies born to poor families "watch" up to three and a half hours of television a day before the age of two, which results in that much less attention from adults and older children. Some researchers have found that this much television viewing is associated with a higher rate of language delay in toddlers.[14] As one young mother, an immigrant living alone with her two-year-old, told me, "TV is a big part of Brian's life because it keeps him busy while I do things around the house." When I asked if she talks to her toddler while she works, describing what she's doing, and if he then responds, pointing things out and naming them for her, her brows knitted with worry. "He's not really talking yet," she said. His world was baby-oriented television programming and videos. Her world was the adult sphere of household chores and responsibilities. As caring as she was, it had never dawned on this young mother to talk to her child as she would if an adult were in the room.

Take, as another example, the experience of nine-year-old Katie Brindle. In 1993, University of Pennsylvania sociologist Annette Lareau observed Katie, a white girl living in a rundown Philadelphia neighborhood, while the fourth-grader attempted to build a dollhouse in the kitchen out of old boxes and tape. While she was playing, her mother watched television. When Katie ran into trouble, she carried the toppling structure into the living room, plopped down the project at her mother's feet, and asked her for help. "Nah," said her mother. Katie was "silent but disappointed," noted Lareau, but that was it. Their worlds didn't intersect.

Katie's was only one of twelve family observations in a larger, long-term study that Lareau was conducting of American families, but her mother's response was an epiphany for the researcher, crystallizing what she had observed in many other working-class living rooms. Lower-class families are less likely to collaborate with their children to solve problems or to engage them in discussion. In contrast, the upper- and middle-class parents "see their children as a project," says Lareau.[15] They burnish their children's language and reasoning skills with a barrage of sophisticated chatter and edifying activities: preschool kindergyms, drama groups, choirs, sports and robotics teams. (*Mea culpa.* I ferried my kids to a bevy of extracurricular pursuits that included years of children's choir, youth orchestra, violin lessons and break dancing classes, as well as music, art, rock-climbing, or wilderness camps during the summers.) This approach costs not only money but time.

Perhaps that's why most of the working-class families Lareau studied were more hands-off. Their preschoolers may spend more time in front of a screen because they have fewer safe places to play outside or, if there are parks nearby, fewer adults to take them there.[16] Still, Lareau observed that these parents often said no to involvement with their children "casually and without guilt, because playtime was deemed inconsequential, a child's sphere and not an adult's."[17] Such a division between the parents' and child's worlds may result in more relaxed and vibrant kids, Brooks notes; children from lower-class areas have more contact with their extended families, more playtime with neighborhood kids, and they complain less about being bored.[18] "Whining, which was pervasive in middle-class homes, was rare in working-class and poor ones," Lareau observes. But this hands-off style also means that adults talk to kids less, children are alone in front of the screen more, and there's a lot less interaction and supervision.[19]

This is not just a North American phenomenon. "Remarkably, in most countries, parents of a low socio-economic status had

almost no rules regarding watching TV," write the researchers leading the Toybox Study, a long-running survey of the TV-watching
habits of children in six EU countries. "Children can watch all day
long or whenever they want."[20] Whether or not parents restrict their
kids' screen time is not a moral issue. Indeed, overly conscientious
parents (usually mothers) who control how their children spend
their out-of-school hours are often lampooned as dragons, helicop-
ters, or worse. Still, when it comes to how much face-to-face interaction a young child gets, the law of unintended consequences
may apply. Differences in parenting style are a fairly good predictor
of which child will have a bigger vocabulary, become a fluid reader,
and years later ace college admission tests.[21] Knowing that this
triage begins early, a growing number of professionals who work
with children are starting to rage against the machine.

TECHNOLOGY IMMERSION

Without early immersion in the latest gadgetry, some parents and
teachers warn that kids will find themselves behind the eightball in
an i-economy. But how hard is it, really, to master a touch screen?
One mother of a two-year-old described the first time her toddler
held her father's iPhone as akin to a religious conversion. "She
pressed the button and it lit up. I just remember her eyes. It was like
'Whoa!'" Natasha Sykes told a reporter. At first the child's parents
were charmed by their tot's instant love affair with new technology.
But then she got serious about the phone, Sykes said. "It was like
she'd always want the phone." She'd beg for it and cry for it. The
family had blocks, balls, Lego, little toy cars, and books, but "if she
knew she had the option of the phone or toys, it will be the phone."[22]
And who can blame her? Why should adults get to have all the fun?

Yet if this interface is easy enough for infants—YouTube features
dozens of film clips of drooling diaper-clad iPhone users—then
commercial apps for babies can't be far behind. Indeed, downloads
for small fry are a lucrative market, and new parents an eager

demographic. Sixty percent of iTunes' bestselling apps are targeted to toddlers and preschoolers, nearly double the number that target adults. One of them, Pull-Ups iGo Potty, sponsored by Kimberly-Clark, has an insidiously memorable soundtrack: "I know how to use the potty, 'cause I know my stuff. I know how to use the potty, 'cause I'm big enough! No more diapers, no more wet pants, no more icky poo!" The app reminds the toddler to use the potty and then, when she does, rewards her with a tinny "Good job!" and a virtual gold star, followed by virtual applause (the adult must key in the information, of course). Featuring cartoon objects that float among airborne wads of toilet paper, the app also helpfully reminds users not to throw ice cream cones or hamburgers down the toilet. Without any evidence that they work, parents download these apps onto their mobile devices and then pass them to their kids, hoping to offload one of the most detested jobs of early parenthood. There is now even an iPotty with a three-position dock for an iPad, so toddlers can watch videos and play video games while they master sphincter control (splash guard and iPad sold separately). For those parents who might want to outsource other aspects of early parenting, there are apps that purportedly teach babies to say their first words. One promotional blurb asks: "What parent hasn't held up items and said their name aloud? You hold up a sock and say 'so-ock.' Now Baby Flashcards has taken that game and made it virtual!"

It's too early to know whether an app can help toddlers control their bladders or kick-start their speech. Right now there's no evidence that they do, nor is there a contingent of researchers seriously investigating the question. That's a telling sign of avoidance, or maybe wishful thinking. Sixty-one percent of Americans now own smartphones, according to the Pew Center on the Internet and American Life, as do the majority of adults in Canada and the U.K. Over a third also own tablet computers. If the parents among them have handed over their mobile devices to their preschoolers, it's not only because toddlers are enthralled by these devices but because they keep them occupied.[23] At least a third of parents also say they believe that using these devices is good for their child's brain and development.[24] "Among the chart-topping products for the iPhone and iPad in the education category of iTunes, apps for toddlers and preschoolers experienced the greatest growth in the last two years," a think tank on children's learning and literacy reported in 2012, adding this chilling proviso: "No voluntary or regulatory standards currently exist around marketing products as educational."[25] In other words, let the buyer beware.

The truth is that electronic media—not just television, but the apps, videos, YouTube clips, games, and "social" networks sites— aimed at young children can't be evaluated because there's no information yet on their impact. There are some fairly strong hints, though. We know from the latest studies in developmental psychology, neuroscience, and social robotics that much of early learning is driven by the motivation to connect face-to-face. The American developmental psychologists Andrew Meltzoff and his wife, Patricia Kuhl, and their colleagues summarized the lay of the land this way in *Science*: "Children do not compute statistics indiscriminately. Social cues highlight what and when to learn. Even young infants are predisposed to attend to people and are motivated to copy the actions they see others do. They more readily learn and reenact an event when it is produced by a person than by an inanimate device."[26] Translation? For a young child, learning is not a passive act, stripped of human contact. Screens just don't do the trick.

In 2001, and again in 2011, the American Academy of Pediatrics issued strongly worded advisories discouraging all television—or any screen time at all—for children under two, and suggested that electronic media be tightly limited for preschoolers. The 2011 report provided ample evidence that TV and videos have little educational value, and can even be detrimental to early learning. Despite these warnings and the media coverage they received, only 6 percent of American parents are aware of the guidelines. Forty percent of

American babies three months of age are already watching some form of electronic media; by age two, 90 percent of them are. According to Dimitri Christakis, a researcher and pediatrician, "many children under two, who are only awake for about 10–12 hours a day, are spending as much as 30–40 percent of their waking hours watching TV." By the age of three, a third of American children have a television in their bedrooms. Preschoolers now spend over four hours a day in front of a screen, more time than they spend on any activity except sleeping. For many of them, this is time spent alone.[27]

Studies of the impact of screen time on child development are sobering. Two-and-a-half-year-olds who watch more than two hours of TV a day are more likely than other kids to have behavioral and social problems when the researchers catch up with them at the age of five, just when they're entering kindergarten.[28] Another study looked at the hours of television watched each week by more than a thousand randomly selected two- and four-year-olds and then followed up on how those kids were doing at the age of ten. The University of Montreal psychology professor who led this study, Linda Pagani, told me in a phone interview that she collected all kinds of data about this group of 1,314 Canadian children. "The kids had their blood drawn; they were tested for IQ, weighed, poked, and prodded. There were lots of parent interviews too." Her study included extensive home observations of the families, and controlled for almost anything else that might be skewing their results—the mother's education, the family's makeup and how well family members got along, divorce or remarriage, the child's sex, IQ, temperament, sleep patterns, and diet—all were factored out of the mix so the researchers could bear down on the effects of TV viewing.[29]

The results were startling. "Every additional hour of TV exposure among toddlers corresponded to a future decrease in classroom engagement, less success at math, increased victimization by classmates, a more sedentary lifestyle, higher consumption of junk food, and ultimately a higher body mass index," said Pagani.[30] Just as the more one drinks, the drunker one gets, there was a dose–response effect. Each hour of TV watched at twenty-nine months of age increased the odds that the child would become more detached and unengaged as a fourth-grade student. Not just detached and unengaged, mind you, but also less successful at math, fatter, and more likely to be bullied at school. "What we see is that a child with an entrenched habit—well, that continues," Pagani went on. "Kids who watch excessively at two watch excessively at age ten. And they don't develop the skills needed for a healthy social life."

BATHTUBS AND TELETUBBIES

If you want to know why early TV watching might be so damaging to growing brains, consider Archimedes. Legend has it that the Greek polymath, born in 287 BCE, discovered the laws of displacement while sitting in the bath. He had been trying to solve a problem handed to him by the reigning tyrant of the time, Hiero, who was concerned that someone was trying to pull a fast one by sneaking some silver into a gold crown he had ordered. Hiero asked the local mathematician and engineer, Archimedes, whether he was being cheated. The answer, Archimedes discovered—after letting his mind wander while he soaked in the bath—was related to the volume of water that overflowed when he sank down in the tub. If his body weight matched the weight of the water he had displaced, he could find out if the gold crown was mixed with dross by dunking it in water. As silver weighs less than gold, a crown made with silver would have to be bulkier and would therefore displace more water than a solid gold crown. "Eureka!" Archimedes supposedly shouted as he ran naked and dripping into the street.[31]

This story may be bunk, the first-ever urban legend. But I mention it here because the link between kids' psychological development and screen time may be as simple as displacement. If *Teletubbies* is on the tube for three hours every afternoon, face-to-face interaction takes a three-hour hit. This is serious, because social interaction is a requirement of early language development. As my brother Steve notes in *The Language Instinct*, there has never been a feral child—a child raised without human interaction—who has learned to speak. Even if a wild child living alone in the forest did produce language independently, who would she talk to? The motivation to connect with another human being is the prime driver of language learning. "Though speech input is necessary for speech development, a mere soundtrack is not sufficient. Deaf parents of hearing children were once advised to have the children watch a lot of television. In no case did the children learn English."[32]

In fact, the reverse is true. The more television sounds a baby hears, the less language she hears from a parent, the fewer words she subsequently uses, and the less likely that child is to take "conversational turns," according to a clever study by Dimitri Christakis and his colleagues. The team discovered this tradeoff by attaching digital recorders to preschoolers. Crunching the content of their digital soundscapes, the researchers discovered that television noise displaced social interaction much the way Archimedes' heft displaced the bathwater. It didn't matter whether the child was left alone in front of a screen or whether adults were there in the room, distracted by the show. For every hour of media entertainment, five hundred to a thousand fewer adult words were directed to the child. And for every hour of screen time, the child said less, too.[33] Perhaps that's why several other studies have found a link between early television watching and lower scores on tests of language and cognitive development as the child gets older. When the TV is on, there isn't that much time for talking, for social interaction, or for much creative play.[34]

Research led by UCLA psychologist Patricia Greenfield revealed that after watching toy-based cartoons, kids were much more likely to use the branded action figures to ape what they saw on the show and less likely to make up their own scenarios.[35] And while imitation is part of learning—as anyone who has ever watched a cooking show knows—for very young children, new language skills are absorbed only if the screen time is combined with face-to-face activities. Vulnerable preschoolers from Mississippi to Tanzania have had their language skills boosted by watching *Sesame Street*–style educational TV, as long as their viewing is supplemented by reading aloud and other hands-on literacy activities.[36]

Studies have shown that watching "educational" programming either has no impact on toddlers' language skills or it has a negative effect, a phenomenon researchers call the "video deficit." Still, not all media are created equal, nor are all kids. Some children need more engaged parenting and stimulation than others, and the amount and kind of screen media they're watching can be a proxy for the type of parenting they actually get. If we follow the data trail, the rule of thumb seems to be that the younger the child, the less he or she gets out of screen time; currently the language heard in baby TV and DVDs is less complex than what toddlers would hear from their parents, the pacing is out of sync with their developing brains, and there is a surprising lack of social interaction written into most scripts directed at the under-three set.[37] Without real practice with real people, that's not real language learning. That's entertainment.

THE ANTI-TV EVANGELISTS

So much for baby-oriented DVDs turning small fry into little Einsteins. The branding of many of these digital products suggests that they prompt baby smarts. Nothing could be further from the truth. and facing accusations of false advertising, a number of companies have been forced by the courts to offer refunds and to strike the word *educational* from their packaging and websites.[38] In the meantime, apps and global 24/7 kiddy cable channels have emerged to expand that niche. There are now millions of adherents to the notion that adults must throw every technological trick in the book at young children in order to stimulate their developing brains—and relatively few detractors.

And yet. Though adults love to watch TV and play video games, conflating entertainment with learning is not a mistake most adults make for themselves. That mental sleight of hand happens mostly with their kids. In one British survey of 345 families, many parents taught their preschoolers to surf the web and use the television remote so that the small fry could become "independent technology users" (the remote was described by one parent as "mum and dad's best friend"), while an American report found that many parents of babies and toddlers "can't imagine how they'd get through the day" without TV.[39] Among people who have choices, the rationale goes something like this: Technology prowess is necessary to succeed at school and work. One day my baby will go to school and work. Better give her a head start now—besides, if she's occupied, I can watch my own shows in peace.

Dimitri Christakis doesn't buy it. A vocal anti-TV evangelist, physician, and child development researcher (he's also the brother of scientist Nicholas Christakis), he ascribes to the displacement theory: that screens suck time away from children's engagement with people at a time when their developing brains most need social contact. That's one reason why there's such a tight relationship between screen time and lackluster language skills, he thinks. But the other reason has to do with what children watch and how old they are when they watch it. If there's a mismatch between the maturity of a child's brain and the fast-paced media she watches, real life will strike her as a bore. Reality's slow scene-changes, Christakis says, will be "underwhelming in comparison."[40]

It's all about timing. In a study of how much television 2,600 American babies watched (which controlled for other culprits that might cause inattention), Christakis and his research team found that for each additional hour of TV toddlers watched before age three, there was a 9 percent increased risk of attention problems at

"She thinks it's a touchscreen."

age seven—a finding that suggests (but doesn't prove) that a lot of early TV watching engenders problems with self-control later.[41]

But one study of preschoolers does show a causal link, at least in terms of television's immediate effects. In 2011, two researchers from the University of Virginia randomly assigned four-year-olds to one of three activities: a fast-paced TV show for preschoolers (*SpongeBob SquarePants*, with frenetic pacing and a scene change approximately every eleven seconds); a slower, educational program (*Caillou*, with scene changes on average every thirty-four seconds); or a control group (they drew pictures for the duration of the shows). Afterwards, the kids were given memory games, spatial and fine motor puzzles, and delayed gratification tests (they were offered a choice between two marshmallows that they could eat right away or ten marshmallows if they waited). The results? Though the kids in all three groups were equally attentive before the experiment began, those who had just watched *SpongeBob* fared significantly worse on the tests of planning and self-control than those in the drawing group, and somewhat worse than those in the educational TV group.[42]

These are immediate, not long-term effects. Still, it's discouraging if you're a parent whose child is restless, demanding, tired, hungry, and whiny—and you feel the same way. That's when a half-hour of TV may seem like a panacea. Dr. Christakis, who works as a pediatrician as well as a researcher, finds TV viewing less objectionable as a stopgap than as a habit. "If parents need a break for twenty minutes I tell them it's fine," he says. "I also suggest alternative ways of getting a break. But most parents think screen time is good for the child. They need to think again because there's no evidence of that."

DOES TECHNOLOGY AFFECT KIDS' HAPPINESS?

We now know that toddlers and preschoolers exposed to a heavy diet of television, videos, and computer games have exaggerated odds of growing up to be fat, fidgety underachievers who are bullied by their classmates. The thirty-odd international studies that suggest as much should be enough to persuade parents to hide the remote. But if that isn't sufficient, over the past decade several studies have suggested that screen time erodes a child's happiness. Well, it's either that, or unhappy children are especially drawn to screens.

Heavy media use in young children is linked to "appearing more sad or unhappy than their second-grade classmates," as Linda Pagani puts it. Those who spend the lion's share of their after-school hours watching TV, playing computer games, or on social networks "consistently reported being less happy and competent than their peers," according to a different study, this one of 1,266 middle-school kids in British Columbia. This was especially the case for the boys. Meanwhile, those kids who felt closely connected to parents, friends, and teachers and who spent time with them face-to-face felt most competent and happy.[43]

The late Clifford Nass discovered the same phenomenon when his Stanford University research team surveyed 3,461 Canadian and American girls between the ages of eight and twelve. Nass wanted to get a clear picture of the time preteen girls spent on media multitasking—watching videos, playing computer games, emailing, posting Facebook updates, texting, instant messaging, cellphone and video chatting—compared to how much time they spent interacting with people in person. Nass is the researcher who published a well-known study showing that adult multitaskers— people who work while dealing with several streams of electronic information at once—don't solve problems or remember facts very well. "They're suckers for irrelevancy," Nass said of media multi- taskers. His colleague and co-author Eyal Ophir added, "We kept looking for what they're better at and we didn't find it."[44]

Segue now to the 3,400 girls. Their media multitasking was associated with another set of disadvantages, this time in the social sphere. Girls between eight and twelve who are media multitaskers felt less happy and socially included than other girls, according to Nass's study. Even media meant to foster interaction, such as online social networks, evoked this paradox. Heavy users were more likely to feel abnormal.

The irony is that parents who spend their hard-earned cash on gadgets so their children will have immediate access to communica- tion networks may also be facilitating their girls' feelings of social exclusion. Girls with televisions, computers, and cellphones in their rooms, for example, sleep less, have more undesirable friends (according to their parents), and are the least likely to get together with their real buddies face-to-face. Yet, according to this study too, it is exactly these face-to-face interactions that are most tightly linked to feeling happy and socially at ease. If North American girls spend an average of almost seven hours a day using various media and their face-to-face social interactions average about two hours a day—less than half that time—then many girls are spending most of their spare time on activities that make them feel excluded and unhappy.[45]

YouTube, Tumblr, and Facebook make girls feel abnormal and excluded? Yup, and the reasons are not that hard to fathom. Online networks are social la-la lands. They're where people post idealized digital personae they've crafted for public consumption. Smiling broadly, with several friends' arms draped around their shoulders, group shots and status updates are uploaded to express—what, exactly? That the social lives of teenage girls are rife with conflict, social exclusion, and shifting allegiances? Yes, actually. The person who isn't in the Facebook photo now knows that not only was she excluded from the get-together, everyone in her circle knows it too.

Still, just as people who live alone use their televisions as "company," media multitasking is often what people do when they're frustrated, alone, or at loose ends. As *New York Times* critic and self-described gaming addict Sam Anderson wrote about video games, "They're less an activity in our day than a blank space in our day."[46] Online networks are the same. As they clue you in to a burnished version of other people's social lives, they can also amplify feelings of loneliness. In 2011, when I spent a solitary summer writing in a cabin in the Laurentian Mountains, my lack of human contact prompted me to check email and Facebook more than usual—and more than I should have. With each hopeful click I learned about everything I was missing—the dinners, jazz festival dates, casual jaunts for coffee with friends and family— all of which made me feel even more isolated.

I chose to hunker down in the woods to get work done. But social isolation among preteens is usually not their choice. Can't go on a school trip because there's not enough money or your parents won't let you? Here are a dozen photos of your classmates having fun. If you didn't feel left out before you checked your phone, you will now. How about that lopsided cake bedecked with burning candles, pictured on a pedestal plate and tagged as the twelve-year-old's birthday offering from her sixteen-year-old boyfriend? It's inexpertly iced but the message, dispatched on a news feed to 350 "friends," is that someone in the group has a boyfriend who cared enough to bake her a cake. How about that?

And these are the anodyne posts. The more sinister ones eviscerate a person's self-respect.[47]

Whether they're lobbed in our direction or at others, most of us are keenly aware of social affronts in our own "villages." But online networks instantaneously expand humiliation's reach. As our species' survival has hinged on group cohesion, we've evolved antennae exquisitely attuned to pick up on hints of exclusion; when such hints are detected, it hurts, as much or more than physical pain. In fact, expressions such as "hurt feelings," "heartbreak," and "rubbing salt into the wound" are not just metaphors. As we saw in Chapter 4, brain imaging studies by Naomi Eisenberger and her team at UCLA have shown that overlapping neural networks are involved in physical *and* social injuries. Shared neural anatomy is why social pain feels visceral.

The dorsal anterior cingulate cortex (dACC) and parts of the right prefrontal cortex, which together constitute the brain's alarm system, become activated when people experience physical pain, according to Eisenberger. Amazingly, the same areas become activated when people feel socially excluded, showing that, biologically speaking, feeling socially isolated is as much a threat to survival as bodily injury is.[48] This is especially true in adolescents, whose brains are uniquely wired to detect signs of social exclusion.[49] Eisenberger has shown that teenagers' individual differences in sensitivity to rejection are distinctly visible on brain scans. Online networks exploit this sensitivity by blitzing users with a steady stream of status updates, which by some unwritten rule, accentuate the positive and eliminate the negative in other people's social lives—making your own social life look so much worse in comparison.

HONEST SIGNALS

Aside from the flaws we purposely omit, what's also missing from our digital personae are the subtle signs that allow us to read each other's minds. When we're in close physical proximity, our emotions leak out, or so I discovered while driving a friend to the airport a few years ago. Straight ahead were road signs indicating which lanes to take for departures, arrivals, short-term parking, long-term parking, very distant parking, valet parking, and curb drop-offs. I'd driven to this airport dozens of times. Yet my feelings about the fact that I would not be seeing this friend again for months, perhaps years, became cognitive overload. I slowed to a halt under the forest of signs. "Am I distracting you?" my friend asked, pausing in mid sentence. I said no, but the answer was yes. My body was sending out honest signals: signs of my awareness that she would soon be three thousand miles away. Suddenly, remarkably, I had no idea where to go.

Honest signals are primarily nonverbal. Much of what is transmitted in face-to-face interactions—whom to trust, who is "hot," who is the most feared or persuasive member of the group—is communicated through nonverbal cues. As primates whose survival hinged on our social bonds, most of us get these messages even if they fly under our radar; we evolved the capacity to transmit them before we evolved the capacity to speak.[50] Even though humans can express sophisticated ideas with symbolic language, the nonverbal leftovers are still with us, adding a layer of communication that mainly happens face-to-face.

Lest you think these signs too primitive to be relevant in a digital age, as I mentioned earlier, two MIT computer scientists, Sandy Pentland and Ben Waber, have devised wearable computers that look like iPhones—"sociometric badges"—to capture these honest signals and make them analyzable. In a phone interview, Waber told me that the masses of data the sociometers capture are not parsed for content but aggregated to detect overarching patterns. "You can't reconstruct what people are saying," he assured me. Equipped with infrared sensors, Bluetooth location applications, and accelerometers to measure body movements, as well as recorders that capture the pitch of people's voices, these sociometers measure tone of voice, posture, and excited or languid gestures—whether a person is unwittingly communicating *"Put your head on my shoulder"* or *"Don't stand so close to me."*

Using the sociometers in large corporations and on university campuses, the team has discovered that honest signals can predict

a group's cohesion, not to mention its productivity levels, and who will assume a leadership role.[51] But I'm getting ahead of myself. The point is that analyzing social signaling provides a "God's eye" view, says Pentland, revealing information that can predict things people desperately want to know.

The question, though, is how rich does the medium have to be for us to "get" these honest signals? For example, can we show emotional support through an instant message or a text?

A sociometric badge.

Leslie Seltzer, Seth Pollack, and their colleagues at the University of Wisconsin explored these questions with stressed-out kids. The psychologists already knew that a mother's voice, like her touch, prompts the release of oxytocin in her children (the hormone is a physiological sign of being soothed by social interaction).[52] What they wanted to know was whether the meaning of the words or the sound of a mother's voice mattered more.

To find out, they induced stress in seven- to twelve-year-old girls by asking them to solve math and word problems in front of an audience. The researchers randomly assigned the girls to one of four groups. The first group met up with their mothers right after the test. The second group received a comforting phone call from her instead. The third group received a supportive text, and the fourth—the control group—had no contact with their mothers at all. The upshot? Being near her mom or getting a call from her prompted similar levels of oxytocin release, which was detected in higher amounts in the girls' urine. The contact also induced a drop in cortisol (a byproduct of stress), in the girls' saliva. Talking to their mothers after a stressful event clearly had a calming effect. In contrast, an instant message from Mom had no effect on oxytocin release. In fact, the girls who received IMs from their mothers had cortisol levels just as high as the girls who'd had no contact with their mothers at all.[53]

Really? An emotionally supportive text has no impact? Seltzer's research subverts what most of us assume: that the content of our messages matters more than the medium. Instead, the sound of a loved one's voice is like her touch—an honest signal that gets lost in translation on a screen.

THE FEMALE EFFECT

To be clear, though, what Mom says actually does matter. When researchers observed the social interactions of fifty-five British families for over a decade, they found that children whose mothers explicitly discussed other people's feelings and intentions grew up to be more empathic than their peers. The researchers tested and controlled for the mother's baseline level of empathy, so it wasn't just a question of sensitive parents passing on their genetic traits to their children. The mother's interactions made a difference. "You can predict, even from when the children are three or four, what their social understanding will be like when they're eight or nine," Dr. Yuill said of the fourteen years she spent being a fly on the wall in British living rooms.[54]

When it comes to communicating face-to-face, research by psychologist Mihaly Csikszentmihalyi reinforces the idea that emotions are contagious within a family. No surprise there. But what is remarkable is that the most powerful route of transmission is from daughters to their parents. And gender matters: mothers convey their feelings, especially their anxieties and triumphs about work, to their children in ways that fathers do not, according to the 500 Family Study, a large, long-term study of American working families.[55] A similar pattern of maternal influence emerged in another naturalistic study, of American dual-income families. From 2002 to 2005, Belinda Campos and a team of researchers from UCLA voyeuristically filmed the interactions of thirty middle-class, two-income American families with two or three children. The team focused on two important features of family life: reunions (the moment when a working parent comes home) and physical proximity (when family members are together in the same room). Their observations confirmed the primacy of working mothers in their children's lives. Mothers were more likely to be enthusiastically greeted when they came home from work than fathers, who often came home an hour or so later, only to find their children already distracted. Mothers were also much more likely to be in the same room with the children than fathers, and fathers were the family members most likely to spend their time at home alone.

The most shocking revelation, though, was the solitary nature of American family life. The members of almost a third of these families were never in the same room at the same time. For this group, there was "not a single instance in which all family members came together," write the researchers. On average, family members were together about 14 percent of the time they were at home. And while mothers did manage to spend time with their children, the most common configuration of all was family members, and especially fathers, "alone together"—each in his or her own space.[56]

In a short evolutionary time, we have changed from group-living primates skilled at reading each other's every gesture and intention to a solitary species, each one of us preoccupied with our own screen. But what if that screen is also a camera, party line, gossip column, television, encyclopedia, megaphone, cheat-sheet, video arcade, and, of course, telephone, all rolled into one hard, shiny package that rides along with you everywhere, stashed away in your pocket? During the clannish teen years, being constantly connected to your pals shouldn't be a problem. As Fran Lebowitz has remarked, "as a teenager you are at the last stage in your life when you will be happy to hear that the phone is for you." Let's now turn to adolescents to see if that's still true.

Teens and Screens

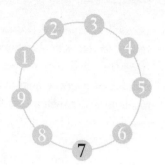

How Digital Technology Has Transformed Teens' Lives

7

When Allison Miller was an eighth-grade student attending Woodside High School in northern California, she sent and received twenty-seven thousand texts a month. Thumbing through about nine hundred digital conversations a day, often keeping as many as seven conversations going at once, the pert blond teenager was nearly always connected to her circle of friends—during the breaks between classes, while being driven to and from school, before and after sports practices, and while studying for tests. "I'll be reading a book for homework and I'll get a text message and pause my reading and put down the book, pick up the phone to reply to the text message, and then twenty minutes later realize, 'Oh, I forgot to do my homework—,'" she told reporter Matt Richtel of the *New York Times*.[1] The human dramas landing on her cellphone's screen often eclipsed other activities, she admitted. If she got wind via text of a ripple of conflict between friends, she would try to intervene. "I can text one person while talking on the phone to someone else," she said, blaming a lackluster report card on her technology multitasking.

Allison, fourteen years old, is hardly unique in transmitting a tsunami of texts to an expanding group of contacts, nor in attributing her peripatetic attention to her online habits. "Once you reach a critical mass in your network of friends, you begin to text them all the time, and they expect you'll do that, and you expect them to do that," said Amanda Lenhart, author of a Pew Internet Project report on teens and texting. Not that there's anything wrong with that, she might have added. Just as most adults are tethered to their wireless devices, so are teens to their cellphones, clinging to them even more tightly than adults, given that developing and grooming a loyal circle of friends is a major adolescent milestone. Four thousand texts a month was average for most teenagers in 2012, according to several reports, which translates to about six or seven for every hour that teenage girls are awake. Meanwhile, the former mainstays of adolescence—phone calls and hanging out in person—are way, way down. Two-thirds of American adolescents text "their people" multiple times a day, more than three times as often as they call them, send emails, or see them in person.[2]

The upside is instant access. The downside is that the medium is even more stripped down than email: brief, no eye contact, no tone of voice to shade or soften a message, and emotion and irony expressed minimally, through emoticons. That's why texting can be wildly fun but also brutal, such as when a guest arriving for lunch instinctively slid her buzzing phone out of her pocket and discovered, in the midst of joyous greetings and hugs, that her best friend had just died of breast cancer. As opposed to real chatting, texting is more like lobbing news bulletins; Clive Thompson, writing in *Wired* magazine, calls it "lightweight contact." While a conversation involves two or more people volleying a number of ideas back and forth, spinning from one topic to the next, each text represents a single thought.

Still, nine hundred texts a day? My incredulity is not about whether texting is good or bad. After all, first there was the Pony Express, then telegrams, then telephones, then IMs and emails, then SMS, etc., etc. Given that I enthusiastically exchange texts and use Skype to connect with my far-flung children, colleagues, and friends, I'm hardly a technology rookie. Wireless communication is just a blip in a series of brilliant inventions that connect people separated by geography who can't—or won't—talk face-to-face. Which brings to mind one of the questions adults think about. Why do teenagers text people who are sitting in the same room when they can have so-called *real* conversations? Does the technology bring them closer, say, by adding a layer of complicity, like a note passed in class? Or does it add a layer of distance, making it easier for shy (or sneaky) kids to express things they can't bring themselves to say to each other face-to-face? Do the Internet and, especially, social networks expand adolescents' social horizons? Or do they make some kids, say, the more vulnerable ones, feel even weirder and lonelier than they did before?

These are fairly urgent questions and they've been tricky to answer, not only because the technology is in flux, but because adolescents' brains are too. The prefrontal cortex is the neural area where planning, problem-solving, and decision-making take place. This is the stationmaster within your brain, the organizer that shifts your attention from place to place, initiates an activity and then stops it, decides what you're going to do and when you're going to do it. But unlike other cortical areas, it's a late bloomer. In the visual cortex, for example, synaptic development ramps up quickly after birth and peaks by six months of age. By age five, development of the visual cortex has wound down completely, meaning that by the time preschoolers enter kindergarten, they are perceiving and parsing visual information as well as they ever will. But synaptic connecting and pruning go on in the prefrontal cortex until late adolescence or even early adulthood, depending on the person.[3] In other words, before their frontal cortices are fully functional, we expect kids to drive cars and make fateful decisions about their careers (enlisting in the army, for example); we expect them to vote responsibly and craft online personae that won't mortify them when they're applying for jobs a few years later. Yet most teenagers won't develop adult levels of planning and self-control until they're twenty-one or older.

Despite this cognitive gap, most of the research about the online world deals with its impact on adults.[4] The received wisdom seems to be that what's true for adults holds for teenagers too, and that all technologies—and all teens—are created equal. But can a fourteen-year-old pinged with twenty-seven thousand texts a month, along with gossipy emails, "sexts," and Facebook updates, focus on algebraic equations or think far enough into the future to imagine the impact of her online postings? In short, at a time of life when friends mean everything to you, what does it mean to have 1,700 of them?

TEENAGE ANGST, MEET THE INTERNET

In the year 2000, a sprightly blond thirteen-year-old girl and her parents came to my psychology office with what was a fairly unusual predicament at the time. A boy from the girl's seventh-grade class was persistently harassing her through IM and email messages. The girl, who lived in a semirural area and came home to an empty house while her parents were still at work, was scared. Her parents were bewildered and came to me for advice, having been referred by their pediatrician. This boy was the son of good friends, and at first they thought their daughter should be able to handle it. She could give as good as she got, they told me. But when they read his creepy messages and realized that their daughter was afraid to stay home alone, they reconsidered.

Cyberbullying was new to me at the time, but I knew that without adult intervention the secret taunts would escalate. Based on my experience with garden-variety bullying and knowledge of the research of Norwegian social scientist Dan Olweus (the first to address schoolyard bullying systematically), I advised the parents to inform their friends, the boy's parents, as well as the school. As parents who'd been trusted with their daughter's confidence, they had a responsibility to help her by letting the boy know that his behavior was out of bounds. And that if his cyberbullying continued, there could be serious consequences, such as a suspension from school or a call to the police.

The parents were stunned. Like many adults—including school personnel—they were reluctant to get involved in kids' online lives. But with digital devices dominating adolescents' social spheres, it had become clear that online interactions had morphed. Whatever went on offline was amplified online. Smartphones are perfectly designed for making and cancelling social plans. But they also serve to draw tight social boundaries, to convey power and contempt, and are being used as a tool to prey on others. According to a survey of 20,766 students in Massachusetts, the real online danger is not kids being contacted by strangers but being victimized by someone they know.[5] In 2007, a study of nearly two thousand randomly selected middle-school students found that those who had faced bullying, including cyberbullying, had more suicidal thoughts and were more likely to have attempted to take their lives.[6] While most online encounters between teenagers are profoundly boring, a single impulsive or vicious post can lead to catastrophe. The suicide of eighteen-year-old Tyler Clementi occurred just two days after his college roommate secretly filmed—and then broadcast via Twitter and live video feed—a sexual encounter between Tyler and another male student. In an instant, the Internet had transformed a commonplace event—consensual sexual exploration on campus—into a global happening with deadly repercussions.

In a 2008 survey, American Internet-use expert Amanda Lenhart found that 32 percent of teens had experienced online harassment. The same proportion (though not necessarily the same kids) had been contacted by strangers online, especially if they were girls.[7] A similar pattern was unearthed by Dutch Internet experts Patti Valkenberg and Jochen Peter in a study of two thousand Dutch teens. They discovered that 22 percent had been bullied online and that two-thirds of those bullied were girls fourteen to fifteen years old.[8] Fifteen is a watershed year for defining one's in-group, as any parent of a girl that age knows. Fifteen-year-olds everywhere, including countries as diverse as China and Iceland, are consistent in their definitions of friendship and mutual trust. Given that it's the apex of bullying, fifteen is also the age for agreeing on what counts as social ostracism.[9]

BULLYING TIMES TEN
In yet another iteration of the Internet's ability to exaggerate, online bullying amplifies what is already going on in the locker room, in the cafeteria, on the playing field—indeed anywhere adults aren't watching, the research shows. And though the two types of bullying overlap, there are differences; cyberbullying is much more common among teens who spend lots of time online, far from the parental supervisory gaze.[10] Two studies, one of 20,000 Boston teenagers and another of 7,500 American teens from across the country, found that 60 percent of cyberbullying victims were also victims of bullying at school, and that cyberbullying was especially rife during transitions—when changing to middle school or high school, for example. Girls and gays are the most frequent targets.[11]

Most parents of fourteen- or fifteen-year-old girls would not be surprised to learn that girls are largely the victims of cyberbullying, given that girls are also the targets of sly snubs, nasty rumors, and cutting comments from other girls. Online or off, mountains of evidence show that boys are more likely to use overt aggression when jockeying for status—insulting or physically attacking their rivals—while girls usually avoid in-your-face attacks. Instead they tend toward covert hostility, demeaning or denigrating other girls in order to exclude them from the group.

Why would they do that? Throughout evolutionary history, large groups were risky for women and experienced as something to be avoided, write David Geary and his colleagues Benjamin and Bo Winegard. The dangers for women and children in traditional polygynous marriages, for example—where multiple co-wives had to compete for food, and where the odds of premature death for children were seven to eleven times higher than for those born to monogamous parents—put a lie to the notion that groups of women will immediately band together to help each other. In addition to neglect and abuse, "it was widely assumed that co-wives often poisoned each other's children," the evolutionary psychologists coolly write.[12] A child's likelihood of surviving was greater if his mother was the bossy, dominant type, as were his chances if the number of women in the immediate vicinity was smaller and the group tighter. The point is that social ostracism among girls emerged as a way of whittling the group down to size. Even now, girls and women (not to mention female chimpanzees) prefer smaller social groups than males do, and use bullying and ostracism to reduce the female competition.[13] What's really interesting is that teenage girls feel the pain of social exclusion so much more acutely than adults do. This makes sense, given that the neural networks that allow teenagers to understand social events are still in flux. One British study showed that teenage girls who feel they're being purposely excluded from a game become much more anxious than adult women would in the same circumstance. The peak year for social rejection and its agonies is fifteen.[14]

Indeed, a low, low point in my parenting career was the day my daughter turned fifteen. That day, as a reverse birthday present, her locker was broken into; the school custodian later found the contents dumped in the trash. Then an anonymous hate letter (there was no Facebook at the time) full of invidious accusations turned up in her backpack. Worst of all, her group of female friends had mysteriously turned against her. Only a couple of stalwarts showed up for her birthday party at our house that evening. We later learned that a "queen bee"—a female bully who targets other girls—had her eye on a boy who was a mutual friend. She wanted my daughter out of the way so that she could make her move.

Building alliances with Eva's friends, then siphoning off the more gullible ones, along with the break-in and the poison-pen letter, were attempts to diminish Eva's social status. Vicious as it is, such psychological hazing is a rite of passage for teenage girls. Add those exclusionary tactics to the instantaneous carpet-bombing power of the Internet, and what you get is cyberbullying.

It's important to keep in mind, though, that texting and online networks don't engender teenage meanness. They simply transmit, without the emotional checks of face-to-face contact, capacities that are already there. Such harassment is a millennia-old primate tradition, especially during popularity contests linked to bids for status or attention, usually from a member of the opposite sex. In their riveting book *Baboon Metaphysics*, American primatologists Dorothy Cheney and Robert Seyfarth write that even if peaceful social hierarchies are the order of the day for female baboons, there are occasional upstarts who try to disrupt the social order. And that's when all hell breaks loose.

One such opportunity seems to have arisen in July 2003, when Leko, the matriarch of the fourth-ranking matriline, innocuously began a sexual consortship with Loki, a middle-ranking male. For reasons still unclear, adolescent females from the fifth-, second-, and third-ranking matrilines responded with indignation. They threatened Leko with head bobs, threat-grunts, chases, and bites. Leko and her daughters, Lizzie and Lissa, responded in kind, but Leko was soon driven to the periphery of the group. The bulk of the attacks involved members of the fifth-ranking matriline—Balo, her daughters Amazon and Domino, and her sister, Atchar. For a week the members of both matrilines, as well as females from other matrilines, fought often and sometimes violently. After a few days Leko's and Loki's consortship ended, and the Leko family's retaliation began in earnest. Lissa seemed particularly incensed by the pretenders' challenge. One morning she was able to isolate Balo, the two tussled in a violent scrum, and Balo received a bloody wound on her eye. Gradually, the attacks abated, and everyone reverted to her former rank.[15]

High-ranking female primates can intimidate other females to the point where the victims can't conceive viable offspring, or if they do, the mothers are so browbeaten they can't raise them to maturity.[16] This is the ultimate evolutionary put-down. Still, female bullying is more common among adolescents than it is among adults. In the case of the attack on Leko, Cheney and Seyfarth remark that it might have happened because an unusual number of sexually mature adolescent females were hanging around, who may have perceived Leko's new relationship as reducing their prospects. *Who does she think she is?* could be one anthropomorphic interpretation, a phrase that might also have characterized the thinking of my daughter's aggressor.

But overt aggression among female primates is rare. "Instead, most female dominance interactions take the form of supplants: one female simply approaches another and the latter cedes her sitting position, grooming partner, or food," Cheney and Seyfarth note. When fights do occur, other females tend to chime in. "Uninvolved bystanders often give threat-grunts while observing other females' disputes, as if indignantly reproaching the tiff from the sidelines," they write.[17] It's an interesting parallel to cyberbullying. "Friends" can add fuel to the fire by posting online comments or photos—an update of the threat grunt. Or they can lurk out there in cyberspace, just watching.

One of the novel aspects of Internet bullying is that the humiliation is public at the same time as the teen's experience is private. Less than 10 percent of cyberbullied teens tell an adult what's happening to them.[18] As for friends, it's hard to marshal your allies when you're home alone in front of your screen at the time you discover that a humiliating image or a rumor about you has just been blasted to your virtual village: several hundred "friends," who each share it with their own networks. With smartphones, cyberbullies can be cowards; they can follow you anywhere, camouflage their identity, and never have to see the expression on your face when the diss hits its mark. Strangest of all, the victim's cyber community often goes along with the ordeal, as if they're paralyzed by a dream or engrossed by the action in a movie. Very few try to stop what's happening.

It shouldn't be surprising, then, that a team of epidemiologists at the National Institutes of Health in Washington found that cybervictims experience higher rates of clinical depression than "standard" victims or bullies.[19] If that weren't sobering enough, a survey of nearly two thousand American teens in middle school (grades six through eight) found that 20 percent of those who had been cyberbullied were seriously contemplating suicide, while another 19 percent said they had already tried to kill themselves.[20] With suicide the third leading cause of death among adolescents, according to the Centers for Disease Control, these figures should strike fear into the hearts of parents.

Also, cyberbullying is common. Seventy-two percent of Internet users between twelve and seventeen have been targeted once and one-fifth have experienced such attacks repeatedly, according to a survey by a pair of UCLA psychologists, Elisheva Gross and Jaana Juvonen. Though the marked overlap between harassment at school and cyberbullying—85 percent—suggests that the Internet simply "extends the school grounds," as the researchers put it, when social media and webcams are used to intimidate, they up the ante on adolescent risk-taking. As with fast cars and alcohol, the use of social networks can become lethal if there is no adult oversight.

MISSING THE FUNERAL

I recently learned on Facebook that a childhood friend's sister had died. But as I check my newsfeed only every few days, I missed the funeral. I should have been there. Had I been contacted directly,

I would have been. My friend's sister lived alone and had fallen down the stairs. She had lain there for a long time before being discovered; it was a solitary, lonely death. I called my friend and left a message on her cellphone. I sent her a supportive email, copying it to her various accounts. I considered sending her a text but thought better of it. I'd known her for forty years, and her sister too. I wanted to hear my friend's voice and for her to hear mine. But by the time we managed to communicate with each other, the week of shivah (in Judaism, the "social" period of mourning, when the bereaved are surrounded by friends and family) had come and gone. She had returned to her home in another city and resumed her daily life. I had gone back to mine.

Even when a life ends abruptly, a conversation with honest signals is no longer that common. The post about the sister's death floated among the electronic flotsam— "likes" for a recently visited hotel, links to cats doing stunts on YouTube. The disconnect is less about the medium than about our outsized expectations of it. Assigning our devices supernatural powers, many of us assume they can create distance when we want it and closeness when we want it. Explaining why he and his long-term romantic partner don't live together, for example, columnist Frank Bruni writes that they don't have to: they can meet in on the Internet. "That's the thing about our wired age: apart is actually the new together, because alone isn't alone anymore. On top of calling, there's Skyping, emailing, texting, sexting: a Kama Sutra of electronic intercourse."[21]

Make no mistake, I enjoy reading the odd article a "friend" has shared as much as the next person, even if the site robotically advertises that I've read it and even if that "friend" doesn't recognize me when I pass her on the street. But in its inability to filter out the dreck and its lack of emotional tenor, a social networking site is neither newspaper nor party line. You can read someone's posts about her Memorial Day weekend or see that she's won an award and hit "like." But for the most part, her fallible, human side is invisible there. You may share a history. You may know a lot about her. But when her sister dies, the two of you might as well be strangers.

THE GOOD NEWS AND THE BAD NEWS

It's reassuring that there is some good news about teens' enthusiasm for screens. Kids with lots of friends use their gadgets to keep their friends close at hand. One type of contact fosters the other, though this idea is an about-face of what the experts initially thought. In the late nineties, social psychologist Robert Kraus and his colleagues gave computers to ninety-three Pittsburgh families and followed everyone over the age of ten for two years, meticulously tracking their activities and moods. The researchers found that computers reduced the teenagers' face-to-face social contact by replacing it with virtual experiences. The more time teens spent on the Internet, the less socially engaged they became and the lonelier they felt.[22] As the team had tested the subjects' moods before the study began, they could impute cause and effect. Instead of making teens feel connected, the machines fostered their isolation. The researchers expected the reverse, so they called this the "Internet paradox."

Today the consensus is more shaded and can be summed up this way: the impact of the Internet on a kid's social life depends on who is logging on. Personality plays a big role. Outgoing adolescents deploy their mobile devices to up the social ante. They contact people they already know, deluging them with pictures, pokes, and jokes that make them feel closer to each other and help them cement their social plans.[23] For those lucky enough to have an expansive circle of friends, instant messaging and email correlate with face-to-face interaction. When one type of contact rises, the other rises in tandem. In other words, wireless communication exaggerates the extroversion of outgoing, well-adjusted teens: the socially rich get richer.

But what about more inhibited kids? Do the poor also get richer? Well, that depends. The Internet allows shy kids to share details about themselves without having to look anyone in the eye, read their body language, or worry about other people's reactions. This is a handy feature for teenage boys who are, by and large, less apt than girls to disclose their feelings face-to-face. And as sharing is a prerequisite for building relationships with girls, this stripped-down medium works quite nicely for many of them.[24] Not only are the emotions of the other person invisible, the machine's limits create a barrier that can be titillating. Think of Ovid's young lovers Pyramus and Thisbe, who grew up in houses that shared a common wall. Forbidden to marry, they communicated through a chink in the wall; that tiny gap became their only way to reach each other. "The more the flame is covered up, the hotter it burns," classicist Edith Hamilton noted of the romantic tension created by a wall.[25]

But without face-to-face contact, the socially poor also get poorer. Teenagers who communicate online with strangers feel lonelier than kids who use their devices to connect with people they already know. And it's precisely the kids who already feel lousy who are most likely to communicate with strangers.[26] Pundits have dubbed this "Facebook depression." If teenagers already feel alienated—a mood that prompts many of them to turn to the online world for connection—their attempts to form relationships in the often anonymous world of the Internet amplify that feeling, making them feel more depressed than they were before. This is more likely to happen to kids with existing psychological problems. An Israeli study showed that teenagers with learning disabilities—who often feel like outsiders—felt more alienated when they used the Internet to connect with virtual friends. Lonely teenagers who look for love or social connection on the Internet (as opposed to using the web for information or bargain-hunting) felt even lonelier than they had before.[27]

Meanwhile, parents of kids with ADHD who remark that their teens' restless minds are calm when they watch television or play video games are definitely onto something, though it's not a negation of the diagnosis, as many hope. The attraction to screens reflects the pleasurable dopamine surge their children's brains get from digital media's constant novelty and unpredictable rewards. These kids often act without stopping to consider the consequences and then are snubbed by peers because of their boneheadedness (I mean, impulsivity). It's so much easier for them to turn to the screen for electronic companionship instead.[28] "Children whose brains need neurochemical rewards seek out an activity that provides it. Children with social problems spend more time alone, facing a screen," as Perri Klass has observed.[29]

In fact, depressed teens leave characteristic cyber footprints. Researchers at Microsoft who mined the Twitter posts of 489 people found that those at risk of a major depression tweet more late at night, and that their posts refer less to real social plans and other people and more to themselves and their own symptoms.[30] Facebook, too, mirrors people's mental states. Twenty to thirty percent of college students' Facebook profiles refer to their profound feelings of depression, which should give parents and university officials a jolt, not only about the state of their kids' mental health but also about their privacy.[31] Even though people can opt out of sharing some of their posts, the Big Brother aspect of data-mining tells us two important things: first, that the number of college-aged teenagers who find themselves too depressed to function is underreported, and second, that teenagers' online behavior may be communicating more about how they feel than what they're actually telling you.

That's because the shallow sips of digital exchange—the texts, emails, downloaded content, and tweets that are so useful in business, politics, and building one's electronic tribe—don't necessarily add up to a real conversation, as MIT psychologist Sherry Turkle points out in her book *Alone Together.* She quotes a sixteen-year-old boy who relies on texting to communicate almost everything he wants to say. "Someday, someday, but certainly not now, I'd like to learn how to have a conversation," he told her.[32] This sounds extreme, but the feeling resonates with many older adolescents, according to a detailed portrait of five thousand American college students published in 2012. Having surveyed two previous decades of undergraduates (students during the eighties and nineties), the researchers found that "contemporary undergraduates are at once more connected and more isolated than their predecessors. . . . The image that comes to mind is a group of students walking across campus, each on their cell phone." Led by Arthur Levine and Diane Dean, the study portrays the current college student as savvy with electronic devices but "weak in interpersonal skills" and often struggling to communicate thoughts and emotions face-to-face. From the book they wrote on the subject, *Generation on a Tightrope*:

> On nearly every campus with residential housing, we were told about roommates having an argument facing back-to-back in the same room, not speaking but furiously texting. . . . A number of students said they preferred to text rather than call people because they felt less vulnerable that way. This was particularly the case with matters of the heart. They feared rejection and texts were less personal. This creates an environment in which things that would best be done in person are relegated to texts and e-mails. Students told of getting break-up texts and messages such as "I don't want to be friends anymore." Almost universally, deans said the current generation of college students had weaker social skills. One went so far as to call them *"socially retarded."*[33]

I'm not suggesting that the majority of teenagers are social Neanderthals. In their ability to keep track of people, the opposite may be true. Social media now allow students to bring the formative friendships of high school along with them to college and to their first jobs. But some are still missing out. Instead of investing in deep relationships in the here and now, many settle for small digital snatches of the familiar, for hookups that don't require much emotional capital. Their "villages" are dense, intense, and

interwoven but not all that local: it's now possible to be hypercon-
nected and extremely lonely all at the same time. Even if alien-
ation is any self-respecting teenager's mantra, one has to wonder
about the impact of diminishing day-to-day social contact on
their learning and happiness. Jay Giedd, a neuroscientist and
chief of brain imaging at the US National Institute of Mental
Health, has pointed out that an enormous amount of the change
in the adolescent brain is due to the impact of real social interaction.[34] Why, then, are so many adults pushing them toward digital
experiences at school?

ONE LAPTOP SAVES THE WORLD

In the early 2000s, seductive new technologies whipped parents,
teachers, school administrators, and even governments into a fund-
raising frenzy. Cupcakes were sold by the thousands to get computers into classrooms. Unbridled optimism made feasibility and
outcome studies—usually the mainstay of ministries of education
and school boards—suddenly irrelevant. Technology would transform education and democratize academic achievement. With
access to a computer and the web at her fingertips, each child
would learn at her own level. Books, not to mention classrooms,
would soon be obsolete, one teacher told me, and her second-grade
students needed to adjust right away. Digital and especially mobile
technology would go where no teacher had gone before.

On the international scene, the One Laptop Per Child (OLPC)
project envisioned a digital utopia in which all kids in developing
countries would be online. Spearheaded by Nicholas Negroponte,
one of the founders of the MIT Media Lab, the project aimed to put
a new low-cost, networked laptop in the hands of every child over
six around the world. The idea was that given a computer, children
from impoverished or remote communities would teach themselves
and their families how to use it. And that's how knowledge would
spread. To quote digital education theorist Mark Warschauer, it

would be drive-by education: adults could distribute the laptops and then walk away.[35]

Already loaded with a unique operating system called Sugar, the machines would be more reliable than human teachers, according to supporters. And as any twelve-year-old could provide tech support, there would be no operation or maintenance costs. "When you go to these rural schools, the teacher can be very well meaning, but the teacher might only have a sixth-grade education. In some countries, which I'll leave unnamed, as many as one third of the teachers never show up at school," Negroponte explained. His MIT colleague and a founding partner of the laptop project, Seymour Papert, asserted that once each kid had a computer, face-to-face instruction wouldn't be necessary. "There are many millions, tens of millions of people in the world who bought computers and learned how to use them without anybody teaching them. I have confidence in kids' ability to learn."[36]

Kids are wired to learn, that's true. But certain basics must be in place before they can learn more than frustration, as many teachers in impoverished communities discovered decades ago. There were One Laptop programs in American urban settings, such as Birmingham, Alabama, where students ultimately spent less time on homework and creative work and more time in online chat rooms after getting their free laptops, according to Mark Warschauer and Morgan Ames, who led the study. The researchers noted that teens in low-income families often get less supervision from adults, many of whom are working long hours, and so use their laptops mainly for entertainment: to play games, to chat, and to download music and movies.[37] Like a television, laptops can be used as an educational tool. But usually they're not.

Negroponte's utopian vision was intended primarily for developing economies where the challenges turned out to be different. Many of the proud new owners of the laptops are children without access to indoor plumbing and electricity. One young American electrical engineer who volunteered with one of the first and biggest OLPC programs, in Peru, noted in his blog that the problems could be big (the kids were often sick) or small (easily broken laptop keyboards), but the accretion of obstacles overwhelmed any educational goals. Uncontaminated drinking water was hard to come by in the village, so his students often had diarrhea and were too sick to learn. Electrical outlets to charge the laptops and Internet connections—a basic tenet of the OLPC program—were sparse. And often there was no one around to repair the buggy laptops when they broke down.[38] These were such common problems that much of the online commentary about One Laptop programs around the world dealt with trying to solve technical bugs as opposed to asking the fundamental question—could kids really learn more from these laptops than they could from a responsive, well-trained teacher?

No one really had the answer when the program was launched. Yet, enticed by the promise of mobile technology and the concrete nature of the gift (a box of brand-new laptops is more palpable than a teacher training program), corporate money poured in. Individual donors followed suit, especially under the North American Give One, Get One program, through which a $400 donation would yield one specially designed laptop for the donor and one for a child in a developing country. In 2012, seven years after its inception, the annual One Laptop Per Child budget was $12 million a year and 2.5 million laptops had been shipped to children in developing countries.[39]

The upshot? Kids' self-esteem seems to rise when they own a laptop, but there's no sign that their reading or writing skills improve.[40] In Haiti, for example, where fifteen thousand laptops have been distributed, half of the country's third-grade kids can't read a single word of French or Creole. That makes sense, given that a third of Haitian children between five and fourteen don't attend school, a figure that is likely higher for older teenagers.[41] In

Nepal, where a subsidized OLPC laptop costs $77 and at least 2,500 laptops have been handed out, the government spends only $61 a year for a student's education, according to 2010 UNESCO figures. Such scant investment in education is one reason why 79 percent of second-grade students in Nepal are illiterate, laptops or not.[42] In comparison, in 2010 the United States spent almost two hundred times that amount: $11,000 a year per elementary school student and $12,000 per high-school student.[43]

Our unabashed love affair with providing mobile technologies for students everywhere prompts serious moral questions alongside the educational ones. Malaria has surged by a shocking 250 percent since 2009, the year the One Laptop program began distributing its new computers in the war-ravaged Democratic Republic of the Congo. Needless to say, laptop programs don't cause malaria or civil wars, and one could argue that children's education should progress while a country faces other problems. But when 200,000 people, including children, are dying of a transmissible disease each year and most families cannot afford a three-dollar mosquito net, much less pay for their children's school fees, medical care, school uniforms, or textbooks, an expensive laptop project seems not only misguided but absurd. "If they have to choose between food and a mosquito net, they choose food," said Kalil Sagno, the region's head of child survival for UNICEF.[44] And who can blame them? The cost of one laptop would buy about sixty-seven mosquito nets or pay a teacher's salary for a month in most OLPC countries.

PROFESSOR GADGET

Closer to home, when laptop initiatives sprang up in schools, I wasn't immune to the hoopla. I enrolled my twelve-year-old son in an experimental program that was launched in 2000, the year he started high school. One of many such laptop programs springing up across North America and Europe, its immediate coup was seducing a committed, technologically savvy group of parents flush enough to shell out the $1,000 for a laptop for just one child in the family. Like the One Laptop program, the idea was that each child would have a computer that wouldn't have to be shared. Its second achievement, if you can call it that, was valuing proficiency in PowerPoint and Excel over low-tech tools such as paper-and-pencil tests and term papers. It soon became clear that I had made a mistake.

My son and his classmates spent their time surfing the web and playing computer games; if the teacher walked by, the students would skillfully toggle to the current classroom screen. Overblown sophomoric PowerPoint presentations became the homework assignment of choice (one of my son's first presentations featured an animated turd that hovered over his subject's head, like a thought balloon in a comic strip). He thought the whole thing fun at first. But soon all the class time the teacher was spending trying to lure the students' attention away from screen distractions became frustrating. After a year he wanted out. The school administration, anxious to prove that the pilot program was working, wouldn't allow it. So committed were they to their experimental laptop program that they wanted empirical proof that it worked, no matter what. They got it by keeping the highest-performing students in the laptop class, sometimes against their will.

The interesting question is why otherwise exacting parents and school administrators have fallen so hard for classroom technology. In his book *When Can You Trust the Experts?* psychologist Daniel Willingham uses research in cognitive science to debunk sacred cows in education. Lying on the junk-heap of no-evidence-to-support-them are such longtime favorites as learning-styles theory (some students are visual learners, others are auditory learners, and each must be taught accordingly), the whole-word method of teaching reading (memorizing whole words is better than sounding them out), and left-brain, right-brain education (analysis happens in the left hemisphere, creativity in the right). None of these approaches has much of an empirical leg to stand on, but they continue to draw fervent support because people gravitate toward simple explanations and glom onto anything that confirms them. But not all popular ideas are created equal, Willingham writes:

> Many such beliefs, though unfounded, are harmless. Maybe they cost us a little time or money, but we find them fun or interesting, and we don't take them all that seriously anyway. But unfounded beliefs related to schooling are of greater concern. The costs in time and money can be substantial and worse, faulty beliefs about learning potentially cost kids their education. Scientific tools can be a real help in sorting out which methods and materials really help students learn and which do not. . . . But even though scientific tools are routinely applied, the product is often ignored, or else it's twisted by people with dollars on their minds.[45]

The shift from student-centered to technology-centered classrooms has been swift, and expensive. In 2005, Bill Clinton asked Congress for $46.3 million for laptops, SMART Boards, and other digital gear for the nation's teachers and administrators. Since then, the US government has spent more than $40 billion to computerize its classrooms; the annual instructional technology bill for its ninety-nine thousand K–12 schools is about $17 billion.[46] The U.K. bought early into the technology juggernaut. In the mid nineties, Prime Minister Tony Blair decided to underwrite SMART Boards for every British classroom, a move that had cost British taxpayers 1.67 billion pounds by 2005, and the money is still flowing.[47] Meanwhile, in 2012, the Australian prime minister of the day, Julia Gillard, allocated $11.7 million to the One Laptop Per Child project, for fifty thousand laptops for students living in remote areas.[48]

When such heads of state, not to mention scores of well-meaning parents like myself, have been persuaded to part with mountains of cash to put the latest technology into the hands of students, one might expect that equally large mountains of evidence exist somewhere to support the venture. But more than a decade after laptops, interactive whiteboards, and tablets were introduced into millions of North American and European homes and classrooms, there's very little evidence that the technology boosts achievement. In fact, the data largely show the reverse. With the advent of new technology programs, most teenagers' academic performance either stagnates or plummets.

You'd think we'd be familiar with this trope by now. High expectations follow the appearance of most new technologies. The telephone was predicted to be the "antidote to provincialism," author Tom Vanderbilt writes, and was credited with the genesis of skyscrapers and the multinational corporation. Grandiose predictions accompanied the television too. Its inventor, Philo T. Farnsworth, thought his brainchild would bring world peace. "If we were able to see people in other countries and learn about their differences, why would there be any misunderstandings? War would be a thing of the past," writes Evan Schwartz, Farnsworth's biographer.[49] Given how ubiquitous and compelling networked devices are to most teens (and adults), we tacitly assume that these machines will teach them what they need to know.

A second assumption behind the vast public spending is that access to technology will reduce any educational gaps between rich and poor. Access to technology would just make learning happen. But does it? In the early 2000s, economists Jacob Vigdor and Helen Ladd decided to test the idea systematically. Over five years, nearly one million American students between grades five and eight were assessed annually in math and reading and were asked to fill out detailed questionnaires about how they spent their time outside school. By tracking the students' academic progress against the dates computers and broadband became available to them, the researchers were able to assess the technology's impact. The news was not good. "Students who gain access to a home computer between 5th and 8th grade tend to witness a persistent decline in reading and math test scores. . . . The introduction of high-speed internet service is similarly associated with significantly lower math and reading test scores in the middle grades."[50] With the advent of home computers, the students' reading, writing, and math scores dropped, and they remained low for as long as the researchers kept tabs on them.

One explanation is that the computers displace other activities such as homework and face-to-face social contact. Many of the kids used their newly acquired networked devices to surf the net, play video games, and download music, movies and porn, rather than attacking that book report on *Great Expectations*. Even worse, instead of leveling class differences in education, access to a laptop and the Internet seemed to widen them. Even within an economically disadvantaged group, the relatively weaker students (boys, blacks) were more adversely affected than other kids. After their computers arrived, their reading scores fell even further.

For the vast majority of students, the impact of the latest gadgets on reading, writing, and math skills—compared to students' performance in less wired classrooms—can be summarized in three words: *no significant differences.*[51] For example, bringing in touch-sensitive digital-projector-ready whiteboards makes class time more entertaining for the students and toggling between video and blackboard smoother for the teacher, a British research team found.[52] But ultimately the data suggest that it's a teacher's ability to weave this new technology into meaningful interactions with students that makes a difference to learning.[53] In other words, it's not the technology, it's the teacher.

Overall, evaluations of experimental laptop programs using different types of software and involving tens of thousands of high-school students have shown anemic results. A perfect example is Michigan's laptop program, loftily named Freedom to Learn. When eight matched pairs of schools in the program were compared after two years, there were no differences between the laptop and the control schools.[54] Lukewarm results were also the outcome of a four-year study of five thousand middle-schoolers in laptop programs in Texas.[55] Confirming research keeps pouring in. No matter how many students are studied and (with the exception of one fourth-grade program) regardless of the software used, laptops in the class-room do not improve students' achievement. In some cases they make things worse. In one huge American study of ten thousand sixth-graders from thirty-three different school districts, for example, the laptop kids' math skills fell behind those of their peers.[56]

Sadly, there seems to be no support for the chestnut that class-room technology allows students to learn at their own pace. "There was no evidence linking technology immersion with student-directed learning or satisfaction with school work," the Texas researchers stated baldly. Just like their classmates, students in laptop programs said they found high school meaningless. And while the laptop-program kids were less likely to act out in class, they were also more likely to be absent. (Other studies, too, show that intense Internet users are more likely to skip school, especially if they're girls.) Like many current university students, they probably surmised that if their instruction was mainly delivered electronically, there was no point in going to class.[57] After all, they could just go online.

IS IT THE TECHNOLOGY OR IS IT THE TEACHER?

One slushy day in early spring I observed a second-grade class to which a parent had donated thirty new iPads, no strings attached. Neither the parent nor the school had suggested how the teacher should integrate these electronic jewels into her teaching, so, left to her own devices, she decided to use them to read an e-book of *The Velveteen Rabbit*. Despite this teacher's excellent intentions and her superb face-to-face teaching skills, the seven-year-olds' first chapter-book reading experience instantly became more focused on adjusting font size, swiping pages, and inserting color-coded Post-it notes than it was on the bittersweet meaning of the story.

As the class was winding down and lining up for gym, the teacher showed the class a dog-eared paperback copy of *The Velveteen Rabbit* and asked if anyone wanted one. One girl lifted her hand tentatively. The rest looked down at their shoes or scanned the perimeter of the classroom so as not to make eye contact. Only when the teacher assured them that they didn't have to trade their free iPads for the book did their hands go up, one by one.

One reason for classroom technology's lackluster impact on learning may be that most teachers haven't received any subject-specific training in how to use it. Indeed, a study of ten thousand classrooms found that class laptops were rarely used to teach something new; they were deployed primarily to display content or to drill skills that had already been taught.[58] On a small scale, though, there have been successes with some kids in some places under certain conditions. For example a selection of schools participating in the state of Maine's universal laptop program for seventh- to ninth-graders showed that after their laptops arrived, the older kids' writing improved, as did some of the students' math skills—as long as their teachers had received "a well-designed and executed professional development program."[59] The training program beefed up the teachers' knowledge of math with face-to-face and online workshops, targeted their classroom practices to improve their teaching skills, provided "professional learning communities" of other math teachers so they could mentor each other, and finally, helped them integrate the new technology into their teaching. If experimental laptop-class teachers participated in such training for two years, their students' math scores improved slightly more than the control group's did (the experimental group improved by 22 percent while the control group improved by 20 percent).

Any teacher who gets all that extra training *should* get better at her craft, laptops or no laptops. The way the study was designed, we can't know whether it was the teacher training or the laptops that made the difference. But based on what we know about effective classrooms—namely, that a highly skilled teacher is the best predictor of learning (mattering more to kids' learning success than any other factor, even class size, race, or financial background)—I suspect that teacher training is the key. Only a skilled teacher who knows how to integrate the technology into her interactions with students gets results.[60]

Being assigned to a more effective teacher can raise a student's math scores by as much as 50 percentile points over three years, according to statisticians William Sanders and June Rivers. In fact, having a great teacher for just one year between the fourth and eighth grade boosts a student's odds of attending college, earning significantly more than other students, living in better neighborhoods, and saving more for retirement, according to a study of 2.5 million American families by economists Raj Chetty, Jonah Rockoff, and John Friedman. That one year with a great teacher—regardless of family income or access to laptops—also predicted a smaller likelihood of a girl getting pregnant as a teenager.[61] Forming a relationship with an inspiring teacher can also attenuate the genetic roll of the dice. A study of identical twins assigned to different classrooms has shown that those with a close relationship to their teachers were less aggressive than their genetically identical siblings. It's not that genes are irrelevant, but that a teacher who establishes a good rapport with a student can damp down his or her belligerence. "Teachers, next to parents, are the most influential adults in a child's life," said Mara Brendgen, the study's author.[62]

Face-to-face contact with a skilled teacher for even one year in a child's life has more impact than any laptop program has had so far. One can only wonder what might happen if the $10.5 million a small state like Maine spends annually on its laptop program each year were spent on teacher training instead. Now, *that* would be an interesting experiment.

Still, many teachers say they like the laptop programs because the computers streamline their administrative tasks and help them cover more material in class. Along with many parents and students, school personnel often believe that building teaching around classroom technology prepares their students for the future and makes their schools more marketable.[63] So far, though, the keyboarding, file organizing, Internet researching, tablet using, emailing, chatting, Skyping, blogging, and link posting that comprise most adults' Internet skills haven't required much prior academic training (my parents, eighty and eighty-six, have become expert at these tasks despite having written with fountain pens in high school). And as for more efficiency, when teachers click through their PowerPoint bullets, they often move more quickly than adolescents' brains do. The tendency for teachers to gloss over complex or controversial topics is the reason why many kids, including my own, call their laptop-based classes "death by PowerPoint."

ENGAGEMENT VERSUS DISTRACTION

One of the virtues of classroom laptop and whiteboard programs is that many teens say the computers make them feel good.[64] In the Maine program, for example, 78 percent of the students agreed that "I am more interested in school when I use my laptop." Like the kids in the developing world's One Laptop program, North American and British teens newly equipped with their own personal laptops report that they feel better about themselves.[65]

If so many teachers and students say that the technology makes them feel more engaged, one might wonder why this renewed interest doesn't lead to crackerjack school performance. Could it be that the technology is so compelling that its bells and whistles distract kids from learning the hard stuff? When I asked this question of Larry Cuban, an emeritus professor of education at Stanford who has written extensively on teaching and technology, he said the only way to know is to ask students what they're thinking about when they're on their devices. Even if teachers and parents report that students feel more engaged when the technology arrives, it's a mistake to assume this will create an uptick in their learning. "Since there is a novelty effect from high-tech devices and software, such engagement may well wear off after a few months or weeks, and then the supposed effects on achievement—if there are any—dampen," Cuban told me. Another prominent American educational researcher, Randy Yerrick, champions using technology in the classroom when it's uniquely suited to the task—in science simulations, for instance, or to teach kids with disabilities. But as an all-purpose academic mood lifter? "That's a fluffy idea," he said.

In short, sometimes digital technology trumps personal attention from a well-trained teacher or therapist. When predictability is key, for example, well-designed devices are indispensable. Students on the autistic spectrum, who have trouble reading other people's emotional states and communicating face-to-face, have benefited from wearable computers that monitor their own physiological signals and the emotions of others. Developed by Rosalind Picard's Affective Computing group at MIT, such applications allow students to function in the social sphere. Like an invisible doppelganger who whispers in your ear what other people are feeling—and what you should say in response—I can't imagine a better use for personal computers. Similarly, laptops and tablets have allowed students with grave illnesses to continue their education while in treatment, while digital devices have distracted young patients enough to stay calm without sedation during chemotherapy.[66]

But such situations are rare. What's more common, among healthy teens at any rate, is that digital technology distracts. Though there's little evidence that constant texting, messaging, streaming movies, and playing video games actually cause attention deficit hyperactivity disorder, there is good evidence that hours spent oscillating between these activities mimics ADHD's symptoms: flighty attention, reduced capacity to harness one's impulses, and, in the case of hours spent playing video games, disrupted sleep architecture and poor verbal memory.[67] The 5 to 10 percent of adolescents who are addicted to gaming, spending eight to ten hours at a time playing them, have shown neural changes similar to those seen in the brains of alcoholics and cocaine addicts. Compared to healthy teens their own age and sex, the Internet addicts' brain images revealed less density in areas related to self-awareness, error detection, and self-control.[68]

The corresponding impairments to thinking and attention suggest why dreadful tragedies have occurred. One British twenty-year-old died of a blood clot that developed during the twelve hours he spent immobilized while playing Xbox games, shortly before he was about to enter university to study game design. Then there was the appalling death of a three-year-old girl who starved to death when her twenty-something mother became so entranced by the hugely popular online role-playing game World of Warcraft that she forgot to feed her. Sometimes, though, the impact of computer game addiction isn't dangerous, it's just bizarre. One young man spent six years at the same screen in an Internet café in northern China, eating, sleeping, and playing at the same seat twenty-four hours a day, leaving only to go to the bathroom or to take a shower. "He's no trouble. In fact we barely hear anything from him at all. He pays his bills and doesn't upset anyone. The staff almost never talk to him unless there's a technical problem or he wants some food," said the café manager.[69]

Of course, it's likely that teenagers and young adults with pre-existing problems such as a flighty attention span are particularly drawn to mobile technology's interruptions and brisk scene changes. But studies that follow kids and their media habits over time and that control for extraneous factors, rule out the idea that the disorder always comes first. It's not just kids with ADHD who become addicted to their screens. And teenagers are not the only ones who can't stop playing online games or checking their phones.[70] It's all of us.

Our wireless devices are addictive for a reason. They connect us, and we're a deeply, profoundly social species. Our big brains grew to their current size, scientists say, in order to process our complex social interactions. Still, most of us need one special person more than anyone else. The reason that one person is on speed dial is the subject of the next chapter.

Going to the Chapel

Face-to-Face Social Networks, Love, and Marriage

8

When Natalie attended an eight-week workshop called Meet the Man of Your Dreams, she didn't think she ever would. At fifty, her romantic dreams were modest: she wanted to meet someone to go hiking with and maybe go out for a bite to eat afterward. "Frankly, I asked myself what I was doing there," Natalie recalled, her expressive mouth turned down in a frown. It was a steamy June afternoon, barely a month after I had attended her magnificent wedding and we were cooling off in my dining room, curtains drawn against the heat, while she recounted some of the stranger episodes of her romantic history. Though I didn't know her very well (I was on the groom's side), I had invited Natalie over to tell me how she and the man of her dreams had become an item. It turned out that the wry wink in the workshop's title didn't negate its meaning. Most people think they *will* find the man or woman of their dreams. Deep down, they believe there is a perfect match for them somewhere out there— a *bashert*, the Yiddish word for a predestined soul-mate.[1] And even though she was a free-thinker and a survivor of the sexual revolution, Natalie, in her heart of hearts, was no different.

Ultimately, Natalie's face-to-face social encounters transformed her life in ways she'd never imagined, particularly when it came to meeting her *bashert*. In that respect she was like nearly three-quarters of all couples in the industrialized world, according to surveys of how people find their romantic partners. Their real-world social connections—the people, places, and occupations they share—are typically what bring them together.[2]

MEETING THE MAN OF YOUR DREAMS

A movement therapist, Natalie had swapped attendance at one of her own dance workshops for the romantic one, as a courtesy to another member of her professional women's network. But her heart wasn't in it. After a brief marriage in her early twenties, which produced a daughter, now grown, she'd had a couple of relationships, each lasting a year or two. Though she'd had a handful of chance encounters (including a fling with someone she met on a subway platform when they both arrived late to meet up with friends), she intentionally set out to connect with new people. As an outsider, she had to. In the nineties Natalie had moved from France to Montreal, and "not being a bar person," she had first tried to meet her soulmate through personal ads. "My priority was listening to the quality of the voice on the recorded message," she said, that being her only honest signal. Then she tried two different Internet dating sites before labeling the online vetting process "disgusting" and giving up on it. She'd given romance her best shot, she thought, and came to the conclusion that what she wanted didn't exist.

When her acquaintance, the workshop leader, asked each attendee to list what she was looking for in a man, Natalie was not only taken aback by the question, she was stumped. "It was the first time I had to write down what I wanted, exactly." After a few minutes of hard thinking, her list looked like this:

1. a man with a lot of life experience
2. who is already a father, so not selfish
3. is educated (with at least a master's degree)
4. knows what a woman is all about
5. is warm and kind
6. speaks at least two languages

7. loves life
8. is interested in leading a spiritual life
9. is comfortable in his own body
10. likes to dance

Little did she know it, but Natalie was describing my friend Lou. A gregarious man who had lived in Egypt, Switzerland, and Canada, Lou was a widower with three grown children; he spoke several languages and had been around the block a time or two. When the workshop leader asked the participants where they hoped to meet their prospective partners, "that's when it occurred to me I wanted to meet him in a Jewish milieu," Natalie said. This surprised her. She was the only daughter of two secular Jews who had met in a refugee camp after having lost their respective families in the Holocaust. They had raised Natalie as a secular citizen of the French Republic. Period. There was no religious observance at all in her house when she was growing up. And aside from some dabbling in Eastern mysticism, there had been none at all for Natalie as an adult. So what was this all about?

BU-JEWS AND HU-JEWS

Natalie and Lou met in the most Jewish milieu of all, a synagogue. But they didn't just bump into each other while making small talk over crusty hummus and stale pita pockets at the post-service kiddush, though to be sure, other romances have been launched that way. They met at Bakol, a biannual weekend Jewish spirituality retreat sponsored by their local Reconstructionist congregation. A progressive movement that split off from mainstream Judaism in the 1940s, Reconstructionists believe in maintaining most of the Jewish traditions, such as lighting Sabbath candles and going to synagogue, while they largely reject the idea of a supernatural, anthropomorphic God (so much for divine intervention in one's love life).

If Reconstructionism is a splinter group of traditional Jewish belief, Bakol is a splinter of a splinter. The participants are spiritual seekers, some of them "Bu-Jews"—Jews who engage in Buddhist practices such as meditation—and some of them "Hu-Jews"—secular humanists (professionals and academics mostly) who enjoy yoga almost as much as they relish dissecting philosophical texts. The important point is that the couple met at a spiritual retreat led by a progressive rabbi, held in the clubhouse of an empty Jewish summer camp.

The milieu wasn't expressly romantic, and for the first few years of the program, Lou was in no mood for love, as we shall see. But it was an intimate environment that brought twenty like-minded people with similar backgrounds together twice a year for weekend retreats. Not everything had to be said out loud; the participants' shared experiences established a baseline of mutual trust. Here, then, was a social network within a social network, a small, tight circle inside an already circumscribed circle.

SHELTER FROM THE STORM

As social support systems go, marriage is unique. One might think that all couples who live together enjoy exactly the same benefits. But compared to cohabiters, married people enjoy stronger, more stable relationships and better physical and psychological health. They are far less likely to be alcoholics or depressed. They live longer, happier lives, even when scientists control for what shape they were in before they tied the knot.[3] This is true in almost all developed countries, no matter how progressive or conservative the common culture. One study published in the late nineties showed that in seventeen industrialized nations—including Canada, Britain, and most of Europe—married couples are substantially happier than those who live together. Meanwhile, couples who live together are happier than people who are single or divorced.[4]

The impact of face-to-face contact on our love lives seems to be on a continuum, with greater commitment bringing greater rewards. Now that nearly two-thirds of American newlyweds live together before they marry—an increase of 1,500 percent over the past half-century, according to the National Center for Family and Marriage Research—it's reassuring to know that the benefits of living together aren't completely nil, as was thought as recently as the late nineties.[5] Still, the commitment of marriage provides an added layer of protection. Whether the couple plans to get married when they move in together is what matters. If sharing a roof and a bed are preludes to marriage, then cohabitation presents no risk to the relationship and, by extension, to the couple's happiness.[6] But if the living arrangement just happened and stayed that way through sheer inertia, couples who live together are more likely to split than married couples.

In a book about twenty-somethings that twenty-something-year-old Samantha Henig co-wrote with her mother, Robin Marantz Henig, the younger Henig describes what she calls "sliding":

> You spend enough nights together that, actually, now that you think about it, doesn't it seem silly that you're paying two rents and constantly leaving the shoes you need at the wrong apartment? . . . Living together has its hardships, but it's also sort of fun, like playing house. You experiment with cooking braised short-ribs and bicker about throw pillows, just the way you always imagined you would one day. The things that concern you about the relationship are still there, but however hard it would have been to break up before, now there's the shared couch to consider, and the fact that you could never afford such a big living room on your own. (And yes, this "you" here applies to "me," the veteran of two live-in relationships that ended in breakups and couch custody battles.) Pretty soon you start to look like a married couple anyway, so maybe it makes sense just to make it official. Suddenly you have a wedding website and you've posted a poll asking if the honeymoon should be in Europe or Jamaica, without ever fully facing the very real

question of whether you actually want to spend the rest of your life with this person.[7]

The difference between sliding and deciding is crucial, and not just because that key distinction is one of the best predictors of the longevity of a relationship. Many Americans say that the only person they really trust is their spouse, which suggests that millions of us are just one person away from having no one at all. This is especially true for men, most of whom depend on their wives not only to give them shelter from the storm, as Bob Dylan put it, but to monitor their health and to build and maintain a web of social relationships that buffers both husband and wife for as long as the marriage lasts. Spouses in good marriages damp down each other's stress levels—a hidden system of emotional outsourcing—and wives are often their husbands' entry ticket into a rich social world. For many men, simply being married induces the village effect.

But women benefit from marriage too, and not just financially. One friend, a highly accomplished professional woman living in a region that recognizes civil unions, recently married the man she had been living with, happily, for thirty-five years. She was surprised to discover that her new status was not just a bureaucratic rubber-stamping of their relationship. Being married made her feel different, she told me: "More confident in myself. More confident in the relationship, and more secure in my ability to make decisions that affect us both."

I was stunned. I knew that a good marriage offers resistance to colds, but to existential self-doubt? This is rarely talked about, even among women. Nor is it measured by epidemiologists, who might measure blood pressure and cortisol levels but rarely the emotional ballast of those who know that someone always has their back.

Other than providing economic stability, at first no one knew why marriage was so protective of individuals' well-being. As of the

Enlightenment, they just knew that it was. By the late 1700s, marriage had become less of a public agreement with often draconian private consequences and more of a private agreement with some public consequences; as the social historian Stephanie Coontz writes, "Ordinary people more and more frequently talked about marriage as the route to happiness and peace."[8] Marriage was morphing from a business transaction between the bride and groom's parents to a public avowal of the couple's love and devotion to each other.

It wasn't until the mid 1800s, though, that William Farr, a physician hired by the British Registrar to keep track of births and deaths, discovered that marriage was also tightly linked to personal health. As France kept better demographic records, Farr set about developing models by looking at the French statistics first. Surveying data from twenty-five million French adults, he separated the population into three groups: married, never married, and widowed. Farr then took a close look at how likely people in each category were to get sick and die, a tragically common occurrence before antiseptics and antibiotics were invented (in the mid 1800s most Europeans were dead before they hit forty).[9] Having observed that the never-marrieds died "in undue proportion" compared to married people, and that the widowed were at the highest risk of premature death, Farr reasonably concluded that "marriage is a healthy estate." Gay, cohabiting, or divorced people weren't included in his Victorian-era roundup, of course, but contemporary epidemiologists who have added them to the mix have largely confirmed Farr's summary statement: "The single person is more likely to be wrecked on his voyage than the lives joined together in matrimony." As long as the lives are peaceably joined, that is—an important proviso that I'll get to in a moment.[10]

Dr. Farr was the first to show that married people have a longevity advantage over singles. However, sampling a population at one fell swoop meant he had simply found a correlation. It might not

be that married life was so salubrious, but that robust types might
be more likely to get married in the first place. It didn't take long
before critics raised that objection. In the late 1800s, only a few
decades after Farr published his paper, a Dutch physician named
Douwe Lubach suggested that people with "physical handicaps,
mental sufferings or infamy" tended to be single, and that it was
their illnesses and disabilities, not their marital status, that jinxed
their lifespans. This argument, called the selection hypothesis, was
later echoed a tad more genteelly by Dutch mathematician Barend
Turksma. An advisor to the city of Amsterdam at the turn of the
twentieth century, Turksma suggested that those in poor health, or
with "the least vitality," could hardly be good providers and thus
"are almost all obliged to spend their life unmarried." His wording
suggested that flawed men (say, alcoholics) were voluntarily with-
drawing from the dating pool. As any evolutionary psychologist
will tell you, though, it was more likely the case that judicious
women wouldn't have them.

Even taking into account women's longstanding preference for
stalwart, dependable guys, as soon as scientists started keeping
track they documented an inexorable trend toward an increasingly
larger gap between the lifespans of married couples and those of
single, widowed, and divorced folks. Barring extraordinary tragedies such as the Dutch hunger winter, which killed a dispropor-
tionate number of single and divorced men, and the Holocaust,
which wiped out entire communities (including statistician Barend
Turksma and his wife, at Dachau in 1942), under normal circumstances married people lived longer. It hardly mattered whether
you were a French laborer in the mid 1800s, a 1970s flower child
in the Netherlands, a Thatcher-era female lawyer in Britain, or an
American software engineer working sixteen hours a day in twenty-
first-century Silicon Valley. If you were married or living in a long-
term relationship with a loving partner, you'd be much more likely
to be happy and healthy—not to mention financially solvent—than

if you were single or divorced. And it wasn't just because you started out that way.[11]

THE MARITAL DOGHOUSE

Of course, sustaining a long, stable marriage is no picnic, as I discovered at the first social event I attended with my husband's colleagues after I returned from my honeymoon in the 1980s. It was a black-tie banquet at a downtown hotel, which I recall as a long evening of stale Henny Youngman jokes. Suddenly trussed up in evening wear, and jet-lagged to boot, I felt adrift in an undifferentiated sea of middle-aged men in ill-fitting tuxedoes. Some of them were gleeful as they trotted out cynical chestnuts like "A marriage is a fortress—those outside are fighting to get in while those inside are fighting to get out." Despite the snide tenor of the teasing, which I found as unsettling as the phalanx of silverware framing my gold-rimmed hotel plate, this predominantly male crowd was predominantly married. Divorce had taken its toll—this was the 1980s after all, when divorce rates were at their peak. But even the men whose first marriages had ended in divorce had been confident enough to marry again.[12] "If you want to read about love and marriage, you've got to buy two separate books," quipped comedian Alan King, who in fact stayed married to the same woman for fifty-seven years, from the age of twenty until he died in 2004, at the age of seventy-seven. Like my dinner companions that night, it didn't so much matter what *he* did; the point was that, out there in the world, the romantic view of marriage had soured.

Their remarks reflected a massive attitude shift. In 1957 an American survey revealed that four out of five people believed that anyone who chose to be single was "sick, neurotic, or immoral."[13] But by the early eighties the situation had reversed: marriage was in the doghouse. "The reasons for the revolution were many," author Kay Hymowitz writes of the trend away from marriage and toward single motherhood, including "the sexual revolution, a powerful strain of anti-marriage feminism, and a superbug of American individualism that hit the country in the 1960s and '70s."[4] Extending well into the twenty-first century, popular culture reflected the ambivalence, if not downright hostility, people felt about marriage as an institution. One-liners, TV sitcoms, and song lyrics mocked the idea that marriage could be the route to intimacy and happiness. The data, though, tell a very different story.

THE SCIENCE OF MARRIAGE

Over the past fifteen years, psychologists and physiologists have joined forces in an effort to show that face-to-face contact with your partner—specifically your level of intimacy and how you deal with conflict—can have a huge impact on your health. Even passable marriages provide a physiological umbrella that bolsters both spouses' immunity and resilience. The benefits accrue to men and women both, though not equally. Unmarried women are 50 percent more likely to die young than married women, while single or divorced men are *250 percent* more likely to die prematurely than married men are at any age.[15]

Being married significantly reduces your chances of being hospitalized, needing surgery, dying in the hospital after surgery or within fifteen years of a coronary bypass procedure; developing pneumonia, rheumatoid arthritis, gum disease, a viral infection, dementia, clinical depression, a serious cardiac event, or a variety of horrible cancers; going to jail, being murdered, dying in a car accident, or taking your own life. Much of this research is new. Though it's long been known that suicide kills four times as many men as women and twice as many single men as married ones (French sociologist Emile Durkheim described the phenomenon in the late nineteenth century), it has taken well over a hundred years to begin to map out the physiological pathways that transform the lack of enduring romantic bonds into a list of identifiable diseases.[16]

Admittedly, it's an impressive list. "In countries as diverse as Japan and the Netherlands, the unmarried die off much faster and sooner than the married" is how sociologist Linda Waite and her co-author, Maggie Gallagher, baldly put it in *The Case for Marriage*. They might have added the United States, the United Kingdom, Canada, France, Israel, Hungary, and the Scandinavian countries while they were at it.[17] Except in developing nations—where, shockingly, pregnancy and childbirth are still the leading causes of death for married women of reproductive age—the longevity gap between married and single people continues to widen, with married men now living an average of seven years longer than single men, and married women living an average of three years longer than nevermarried women. Clearly there is something about the special attention spouses offer each other that trumps being footloose and fancy-free.[18] The lifesaving properties of marriage could be as concrete as having someone there to call an ambulance in the middle of the night or to notice a new mole right between the shoulder blades. Or it could be as mysterious as stress hormones hitching a ride in our blood cells as they move through our bodies, touching every nerve, joint, and muscle within.

BETTER THAN YOGA, BLACK COHOSH, AND ECHINACEA COMBINED

In 2008, psychologist Julianne Holt-Lunstad and her colleagues strapped blood pressure monitors onto three hundred adults. Though some were single and others were married, their levels of physical and mental health were fairly similar; at the outset of the experiment there were no measurable differences between married and singles in how stressed out or depressed they were. The group wore the monitors nonstop for twenty-four hours, the blood pressure cuff automatically inflating and deflating as the subjects went about their day, eating, working, walking, talking, resting, arguing.

The results showed that adults who were happily married had lower nighttime blood pressure, and thus a lower risk of being cut down by a catastrophic cardiac event, than single people did. Their marriages were literally protecting their hearts while they were sleeping. Though singles were better off than those in miserable marriages, there was also something uniquely protective about simply being married. While the singles' happiness was closely connected to being surrounded by friends and extended family, the researchers found that this type of social support didn't have the same protective effect on the thrumming of their hearts as a long-standing, stable marriage.[19]

A happy marriage also has an invisible impact on whether women sleep well. A team led by Wendy Troxel, a psychiatry professor at the University of Pittsburgh, interviewed nearly two thousand married middle-aged American women about their sleep patterns. They found that happily married women had far fewer sleep problems, even when the researchers controlled for other sources of insomnia such as money or work worries, their husbands' snoring, their sex lives, or their caffeine consumption. Being happily married meant falling asleep quickly, waking less, and sleeping more peacefully. Interestingly, compared to women who had lots of social support from friends and family, only a good marriage predicted whether they were getting a good night's rest. "Those marriages that provide a sense of security should promote sleep," Dr. Troxel said, "whereas those that are a source of stress should promote vigilance, which is the opposite of falling into a deep sleep." As in Julianne Holt-Lunstad's study of nighttime blood pressure, a particular type of face-to-face relationship allowed women to let down their guards and let their bodies rest. But a prior history of instability in their romantic relationships—being separated, widowed, or divorced—scuttled that possibility.[20]

SEX DIFFERENCES AND MARITAL STRIFE

If a good marriage protects your health, does a hostile or hollow marriage damage it? Sadly, the answer is yes. An unhappy relationship is physiologically corrosive; it's not simply experienced as less support, fewer lifts to the doctor, or bowls of chicken soup.[21] "When love was strong, we could have made our bed on a sword's blade; now when it has become weak, a bed of sixty cubits is not large enough for us," a second-century rabbi commented in the Talmud. That emotional distance, whether writ in separate beds or separate custody arrangements, can be read in one's vital signs. But, by and large, men and women don't have the same physiological reactions to marital distance and distress.

Women are more likely than men to register the effects of stonewalling, contempt, and conflict directly in their vascular and immune systems. In fact, just thinking about a long-past marital conflict can raise a woman's (but not a man's) blood pressure. For women, emotional memory is so transformative that it can activate the same damaging neural networks as experiencing the conflict did in the first place.[22] This happens automatically and without our consent.

As we've seen, people who have a low opinion of their marital togetherness have higher nighttime blood pressure and thus a higher risk of heart attack and stroke. This is especially true for women, whose heart rates and blood pressure are more sensitive to social cues.[23] In fact, the quality of their marriage is so predictive of women's cardiovascular health that a long-running Finnish study showed that women whose marriages were colored by "considerable conflict" were two and a half times more likely than other women to be classified as physically disabled when the researchers followed up on them six years later. These findings were replicated by a Swedish team, who found that middle-aged women with a history of heart disease had three times the risk of another heart attack if their marriages were unhappy.[24] Conversely, another study found that women with the same type of medical history were less likely to die if they had found true companionship in their marriage.[25] All evidence points to irresolvable marital conflict being experienced by women as an illness with long-term physical consequences.

For men, marital conflict wasn't the issue. It was keeping their cards close to their chest that proved dangerous. Men with a cardiac history are less likely to have chest pains, to be re-hospitalized, or to die if they are able to confide in their wives, according to work by Carnegie-Mellon University's Vicki Helgeson.[26] More than anything else, it was emotional bonding that predicted their survival— a theme I'll return to in a moment. For now, though, consider that problem marriages affect men and women differently. The doyenne of research on marital stress, psychologist Janice Kiecolt-Glaser, put it this way: "Wives demonstrated greater and more persistent physiological changes related to marital conflict than husbands." This was true whether the women were newlyweds or veterans of fifty-year marathon marriages.[27]

Janice Kiecolt-Glaser, whom I met at a psychology conference in 2010, is a petite blond with a no-nonsense style. She is also a powerhouse of scientific productivity. She belongs to an elite club of social scientists who have teamed up with their spouses to answer some basic questions about human nature, such as why we need another person's love to survive. Kiecolt-Glaser works closely with her husband, viral immunologist Ronald Glaser, to explore the science of love and attachment. Other married social psychology club members have spent their work and married lives investigating why our long-term bonds matter. They include developmental psychologists Andrew Meltzoff and his wife, Patricia Kuhl (whom we met in Chapter 5), who have shown that babies need face-to-face contact in order to acquire the specifics of human language and empathy; social psychologists Roy Baumeister and

Dianne Tice, who share a research lab in Florida and together have mapped out much of what we know about why people feel the need to belong; and behavioral neurobiologist Sue Carter—the person who discovered that oxytocin fosters monogamy—and her husband, neuroscientist Stephen Porges, who have forever changed the way we think about the brass tacks of romantic commitment. And we've already met married primatologists Dorothy Cheney and Robert Seyfarth, who have made it patently clear that our complex web of social relationships—including our interest in who is sleeping with whom—is hardly uniquely human if it's shared with the chacma baboon.

But let's get back to Kiecolt-Glaser and Ron Glaser for a moment. The couple has found that recurring marital conflict leads to wild fluctuations in a woman's production of epinephrine, norepinephrine, and corticotropin—hormones that register fear and stress. Long-term high levels of these hormones impair the cardiovascular and immune systems. It's different for men, for whom lack of companionship in marriage is far more damaging, especially as many can't get that feeling of closeness anywhere else.[28] For many men, their one and only intimate friend is their wife. Meanwhile, their wives are more likely to surround themselves with a tight circle of close friends and family. This "village" is not only indispensable to their own health and happiness but provides a protective umbrella for the men they marry.

Interestingly, women don't have a monopoly on close circles of female friends who are always there backstage to bolster their spirits—and immune systems—when the chips are down. The bonds formed among nonhuman female primates are legendary. And the female chacma baboons with the strongest, most enduring female relationships also secrete lower levels of stress hormones than others, according to research by UCLA primatologist Joan Silk and her colleagues. These highly social baboons also raise more offspring to adulthood and live longer than their more solitary sisters.[29]

In the longest-running study of baboons to date, Silk and her team monitored 108 females from two groups of baboons, one living in Kenya's Amboseli Park, at the foot of Mount Kilimanjaro, and the other near the Okavango Delta, in Botswana's Moremi Reserve. The researchers discovered that the most social baboon mothers, the ones with a tightly integrated circle of friends and family members, had the highest number of surviving offspring. Social integration trumped rank and even environmental conditions in predicting which baboon's infants would make it to their first birthday. The size of the baboon sisterhood numbered around six. "To have a top three seems to be what's important here," Joan Silk said of the "strong, stable relationships that help females cope better with stress."[30]

How do baboons demonstrate friendship? They stay near each other, groom each other's fur, and help out when there's a conflict, much as human girlfriends do. They also share food, as we learned in Chapter 4. Still, tokens of friendship don't always resonate. When I was in Moremi in 2007, I observed a pair of female baboons squatting face-to-face with a pile of fresh elephant dung between them. They were carefully extracting undigested nuggets of fruit and nuts with their fingernails and feeding them to each other.

Other species have more appealing habits. Female elephants keep in touch with their chums through frequent exchanges of low-pitched vocalizations called rumbles. "We liken it to an elephant cellphone," said Joseph Soltis, a research scientist who works with elephants at Disney's Animal Kingdom in Florida. "They're texting each other, I'm over here. Where are you?" science journalist Natalie Angier wrote in an article about female connections in nonhuman species.[31] British primatologist Julia Lehmann has discovered that female West African chimpanzees stay within eye contact of their friends while foraging during the day, and rest with their backs propped up against each other at night.[32] Clearly women have a long evolutionary history of forming tight social networks. Those intimate female bonds act as catalysts for the village effect, and being married allows men to share the health benefits.

BLISTER STUDIES

If you were a young couple, probably the least romantic activity you could think of would be to check into a hospital together so researchers could observe your marital fights. Yet eighty healthy American couples did just that, not just once, but twice.[33] After agreeing to two twenty-four-hour hospital stays and a post-hospital week of daily checkups, the couples allowed a nurse to insert heparin wells in their arms. These are like IV ports, but instead of enabling fluids to enter the body, they allow blood samples to be taken without the subjects having to face a hypodermic needle each time. "People don't notice it at all once it's in," Dr. Kiecolt-Glaser told me.

The second step: nurses used a small tube to suction up the skin on the tender undersides of the couples' forearms. The suctioning process went on for at least an hour, until eight blisters had popped up. The size of plump blueberries, the blisters were hard to ignore, especially as the researchers then sliced the skin off the top of each, covered it with plastic, and then injected the blister with saline solution. Finally the researchers positioned the couple in chairs facing each other and asked them to discuss neutral topics (first session) or disagreeable ones that engendered conflict (second session). The scientists watched what happened from behind a curtain while videotaping the proceedings. Later they analyzed the couples' interactions, along with their blood and blister samples.

Though it sounds like some twisted episode of *Survivor*, this scenario was a way to simulate, under controlled conditions, what happens when married couples bicker about money, sex, badly behaved kids, meddling in-laws, dirty laundry, or whatever it is that makes them angry—sometimes for years on end. The point was to see how their face-to-face interactions might influence inflammation and wound healing. "Some were supportive and helpful. Some were downright nasty," is how Dr. Kiecolt-Glaser described the inter- actions. Marital hostility was measured as expressing disgust, con- tempt, or belligerence by glowering, stonewalling, or talking in a threatening way—all cues to that marriage's short shelf life.

Along with Sybil Carrère, psychologist Jack Gottman and his team found that they could reliably predict whether a couple would divorce within the next six years, based on three minutes of their conversation when they were newlyweds. Did the couple try to solve a problem during a conflict, or did they try to wound their partner or create distance with sarcasm or disdain?[34] If such hostil- ity—or its converse, supportive comments—gets under our skins somehow, how do our bodies register these interactions?

Part of the answer to that question is what was in those fluid- filled blisters. Kiecolt-Glaser and her researchers expected that couples who showed more marital hostility would produce fewer pro-inflammatory cytokines in their blisters, but higher cytokines in their blood. Cytokines are proteins that act as messengers between immune cells. With fewer pro-inflammatory cytokines at their blister sites, hostile couples would heal more slowly, while higher amounts of these compounds in the bloodstream have been linked to a host of age-related diseases. The researchers also expected that, compared to men, women would show more physi- ological evidence of marital conflict.

The results? The blisters of the couples who were more hostile to each other did, in fact, take longer to heal: seven days versus five days. The hostile couples had more cytokines circulating in their bloodstream and fewer at the blister site. Interestingly, their sores hung around longer after the session when they discussed divisive issues, compared to when they just chatted with each other. "It destroys one's nerves to be amiable every day to the same human being," former British prime minister Benjamin Disraeli is reputed to have said. The evidence proves just the opposite.

The difference between the couples' communication styles was significant too. The hostile couples' blisters healed at 60 percent the rate of the other couples.[35] In other words, if you're married, don't fight dirty. Even thirty minutes of marital hostility can have a dramatic impact on your ability to fight infection and how quickly your wounds will heal.[36]

Given this evidence, it's a wonder that doctors don't ask about the state of their patients' marriages as a matter of routine, along with checking their vital signs and palpating their prostates. Dentists should ask too. After all, people with a low opinion of their marriage are more likely to have gum disease and cavities than those who are happily married. Patients with Parkinson's disease, rheumatoid arthritis, and Alzheimer's disease who have critical or over-involved spouses have more debilitating symptoms than those with supportive, responsive ones.[37] Even physical pain is moderated by marital love, especially in women. One Finnish study found that women with back problems who were unhappily married had more acute pain and disability than matched controls. Conversely, being close enough to be touched by one's partner attenuates physical pain. California neuroscientists Naomi Eisenberger and Shelley Taylor have found that a woman who holds her loved one's hand (as opposed to the hand of a stranger) during an invasive procedure feels less physical pain.[38]

We can all hum "All You Need Is Love," but these results are still surprising. Who would expect that snide remarks from a spouse can rot your teeth? But it makes sense. If human infants and other primates are hardwired to react to the presence of a loving parent (versus a careless, anxious, or absent one), and if other face-to-face relationships buttress our immune systems, then the endocrinological armature that registers the tenor of one's romantic relationships must be able to write its signature on adults' bodies too. The evidence is building that a spouse has a direct, biochemical impact on the production and migration of our white blood cells and the way our genes are expressed.[39] And nowhere is this more obvious than in the acute suffering of widowed men.

THE WIDOWHOOD EFFECT

My friend Lou is a handsome man in his early sixties with a silvery beard, a receding hairline, and large aviator glasses. When he laughs, which is often, his mouth opens wide and his blue eyes crinkle up so that there's just a glint of pupil showing. Solidly built, with a powerful chest and a rumbling bass voice, Lou has a reassuring physical presence, which is a very good thing, as he's a psychologist who works with substance abusers. He seems at home in his own skin, and that easygoing affability is probably what attracted Natalie to him in the first place.

But Lou didn't feel all that affable when they met. Though he was participating in his usual activities—going to work, visiting with his grown kids and their partners, swimming regularly, and going to synagogue—in early 2008 he was mainly spending time with his wife, Anna, whose breast cancer had returned after a five-year remission. When she first became ill, they had decided together that she should have a mastectomy to ward off a future recurrence; they would celebrate together after the surgery was over. "What can I say? It was a time of closeness. We were so close. And we traveled to China after that. We did things, we went down the Yangtze River, and it was wonderful," Lou recalled wistfully, also remembering the boisterous family dinners they hosted between Anna's first breast cancer diagnosis and its recurrence.

But within four months of the cancer's return, Anna was gone. It seemed inconceivable. Her parents, both Holocaust survivors, had lost their only child. The youngest of Lou and Anna's three kids was eighteen and not yet in college—not ready to lose his mother, if one ever is. And Lou had lost his *beshert*.

"I knew who she was," he said of Natalie when I asked where they'd first met. "But I was not available in any way to meet or speak to people in a romantic kind of way. I still continued in Bakol. But I was all in my grief and I was not listening to what was going on. As a matter of fact, I went to one of those retreats and was wondering, *What the hell am I doing here? I really feel so shitty. All this spiritual stuff, my mind is not in it at all. All I am is in my grief.* So I told her—just the way I would feel comfortable telling you—and she listened and she was nice. And I went off by myself in the woods."

Four years later, Lou and I were chatting in my backyard after a midweek dinner, just two months after Lou and Natalie's spring wedding. Natalie was away in France visiting family, and Lou, my husband, and I had just demolished a zucchini frittata, a salad, and a bottle of Chianti while the fireflies flashed in and out of the azaleas. The sun had set and Martin had generously offered to do the dishes so Lou and I could talk. Among other things, I wanted to know how he had emerged from the dark tunnel of widowhood—a place that swallows up so many other men. At any age, widowhood increases a man's risk of dying within a year of losing his spouse by 20 to 40 percent. A powerful gender difference tells us that hormonal and social factors are at play, though it's not clear exactly how.[40]

It's more than just the loss of homecooked meals, or the solicitous care they received when they were married.[41] When they lose their spouses, men are at a heightened risk of sudden death or suicide because of extreme loneliness. Women, who tend to have more social supports, are not.[42] And though the phenomenon hits men of all ages, the impact is far more dramatic among those over sixty. The risk that an older married man will die within a few months of his wife's death increases by *30 to 90 percent*, a danger that ratchets even higher among more educated men.[43] Called the widowhood effect, I'd witnessed this disaster in my father-in-law, Charlie. He dropped fifty pounds, became disoriented, and experienced multiple life-threatening cardiac events in the months after my mother-in-law suddenly died.[44] A dapper Clark Gable lookalike with trimmed moustache, felt fedora, and a wry sense of humor, Charlie had had a mild heart attack in his mid-forties, but then had been healthy for more than three decades. Losing his wife literally unhinged his heart. He lost not only the physical presence of his loving wife but the structure of his days: driving her to the grocery store and to the hair salon, their card games and movies with friends, their family dinners. Like many men, his primary social contact was his wife, and when she was gone, their joint social network disappeared with her.[45]

Unacknowledged while they're married, this warm web of connections often evaporates once a man becomes widowed. Not only has the man in question lost his only confidante and main source of social support, but after the post-funeral casseroles are gone, the invitations often vanish too.

Though Lou felt miserable for a long time after Anna died, his health hadn't taken a hit. What protected him? There are likely lots of factors, including the genetic recipe that fostered his easygoing nature, being somewhat younger than many widowers, and his commitment to a regimen of regular exercise. But there was also something else. Lou's daily routine included a variety of social encounters. He participated in a handful of community, religious, therapeutic, and team sports activities. And if there's any scientific consensus at all about the impact of our relationships on our health, it's that a single bond—no matter how intimate—isn't sufficient on its own to protect us. When epidemiologists make mortality predictions based on decades of data, it's social integration that matters most: being married *and* belonging to a religious group *and* playing bridge every Wednesday *and* volunteering at the church. The more types of face-to-face ties you sustain—both close relationships and the weaker ties with people who regularly cross your path—the better you will be at warding off the Grim Reaper.[46]

Lou was surrounded not just by close family and friends but by a coterie of supporters with whom he connected, even if they weren't billed as such. He was a joiner. Like Sylvie, whom we met in Chapter 1, Lou was connected to a large network of people who were there when the chips were down. "When I was afraid of sinking into a depression," as Lou put it, they propped him up even if they didn't know that's what they were doing. "One of the things that I did throughout Anna's illness and afterwards is that I kept on swimming," he told me when I asked how he had fended off the physical assaults of grief. "When my father got sick and went through many months in the hospital and then died, I would also go swimming. It helped me. And I even competed. I competed during Anna's illness," he told me, "though there was one year when Anna was very sick that I missed the championships."

Two years after Anna died, Lou prepared for his first date with an odd ritual. "I remember that I called the synagogue first. First buy my burial plot next to Anna, pay for it, and only then go out on a date," he recalled. When I asked why, he sighed. "Now we're getting to the heart of things. This has nothing to do with Natalie, whom I hadn't met yet. But the idea was that whoever the woman is who is going to come in the future has to understand that I had a life before—thirty-seven years—and even though I'm going to continue living, they have to realize that I'm still part of . . . that I'm still close to Anna. And I want my kids to see that."

Apparently four years was long enough after Anna's death to be able to discuss it, but not so long that the pain of losing her had dissipated. And even though he had just remarried, he still felt a "tug-of-war between letting myself enjoy life with Natalie and being in mourning." Fortunately, he said, Natalie could tolerate this ambivalence. They could talk about the tough stuff without too much preamble, he told me. "From the very first, I brought up the question of how she could go out with me when I am still so attached to Anna. But that was discussed! On the first date! And she said to me that as long as I can be present for her in the now, it doesn't matter to her if I have an attachment in the past. She can live with it. That is what she said, and that was huge for me."

Lou didn't have to give anything up—not his feelings about Anna, nor his relationship with his adult kids, nor his ties and responsibilities to Anna's parents, who were still grieving and fragile. "Still, I am more and more allowing myself to enjoy life again with Natalie, while still dealing with the loss," he said. After Anna's death, Lou made paintings and composed a love song as a tribute to the woman with whom he had built the first part of his adult life. "But now I must start my romance with Natalie. Part of that is I tell her that I will love her more every year, and that I am very lucky to have her. I feel a lot of gratitude not to be alone."

RELIGION AND THE FIRST DATE

Natalie and Lou got married, at least in part, because they happened to find themselves at synagogue on the same Saturday morning, observing their fathers' yahrzeits (the yearly anniversary of a loved one's death, according to the Hebrew calendar). They had known each other superficially from Bakol retreats, and when they met up again two years after Anna's death, Lou felt a little less raw and a little more willing to take a chance on a post-synagogue walk in the freshly fallen snow with an attractive woman.

You might not expect matching yahrzeit dates to be an auspicious omen. But as the astute British writer Alain de Botton points out in *Religion for Atheists*, religion seems tailor-made to foster trust between strangers—even strangers who do not believe in God.

> A church, with its massive timber doors and 300 stone angels carved around its porch, gives us rare permission to lean over and say hello to a stranger without any danger of being thought predatory or insane. We are promised that here (in the words of the Mass's initial greeting) "the love of God and the fellowship of the Holy Spirit"

belong to all who have assembled. The church lends its enormous
prestige, accrued though age, learning and architectural grandeur,
to our shy desire to open ourselves to someone new.[47]

Say what you like about religion, it has a way of bringing like-
minded people together and binding them with songs, prayers,
stories, and acts of kindness that make them feel good about themselves and the people around them. When congregants get together
they often sway, bow, kneel, chant, or rock, as if moving as one
organism. Indeed, synchrony is a well-known evolutionary trick.[48]
Neuroscientist David Eagleman writes that religions "define
groups, coordinate behavior and suppress selfishness in favor of
cooperation," which, like other signs of group cohesion, grease the
wheels of survival and make us feel like "the smartest, boldest, best
guys that ever were."[49] That feeling, a byproduct of the village
effect, can be one hell of an aphrodisiac.

It makes sense. Religious rituals lean heavily on the honest signals that establish mutual trust. At one California megachurch
service I attended, along with about 2,500 parishioners seated com-
fortably in red plush seats, the pastor, Dick Bernal, peppered his
sermon with regular entreaties to make eye contact with adjacent
strangers. "Look at your neighbor and say, 'You and me are a majority,'" he intoned. Then he paused so everyone could do just that, as
a huge video camera on a twenty-foot boom zigzagged slowly over
the huge sanctuary. After some storytelling and vamping from an
R&B band on the podium, he asked us again. "Look at your other
neighbor and say, 'We've got a job to do.'" Then, after some scrip-
ture reading, another entreaty: "Turn to your neighbor and say, 'I
need you and you need me.'" And again: "Your neighbor is right
there for you. So say, 'Hang on, baby, hang on.'"

It was as if the pastor were applying research by neuroscientist
Andrew Newberg and his wife, Stephanie. They devised a ten-minute
exercise that trains strangers to make eye contact and hold a

"compassionate thought about the person with whom they are sitting." Practicing this several times resulted in a 20 percent increase in participants' willingness to feel close to and spend time with an unfamiliar person.[50] Simply making eye contact and empathizing with a stranger relaxed their anxieties about meeting someone new. I wonder if religious gatherings have the same effect. By bringing potential couples together in an environment that relieves their standoffishness, they're acting as de facto matchmakers.

I checked out my hypothesis with Michael Inzlicht, a Canadian psychologist who studies the neural underpinnings of religious belief, and he thought it plausible. Inzlicht's research has shown that people with religious faith show more sluggish activity in the anterior cingulate cortex, or ACC, a neural area that registers social anxiety. The distress that accompanies social rejection and anxiety about making social blunders, as well as its converse—the feeling of complete existential acceptance that is part of romantic love—is observable via the rate of activity in the ACC.[51] Interestingly, Inzlicht and his colleagues found it is also implicated in religious conviction. The ACC becomes activated during periods of social exclusion; it is quieter during religious observance, which believers find soothing.[52]

Whether it's a romantic or a religious experience, the ACC helps us monitor where we stand in relation to others. Being included is adaptive and therefore feels good in the here and now, while being ostracized rings physiological alarm bells.[53] The role of belief and ritual in stilling these alarms may be one reason why religious practice has persisted. Having linked attendance at religious services to greater happiness and lower rates of cardiovascular disease and death, some epidemiologists have suggested that going to church is more effective than Lipitor, adding an average of two to three years to a person's life.[54]

But religious practice also works at the group level, helping people stick together and solve internal conflicts.[55] In *The Righteous Mind*, psychologist Jonathan Haidt quotes a study showing that of two hundred utopian communes founded in nineteenth-century America, only 6 percent of the secular ones survived, compared to 39 percent of the religious ones. The groups with the highest rates of survival required their members to visibly alter their behavior or appearance to show that they belonged, by changing their hair, dress, or diet, or by giving up alcohol, meat, or tobacco.[56] This brings to mind the extraordinary longevity of the socially cohesive, vegetarian, nut-eating, teetotaling Seventh-day Adventists we met in Chapter 2, and the survival, despite centuries of persecution, of the ultra-Orthodox Jewish "black hat" communities that maintain the strict diet, style of dress, and moral codes of their ancestors in medieval Europe.

As a face-to-face activity that could set the stage for love, religions have a head start. They quell social and existential anxieties. They regularly gather similar people in the same place and make them feel that they belong together. In church, synagogue, temple, or mosque, everyone coordinates their activities, believing their efforts to be in the service of something bigger than themselves. And religious practice encourages the exchange of honest signals. But what happens if you're having trouble meeting people and you don't belong to a religious group? Extending the romantic options beyond the immediate locale and capable of sorting people in a number of ways, the Internet seems perfect for putting the right people together. But along with its obvious matchmaking successes come a few tradeoffs.

ONLINE DATING

I confess that I have occasionally acted as a behind-the-scenes social connector. Having watched many of my single friends struggle to meet partners, I introduced a longtime writer friend to one of my former newspaper editors, a delightful fellow who had suddenly found himself single again. As if to illustrate the power of three degrees, I then received this email from a friend of my writer friend:

Jan, at whose party we met a while ago, mentioned that you occasionally ventured into matchmaking, and from her latest report she and Bruce are coming along very nicely. And that's why I'm writing to you. I would love you to help me find a match. Let me know when we can talk and I can tell you everything I've tried.

We met at my local café on a rainy afternoon. Like millions of other people around the globe, one thing she'd tried was online dating—venturing into the questionnaire-heavy waters of PlentyOfFish (POF), eHarmony, OkCupid, and Yahoo Friends. Her best prospect, "Vic," whom she'd met on POF, seemed promising after some online and telephone banter, jibing nicely with her list of requirements: over six feet tall; currently employed; no health problems; liked the arts and, in particular, photography. But she ultimately discovered that he was mainly interested in phone sex. "I kept saying, 'Tell me where you are and I'll meet you.' But he wasn't interested in a face-to-face. All he wanted to know was, 'What room are you in now? Why don't you describe your sheets to me?' And that's the thing about online dating. You can have the most wonderful email exchanges, but then the guy doesn't turn out to be who he says he is."

If there's one constant on the Internet, it's dissimulation. On Second Life, for example, your (much more attractive) digital avatar can have an affair with another avatar, or a one-off with a virtual prostitute. Catching him doing just that is what sparked David Pollard's wife, Amy Taylor, to file for divorce in 2008. The British couple had met online and married—twice. First their avatars married; the well-toned, topcoat- and medallion-wearing "Dave Barmy" wedded "Laura Skye," a svelte and busty six-foot-tall DJ clad in a skintight purple gown. Their vows were exchanged on a tropical fantasy island. Somewhat later, the couple married in real life, at the more lackluster registry office in Cornwall. But when Taylor, an unemployed waitress originally from London,

Former couple Amy Taylor and David Pollard with their avatars, Laura Skye and Dave Barmy.

woke from a nap one afternoon to find Pollard's avatar having virtual sex with a prostitute on Second Life, it was the beginning of the end of their real-world marriage. "It's cheating as far as I'm concerned, but he didn't see it as a problem and couldn't see why I was so upset," Taylor told the *Times of London*.[57]

Bizarre as this tale is, it illustrates the ease with which people blur fact and fiction in cyberspace. This is especially true of online dating sites, where most people lie about themselves, some shading the truth just a little, others quite a lot. Ron James, who over an eighteen-month period emailed six hundred women he had "met" through JDate (ultimately dating forty to fifty of them), discovered that many of the women had lied about their ages, posted old photos, and misrepresented what they did for a living. "I learned to watch out for sunglasses," James said.[58]

"Four out of five people misrepresent themselves," Eli Finkel, a Northwestern University psychology professor, told me after he had analyzed all the science on online dating he could find. One of the studies, led by Catalina Toma at the University of Wisconsin–Madison, surveyed eighty online daters. After they had created their profiles, the researchers followed up with a tape measure, a scale, and a request to see their driver's licenses. The results? Eighty-one percent of the online daters had fibbed, inaccurately reporting their basic details in ways they hoped wouldn't be detected (women made themselves 8.5 pounds thinner, on average).[59] Together with several colleagues, Finkel conducted several lab experiments that mimicked the main features of online dating. In the process he happened on some unsettling findings. "Women are heavier than their profiles say they are. Men are a bit shorter and have fewer resources than they say they do. But the biggest problem," he said, "is not that people misrepresent themselves, but that we're not very good at describing what attracts us. When you meet someone you're attracted to, you just don't have the insight about why."

Sexual attraction is a lot like what they say about art. Or wine. Or porn. You can't put into words what you like about it, but you know it when you see it.[60] One of Finkel's experiments asked 106 research subjects to come up with three essential traits in an ideal romantic partner. They also asked for three of the least important or least desired qualities in a mate. Would you absolutely require your future beloved to be ambitious? Affectionate? Broadminded? Generous? It was like the task Natalie faced in the Meet the Man of Your Dreams workshop, and a lot like what dating sites ask of us—to describe exactly what we want. "You fill out a bunch of questionnaires about an ideal partner, then later you encounter something like that person. We rigged it so that the person matches or mismatches your ideal mate," is how Finkel explained his experiment.

The results showed that their university-aged subjects were predictably keen to meet someone whose profile matched their must-have criteria—at least on paper. But when they were actually thrown together in a room with that perfect match, the subjects weren't all that attracted to their dreamboats. In a live, face-to-face situation, their criteria didn't predict who they found hot any more than their list of "avoids" predicted revulsion.[61] It turns out that most of us don't know who will turn us on any more than we can predict what will make us happy in the future.[62]

WHAT A PIECE OF WORK

When it comes to attraction, something mysterious is going on. Before I get to that, though, consider that online dating sites ask people not only to list the traits they hanker after in a mate but also to describe themselves faithfully. But as we've seen, humans are not particularly gifted at either task, perhaps one of the reasons why marriage rates haven't budged since the online dating revolution began. We lie outright or unconsciously delude ourselves about how slender, accomplished, and winsome we are. Notwithstanding the ancient Greek maxim "Know thyself," self-awareness is not really our strong suit.

"What a piece of work is man!" Hamlet observes, "How noble in reason! how infinite in faculties! in form and moving, how express and admirable! in action, how like an angel! in apprehension, how like a god! the beauty of the world! the paragon of animals! And yet, to me, what is this quintessence of dust?" While Shakespeare asks you to acknowledge the ineffability of human nature, eHarmony asks you whether you often leave your socks on the floor. Among its several hundred questions, I was asked to click a box indicating whether I prefer that a future partner "do things according to plan." Well, yes, if there's a plane to catch. But no, once we've touched down in Venice. And while I like a tidy environment, my husband of thirty years surrounds himself with leaning stacks of yellowing paper and assorted musical instruments in various states of repair. Still, I'd trade a clean surface any day for a taste of his sly humor.

And there's the rub. "People are incredibly complex and are not reducible to a set of characteristics you enter into fields," says Eli Finkel. "You may say you like someone who's proud, but it's hard to differentiate between arrogance and confidence without face-to-face contact." Distilling what a person is like from their online profile is like knowing what a meal will taste like from a list of ingredients, he told me. "That's just not how the mind works." Yet all dating sites profess an oracle-like ability to match up future couples based on lists of their self-reported personality traits. For example, eHarmony advertises a "patented Compatibility Matching System™ that narrows the field from millions of candidates to a highly select group of singles that are compatible with you."

But if you're lonely and believe such claims, you've succumbed to "smoke and mirrors," says Harry Reis, a psychology professor at the University of Rochester who has spent his career researching successful relationships. "There's just no evidence that any dating algorithm that's ever been used is any better than chance." Meeting someone who elicits that flash of mutual attraction and finding a long-term partner with whom to build a life together are two completely different things. Though most dating sites (and most of us) conflate them, there's no evidence that online dating sites can predict either one, he tells me.[63] True, 5 percent of people who meet each other on eHarmony get married (well, according to a study conducted by eHarmony). "But if thirty million people sent me their names and I randomly paired them up and sent them an email saying, 'This person is your soulmate,' I might do just as well. But no one has ever tested that," says Reis, chuckling at the thought.

Though the evidence is deflating, I learned some facts every single person should know. First, one of the bedrock claims of dating sites—that parallel personality types will be compatible—is "pseudoscience" and "monkey business," according to Reis. Matching people based on paper or screen-based personality assessments has not been shown to be a useful metric in the real world, so why would it work in a virtual universe? Plus, the cues available online are too paltry to assess what *really* matters: whether there's a sense of rapport between two people. "It's very clear that compatibility is determined by things that can't be assessed on paper or on the screen. Hundreds of studies show that nonverbal rapport predicts relationship happiness," Reis said, referring to whether someone looks you in the eye during conversation, synchronizes his emotions or movements with yours, and confides in you when you're together. Second, the fact that you're both introverts or both love *Seinfeld* reruns says a lot about initial attraction, but nothing about how long your union will, last or how happy it will be.[64] Similar personality traits and interests mean that you may fight less over the TV remote. But this basic sorting process doesn't predict how much TLC you'll get from your main squeeze when the chips are down.

THE HOLY GRAIL

What does predict whether a romantic union will last? "How do you react when you taste my cooking? Do you like my family? How well do you solve problems together? Do you help each other through personal issues and share in each other's pleasures and good fortune?" Reis asked me, adding a string of other rhetorical questions to the list. Enjoying sex together is in there, but it's not number one. Being able to solve problems is. "How do you deal with a very sick child or a dying parent together? How do you help each other with personal problems?" It turns out that the ability to face adversity together and its converse—to have fun as intimate buddies—is more important in the long run than being matched on eHarmony's 29 dimensions of personality.[65] When I asked him whether dating websites can assess any of those things, Reis responded with another question: "How can you measure any of that without putting people together to solve problems, face-to-face?"

Despite the downsides of the medium—the never-satisfied, Christmas shopping feeling it instills, the commodification and unrealistic expectations of future love objects it promotes—one indisputable advantage of online sites is that they do increase your chances of meeting new people. And it can also be expedient in ruling out gross mismatches and false starts. "Before you've even had an email contact, you can find all sorts of red flags to tell you they're not a good match, such as their political bent, their degree of religiosity, and how rough they like their sex," wrote one friend in an email. "People can be surprisingly open in an anonymous forum." As JDate posts on its site, "This is WAY better than the bar scene. For the price of a few drinks, you can subscribe for a month and meet a new person every day if you like."

But meeting is key. Prolonged online interaction promotes a false sense of intimacy, Jan told me ruefully (she's the friend I fixed up with my editor). Confidences can be shared online by people who can't manage intimacy in a real encounter. Insults, too. (Like many writers, I've faced lurid venom from online attackers—trolls—who would not exist without the shield of anonymity the Internet provides.) Helen Fisher, a biological anthropologist who is an expert on sexual attraction, puts it bluntly: Online sites just provide the introduction. You have to do the rest. "You've got to get out there. You've got to meet them yourself. You've got to bring your own algorithm to the party," she told me.

When it comes to love and trust, research confirms Fisher's assertion that the human brain has evolved its own inimitable algorithms. Studies have shown that people who interacted face-to-face "felt greater oneness with their partner than did participants who interacted over the computer," according to research led by psychologist Bradley Okdie. The effect is cumulative: the more real, live interaction, the greater the attraction. Apparently familiarity does *not* breed contempt.[66] In the study's comparisons of screen versus live interaction, the couples who first met each other in person (as opposed to online) liked their potential partners more and found the dating experience more fun than the digital discovery process. For one thing, it didn't involve building up one's hopes based on an online profile, only to have them dashed—or being summarily rejected—once you meet face-to-face.[67] In some ways, though, meeting someone at the laundromat or at a supermarket checkout line is also a challenge, especially for introverts. Processing a blast of simultaneous information from eye contact, facial expressions, and the social environment is far more taxing, cognitively, than reading text on a screen, not to mention the fact that approaching an attractive stranger doesn't guarantee that she's single or interested in meeting people.

But courting face-to-face can also be more rewarding. Tim Kreider, a New York–based writer, decided to try online dating "after meeting my one millionth attractive, intelligent, funny woman who turned out to be married." But reviewing women's online profiles turned out to be a depressing type of channel surfing, he wrote, the vetting process being "driven by the anxiety that you might be missing out on something just a little bit better." Eventually he left the site to go back to what he called the analog approach. And that's when he fell in love with a woman he met at a friend's brunch. Until he looked up her work online and saw her photo there, he didn't realize they'd already "met" each other once before—on the dating site. Kreider writes:

> The whole, warm, complex animal gestalt of her was unlike anything I could've gleaned from e-mails or JPEGs. The difficult love in her voice when she talked about her father contained a compressed terabyte of information. The things that happen online have some of the same quality as things that happen in dreams, feeling unreal and disconnected from real life, melding together and paling in memory, evaporating within moments after you wake up or sign off. It was strange to meet someone from the internet out in the world and realize that she'd been real all along.[68]

MAGNETS VERSUS GLUE

Returning to my friends Lou and Natalie, I could ask whether this couple, who met through face-to-face social networks, has a better chance of succeeding as a unit than two strangers who meet online. No one has the answer to that question—no scientist has ever asked. But we do know that Lou and Natalie survived their first test. Before they married, the two wilderness lovers decided to go on a camping trip. The destination was a family wedding, where Lou was to introduce Natalie to his extended clan for the first time. The night before the wedding they stopped to pitch their tent at a campsite not far from the event. It was eleven p.m. and raining hard. "And we arrive to discover that we forgot the tent poles," recounts Lou, his brow furrowing. "But we managed, in the dark, to make a makeshift thing with ropes tied to the trees. What I liked is we really cooperated quickly and there was no 'Who forgot the poles?' There wasn't a whole story about it. And I thought, *This is a woman I can live with.*"

Similarity and common social bonds were likely Lou and Natalie's first magnets. But they'll likely stay together not because they're similar but because they *see* themselves as like-minded. This is what the research tells us. Similarity may bring couples together at first, But being similar to your partner is not what matters to your success and happiness as a couple. *Perceiving* yourselves as sharing common values and traits is what matters to a relationship's success. In Chengdu, in western China, couples have even pursued matching cosmetic surgery because they see themselves as similar and want to look more alike.[69] Whether or not you're literally a matching pair, thinking that you are makes a couple feel *bashert*—like they belong together. That, along with the ability to solve problems and have fun together, forms much of the glue.[70]

"Sharing a life's journey is more pleasant if you and your partner are on parallel paths—literally," says Irene Huang, a social psychologist. After running tests in both countries, Huang found that American and Chinese couples who chose to take exactly the same route to work—whether or not they left home at the same time— were the happiest with each other.[71] Their matching journeys implied matching goals. This synchrony resonated with the couple as yet another confirmation of their bond. Every seemingly coincidental overlap in their thoughts, habits, or behavior reminded them of what had attracted them to each other in the first place.

Like attracts like, homophily, assortative mating, birds of a feather—whatever you want to call it, we know that people who are already similar are drawn to each other. They live in the same neighborhoods, eat the same foods, have similar worries, pray in the same way, and often do business together. The question we'll explore in the next chapter is whether this magnetic attraction is always a force for good.

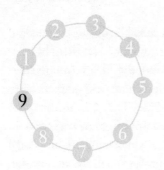

When Money Really Talks

Social Networks, Business, and Crime

Located in the good part of town, Mary Coughlan's living room looks like a cross between a private library and a gallery of Asian and African art. Floor-to-ceiling bookshelves line one wall, and two massive armoires, inlaid with miniature netsuke-like ivory animals, are positioned on either side of her velvet armchair. Her ground-floor apartment gives onto a fenced green space, so it's easy for Mary to open the sliding glass doors to let out her golden Labrador retriever, Olivia, for some late afternoon exercise. As the dog pads by me, she stops to nuzzle my hand and then lifts her paw. We shake. "She doesn't do any tricks," Mary says quickly from her corner, where she's sitting in the sage-colored velvet chair with her feet perched on a matching ottoman. "That's beneath her dignity."

Regal and dignified herself, Mary Coughlan, seventy-seven, has invited me over to talk about how she was swindled out of her life savings—about a million dollars of retirement funds—by someone she had known for thirty years. She first met Earl Jones, a financial planner, in 1979. She was in her late forties at the time, recently widowed and raising four children on her own. She wanted to learn how to handle her own money, and an evening course at the YMCA on financial management for women seemed to be just the thing. "I saw Earl speaking in that series," she told me, when I asked how she first met him. "I had some money that my father had left me. I was forty-seven when my husband died, and I wanted to get away from my family handling my money." She thought Earl Jones "was such a nice guy." A mutual friend she knew through her mother and through her church connections had worked with Jones, too. "So I trusted him," she told me.

For the better part of thirty years the arrangement worked well. Investment income arrived regularly, which covered her daily expenses and then some. When her mother died, the money she inherited went directly to Jones. "Seven years ago I sold a house in Westmount"—an upscale neighborhood in Montreal—"and the proceeds went to him." She did not know at the time that the check he deposited in her account from the sale was a fraction of the agreed-upon price. Though her house had been paid off, Jones had taken out two new mortgages on the property that she knew nothing about. The borrowed cash from those mortgages had landed in Earl Jones's slush fund. She'd been scammed by a friend.

Other horrors soon surfaced. On July 6, 2009, Los Angeles architect Kevin Curran got a call from an old buddy, telling him there was a possibility that both of their mothers had been swindled by the same con artist. Curran flew to Montreal, intending to spend a week unraveling the mess. One year later he was still there, trying to help his mother and other victims of the fraud, who were mostly older women. "When I saw how Earl had flipped my mother's mortgage from $150,000 to $350,000 and taken her $500,000 inheritance, I knew we were screwed. She didn't have the money. I vowed to stay until we had secured mortgage relief," he told a reporter for the local paper. "That was what initially kept me here."

Working as the victims' financial sleuth, manager, and problem-solver, Curran (along with two other adult children of Jones's victims, Ginny Nelles and Joey Davis) discovered that this was one tightly interwoven social group, but it was also an aging and fragile one. By July 2010, one year after Earl Jones's Ponzi scheme was revealed, three of Jones's elderly victims had died, one had been diagnosed with breast cancer, five had lost their homes, and another eleven were about to lose theirs as the one-year grace period negotiated with their banks expired. Thirty-five others were forced to accept handouts to pay for rent, food, Ensure, and adult diapers from the charities they had not long before supported with their own donations.[1]

No one wants to spend their golden years financially vulnerable and dependent on others. And for a proud generation of savers, most of whom had cut their teeth during the Depression and who had spent their adult lives intent on being self-supporting, becoming penniless was the ultimate disgrace.

How did Earl Jones pull it off? As was the case with Bernie Madoff, the trust inherent in a tightly knit, homogeneous social network at first helped Jones build a legitimate career. As a member of the community, it's easy to establish one's bona fides. And once he had earned other members' confidence, he no longer had to prove himself. The pressures and temptations built. "I can see him sitting in that chair," Mary Coughlan said, pointing to where I was sitting. "He used to come here about four times a year. He'd come in and say, 'How are the kids?' Then he'd spend two hours here. It was a social visit." Coughlan said she still thinks of him as a friend—a sociopathic one perhaps, but one she'd trusted. "He'd say, 'I need your signature,' and I'd say yes. I had been paying him to look after me."

And he had. In the early 1980s, when Coughlan began investing with him, Jones issued regular dividend checks and monthly statements detailing her investments in stocks and bonds. But by the late eighties the statements had become less regular and less detailed, appearing only if she asked for one. By the early nineties, not only had his reporting style changed but his investment strategy had shifted, too. He offered clients opportunities to invest in loans on estates and mortgages extended to other clients—often other members of their churchgoing, golf-playing, Maine-summering social circle. These were people they knew who he said were in a fix, perhaps waiting for a will to be probated so they could buy a big-ticket item like a house or a car; in the meantime they needed some cash to tide them over. The interest would be upward of 8 percent, and sometimes there was a signing bonus of a few thousand as well. "One of his tricks was to say that so-and-so needed money until the will went through," Coughlan explained, adding that the sad stories Jones told were all too credible. As the loan would be secured against the borrower's estate, it seemed a safe thing to do. Over fourteen years, Mary Coughlan said yes five times.[2]

In reality, Jones had never invested a cent of her nest egg. Her capital, along with everyone else's, had been distributed as interest to maintain the illusion that the fund was growing. Jones's payroll was $200,000 a month—the monthly "dividends" he disbursed to his core clients. And then there were his own expenses, such as mortgages on four condos, including one in Boca Raton and another on a golf course in Mont-Tremblant, a Quebec ski resort. There was also a condo in Maine that he'd bought for his intellectually handicapped daughter Kimberly. There were private school fees, cars, and cruises, too, all bankrolled by his clients' nest eggs. He had been running a Madoff-like Ponzi scheme built on his own community's life savings.

Coughlan was on holiday with her family in Maine in early July 2009 when she got a call from her bank. Her checks were bouncing. Soon other members of her social set were discovering that their money was mysteriously inaccessible. With a trip to New York planned, forty-two-year-old Ginny Nelles—whose late father had for decades been a close friend of Jones's—discovered that the money she wanted to withdraw from her account with "Uncle Earl" was out of reach, just when she needed it for a family holiday. Then it turned out that Uncle Earl, whose career her own father had launched when they both worked at Montreal Trust in the 1970s, had skipped town.

In the meantime, Earl Jones was frantically scrabbling for fresh money. A longtime client had asked for his capital to buy a house.

Unfortunately, Jones had already spent it. When other clients called his office to inquire about their funds, they encountered not his usual office staff, who were known as Earl's girls, but a recorded message saying there would be no payments for thirty days. Jones had gone on the lam. He evaded capture for three weeks but was eventually apprehended, tried, and sentenced to eleven years in prison for fraud.[3] Until that moment, though, he had been seen as a family man, a pillar of the community, a trusted financial advisor, and a friend.

Between 1982 and 2009 Earl Jones had stolen more than $51 million from 160 victims. Eighty percent were women, many of them widows. "He deals with a lot of little old ladies. He had the looks and the gift of the gab," said Doris Babbington, a former high-school friend who'd "invested" all of her savings (about $100,000) with Jones.[4] She'd known Jones and his wife for sixty years.

A socially skilled man with a large, homogeneous social network, Jones saw a niche that had been neglected by other money managers, who were more interested in snagging high-rollers. His targets were midlevel earners like himself, who had modest roots but harbored high hopes for the future: early retirement, perhaps; membership in a private golf club; Caribbean cruises now and then. More important, though, was establishing a bond with their wives, who would be emotionally vulnerable after their husbands had died. As a rule, these women were financially naive. Having grown up in the 1940s, most had missed out on the feminist revolution. They were not only the beneficiaries of their husband's or parents' estates but also the owners of family homes worth at least a couple of hundred thousand. Aside from government pensions, the assets were all they had. They were grateful to Jones for his offer of assistance.[5]

When Ginny Nelles's father died in 2004, Earl Jones, once a close friend of the family's, reappeared at the funeral. The men had been colleagues at Montreal Trust and their families had vacationed together for at least twenty-five of the fifty years they'd known each other. Jones was the godfather of Ginny's brother. But he and Nelles's father had had a falling out in the early nineties. Until he approached them at the funeral, Ginny and the rest of the family hadn't seen much of him for ten years. Reminding the siblings that he was an estate planner, Jones told them, "If I can help you in any way, I'm here for you." He reassured Ginny's mother, Wendy, "Don't worry. I'll take care of you."

Five days after the funeral, Jones persuaded Wendy Nelles to move her husband's estate planning from the bank to Jones's own account. "He told her ScotiaBank wasn't doing much with the money and that the laws had changed. He was a vulture. He swooped in," Ginny said ruefully.

Four years after that, Jones persuaded Wendy to remortgage her paid-off home for $327,000—to be paid off over forty years. The money was ostensibly invested in her account with Earl to give her an immediate high rate of return; Wendy wanted to share this income with her children and grandchildren. On Jones's advice, and against the diversification mantra of most financial planners, she collapsed all her accounts in other banks in order to consolidate her money with him.

I met with Ginny Nelles in November 2009, five months after Earl Jones's Ponzi scheme had been exposed. Her mother was about to lose her house and had no source of income. Ginny and her brother would likely never recover their inheritances from their father, much less their own savings. And this blow had struck after grave health crises for both Ginny and her brother. Yet little of this psychological wear and tear was evident at first glance. Ginny was poised and articulate, crisply dressed in a white blouse and pearls, her highlighted blond hair neatly tied back. Clearly she had experienced certain privileges—attendance at the British-styled private girls' school that served the upper-crust Anglos of Montreal, Miss Edgar's and Miss Cramp's (where Earl's daughters had also gone to school); a winter ski house in the Laurentians; entire summers spent at their beach house in Kennebunk, Maine, hanging out with other families much like hers. She seemed perfect to me—a card-carrying member of a cultural and socioeconomic subgroup that had always seemed effortlessly polished, exclusive, and preternaturally Canadian.

Though Jones had the right background, he couldn't afford the lifestyle. That was the opinion of those speculating about his motives. There is recent evidence, too, that repeatedly getting away with something illicit prompts exhilaration, not guilt. The economists who conducted this revealing study call this the "cheater's high".[6]

Still, most of Jones's victims were middle class, and they had little in common with other victims of Ponzi schemes. That is, nothing except the fact that they—along with the scammer—belonged to a tightly knit social group with a shared language and religion, not to mention the same cultural mores and interests. (In this case, the members of this "village" shared a deep interest in sports. As a young man, Jones was a gifted, semi-professional hockey player, which further boosted his credibility.) During the decades they were being duped, this group of suburban English speakers also felt themselves to be a beleaguered minority in Quebec. Those who hadn't moved out of the province lived in the same neighborhoods, went to the same churches, and sent their kids to the same schools. From a social-network perspective, homophily intensified, as did mutual trust within a group that had battened down the hatches. If you were an insider who knew the code, it wasn't hard to gain the confidence of other insiders.

This was a classic case of what's called affinity fraud: when common social and religious ties offer con artists a shortcut to a group's trust. In this book so far, I've shown face-to-face interaction to be a vector of health, happiness, academic achievement, and longevity. But trading in honest signals—the lingua franca of close social contact—is not always a force for good. Getting up close and personal can swing both ways, especially in business. While face-to-face contact can bring increased performance, customer loyalty, satisfaction, and profits, it can also lead to big-time betrayal.

AFFINITY FRAUD

How could so many people fall for the outsized promises of Earl Jones—or Bernie Madoff, for that matter? As social animals, "the default is to trust until there's a reason not to," said the late Robyn Dawes, a psychologist at Carnegie Mellon who was one of the pioneers of behavioral economics.[7] When it comes to having confidence in other people, our group or religious affiliations work as a stand-in for family relationships. Trusting others who look and sound like us feels natural; there's a visceral satisfaction that accompanies letting down one's guard. Believing and helping others within a family or its extension, the group—even if such altruism means there will be less food, money, energy, sexual opportunity, or other goodies for ourselves—just feels good. Evolutionary biologists explain this paradoxical phenomenon through the idea of kin selection. (It's a paradox because every individual in the species should have evolved to maximize the survival of its own genes, and no one else's.) Even though it reduces an individual's advantages, people trust and sacrifice for each other to the degree that they're genetically related—or suspect that they are—even if there's no clear benefit to themselves, according to British geneticist J. B. S. Haldane. He pointed out that you would be likely to leap into an icy river to save a drowning sibling (who shares half your genes), because even if you die in the process, a copy of your genes would survive in each of her future offspring.[8]

Many animals do the same. Elephants, chimpanzees, baboons— even vampire bats and naked mole rats—recognize their own relatives, especially female ones, and act accordingly, meaning nepotistically.[9] We've already seen that a Japanese macaque will allow another macaque that wanders by to nibble some of her food as long as the two are directly related.[10] Meanwhile, adult female baboons spend up to five hours every day grooming different partners, but primarily their female relatives, write Dorothy Cheney and Robert Seyfarth, who add that time spent grooming forges sisterly bonds that come in handy when food is scarce or the temperature suddenly drops.[11] Such oxytocin-releasing intimacy not only feels good, it pays off.

You might be wondering what all this monkey business has to do with con artists scamming their own. Not just among nonhuman primates but in every culture in the world, people form kin- and belief-based social networks, cooperating with other people as if they were family.[12] That baseline trust allows in-group members to escape the scrutiny that any outsider would face. Signs of shared identity and status—accents, tattoos, tight pants or baggy ones, hairstyles, sock colors—are more persuasive face-to-face than they are over the Internet. That's why we're more vulnerable to in-group scammers whom we meet in person than to faceless Nigerian princes who, like Earl Jones, want our bank account details. No matter what our culture, we all have the same inclination to trust members of our tribe, and the same feelings of indignation and shame when that trust has been betrayed. Iris Bohnet, a Swiss behavioral economist who is now dean of Harvard's Kennedy School of Government, has shown that in countries with dramatically different social mores—including the United States, China, Turkey, and Oman—people everywhere are so averse to being betrayed that they are far less likely to trust another person with their money than they are to trust to nature or chance.[13] Only a member of the in-crowd can circumvent this betrayal aversion.

WHAT GOD WANTED

"God wanted the Brazilian community to be prosperous," Sann Rodrigues and Victor Sales told the Brazilian-American community in a hotel near Boston in 2007. Promising their countrymen, most of whom were also evangelical Christians, that they could earn as much as $17,000 a month if they paid $2,000 to $5,000 up front to become members of a prepaid phone card company called Universo FoneClub, they showed a PowerPoint presentation with images of golfers and large, pricy houses. They even floated the suggestion that Universo investors could buy their own island. "God did not want the Brazilians to spend their lives working as house cleaners, dishwashers, and landscapers," the duo said in Portuguese, according to court documents recording the details of their pyramid scheme. "God did not want the Brazilians to be poor." To underscore that point, checks of up to $7,000 were handed out to members of the audience, which included shills who testified that they'd earned ten grand in eight days. More than $3.2 million was raised from the community, about half of which was later returned, according to a civil suit brought by federal regulators.[14]

The Amish of Sugarcreek, Ohio, weren't as lucky. They trusted an elder with their savings, as did about 2,500 other members of the plain community, as the Mennonites and Amish call themselves. Monroe Beachy, now in his late seventies, was a respected financial advisor who lived a modest lifestyle and acquired his financial bona fides in H&R Block classes. Through his company, A&M Investments, Beachy took in about $33 million from his community over twenty-odd years. Much like Bernie Madoff and Earl Jones, Beachy promised a rate of return that was better than the bank's— and all through risk-free government bonds. "Word spread about his safe, steady returns. Parents encouraged their children to practice thrift by opening A&M accounts, too," wrote business reporter Diana Henriques. When the Ponzi scheme broke, Beachy's own family members and more than a dozen churches, nonprofits, and charities lost their shirts. Though Beachy was accused of fraud by the Securities and Exchange Commission and lost at least $16 million of his community's personal savings, many of his investors testified in court that they'd rather forgive him than recover their money. But their extraordinary social cohesion couldn't protect him from the consequences. In June 2012, Beachy was sentenced to six and a half years in prison.

Affinity fraud within tightly knit groups is universal. Betraying the trust of Christian pacifists who ply Ohio's back roads via horse and buggy is one thing, but pulling the wool over the eyes of Hezbollah's leaders is quite another. When entrepreneur Salah Ezzedine defrauded the advisor to the Hezbollah leader, Hassan Nasrallah, to the tune of $200,000, people started to refer to him as the Lebanese Madoff. Reputed to have personal ties with the Shiite movement's top brass, Ezzedine was known as a pious man who was generous with his oil fortune. He had built a mosque as well as the Stadium of the Resistance and Liberation Martyrs near his home town in Maaroub. He organized pilgrimages to Mecca through the travel agency he owned. That apparent civic-mindedness, combined with his links to Hezbollah, is likely why so many of the region's residents entrusted their life savings to what turned out to be his $1.2 billion Ponzi scheme.[15] (Being promised a 40 percent return on their investments didn't hurt either.)

To perpetrate such a scam, Ezzedine banked on honest signals—the shortcuts that tell our brains who to trust in the real world. In most cases, as we've learned in previous chapters, honest signals help us to find lifelong friends, lovers, neighborhoods, and spouses. Piggybacking on the same neuroendocrine infrastructure, affinity fraud takes advantage of the human tendency to migrate toward others much like ourselves, and to relax our suspicions in their company.

Encountering another member of our in-group triggers automatic feelings of confidence and security. There is also such thing as having an honest face. In a series of amazing experiments, Alexander Todorov, Nikolaas Oosterhof, and their colleagues at Princeton University have shown that we make snap judgments about whether to trust someone after as little as a tenth of a second. Having more time—indeed, unlimited time—simply confirms our first impressions.[16] The researchers devised a brilliant way to test the idea that many important decisions hinge on a brief glimpse of someone's face. They showed potential voters pairs of black-and-white headshots of candidates who were completely unfamiliar to them. After seeing these candidates' faces for as little as one second, the observers made judgments about the competence of the candidates that predicted, with a fair degree of accuracy, the outcome of the elections. Indeed, a quick glance at someone's face was all it took to predict over 70 percent of the winning candidates in several consecutive US senatorial races, on average, and about 68 percent of those sitting in congress.[17] Lest one think that Americans are particularly swayed by appearances, these results were later replicated in elections held in England, Finland, Australia, Germany, and Mexico.[18]

Neuroscientists now think the ability to pick up such emotional cues evolved in the amygdala, an almond-shaped neural area linked to fight-or-flight behavior in our reptile ancestors.[19] Though fMRI images underscoring the amygdala's role in processing people's faces only appeared in the 1990s, psychologists have long known that snap judgments made during face-to-face encounters can be life-altering. In one study from the early 1980s, several social psychologists closely examined the *Howitzer*, the yearbook of the West Point class of 1950, to see if the cadets' facial features, height, athleticism, or other aspects of their appearance predicted their eventual rank. It was no surprise that the few blacks and Jews at West Point in 1950—no matter how chiseled their features or their jock quotient—didn't rise very high. But the physical features of the rest of the cadets, such as whether or not they had a prominent chin and eyebrows, deep-set eyes, and flat, non-obtrusive ears (and were generally handsome and hunky), turned out to be fairly good predictors of the promotions they'd get within the military hierarchy.[20]

Remarkably, these facial feature studies also confirm one of the first concrete bits of information I learned in graduate school. In my first clinical interviewing course, I was taught that hiring decisions are made within thirty seconds of the first handshake, a factoid that I came to regard as a myth. Yet a generation later, imaging studies validate two basic principles in psychology. First, beauty pays.[21] And second, after we've make a snap judgment, we don't usually change our minds. This is known as confirmation bias. We make decisions based on something as arbitrary as the shape of someone's eyebrows or an inch more or less of height, and then we selectively pay attention to whatever confirms what we've already decided. Though it's probably nothing more than the residue from a time when one glimpse—signaling whom to trust or who would be a good mating partner—gave us a survival advantage, our brains have clearly developed shortcuts that tell us when to raise our hackles and when to lower them.

By incrementally manipulating the features on computer-generated faces, the Princeton researchers were able to test exactly which facial features engender that automatic trust. They found that a slightly feminine, baby-faced appearance, with arched inner eyebrows, prominent cheekbones, and a cheerful demeanor, increases the impression of trustworthiness.[22] In fact, the happier looking the face, the more trustworthy it seems. Meanwhile, a more dominant, masculine-looking face, with lower inner eyebrows and cheekbones, engenders fear and the impulse to keep one's distance. This is not something we think about—it just happens. In fMRI studies of people looking at a series of faces, the amygdala became increasingly active as the experimenters gradually decreased the trustworthy features in the faces subjects were viewing. And lesions to the amygdala can "turn off" our ability to track the trustworthiness in people's faces.[23]

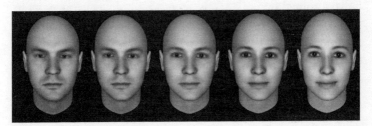

Facial features that elicit trust.

HOW THIN SLICES CAN LET YOU DOWN

It seems we've evolved an automatic, visceral response to human faces. This is just one part of a deception-detecting mechanism in the human brain. So why didn't it protect the victims of those pyramid scammers? One reason is that the criminals' facial features likely conveyed a level of trustworthiness. Combined with their social skills—a natural ability to mimic what their friends

were thinking and feeling, for example—they were able to create an illusion of sincerity that psychologist Daniel Kahneman calls psychopathic charm.

The faces of fraudsters Salah Ezzedine (left) and Earl Jones.

These men may have started out on the straight and narrow. But when financial pressures mounted, they likely pulled the wool over someone's eyes just to keep the money flowing. With each successful foray into deception, they learned to be more successful liars, perhaps even deceiving themselves in the process. To top it all off, they were then amply rewarded for their fabrications.[24] Their appearance offered them a competitive advantage, not in the usual evolutionary sense of an ability to snag food, sex, or resources that might have gone to someone faster or stronger, but in the realm of getting others to trust them.

This is just one way that intuition in social contexts can let us down. Psychologists Robert Rosenthal and the late Nalini Ambady coined the term "thin-slicing" in the early 1990s, when they discovered that even subliminal glimpses of someone can stand in for more considered judgments.[25] Kahneman calls it "System 1" in his book *Thinking Fast and Slow*, while Malcolm Gladwell calls it "blinking" (instead of thinking) in his bestseller about the power of first impressions. Whatever you call it, first impressions are handy cognitive shortcuts that allow precious brainpower to be saved for other tasks. But basing decisions on thin slices of information can backfire, as social psychologist Robert Cialdini points out in his book *Influence*. To make that point, he quotes an exchange between the abrasive sixties-era talk show host Joe Pine (who wore a prosthetic leg) and his guest that day, rock musician Frank Zappa:

PINE: I guess your long hair makes you a girl.

ZAPPA: I guess your wooden leg makes you a table.[26]

But "thin-slicing" doesn't just leave one open to ridicule or deceit. Like other trends that are transmitted face-to-face, social deception can be contagious. I was researching this book during the 2008–09 financial crisis and could barely keep up with all the Ponzi scams that were surfacing in the news. First there was the Madoff scandal, of course. You've just read about how upstanding members of the WASP English minority in Quebec were swindled by one of their own, as were American Mennonites and Amish, the expat Brazilian community in Boston, and Hezbollah supporters in Lebanon. There were also scams involving Mormons, Chinese Canadians living in Toronto, and members of the Church of the Open Door in Elyria, Ohio. In their scramble to survive after the bottom of the market fell out, did people lose their moral compass? Or had cheating become contagious?

CHEATING GOES VIRAL

After a string of scandals involving corporate cheating at Kmart, WorldCom, Tyco, Halliburton, Bristol-Myers Squibb, Freddie Mac, Fannie Mae, and Bernard Madoff Securities, Dan Ariely, a Duke University behavioral economist, wondered whether someone could catch an immorality bug, the way he might catch his seatmate's cold on an airplane. In his book *The Honest Truth about Dishonesty*, he explains his question a bit further:

If there was a real increase in societal dishonesty, could it be spreading like an infection, virus, or communicable bacteria, transmitted through mere observation or direct contact? Might there be a connection between this notion of infection and the continually unfolding story of deception and dishonesty that we have increasingly seen all around us? . . . At the risk of overstretching the metaphor, I thought that the natural balance of social honesty could be upset, too, if we are put into close proximity to someone who is cheating. Perhaps observing dishonesty in people who are close to us might be more "infectious" than observing the same level of dishonesty in people who aren't so close or influential in our lives.[27]

To test whether dishonesty is contagious, Ariely and two colleagues (one of whom was Francesca Gino, the Harvard researcher who found that cheating gives people a little buzz) rigged up the following experiment. Student volunteers received a sheet of paper printed with a series of matrices with numbers in each cell. Their job was to find as many pairs of numbers that added up to 10 as they could. Each number included decimal points, so it wasn't like adding 2 + 3. Some effort was required. The students had five minutes and could take fifty cents for each correct answer from an envelope they were given that contained ten dollars in cash.

Here comes the interesting part. Three groups had mildly different experiences when taking the "test." In the control group, students counted the number of problems they had solved, took the cash they were owed, and brought their solved matrices and the remaining change in the envelope to a research assistant to be checked. The second group, called the "shredders," followed an honor system. Believing they weren't being observed, these students counted their answers, paid themselves from the envelope, then shredded their work and dropped the envelope with any remaining change in a box by the door before they left. The third group was subjected to what Ariely called "the Madoff condition." An attractive confederate was planted in the room. Sixty seconds after the task began, this tall, blond-haired actor stood up and declared, "I've finished! What should I do now?" As few of the other students had completed even one pair, much less seven or eight, this was obviously a ruse. The instructor told the actor to shred his worksheet and pay himself whatever he was owed from the envelope. "I solved everything, so the envelope is empty. What should I do with it?" he asked. The instructor told him to put the empty envelope in the box and feel free to go, which the student did, after visibly pocketing all the cash.

So which of the three groups "solved" the most problems? Ariely and his colleagues found that those in the Madoff group summed almost twice as many pairs as those in the control group. They also completed more than the shredders, who had an opportunity to cheat but no model to show them how it could be done—and that they could get away with it.[28]

If people believe that a man with a soft, feminine-looking face is trustworthy, and if cheating can be contagious, then face-to-face social networks clearly have a dark side. We are easily fooled by signs of shared identity and status, though the brain's cues about whom to trust—the right facial features and expressions, appropriate eye contact and body language for each context—are notoriously hard to fake. Deploying these signals with panache, perpetrators such as Earl Jones, Bernie Madoff, and Monroe Beachy had long generated the respect due to upstanding members of their communities, and as a result they became insulated from suspicion. Ironically, it was their close, interconnected relationships with friends, family, and financial professionals that shielded them from scrutiny for decades. Trust was embedded in their face-to-face relationships and became transitive, moving imperceptibly from one agent to another in the social network.

Ponzi schemes share many of the same features as other face-to-face social networks. Their size, structure, and the way trust is transferred are recognizable, so much so that criminologists can now parse drug cartels the way epidemiologists track AIDS or suicide epidemics: through nodes in the network. For example, when criminologists Rebecca Nash, Martin Bouchard, and Aili Malm investigated the British Columbia–based Eron Mortgage Corporation, which defrauded more than 2,200 investors of $240 million in the nineties, they discovered that a few key victims had spread the word to their friends and family members. As with the Earl Jones fraud, these 150 bridge contacts, or infectors, as the researchers dubbed them, not only jumpstarted the project but unwittingly gave it a patina of legitimacy.[29] Influenced by their personal contacts, dozens of stockbrokers then sold it to others as a bona fide investment opportunity, much the way that Earl Jones's friends and family members recommended him as an investment and estate planner to their close contacts.

THE FEMALE EFFECT AGAIN
Though this is less the case with drug-related criminal networks, a female effect is key to many Ponzi schemes because they hinge on relationships. For example, 80 percent of Earl Jones's victims were female. To wit, Mary Coughlan put her daughter onto Earl Jones, and Wendy Nelles, whose mother and Coughlan were good friends, referred her daughter to him, too.

In small groups, women are more eager communicators than men, on average, and more likely to share details or tips about an expert with their close friends and family, most of whom are other women. As their social groups tend to be smaller than men's, their relationships are more intimate and more intimate information is shared.[30] "For most women, getting together and talking about their feelings and what is happening in their lives is at the heart of friendship. Having someone to tell your secrets to means you are not alone in the world," Deborah Tannen writes in *You Just Don't Understand*. (Filled with juicy tidbits from Tannen's own life alongside her favorite literary quotes, this engaging book creates its own aura of intimacy.)[31]

But women's tendency to communicate and confide in each other is more than anecdotal; it's also validated by reams of data. In a 2012 analysis of 1.9 billion cellphone calls and 489 million text messages from British cellphone subscribers, several European scientists found that women over the age of fifty (Earl Jones's target group) communicate at a higher rate than men, and primarily with a small group of other women. They were in touch more often with their best friends (who after the age of fifty tended to be their adult daughters) than with anyone else. Meanwhile, throughout his life, a man's most frequent contact was with a single person, who in many cases also happened to be a woman—his wife.[32] As a Ponzi scheme depends on a constant supply of new investors to fund the first ones in on the deal, women are unwitting but effective diffusers. Their personal networks may be smaller, on average, than men's, but they're denser and more intimate.[33] Tellingly, Jones kept his distance from men, especially those with financial savvy. "He was very careful. He never approached my son Jerry, who's in investment banking. My daughter was much more trusting," Coughlan said.

This type of betrayal is more corrosive than identity theft and faceless cybercrime, precisely because the crime spreads through people's relationships as opposed to the anonymity of the web. There is good evidence, too, that the psychological impact of such predation is felt more keenly by women than by men.[34]

DUNBAR'S NUMBER

But let's talk about size. An arresting fact about the Earl Jones and Eron (not to be confused with Enron) scandals is that 150 was the magic number. There were just over 150 victims in Jones's pyramid scheme before it collapsed, most of whom were members of the same social network, and just under 150 prime connectors, or "infectors," in Eron. This isn't some weird departure into numerology, nor is it a firm rule (Madoff's victims numbered in the thousands). Still, 150, give or take, has been posited by Oxford evolutionary psychologist Robin Dunbar as the maximum number of meaningful relationships that the human brain can manage.

Dunbar's Number:
Examples of human communities averaging 150 members

- Average clan size in 20 traditional hunter-gatherer societies: 153
- Population of Neolithic villages in the Middle East, circa 6000 BCE: 120–150
- Average size of villages wiped out by William the Conquerer: 150
- Average size of an English country village in the eighteenth century: 160
- Size of Roman fighting units during the republic: 130
- Current company size in the Canadian and US military: 130–150
- Christmas card recipients on a typical list: 150 people (living in 68 households)
- Average number of freelancers at co-working sites: 150–200
- Average number of core scholars within a single sub-discipline: 100–200
- Average size of an Amish or Hutterite community: 110–150
- Number of swimmers on the author's Masters team: 140–150
- Number of employees a business can manage without absenteeism or hierarchical management structures: 150–200[35]

Dunbar is not referring to Facebook or Twitter contacts but to people you know well enough to invite for a cup of coffee—and who would be likely to say yes. I am not alone in having crossed paths with a Facebook friend who showed not a glimmer of recognition as she passed. In contrast, the number of real social bonds a human brain can support has remained fairly static over the past ten thousand years, Dunbar argues, Facebook or no Facebook.

Even if many of our relationships are now sustained online as well as off, and electronic communication coordinates when and how we'll meet, face-to-face get-togethers are essential to keeping the relationship alive and breathing.[36]

One study of students leaving home for university showed that friendships require real, face-to-face contact so as not to decay. To put it bluntly, if you haven't seen a friend for dinner or a movie over the past eighteen months, chances are that your slot in her inner circle has been filled by someone else (though relationships with family are remarkably more durable).[37] "Put simply, our minds are not designed to allow us to have more than a limited number of people in our social world. The emotional and psychological investments that a close relationship requires are considerable, and the emotional capital we have available is limited," Dunbar writes.[38]

A primatologist by training, Dunbar is a mild-mannered, sixty-ish Oxford academic with a graying chinstrap beard, large rimless glasses, and a tendency to sprinkle "as it were" into his speech every few minutes. He should have added "as it were" to that previous statement about the mind: I doubt that he meant our minds were *designed* per se but rather that they evolved over time to support the size and complexity of our social groups. The social intelligence hypothesis explains why primates, and humans in particular, developed brains large enough for them to develop the capacities for language and empathy.[39] In order for primates to survive in larger groups, they needed supercharged brainpower to keep track of who was sleeping with whom, who was whose momma, who was the Big Cheese at any given moment (and who he had just deposed), who was his right-hand man and who were *his* allies, and which young whippersnapper was planning to depose him.

But the cognitive demands of living in groups don't just revolve around parsing the group and remembering who belongs to whom; they're also about mind reading. In order for a primate's group size to increase, that species' cerebral cortex—the thin sheath covering the brain that is responsible for the ability to problem-solve and imagine what other minds are thinking and feeling—must increase, too.[40]

Clearly there is no such thing as a free lunch in the intensely social world of primates, human or otherwise. Nonhuman primates such as baboons spend 45 percent of their waking hours engaged in one-to-one social interaction—namely grooming each other, a hands-on experience to say the least. We humans spend only about 20 percent of our time socializing, and it has to be quality time for us to reap the benefits. The evidence shows that collecting a list of contacts and then keeping in touch via one-way broadcasts may satisfy one's acquisitive urges, but it doesn't count as true connectedness. In a study of the effect of Internet use on social relationships in adults aged eighteen to sixty-three, Dutch psychologist Thomas Pollet found that time spent using online social networks resulted in more online contacts but didn't translate into genuine offline connections or a feeling of closeness.[41] Indeed, not only is online contact experienced as less fun, but without face-to-face contact, social relationships decay and are soon replaced by others.

Depressingly, without an opportunity to meet, it takes as little as eighteen months and as long as seven years for our friendships to fall away and be replaced by other local ones, according to two studies, one in Britain and one in the Netherlands.[42] Though these data confirm the out-of-sight-out-of-mind cliché, they're a letdown, given the promising language of global connectivity. "Emotional closeness declines by around 15 percent a year in the absence of face-to-face contact, so that in five years someone can go from being an intimate acquaintance to the most distant outer layer of your 150 friends," says Dunbar.

What does relationship decay mean for business? If we have only so much neural real estate to devote to our "village," then our *real* social networks may be a lot smaller and more fragile than we've been led to believe. The promise of technology—that one need not be there to talk to and see colleagues and clients in person—may be the message we all want to hear. It's certainly cheaper, more convenient, and in many ways easier on the psyche to blast out electronic bulletins than to communicate and manage in person, or to hire enough staff to do it for you. It's not only more cost-effective, it's aspirational to be able to process training, marketing, and customer service with the same detached efficiency that we apply to other types of digital information. But how well does it work? Let's look at a few stories, and more evidence.

I SAID, COME BACK TOMORROW

Paul English is a dedicated techie. With a graduate degree in computer science and decades of programming behind him, he has co-founded several tech ventures, including KAYAK.com, where he is currently chief technical officer. In late 2006, after posting a cheat sheet on his blog that revealed how to crack the code of several corporate voice-response systems, he unleashed an online stampede. "He named the companies and published their codes for reaching an operator—codes they did not share with the public," *Fast Company*'s William Taylor wrote. Less than six months later, English's blog was getting more than a million visitors a month, many contributing their own code-breaking secrets.[43] English had unwittingly launched a movement. "I've been a programmer for more than 20 years. I'm not anticapitalist. I'm on my fifth start-up. But I am anti-arrogance. Why do the executives who run these call centers think they can decide when I deserve to speak to a human being and when I don't?"

English had channeled a torrent of frustration with automated customer service. If my experience is typical, many companies— especially those in telecommunications, insurance, health care, and travel—are forgoing human contact in order to cut costs, deploying either robots or foreign call centers whose agents know nothing about the business and are paid per call (so they try to make it fast by passing you off to someone else). An attempt to correct a recursive cellphone billing error, for example, required first keying in my ten-digit number and then more than a dozen voice prompts from Emily, the robot customer service representative of my wireless company, which asked me to say my name over and over and over again, enunciating more clearly into the receiver to "confirm my voiceprint." I was then transferred four times to different call-center agents. Each one requested that I give my phone number, address, and date of birth and describe yet again why I was calling. After twenty minutes of this I was put on hold for another forty minutes, at which point my phone battery died. I never did call back. I switched carriers instead.

Paul English got his revenge by way of the Internet. Within two years of his inflammatory blog post he had launched GetHuman.com, a website that publishes companies' secret cheat sheets, on-hold wait times, and a monthly best and worst ranking. By the fall of 2012, the GetHuman site listed the codes for eight thousand companies in forty-five countries, and was growing. Had I known to call a different number than the one my wireless company provided, then press zero at each prompt, I could have reached a live person in less than two minutes. Instead I felt like Dorothy approaching the Wizard of Oz, who thunderously rebukes her when she gets too close: "Do not arouse the wrath of the great and powerful Oz! I said come back tomorrow!"

It would be funny if it weren't so infuriating—and such bad business. But there's more to this story. By deploying technology to keep down labor costs instead of to enhance the client's or employee's experience, businesses are ignoring one of the most critical findings offered by cognitive neuroscience in the past decade, namely that mood, social interaction, and productivity are bound tightly together and multiply each other's effects.

HAPPINESS

Let's start with a few findings about mood and productivity. When Daniel Kahneman and his colleagues set out to evaluate mood, they put handheld computers in the hands of about a thousand working women, who were prompted by their devices throughout the day to log what they were doing at that very moment and how happy they felt while doing it. It turned out that their happiest moments were spent socializing or having sex. They were most miserable while commuting or working.[44] Kahneman took this finding one step further in *Thinking Fast and Slow*, when reviewing the work of two German psychologists, Sascha Topolinski and Fritz Strack, who found that mood has a powerful effect on performance. Banking on the notion that creative intelligence revolves around finding associations among seemingly disparate ideas, the researchers attempted to see if people could come up with associations between triads of words such as these:

COTTAGE	SWISS	CAKE
SKUNK	KINGS	BOILED
BALD	SCREECH	EMBLEM
BLOOD	MUSIC	CHEESE

For example, the common element tying together *cottage, Swiss,* and *cake* is the word *cheese,* while the idea common to *bald, screech,* and *emblem* is *eagle.*

Before testing them, Topolinski and Strack asked their subjects to recall either a happy or sad moment in their lives to see what effect their mood would have on their problem-solving. Remarkably, the experimenters could influence how well people did on the test by first eliciting pleasant or unpleasant memories. It sounds too simple to be true. But asking people to think happy thoughts increased their accuracy by more than 100 percent. "An even more striking result is that unhappy subjects were completely incapable of performing the intuitive task accurately; their guesses were no better than random. Mood evidently affects the operation of System 1: when we are uncomfortable and unhappy, we lose touch with our intuition," Kahneman writes.[45]

Now, feeling lousy might be a good thing for your bottom line if a con artist like Earl Jones were trying to persuade you to collapse your retirement savings accounts and sign over the proceeds to him. A stinky mood would make you more suspicious. But if, as an entrepreneur, you wanted your staff to connect with clients to sell them stuff or to come up with creative solutions to their problems, then you'd want them to be in a good—if not a *fabulous*—mood, which, with any luck, would be contagious. Social contact would facilitate matters at the front end, making staff at all levels feel relaxed and happy about their work. And it would also affect their output as they extended that feeling of magnanimity and connection to clients.

Tony Hsieh, cofounder of the online shoe retailer Zappos, discovered this for himself early on. After selling his Internet banner business LinkExchange to Microsoft for $265 million in 1998, he was asked to stay on to help with the transition, a scenario that would net him $40 million. If he left, he'd forfeit 20 percent of that sum. He was twenty-four at the time. "The practice of sticking around but not really doing anything was actually pretty common practice in Silicon Valley in acquisition scenarios. In fact, there's even a phrase that entrepreneurs use for this: 'Vest in Peace,'" he writes in his autobiography, *Delivering Happiness*. But the prospect bored him. Instead of "vesting," he wanted to do something new, something that would make him happier than doing the same old thing. But what, exactly, would make him happy?

"I made a list of the happiest periods of my life, and I realized that none of them involved money. I realized that building stuff and being creative and inventive made me happy. Connecting with a friend and talking through the entire night until the sun rose made me happy. Trick-or-treating in middle school with a group of my closest friends made me happy. Eating a baked potato after a swim meet made me happy." He concluded that, along with creating something new, social contact was key to his happiness.[46]

He turned his back on that $8 million and moved to Zappos, which he had helped launch as an investor a year earlier. He couldn't care less about shoes and cared even less about fashion. "Long term, it's not even about e-commerce necessarily," he told the *New York Times*. "I guess it's about an experiential brand that's really about making people happy, or improving their life somehow." To delight his customers with just the right pair of shoes at just the right time, he created a corporate culture that fostered a gleeful, self-directed, zany social atmosphere among his sales staff, which he hoped would spill over into their connections with clients. "It was about: what kind of company can we create where we all want to be there, including me?" There were no time limits on phone calls; instead his employees tried to make connections with customers—and to make them happy. "Deliver WOW through service" is the first of the company's core values (one customer service call took six hours). "By imposing an ethos of live human connection on the chilly, anonymous bazaar of the Internet," as one journalist put it, Hsieh succeeded. He sold Zappos to Amazon for more than a billion dollars in 2009, right in the middle of the recession.[47] Meanwhile, larger and leaner online retailers were continuing to crash and burn.

WE SPEAK HUMAN

Hsieh may be a rarity in the stripped-down post-meltdown business environment. But he's not the only one to realize that securing customer loyalty is the Holy Grail. Now that people can bank or shop anywhere, why should they choose you? One reason might be that someone answers the phone at your place. Businesses that are amply staffed with well-trained, well-paid employees who like their work, and who like to work together, generate bigger profits, according to a 2012 study in the *Harvard Business Review* by MIT management professor Zeynep Ton. She found that four discount retailers—Costco, Trader Joe's, QuikTrip, and Mercadona (a Spanish supermarket chain)—violated the common assumption that to keep prices low, labor costs must be kept way down, too. Instead of offering little to no training, basement-level wages, constantly changing schedules, minimal benefits, and no opportunities to move up (as experienced by nearly 20 percent of the American workforce), they "eliminated waste in everything but staffing, and let employees make some decisions," she wrote.[48] Their stores are better places to work, obviously, but they also generate more profit per square foot than their bare-bones competitors. Citing a study showing that every extra dollar a five-hundred-store retailer spent on payroll netted it between $4 and $28 in new sales, James Surowiecki, author of *The Wisdom of Crowds*, points out that the opposite is also true: cutting back on human resources can harm a business.

> Of course, if you have a lousy product selection, a bigger payroll won't help much. But there's a strong case to be made that corporate America's fetish for cost-cutting has gone too far. . . . When Bob Nardelli took over Home Depot, in 2000, he reduced the number of salespeople on the floor and turned many full-time jobs into part-time ones. In the process, he turned Home Depot stores into cavernous wastelands, with customers wandering around dejectedly trying to find an aproned employee, only to discover that he had no useful advice to offer. The company's customer-service ratings plummeted, and its sales growth stalled.[49]

Clearly, scrimping on the human element can hurt business, and since the recession, banks and credit card companies have learned this the hard way. Research shows that when cardholders (who on average own more than five credit cards) are struggling to pay down their debts, they're more likely to pay the companies whose employees try to form an emotional connection with them. In 2010 a woman from Missouri named Donna Tiff was being aggressively pursued by several card companies for outstanding balances of $40,000. "The phone would ring nonstop," she told writer Charles Duhigg. "I would get on, crying, and tell them I don't believe in suicide, but I'm close." She threatened to file for bankruptcy, at which point the creditors would get nothing. Then a Bank of America customer service agent named Tracey called, chatted with her sympathetically, and pointed out that an error in her account meant that an automatic payment was being deducted twice.

Tiff stopped panicking and started listening. "I told her, thank you so much for catching that. And then we talked for over an hour about my problems and raising kids. She was amazing. She was so similar to me. She gave me her direct number and said that I should call her directly anytime I had questions or just needed to talk about what was going on." Duhigg reports that over the next three years Donna Tiff paid off the $28,000 she owed Bank of America, all the while chatting regularly with Tracey. The $12,000 she owed the other card companies? That was never fully repaid.[50]

It's easy to think that corporations are exploiting our social responsiveness just to get something out of us. Despite this cynicism, when I saw a full-page magazine ad with the two-inch tagline "WE SPEAK HUMAN," I tore it out. "There are times when you just want to speak to a real, live person about your money," it read. *You bet I do,* I thought. "And at Ally Bank you can, anytime, 24/7. You just push 'o' to speak to a real person. No complicated phone trees to navigate, no repeating yourself three times to a robot." Whether some executive somewhere realized this was the right thing to do or saw it as good business practice, or both, allowing real human contact within your technological fortress may well give you a competitive advantage, as we shall see.

BADGE OF EXCELLENCE

Imagine wearing a tasteful piece of jewelry, like a watch, that discreetly records whom you're talking to, how excited you feel about the conversation, how animated you get, how long the two of you keep chatting, and whom you talk to afterwards. Though it sounds Big Brother–ish, our brains already do this. They parse a social situation by reading the emotions and subtle movements of the other person, registering your own reactions as well as her level of interest, all the while executing a subtle, highly coordinated dance. When you lean forward, she does; when you cross your arms, so does she. Your averted gaze tells her that you've lost interest and are ready to move on, so she closes off the discussion and directs her attention elsewhere. The sleek little sociometric badge I mentioned earlier, invented by Sandy Pentland, Ben Waber, and their team at MIT, does what our brains do automatically: it registers all these social intricacies and records them so they're analyzable.

In a paper Pentland published in *American Scientist* in 2010, he characterized the four honest signals that the badges record:

- **Mimicry and synchrony:** when people unconsciously match each other's smiles, nods, gestures, and wry expressions, reflexively signaling to the other person that they're of one mind.
- **Activity level:** the level of interest that's evident in the way we move.
- **Influence:** the degree to which one person's expressions and movements affect those of the person they're talking to.
- **Consistency:** the fluidity of speech and movement that suggests self-confidence and expertise.

Together these social signals convey how much people trust each other, how happy they are in each other's company (which we now know is related to their productivity), and how cohesive a group is. This is valuable but usually hidden information. What's more, these nonverbal signals predict about 40 percent of what transpires in job interviews and salary negotiations. "That is equivalent to some estimates of the influence of genetic makeup on individual behavior and is far too large to ignore," Sandy Pentland writes.[51] Nevertheless, most businesses ignore it.

Despite the fact that emails, texts, and tweets are devoid of honest signals, most people conflate face-to-face with electronic social networks (this is like confusing a real kiss with the xx at the bottom of an email). The evidence also highlights that the two types of networks function in discrete ways, each with its own M.O. For example, one study from Pentland's MIT lab had IT specialists wear sociometric badges while they were at work. What the scientists wanted to know was whether face-to-face get-togethers would predict better work performance in these techies. And, indeed, they found this to be true. Smaller groups that communicated face-to-face were more cohesive. There was more trust within the group, which made it easier for people to ask questions and seek help when they needed it. As a result, those groups were more productive, especially when a problem was complex. The rich signaling within the team meant that actual conversations propelled the work forward.

But the opposite was true in email networks.[52] These work best when a larger, more diverse and loosely knit network shares information that can be "written into succinct rules," as the researchers put it. In other words, if everyone shares the same tacit knowledge and the problem is not that complex, there's not much advantage to getting together in person to brainstorm solutions. What's needed in those instances is what Mark Granovetter calls the power of weak bonds: the Internet's unique capacity to assemble diverse groups of people so they can fill in each other's gaps in knowledge.[53]

THE VALUE OF A COFFEE BREAK

The face-to-face advantage wasn't seen only among techies. The MIT research team has tried out their wearable sensors on all sorts of employees, including those who work in banks, on farms, in hospitals, and at call centers. They've found that the happy buzz of workplace chatter predicts productivity everywhere they've looked.[54] Of all the worksites, their call-center study piqued my curiosity most because working in one can be such a soul-deadening job. Employees face rigid schedules and scripts, social isolation, and an emphasis on quantity over quality, and as a rule, they can't rise much in the organization. In terms of tedium and lack of control, it's the twenty-first century's equivalent of a coalmine.

Yet when the badges were handed out at a call center with more than three thousand agents who worked for a major American bank, unexpected patterns emerged. "In the first phase, we just measured what happened. And we found that the more people talked to other people on their team—who were mostly people they were sitting with—the more productive they were," Waber told me. The researchers decided that during the second phase of their study they would try to elicit that effect. If the structure of the workday were tweaked to make it easier for team members to chat, would productivity go up? That was the experiment.

Waber is a young computer scientist who got his PhD in 2011 while working in Sandy Pentland's Human Dynamics lab at MIT. A smiling, compact young man with a neatly trimmed red beard, he is now CEO of a management consulting company that uses the badges to provide clues to leadership potential or to boost productivity. In other words, he's achieved what most young researchers only dream of: making their PhD theses useful. The wearable sensors Waber developed with Pentland and other MIT colleagues have already garnered attention in the *Economist*, the *New York Times*, and on NPR and the CBC, among other outlets. Waber has given talks to think tanks on the link between the bonding that goes on outside formal meetings and the bottom line. One leads to the other, apparently. What employers used to think of as dead time, such as gossip exchanged at the coffee machine during union-mandated breaks, turned out to be critical to profits. "The more cohesion there is, as measured by how much you interact with people within your team, the more productive it is," Waber told me. It's that simple.

The researchers found this out by changing the way half of the call agents worked. Typically, call agents get staggered breaks. "The way the breaks are structured, no one had a break at the same time, which is just a relic from the past. That's the way they've been doing it, so they keep doing it that way," Waber explained. So Waber, Pentland, and the team altered the routine to give half the agents a break at the same time. "We're not going to tell them what to do," he said, speaking in the present tense, as if he could see the call agents arrayed in their cubicles at that very moment. "So we made that change for half the groups, then let them work that way for three months. And we saw a dramatic change in their behavior, even though we're only talking about changing fifteen minutes of their day. There was this new opportunity for interaction and it changed their mindset for the whole day."

After trading hockey scores or juicy bits of gossip, the call agents were more productive, apparently. But that's not all they talked about. Like the spouses we met in the previous chapter, the transformational aspects of social contact came in several flavors. These agents had an opportunity to vent with someone who shared their experience—someone who sat near them and did the same job. "This is a stressful environment, so having those close relationships with a group of people is very important. You can say just a few things, and it makes a difference," Waber said. But physical proximity—being there in person—was key. They could also trade tips: "If they're less stressed, it's easier to deal with customers. They have a friend who said, 'Okay, this is how I dealt with this problem. I figured out how to solve it,' or 'This is how to pitch this new product,'" he continued. Even he seemed amazed that something as simple as changing the break schedule could have such a dramatic effect.

As a result of their experiment, the bank's call-center manager shifted to coordinated coffee breaks—and the plan worked. Recognizing that employees, like the bank clients they serve, are driven to make genuine human connections has led to vastly better outcomes. Coordinated breaks at all ten of the bank's call centers (involving twenty-five thousand employees) improved the weak teams' performance by more than 20 percent, increased performance overall by 8 percent, and boosted employee satisfaction by more than 10 percent, Sandy Pentland reports. Based on these boosts in performance, the bank is predicting $15 million in increased profit.[55] "We have the data to show that small changes can have very large effects," Waber told me. "The things that matter are these social interactions." And if they're truly immersed and embedded in the company, excellent managers know this intuitively. Interestingly, the critical element has nothing to do with what the workers are saying, and it can't be communicated via text or email. You have to be there.

THE LITTLE CHEMICAL THAT COULD
To find out why hanging out with teammates fosters trust and better performance we have to dig deeper, moving from the honest signals communicated through body language and tone of voice to microscopic neuropeptides circulating in the blood. Oxytocin is one of those neuropeptides, and it has become one of the stars of the neuroscience show in recent years because it has been found to grease the brain's wheels of attachment and trust.

Historically, this was considered women's stuff and wasn't taken very seriously. No longer. Within the past decade, several European research teams have shown that oxytocin doesn't just play a cameo role in the physiological backrooms of sex and breastfeeding. Its tentacles reach into all social relationships, stretching from the bedroom to the boardroom. In 2005 a handsome quintet of behavioral economists—Michael Kosfeld, Ernst Fehr, Markus Heinrichs, Urs Fischbacher, and Paul Zak—published an astounding finding. If young men sprayed oxytocin up their noses before playing an investment game, they were more willing to take social risks. More specifically, those who were infused with oxytocin handed over more money to an investment partner compared to men whose nasal spray contained a placebo. What's the significance of this? Oxytocin facilitated their trust. It lowered their natural aversion to the possibility that they might be cheated by someone they didn't know that well.[56] It made them better team players and more willing partners.

There were many reverberations to the finding that the "cuddle chemical" influences investment behavior. The first was that it raised the profile of this little hormone. The revelation that it affected people's readiness to take on risk revolutionized the field of economics. Formerly obsessed with the "me, myself, and I" type of decision-making, economics had been about purely rational thinking. Suddenly social relationships had come into play.

Other experiments showed that when people connect—and especially when they touch each other—oxytocin is released, which damps down their stress and enables them to trust each other. We're not necessarily talking about what Marvin Gaye called sexual healing. A simple handshake, a pat, a fist-bump, a friendly nudge, or a high five does the trick.[57] The effect isn't limited to one-on-one interactions, either. All evidence points to social contact lowering stress among colleagues and making a team more cohesive. This brings us back to the puzzle of why coordinated coffee breaks increase productivity.

In an experiment about group loyalty, Carsten De Dreu, a professor of organizational psychology at the University of Amsterdam, used oxytocin nasal spray to test how it might affect someone's commitment to his team. Two groups of men were recruited to play a classic economics game that revolves around how to spend a windfall. The men were randomly divided into two teams. One team sprayed oxytocin, the control group sprayed a placebo, and then the players were given three choices. They could spend the windfall on themselves, they could spend it on their team (which would give each member a smaller amount than if they spent the sum on themselves), or they could invest the money in a third option that would not only pay each of the investor's team members a token amount, but would also deduct the same amount from the competing team.

The results were dramatic. Almost 60 percent of those infused with oxytocin spent the money on their team, compared to 17 percent who invested in themselves. This scenario was reversed in the placebo group (20 percent invested in their team, while 50 percent invested in themselves). "The implication for business is that people have a strong, almost hardwired tendency to commit to their in-group," De Dreu told me over the phone. "And you can play around with the conditions that make them more loyal"— such as ensuring they have the time and place to socialize. "If people share their time and secrets with each other, that promotes oxytocin secretion," which prompts them to put aside their own self-interest. "This requires a psychologically safe climate, where you don't have to fear each other."[58]

It turns out that the business world runs on the same biological tracks as other face-to-face social networks, the ones that bind people together in Italian hilltop towns, in real neighborhoods, and in "intentional" communities—in churches, synagogues, college dorms, golf foursomes, and swim teams. Given that the same wiring cements together mother and child, not to mention loving spouses, it shouldn't be surprising that face-to-face social bonds trump the electronic kind when it really matters: when lives, loyalty, or lots of money is at stake.

Earl Jones knew that. The question is, why doesn't everybody else, and what does that mean for the rest of us?

Creating the Village Effect

In August 2010 I spent a day nosing about a cohousing community in Pleasant Hill, California. I drove there from Berkeley, crossing over some stinky sulfurous salt ponds, then spiraling through the arid Orinda Hills while the air outside my car got hotter and hotter. Many of the ranch-style houses I passed had signs on their garage doors—PROTECTED BY SMITH & WESSON— which made me a little nervous about dropping in on a group of people I'd never met. But as soon as I stepped out of my car in the community's parking lot, I was greeted by a middle-aged woman unloading groceries from her trunk into a wheeled cart. She smiled at me and asked who I was looking for. When I said Bob Fynn, she pointed me toward a wooden shed about fifty yards away. And that's where I found Bob, a connection I'd made through a friend, tidying the tool bench in the community's workshop.

Pleasant Hill is a cluster of about thirty-two tangerine stucco houses that reminded me of a cross between Mayberry R.F.D. and the kibbutz where I spent a year when I was eighteen.[1] This particular community's goals, though, are less about sharing material resources than about sharing social capital.[2] In an era when more people are living, raising children, and aging alone than at any time in history, these formerly unacquainted folks—numbering about fifty adults and their kids—wanted more from life than they were getting from going it alone. So in 1999 they bought two acres

285

of land and created a village where none had existed before. The aim was to design housing that fostered social contact, or as the American Cohousing Association website describes it, "Old fashioned neighborhoods created with a little ingenuity."

According to a 2011 survey sponsored by the association, cohousing residents say they want the sense of belonging that comes with village life and are willing to give up their own backyards to get it.[3] "I grew up in an apartment building where maybe you knew one person on each floor," Bob Fynn told me. This was a distinct shift from his parents' childhoods, when everyone sat out on the front stoop. "People now put such a premium on privacy that it's hard to get to know your neighbors," he added. So he and his wife decided to help create a neighborhood.

It's not easy to fast-track a real sense of village, and often the reality is far from the perfect community the founding members imagined. I wouldn't want my weekend hours to be whittled down by a community chore roster (it suddenly dawned on me why Fynn was spending his Sunday afternoon cleaning up the communal work bench). But, like co-working sites—former industrial spaces where telecommuters and freelancers are increasingly converging to share office space and an espresso machine—cohousing is a twenty-first-century response to an increasingly solo world. "If our future depends on being clever not individually, but collectively," as British science writer Matt Ridley aptly put it, then how are we going to get together?[4] Because, despite the clear-cut advantages of the Internet, if we want to be happy, healthy, long-lived, and learn more effectively, then we need to find ways to spend more time with each other face-to-face.

This book has shown that intimate contact is a basic human need. Indeed, most of us not born in Sardinian mountain villages still hanker for the feeling of belonging—not to mention the extra twenty years of life—that those villages bestow. Though few of us are willing to give up the educational and occupational opportunities of the present for the inequalities of the past and the very real privations of old-style rural life, at some level we still want a piece of it. The most common reaction to a 2013 radio documentary I wrote about the phenomenon of Sardinian super-longevity was *I want to live there*—even from people in their twenties and thirties. American historian Christopher Lasch captured the digital generation's yearning for real connection when he wrote this little ode to social contact in the early 1990s, not long after the word *cyberspace* was coined:

> We wanted our children to grow up in a kind of extended family, or at least with an abundance of "significant others." A house full of people; a crowded table ranging across the generations; four-hand music at the piano; nonstop conversation and cooking; baseball games and swimming in the afternoon; long walks after dinner; a poker game or Diplomacy or charades in the evening, all these activities mixing adults and children—that was our idea of a well-ordered household and more specifically of a well-ordered education . . . Home was not to be thought of as the nuclear family.[5]

Lasch wasn't engaging in some loopy utopian fantasy as much as he was voicing some cognitive dissonance about the future. Despite our being increasingly tethered to the devices that connect us virtually, there has not been a corresponding uptick in well-being. In fact, it's the reverse. By and large we're lonelier and unhappier than we were in the decades before the Internet age.[6] Psychologists don't know why that is exactly, though we do know that close relationships are the strongest drivers of happiness, and that being alone and unaffiliated makes us the most unhappy. The evidence is pretty clear that we are wired for frequent and genuine social interaction. As humans, we need to know that we belong.[7]

There's no going backwards, of course. No one, least of all me, is about to trash their laptops, smartphones, and tablets. But given the sobering impact of decreasing intimate contact on public health, among other things, it seems that it's time for a slight course correction.

1 Live in a community where you know and talk to your neighbors.

MAKING TRADEOFFS

The digital revolution, like the automotive revolution that preceded it, has enhanced society in countless ways. But it has also had unintended consequences. Many of the hangouts where people used to meet (which sociologist Ray Oldenburg called third places and techies call meatspaces) are disappearing.[8] And given the impact of less social contact on people's health and morale, not to mention on the bottom line, it's no wonder that employers such as Yahoo and Bank of America are calling their remote workers back to the office. It's not that their employees are less productive at home. It's that without the opportunity to bump into colleagues and have real conversations, innovation and social cohesion take a hit. One 2010 study led by Harvard's Isaac Kohane shows that the farther scientists are from each other geographically, the less influential their work is on their discipline, and on society. Indeed, the medical studies cited most often by scientists are more likely to be the work of researchers who work together in the very same building, within two hundred meters of each other.[9]

Evidence like this is why Google designed its Mountain View campus as a series of weirdly angular buildings, all clustered around a common green space equipped with seating and shade, much like the village square I described in Chapter 2, as well as the Pleasant Hill cohousing site. The Googleplex is an effort to promote the "casual collisions of the workforce," says David Radcliffe, the civil engineer in charge of Google's real estate. Roughly eight thousand employees are housed in sixty-five connected buildings (averaging a Dunbar's number–like 123 people per building), none of whom are ever more than a two-minute walk away from any other employee. The headquarters also features 960 micro-kitchens, nineteen cafés, connected walkways, and several dozen "land-marks"—common spaces where people naturally cross paths. As urbanist Greg Lindsay points out, "Our overwhelming preference for face-to-face interaction" is why we are four times as likely to exchange ideas with someone sitting six feet away as sixty feet away.

Build real human contact into your workday. Save email for logistics. Use phone or face time for more nuanced interaction.

2

A MATTER OF LIFE AND DEATH

It's fitting that a giant search engine prioritizes interpersonal con-tact for its own employees, and no surprise that high-tech maver-icks, who were likely the first to feel the dispiriting effects of their ballooning screen hours, would also be the first to start valuing their own face-to-face relationships. But not everyone can work at Google, and in any case this book is about more than work.

The first question I raised is whether we can improve our health by improving our social lives. As the emerging evidence I've laid out from the fields of social neuroscience and epidemiology confirms, the answer is yes. Daily face-to-face contact with a tight group of friends and family helps you live longer—by fortifying your immune system, calibrating your hormones, and rejigging how the genes that govern your behavior and resilience are expressed. But not just any social contact will do. The quality, type, and frequency of contact really matter. A smorgasbord of face-to-face relationships protects you from catching viruses such as colds, for example. Simply being married or having a small clutch of loyal buddies doesn't.[10] The same goes for your likelihood of surviving heart attacks, strokes, HIV/AIDS, or cancer. People with the most integrated social lives—meaning those who have overlapping relationships among friends, family, sports and other recreational or religious pursuits—have the best prognoses. I don't mean to imply that the right social cocktail means you won't ever be diagnosed with a dread disease; John McColgan couldn't ward off polycystic kidney disease, no matter how large his social circle. But if you're buffered by a tightly interwoven web of friends, neighbors, a caring spouse, and colleagues, you'll be far less likely to die from those things.[11]

And the power of social contact extends beyond individuals. Who survives a disaster also hinges, in large part, on the nature of their social bonds. Hurricanes, typhoons, tsunamis, earthquakes, and ferocious winter storms are coming at us fast and furiously, bringing with them devastating loss of life. The official response to these calamities has so far been about building better infrastructure and communication systems: fortified power lines, buildings, dams, bridges, and cell networks. These changes are badly needed. But what about focusing on our social ties as well? Because the evidence is clear. From the Chicago heat wave to Hurricanes Sandy and Katrina and the earthquakes in Japan and India, those most likely to make it had people in their circle who cared enough to check up on them and lend a hand. Those who were isolated—during or after the crises—were more likely to die.[12]

In order to build what I've called the village effect, you need a community of real friends you see in the real world. That community may overlap with your online networks, but is almost certainly smaller and more intimate (even for the most gregarious among us, likely no more than 150 to 200 people). A face-to-face network is not only more intimate, it is also more dynamic. As people fade away or your needs change, you really do need to repair or replace the face-to-face relationships you've lost, for the sake of your well-being, health, and longevity. Like a perennial border that develops gaps when certain plants don't come back after a dormant period, you have to fill in the empty spaces. And much like gardening, cultivating a personal village comes naturally to some people and takes more planning for others.

Researching this book has changed my own habits. In the past, my preferred plan for the evening was to stay home, reading or working. Now I build in social contact the way I build in daily exercise. I swim on a team—some of whose members you've met in these pages—because I've discovered that exercising with a group gives me more bang for my buck than I could ever get from swimming laps alone. Like Marietta Monni, the longtime friend and neighbor of Sardinian centenarian Zia Teresa, I make a point of attending social events and engaging with the people I happen to meet, exchanging more than just hello. And now that I'm paying attention, I can detect an upswing in mood when I extend my inner circle past the tight boundaries of my family and my three or four close friends.

One of these social outlets is not enough. You may be married to the person of your dreams. But if he or she is the only person you feel close to and can confide in, you're one person away from having no one at all. Immunologically speaking, you're almost naked.

Create a village of diverse relationships. Build in social contact with members of this village the way you work in meals and exercise.

3

INTROVERTS AND EXTROVERTS

Is regular face-to-face social contact good for everyone? What about introverts, who can find too much social contact painful? In *Quiet*, author Susan Cain makes a strong case for leaving introverts to their own devices. Defining them as "reflective, cerebral, bookish, unassuming, sensitive, thoughtful, serious, contemplative, subtle, introspective, inner-directed, gentle, calm, modest, solitude-seeking, shy, risk-averse, and thin-skinned," Cain argues that "in a world that can't stop talking," introverts should be allowed to think and create in peace. That certainly sounds sensible, and given that flattering list of attributes, many of us, including me, may now identify as introverts (sensitive, unassuming, thoughtful, and cerebral? Hell, yes).

As in Garrison Keillor's Lake Wobegon—where all the women are strong, all the men are good-looking, and all the children are above average—there may be some truth to this list, but also some wishful thinking. True introverts amount to roughly 25 percent of us, and the evidence shows that they too, need face-to-face contact to be healthy and happy. Though Cain argues that gregariousness should be optional for introverts, the evidence tells us that introverts have a greater risk of dying from cancer, and even an increased susceptibility to catching colds, if they hunker down alone. For example, expressive social activities— talking about your inner world with other people (exactly the kind of thing that introverts often avoid)—are associated with longer survival time in cancer patients. Meanwhile, the more homogeneous social groups that introverts often cultivate are linked to a higher risk of viral infection.[13]

Being human, introverts still need people. Though they may find it harder to initiate and cultivate relationships, they should consider attending social events with the option of slipping out when they've had enough. An introvert I know prefers large gatherings to small ones for precisely this reason. Bob Fynn chose to buy a townhouse in Pleasant Hill because he sees himself as an introvert. "At some point someone did some personality tests [of cohousing residents], " he told me, "and discovered that the overwhelming majority of us are introverts. Extroverts make friends anywhere. But introverts need the help of structure."

Still, even though we all need face-to-face contact, one size does not fit all when it comes to sociability. Those who tend toward introversion need a way to control the time, place, and duration of their social contact. With this principle in mind, university administrators should plan for enough single rooms to accommodate introverted college students, for example, instead of assuming that all undergrads want the company of strangers every minute. (This would be a more thoughtful approach not only for the introverts but for their roommates.)

Some people say they feel more competent online than off.[14] This is especially true for those on the autistic spectrum. Intuiting others' internal states from eye contact and context is not their strong suit, which can make social interaction a minefield. As digital forms of expression afford better predictability and control, many people on the autistic spectrum prefer emoticons, social media, and online gaming over the often overwhelming world of face-to-face interaction. Digital technology has proven to be a huge boon to this community, providing hours of entertainment, an outlet for their talents, and new forms of treatment.

But a question remains. Can screen activities attenuate the loneliness that is a byproduct of their social deficits? Or does it increase their sense of social isolation by reducing their opportunities for face-to-face contact? The evidence in this area is just starting to emerge, but we do know from research led by American psychologist Micah Mazurek that adults on the autistic spectrum who use social networking sites are more likely to cultivate online friendships. "I can connect with others while maintaining a level of detachment," wrote one of Mazurek's study subjects, when asked why he uses social networking sites. "I can communicate with people in a format I am comfortable with—limited emotion and no dumb small talk," wrote another. With no need to process body language and facial expressions, these autistic adults were able to make new friends online. But here's the kicker: There was no connection between their social media use and their ability to make offline friendships, nor did their online social activity reduce their loneliness. Only face-to-face relationships did that.[15]

4 Everyone needs close human contact. Adjust the ratio of your face-to-face to screen communication according to your temperament, just as you adjust how much and what you eat according to your appetite.

UNHOOKED

My home province of Quebec has one of the highest high-school dropout rates in the country—indeed one of the highest in the industrialized world. Nearly 40 percent of teenage boys drop out of high school here (the national average for boys is just under 10 percent, while the OECD average is 20 percent).[16] Called *décrochage* in French, which literally means "unhooking," the issue is so politically charged that when the school year ended in 2012, the provincial education minister explained that the pass rate in more than 250 high schools would be kept under wraps. "If we made the data public, one would realize that many institutions have a 100 percent dropout rate," Line Beauchamp told the press. "It would have a significant impact on the students' self-esteem and staff morale."[17]

Without a high-school diploma, the majority of these teenagers are consigning themselves and their children to a life of poverty. There is also the shadow that deprivation casts on their long-term health and cognitive ability, as we saw in Chapter 5. Yet instead of intervening, politicians tried to conceal the bad news. It's a complex issue, to be sure. Still, policymakers and educators would have a far greater impact on these vulnerable kids if they were to apply what we now know about the value of face-to-face contact. A fairly simple act—reaching out to make a personal connection with a struggling student—can reverse what seems inevitable to a discouraged sixteen-year-old.

In August 2012, four retired teachers and guidance counselors in Toronto used a $12,000 provincial grant to do just that. For two weeks solid they called each high-school student who had disappeared at the end of the school year and hadn't re-registered, and then called again, abandoning the more common administrative approach of dispatching emails and robocalls. The team refused to settle for leaving a message on voicemail; they wanted to speak to the student personally, to find out what had gone wrong and how they could help. This low-tech approach brought 864 out of 1,800 prospective dropouts back to the classroom—a success rate of nearly 50 percent.

One of them was Davia Jackson, whose family had moved during eleventh grade. She didn't want to switch schools for her final year, but when she tried to register at her old school, she became entangled in a bureaucracy that she just couldn't figure out. She was about to give up when the team made contact. "That one call made a difference," she said. "It gave me that push when I was beginning to get hopeless." Another student, Ashley, who has a learning disability and a hearing impairment, was about to fail her senior year because of a single missing course credit. When she received a call from a retired teacher asking her to return to school, she had not only given up, she was shocked that anyone had even noticed she was gone. "I'd been out of school for almost two months, so it made me feel taken aback," she said. "I was like, 'Someone cares.'" The reengagement team helped her register for night school to earn the missing credit. She graduated a few months later, and several months after that registered in a public relations program at a community college.[18]

It's hard to believe that such a simple intervention could work. But social contact is like a vaccine: a little can go a long way when it comes to preventing pain and loss of opportunity, while saving billions in health and social service costs. "We were reaching out and saying basically, we miss you, come back," said Christopher Usih, director of the project.

THE POWER OF PROXIMITY

In the Western world, it is mostly boys who have trouble staying in school. In the rest of the world it's girls. Despite the UN's goal of universal primary education by 2015, it is a few months into 2013 as I write this and more than ninety-three million children are still not in school, the majority of them girls from developing economies.[19]

Even when there are schools in the district, sometimes they're far from home and parents believe that it's unsafe for girls to travel. Or they expect their girls to stay home to do chores. There are plenty of other reasons why girls aren't in the classrooms of sub-Saharan Africa and South Asia, including assumptions about the purpose and outcome of an education. When fifteen-year-old Malala Yousafzai, an activist for girls' education in Pakistan, was shot in the face by the Taliban in 2012, it seemed like universal education might be an intractable problem. The jubilant international response to Malala's recovery and her continued activism haven't altered the dire facts on the ground: Pakistan has the second highest number of unschooled children and, at fifty million people, one of the highest illiteracy rates in the world.

Laptop programs haven't solved the problem of access to education, as we discovered in Chapter 6. But a teacher's proximity to students provides a hint at what works, for school attendance in general and for girls' achievement in particular. In the province of Ghor, in northwestern Afghanistan, only 28 percent of children live within five kilometers of a school, one reason why two-thirds of the area's children don't go. In a 2012 study, two American economists, Dana Burde and Leigh Linden, looked at what happened when small schools were built right in their villages. In 2008, schools were built in thirteen out of thirty-one randomly selected rural villages in the province; students living in the other eighteen villages were assigned to traditional district-based schools. (Attended by 95 percent of the school-going population, the latter were long thought to offer a superior education due to economies of scale and better resources.) The attendance and performance of the roughly 1,500 children in the different types of schools was then compared after a full academic year.

It turned out that the village schools increased girls' attendance by 52 percent and their academic achievement by 1.3 standard deviations, compared to the more distant district schools. All the students benefited from village-based schools (boys' enrollment increased by 34 percent), but girls' attendance and learning benefited the most. Close proximity to the school and its teachers "virtually eliminated the gender disparity in enrollment and improved the disparity in test scores by a third in a single year," Burde and Linden write.[20] Cutting the geographic distance between students and teachers increased enrollment at the rate of more than 16 percent per mile.

This is a literal example of the village effect—the transformative power of proximity. Another example is the reading program I described in Chapter 6, which helps low-income parents (whose kids are at the highest risk of school failure) feel good about yakking with their toddlers and small children while turning the pages of a book. Ongoing close contact with parents really ramped up their kids' language and reading skills later on.[21] In fact, programs that promote face-to-face conversations and interactive reading between parent and child have had *more than twice* the impact on the language and literacy skills of kids from impoverished backgrounds than laptop programs have had. Meanwhile, research shows that face-to-face contact with a skilled teacher for even one year of a child's life has more impact on the child's learning than any laptop program has had so far.[22] If policymakers want to use resources wisely, it is clear that you get a lot more from parent and teacher training programs than you do from investing in expensive—and highly perishable—classroom technology.[23]

To be sure, there are wonderful pieces of educational software on the market, and well-trained teachers who know how to use them to advantage—mostly to target specific skills.[24] But among the most vulnerable kids, the ones who most need a leg-up to succeed—primarily lower-income children, those with ADHD, and impulsive boys—what boosts achievement the most are initiatives that help them develop self-discipline and what psychologists call executive function, namely the ability to plan, to hold key bits of information in memory, and to be cognitively flexible, all while inhibiting their impulses. So, what helps school-age kids master those skills?

Adele Diamond and Kathleen Lee, two Canadian psychologists, asked that question in a recent meta-analysis published in *Science*. They discovered that even the best computer programs, which build in increasing challenges as the child gains competence, succeeded at training kids one skill at a time. But that one skill didn't transfer well to other areas. In other words, a program that trained kids on short-term memory didn't help them with other types of tasks, including ones that included memory skills. A computer program that trained kids to practice a particular type of nonverbal problem-solving improved their skills on *that type of task* but no other. As the authors put it, "those trained on reasoning did not improve on speed, and those trained on speed did not improve on reasoning." In contrast, they found that any program that combined social interaction with a trained teacher and aerobic exercise, music lessons, martial arts training, or mindfulness programs improved different types of executive function in school-aged kids.[25] Even without expensive equipment, kids can learn to plan, wait their turn, control their emotions, solve problems, and rein in their impulses—as long as their teachers are given evidence-based training and support.

There are a few leaders who get this. Barack Obama is one of them. "The need for good teachers deserves emphasis," he wrote about the American educational system in *The Audacity of Hope*. "Recent studies show that the single most important factor in determining a student's achievement isn't the color of his skin or where she comes from, but who the child's teacher is."[26] He wrote this at least five years before some of the most persuasive evidence on the impact of face-to-face interaction surfaced. Still, Obama was on to something. According to a 2011 study of 2.5 million American children, students taught by a *great* (rather than an average) teacher for just one year

- are more likely to go to college;
- are more likely to go to an excellent college;
- are less likely to be teenage mothers;
- earn more as adults (averaging $250,000 more over their lifetimes);
- live in nicer neighborhoods as adults;
- are more likely to save for their retirement.[27]

These outcomes were not just a question of privileged parents choosing schools with great teachers (tax returns in hand, the researchers stripped out the effects of family income). No, the lesson is that we have underestimated the power of interaction. A great teacher can change a child's future. "That's especially true for needy kids, who often get the weakest teachers. That should be the civil rights scandal of our time," Nicholas Kristof writes in a column describing how a perspicacious teacher transformed the future of one Olly Neal, once "a poor black kid with an attitude," who ultimately became an American appeal court judge. Noticing the back-talking sixteen-year-old Neal steal a book with a racy cover from the school library, the teacher, Mildred Grady, used her own time and money to ensure there would always be a new novel by that author on the shelf, secretly stoking what became Neal's lifelong reading habit.[28]

We may not pay them well or respect them as much as we do Internet barons like Mark Zuckerberg or Sergey Brin. But if a gifted teacher can turn resistant kids into readers—if an excellent teacher can be parachuted into a class and learning and achievement spike as a result—then we should start investing at least as much in teachers' wetware as we do in software and hardware.

5 Make parent, teacher, and peer interaction the priority for preschoolers and young children. Combine live teaching with online tools for older children and teens.

FACE-TO-FACE CONTACT AND THE CLASS DIVIDE

The reason I mention the Olly Neal story is that being educated by a wonderful teacher who cares about you may soon become a thing of the past, especially for kids from poor backgrounds. There is a growing opportunity gap between middle-class and working-class kids in North America and Europe. Financially comfortable kids now get reams of what political scientist Robert Putnam calls "*Goodnight Moon* time," compared to children from less affluent backgrounds. To wit, college-educated parents now spend four times as much time, energy, and money on their kids as their parents did in the seventies. During that same time span, high school–educated, often financially pinched parents have barely increased the resources and attention they devote to their kids. This activity and attention gap was less dramatic three to four decades ago. Now the rich–poor rift in reading and math test scores is about 40 percent larger.[29]

Given that providing a virtual education is cheaper than training excellent teachers, I fear that the push toward digital classrooms will exaggerate this class divide. This is not scaremongering. School laptop programs, virtual classrooms, and MOOCs (massive open online courses) are often floated as magic bullets for underprivileged or underserved school populations, whether in Birmingham, Alabama, or Fort Portal, Uganda. MOOCs have gained traction at a galloping pace. Slickly produced virtual courses have generated astronomical registration rates, with students in some courses numbering in the hundreds of thousands. Yet the reality of an inter-action-free education is sobering. On average, 90 percent of these students drop out. Only 3 percent of MOOC students say they feel satisfied with the experience. Without a schedule or any classroom structure, lacking the opportunity to ask questions or receive any encouragement or personal evaluation, it is poor, inexperienced, or disenfranchised students—precisely the ones targeted by many MOOC promoters—who are the ones most likely to flounder and fade away.[30] Meanwhile, parents and students who can afford it are moving in the opposite direction, paying a premium for real human contact with well-trained teachers in small classrooms, teachers who offer plenty of guided discussion, individualized instruction, and hands-on opportunities to learn.

Investing in tools that you hope will prevent your child from falling off the social mobility ladder is nothing new, of course. What's new is that what used to be free—the human element in the classroom—now costs. Parents of kindergarten children in China now pay a monthly fee if they want them to receive hugs from teachers, according to the *Huffington Post*. Closer to home, many parents with choices are opting to pony up for more classroom teaching and less classroom technology. "The idea that an app on an iPad can better teach my kids to read or do arithmetic, that's ridiculous," says Alan Eagle, the chief technology officer of eBay. Eagle has a point, one shared by many well-educated, well-employed parents—especially in Silicon Valley. If you can afford good teaching, why would you entrust your kid's education to an operating system? Digital skills are now so basic they're "like learning to use toothpaste," says Eagle, whose children attend a low-tech Waldorf school (annual tuition: $20,000 per child). "We make technology as brain-dead easy to use as possible. There's no reason why kids can't figure it out when they're older."[31]

This is not what we expected of the digital revolution. Technology was not only supposed to free us, it was expected to be the great equalizer. But simply giving marginalized kids networked computers actually widens existing academic gaps between rich and poor kids. When economists Jacob Vigdor and Helen Ladd followed the school progress of one million American kids from disadvantaged homes for five years, before and after Internet-enabled computers appeared in their lives, this is what they found: "Students who gain access to a home computer between 5th and 8th grade tend to witness a persistent decline in reading and math test scores."[32] We don't know why this is, exactly. One possibility is that without parents at home to supervise—after all, poor and single parents often work long hours— kids do what they often do in school laptop programs: use their gadgets to play games, chat, or download movies and porn.

Now imagine what could happen if children whose parents have less money or moxie are shunted to virtual classrooms. Alongside high attrition rates, this is the dark side of virtual schooling. As education researcher Mark Warschauer points out in *Learning in the Cloud*, budget-driven, as opposed to evidence-based decisions about virtual classrooms are already here.

> Florida has demonstrated some of the benefits of targeted virtual education. . . . However the dark side of virtual schooling is also on display in the state, with students in Miami-Dade County now being placed into teacherless online classes against their will. When students report to class, a "facilitator" assigns them to work at a computer. The new system was put in place not to improve instruction but to save money, since virtual classes in Florida, unlike classes with teachers, have no maximum class sizes. Indeed, an administrator admitted to the *New York Times* that even if students were struggling, mandatory virtual instruction was necessary since "there's no way to beat the class-size mandate without it." One parent said that her "jaw dropped" when she found out that her daughter was assigned to a virtual rather than an actual Spanish class. . . . "None of them want to be there,"

said a girl speaking for the 35 to 40 students who were forced into a teacherless class.[33]

In a state that spends the least on public education in the United States and at a time when increasing scientific evidence stresses the necessity of face-to-face interaction in education, and especially in early learning, limiting kids' interaction with teachers is a chilling development.[34]

As more of our interactions migrate to digital platforms, face-to-face contact in education, medicine, and child care has become a luxury commodity. As a fundamental human need, it should remain accessible to all.

6

FEMALE INFLUENCE

It's not too late. Far more intractable social trends have been reversed, often with women's help. At the turn of the twentieth century, for example, 99 percent of women born in an area south of Beijing had bound feet. None born after 1919 did. "The campaign against foot-binding didn't work immediately. But when it took hold, that thousand-year-old practice essentially vanished in a single generation," writes philosopher Kwame Anthony Appiah in *The Honor Code*.[35] After previous attempts to abolish it had failed, how did this debilitating practice change so quickly?

The short answer is that women's social bonds played a critical role. When a British clergyman called a meeting of women in Xiamen in 1875 and asked them to sign a pledge against foot-binding, at first only nine agreed. Gradually those nine reached out and connected to hundreds more, and ultimately the Unbound Foot Association had ten thousand members. Changing "what was normal," as Appiah puts it, required several catalysts: Protestant clergymen agitating against the barbarity; prominent intellectuals

calling the practice ridiculous; the return of the first wave of
Chinese women to be educated abroad, where they saw that hob-
bling women wasn't done; and perhaps most important of all, the
growth of organizations whose female members pledged not to
bind their daughters' feet or allow their sons to marry women
whose feet were bound.

At a time when they didn't have much political muscle, women
helped promote huge changes, often behind the scenes, through
social contagion and peer pressure. Similar shifts occurred when
women led the temperance movement. And they continue to
happen. Whether working to dramatically reduce infant mortality
in India through face-to-face coaching of new mothers; to change
the rate of HIV transmission in Uganda; to encourage condom use
among their female friends in Cameroon; or to keep their aging
husbands alive and breathing, women everywhere use their tight
social networks and social influence to alter the welfare of people
in their literal and metaphorical villages.[36]

I'm not delivering a "women are wonderful" (also known as
WOW) message but rather a last reminder about the potency of
face-to-face contact. As we've seen, women's social circles tend to
be smaller, tighter, and more intimate than men's. Why that might
be is where this book began. When I learned that women's complex social lives are critical to their better health and longer lives, I
wanted to know why. Exchanging crucial bits of information within
close female networks is key, I discovered. But a commitment to
human contact for its own sake is also keeping women and their
minds alive. Meeting in pairs or small groups, or simply talking on
the phone, women pass on essential nuggets of information. They
also get a neurochemical boost from the interaction. Perhaps most
important of all, women are more likely than men to sustain a
variety of relationships, surrounding themselves with people who
matter and replacing the friends, neighbors, and spouses they may
lose over time with new bonds. In a digital age and at a time when

people are living longer, more mobile, and in many cases more solitary lives, taking the time to build, sustain, and rebuild this village is crucial.

We—both men and women—are happier, healthier, and more resistant to disease and despair if we satisfy the need for meaningful human contact. Our loads seem lighter, the hills literally less steep.[37] Genuine social interaction is a force of nature; we all need some, every day we eat. Given the powerful evidence, the capacity of intimate interaction to jumpstart learning and rejig lifespans is not that hard to fathom, and not that hard to integrate into our daily lives. All we need to do is picture what our own real, in-person villages might look like, and then reach out to create them.

Acknowledgments

The germ of the idea for this book came to me while sitting in a dark Toronto auditorium. That's where I first heard about a far-off place where men live as long as women and that a digital interface has been designed, in all seriousness, to be your perfect mate. My first thanks go to Moses Znaimer and Idea City for putting these apposite ideas together, thereby jumpstarting my thinking about the transformative nature of our social bonds.

The late Mavis Gallant once commented that writing "is like a love affair: the beginning is the best part." And right from the beginning my friends and family—and even a few strangers and *their* families—good-naturedly accepted my incursions into their lives. Generous and candid while I was researching the ideas in this book, I am deeply grateful to Claudia Aristy, Judith Berman, Danielle Brown, Kate Browne, Diana Bruno, Teresa Cabiddu, Giovanni Corrias, Mary Coughlan, Joseph Douek, Arden Ford, Bob Fynn, Jessie Goldberg, Fred Janosy, Sylvie La Fontaine, Kathe Lieber, Ben and Kaz Mattes, John McColgan, Giuseppe Murinu, Ginny Nelles, Claudie Pfeiffer, Francesca Pittau, Florence Velly, and Matt West. If their stories ended up in these pages, I used first-name-only pseudonyms for those who preferred them, and complete names for people who didn't mind being identified. To all those who helped me in my community, including the members of my swim team and the reference librarians at the Westmount Public Library, I say thank you, thank you.

My remarkable literary agents, John Brockman and Katinka Matson, showed keen interest in this book from the start and I thank them for their advocacy and expertise. This is the second time that I have had the good luck to work with the insightful Anne Collins, my editor at Random House Canada, who read and responded to a zillion drafts and queries with alacrity, good sense, and unfailing good humor. Cindy Spiegel, my editor at Spiegel & Grau, was passionate about the book and left no stone unturned to ensure its success. I can only thank their teams collectively here, but Michelle Roper at Random House Canada and Annie Chagnot at Spiegel and Grau, deserve special gratitude and recognition.

While any errors are mine alone, the following experts and friends read early drafts of chapters and generously provided comments that helped me aim for accuracy and style: Barbara Baker, John Cacioppo, Steve Cole, Alison Gopnik, Michael Kramer, Gianni Pes, Laura-Ann Petitto, Steve Pinker, Michel Poulain, Andrew Meltzoff, Harry Reis, Sherry Turkle, Linda Waite, Mark Warschauer, and Joel Yanofsky. Careful reading is an invaluable gift and I am very grateful for their help. On that score, Steve and I may well be the only siblings in the world who find discussions about the function of the passive voice and the amygdala equally compelling. These shared interests are a source of great pleasure and support.

A phalanx of scientists sent me their research and patiently answered my questions about the nature of the social mind. They include Roy Baumeister, Matthew Brashears, John Cacioppo, Sue Carter, Bernard Chapais, Dimitri Christakis, Steve Cole, Eli Finkel, Helen Fisher, James Fowler, Howard Friedman, Paolo Francalacci, David Geary, Keith Hampton, Julianne Holt-Lunstad, Celeste Johnson, Janice Kiecolt-Glaser, Perri Klass, Andrew Meltzoff, Alan Mendelsohn, Carlo Morselli, Linda Pagani, Giovanni Pes, Michel Poulain, John P. Robinson, Niels Rosenquist, Robert Sapolsky, Alex Todorov, Tom Valente, Jacob Vigdor, Ben Waber, Barry Wellman, and Elizabeth Walcot.

Gratitude goes to a series of wonderful research and archival assistants who helped me in numerous ways, including Yanick

Charette, Carl Boodman, Beth Cruchley, Terri Foxman, Damon Hancoff, Gaëlle Hortop, Sara-Lynn Moore, and Roslyn Pinker. Gabrielle Jacobs and Beatrice Toner helped with interview transcriptions; Axel van den Berg, Joseph Helfer, Michelle Roper, and Julia Waks with image translations and tweaks. Deep appreciation goes to a short list of researchers who have been with me now for *years*, including the indefatigable Terri Foxman and Gaëlle Hortop, as well as my immunology and primatology tutor, Carl Boodman, and Roslyn Pinker—clipper and reader extraordinaire, also known as Mom. Martin Boodman, my husband, heard about the minutiae of this book at every stage, and graciously offered feedback and encouragement all along.

By now it's clear that *I couldn't have done it without you* not only describes this book's theme but the process of writing it. My friends and family, including my brothers and sisters-in-law, Steve and Rob Pinker, Rebecca Newberger Goldstein and Kristine Whitehead, along with their children, form the contours of my village. My parents, Roslyn and Harry Pinker—to whom this book is dedicated— cheered me on from behind the scenes, and were the first to to show me why face-to-face relationships really matter. This brings me to the reason I keep breathing and working. I deeply thank Martin, who is the love of my life, and my three children, Eva, Carl, and Eric, who light up my life.

Notes

INTRODUCTION: PEOPLE WHO NEED PEOPLE

1. All American waiting list figures are gleaned from the US Department of Health and Human Services Organ Procurement and Transplantation Network, http://optn.transplant.hrsa.gov/data/. The number of Americans who died while waiting for a kidney was provided by E. Schlam, spokesperson for the National Kidney Foundation, September 12, 2010. Figures for the number of Canadians on the transplant list waiting for a kidney in 2009 are from the Kidney Foundation of Canada Fact Sheet, http://www.kidney.ca/Document.Doc?id=102

2. In 2009 at least a dozen British people were advertising the sale of their kidneys on the Internet. One of them, a nurse with a two-year-old daughter, who was in dire financial straits, had advertised his kidney for $40,000, plus medical and travel expenses. He expected most of the offers to come from Americans, who at the time of writing this book could purchase sperm and ova for in vitro fertilization, as well as a surrogate to gestate their baby, but who were not permitted to offer incentives to spur the donation of healthy organs. This warning was appended to the bottom of the *Sunday Times* article titled "I've Got Debts, Please Buy My Kidney": "Selling human organs in Britain or offering them for sale, is an offence under the Human Tissue Act 2004, punishable with up to three years in prison. Donors can give a kidney to a relative or close friend, but they must demonstrate a close relationship. They must also convince a panel of assessors that they have not been coerced into donating an organ and will not be paid."

3. Giving a kidney to a stranger has become possible in recent years, a phenomenon facilitated by donors and recipients finding each other on

websites such as matchingdonors.com, and by changing attitudes on transplant boards, which until recently discouraged the practice. Altruistic donations—when someone donates an organ to a person they have never met—tend to make headlines, giving the impression that they are becoming common. Not so. Though the incidence of anonymous organ donation is increasing, it is still very rare. In Britain, altruistic donations became legal in 2007, but in 2009–10 the probability of someone with end-stage renal disease receiving a kidney from a living donor with whom they'd had no face-to-face contact ranged from 0.02% to 0.006%, according to the Human Tissue Authority—so hardly a fad. The situation is similar in the United States. According to figures released by the Organ Procurement and Transplantation Network for that period, less than 0.02%—two out of ten thousand—of living kidney donors were anonymous donors found on the Internet (National Health and Nutrition Evaluation Survey, 2009).

4. This is an average, computed on February 8, 2013, from kidney transplant waiting lists in the United States: 0.03% of the population, according to the government census, http://www.census.gov/main/www/popclock.html; Canada: 0.0068% of the population, according to the Canadian Institute for Health Information; the United Kingdom: 0.0098%, according to the UK Office of National Statistics; Germany: 0.0014%, according to German government statistics, http://www.statistik-portal.de/Statistik-Portal/en/en_zso1_bund.asp; and France: 0.0019%, according to the Agence de la biomedicine.

5. This is not hyperbole. MRI scanners, which became commercially available in the early 1980s, while I was in graduate school, cost $1.5 million to more than $2 million at the time, as did a basic Learjet. Michael Bates, "Bill Lear's 'Baby Jet' Celebrates 20 Years in Aviation," *The Dispatch*, October 8, 1983; Martin Stuart-Harle, "Hospitals Seeking Magnetic Imagers Agonize over Choice of Costly Devices," *Globe and Mail*, October 13, 1985.

6. Bureau of Labor Statistics, "American Time Use Survey, 2011 Annual Averages" (Washington, DC: BLS, 2012). The ATUS web page states:

"a primary activity refers to an individual's main activity. Other activities done simultaneously are not included," which would explain why Americans apparently spend a total of 23 minutes a day eating. Whatever goes down the hatch while they're watching TV, at their computers, or in their cars isn't counted. Thanks are due to sociologist John P. Robinson, who clued me in to the ATUS and talked to me frankly about measuring how Americans spend their time.

7. NM Incite, "The Social Media Report" (New York: Nielsen McKinsey, 2012).

8. Bill Bryson, *A Short History of Nearly Everything* (Toronto: Random House Canada, 2003).

9. J. Cacioppo, L. C. Hawkley, G. J. Norman, and G. G. Berntson, "Social Isolation," *Annals of the New York Academy of Sciences* 1231 (2011): 17–22.

10. This research is fully documented in the following chapters.

11. L. F. Berkman et al., "Social Integration and Mortality: A Prospective Study of French Employees of Electricity of France–Gas of France: The GAZEL Cohort," *American Journal of Epidemiology* 159, no. 2 (2004); L. Fratiglioni et al., "An Active and Socially Integrated Lifestyle in Late Life Might Protect Against Dementia," *Lancet Neurology* (2004); S. W. Cole et al., "Social Regulation of Gene Expression in Human Leukocytes," *Genome Biology* 8, no. 9 (2007); Candyce H. Kroenke, Laura D. Kubzansky, Eva S. Schernhammer, Michelle D. Holmes, and Ichiro Kawachi, "Social Networks, Social Support, and Survival after Breast Cancer Diagnosis," *Journal of Clinical Oncology* 24, no. 7 (2006).

12. K. Hampton, F. Lauren Sessions, and Eun Ja Her, "Core Networks, Social Isolation, and New Media," *Information, Communication and Society* 14, no. 1 (2011); J. S. House, K. R. Landis, and D. Umberson, "Social Relationships and Health," *Science* 241, no. 4865 (1988); Fratiglioni et al., "Active and Socially Integrated Lifestyle"; M. E. Brashears, "Small Networks and High Isolation? A Reexamination of American Discussion Networks," *Social Networks* 33 (2011); M.

McPherson, L. Smith-Lovin, and M. E. Brashears, "Social Isolation in America: Changes in Core Discussion Networks over Two Decades," *American Sociological Review* 71, no. 3 (2006); Miller McPherson, L. Smith-Lovin, and M. E. Brashears, "Models and Marginals: Using Survey Evidence to Study Social Networks," *American Sociological Review* 74 (2009); American Association of Retired People, *Loneliness among Older Adults: A National Survey of Adults 45+* (Washington: AARP, 2010); Christina R. Victor and Kemang Yang, "The Prevalence of Loneliness among Adults: A Case Study of the United Kingdom," *Journal of Psychology* 146, no. 1/2 (2012).

13. Jo Griffin, *The Lonely Society?* (London: Mental Health Foundation, 2010).

14. Robert D. Putnam, *Bowling Alone: The Collapse and Revival of the American Community* (New York: Simon & Schuster, 2001); Jennifer Senior, "Alone Together," *New York Magazine*, November 23, 2008.

15. Kemang Yang and Christina Victor, "Age and Loneliness in 25 European Nations," *Ageing and Society* 31 (2011).

16. Canadian Community Health Survey, "Prevalence of Positive Self-Perceived Health, Loneliness and Life Dissatisfaction, by Selected Characteristics, Household Population Aged 65 or Older, Canada Excluding Territories 2008–2009" (Ottawa: Statistics Canada, 2012).

17. Eric Klinenberg, *Heat Wave: A Social Autopsy of Disaster in Chicago* (Chicago: University of Chicago Press, 2002); Rebecca Solnit, *A Paradise Built in Hell: The Extraordinary Communities that Arise in Disaster* (New York: Penguin, 2009); Shankar Vedantam, *The Key to Disaster Survival? Friends and Neighbors* (National Public Radio, 2011).

18. Leo Tolstoy, *War and Peace* (New York: Vintage Reprint, 2008); William Deresiewicz, "Faux Friendship," *Chronicle of Higher Education*, December 6, 2009.

19. Anthony Storrs, *Solitude* (New York: HarperCollins, 1997); Susan Cain, *Quiet* (New York: Broadway, 2012).

20. Ye Luo et al., "Loneliness, Health, and Mortality in Old Age: A National Longitudinal Study," *Social Science and Medicine* 74 (2012).

21. A. Steptoe et al., "Loneliness and Neuroendocrine, Cardiovascular, and Inflammatory Stress Responses in Middle-Aged Men and Women," *Psychoneuroendocrinology* 29, no. 5 (2004); Ruth Hackett et al., "Loneliness and Stress-Related Inflammatory and Neuroendocrine Responses in Older Men and Women," *Psychoneuroendocrinology* 37, no. 1801–9 (2012).

22. M. Iwasaki et al., "Social Networks and Mortality Based on the Komo-Ise Cohort Study in Japan," *International Journal of Epidemiology* 31, no. 6 (2002).

23. J. Cacioppo, James Fowler, and Nicholas A. Christakis, "Alone in the Crowd: The Structure and Spread of Loneliness in a Large Social Network," *Journal of Personality and Social Psychology* 97, no. 6 (2009).

24. L. C. Hawkley et al., "Loneliness in Everyday Life: Cardiovascular Activity, Psychosocial Context, and Health Behaviors," *Journal of Personality and Social Psychology* 85, no. 1 (2003); J. Cacioppo et al., "Social Isolation," *Annals of the New York Academy of Sciences* 1231 (2011); J. Cacioppo and William Patrick, *Loneliness: Human Nature and the Need for Social Connection* (New York: Norton, 2008).

25. Sarah Hampson, "Get Over Your Loner Phobia," *Globe and Mail*, January 18, 2013.

26. Lee Rainie and Barry Wellman, *Networked: The New Social Operating System* (Cambridge, MA: MIT Press, 2012).

27. Ibid.

28. Ellen Goodman, "Friendless in America," *Boston Globe*, June 30, 2006.

29. Rainie and Wellman, *Networked*; Hampton, Sessions, and Her, "Core Networks."

30. K. Hampton, C. U. Lee, and Eun Ja Her, "How New Media Affords Network Diversity: Direct and Mediated Access to Social Capital Through Participation in Local Social Settings," *New Media and Society* 13, no. 7 (2011); K. Hampton et al., *Social Isolation and New Technology* (Washington, DC: Pew Internet and American Life Project, 2009). Keith Hampton speculates that avid users of social networking sites may have used them *because* they were not socially integrated;

their use of electronic networks may be the source of increased network diversity. A subsequent study of social network users—when the technology was more widespread—did not reveal a connection between social media use and disconnection from neighbors (email correspondence with Keith Hampton, July 7, 2013).

31. Claude S. Fischer, *Made in America: A Social History of American Culture and Character* (Chicago: University of Chicago Press, 2010).

32. "Dinner for One: Solo Britons Send Sales of Single-Serve Cookware Soaring by 140%," *Daily Mail*, July 22, 2010; United Kingdom Office for National Statistics, *U.K. Labour Force Survey* (London: ONS, 2011).

33. P. E. Routassalo et al., "Social Contacts and Their Relationship to Loneliness among Aged People: A Population Based Study," *Gerontology* 52 (2006); R. S. Tilvis et al., "Suffering from Loneliness Indicates Significant Mortality Risk of Older People," *Journal of Aging Research* (2011).

34. Iwasaki et al., "Social Networks and Mortality."

35. When I refer to face-to-face interaction in this book, I don't necessarily mean nose-to-nose and eyeball-to-eyeball, but in the same room or at the same table, interacting with one another.

36. T. W. Valente et al., "Variations in Network Boundary and Type: A Study of Adolescent Peer Influences," *Social Networks* 35, no. 3 (2013).

CHAPTER 1: SWIMMING THROUGH THE SCHOOL OF HARD KNOCKS

1. The exceptions include cancers related to smoking or working with asbestos.

2. Elaine Louie, "After the Years' Ups and Downs, Beginning Again," *New York Times*, December 4, 2011.

3. Reading a draft of this chapter, Dr. Steve Cole, of the UCLA Medical Center, made the following observation: "It is true that social contact bolsters immunity. But the health benefits go far beyond the immune system to include growth of blood vessels, the activation of genes in cells throughout the body, changes in brain function, etc." (personal communication, December 13, 2012).

4. J. S. House, K. R. Landis, and D. Umberson, "Social Relationships and Health," *Science* 241, no. 4865 (1988).

5. In his review of Mukherjee's book, the late Canadian oncologist Robert Buckman wrote: "Just as a car can fail in hundreds of different ways, each of which may need a different type of remedy, so the cancers can be triggered by hundreds of different causative factors, creating (or being created by) many different flaws, and combinations of flaws, in cellular pathways and mechanisms."

6. Though reported rates of breast cancer tend to be highest in Western democracies, developing economies are beginning to catch up. One reason for the disparity in diagnosis rates is that women in countries with spotty or expensive health-care coverage often discover breast tumors only at an advanced stage of growth. As timely access to diagnostic resources such as ultrasounds, mammograms, and biopsies is not available to many women, their breast cancers are not counted in the statistics and seem invisible. Thus the national incidence of the disease may be underreported in these countries.

7. Sandra Levy et al., "Perceived Social Support and Tumor Estrogen/ Progesterone Receptor Status as Predictors of Natural Killer Cell Activity in Breast Cancer Patients," *Psychosomatic Medicine* 52 (1990); David Spiegel et al., "Effects of Psychosocial Treatment in Prolonging Cancer Survival May Be Mediated by Neuroimmune Pathways," *Annals of the New York Academy of Sciences* 840 (1998); K. R. Ell et al., "Social Relations, Social Support and Survival among Patients with Cancer," *Journal of Psychosomatic Research* 36, no. 6 (1992).

8. Peggy Reynolds and George Kaplan, "Social Connections and Risk for Cancer: Prospective Evidence from the Alameda County Study," *Behavioral Medicine* 16, no. 3 (1990).

9. In physician and *New Yorker* writer Atul Gawande's remarkable account of solitary confinement, he cites a US military study of nearly 150 naval aviators who returned from imprisonment and torture in Vietnam; they reported that they had found social isolation far more agonizing and damaging than any of the physical abuse they were subjected to.

Gawande's article reports that prisoners put in "the hole" (solitary confinement) in American prisons, often become psychotic, catatonic, or suicidal when deprived of all social contact. Atul Gawande, "Hellhole: The United States Holds Tens of Thousands of Inmates in Long-Term Solitary Confinement. Is This Torture?" *New Yorker*, March 30, 2009.

10. Richard A. Gibbs, George M. Weinstock, and et al., "Genome Sequence of the Brown Norway Rat Yields Insights into Mammalian Evolution," *Nature* 428 (2004).

11. G. L. Hermes et al., "Social Isolation Dysregulates Endocrine and Behavioral Stress While Increasing Malignant Burden of Spontaneous Mammary Tumors," *Proceedings of the National Academy of Sciences of the United States of America* 106, no. 52 (2009). Martha K. McClintock, Suzanne D. Conzen, Sarah Gehlert, et al., "Mammary Cancer and Social Interactions: Identifying Multiple Environments That Regulate Gene Expression Throughout the Life Span," *Journals of Gerontology Series B*, 60B (2005).

12. J. Bradley Williams et al., "A Model of Gene-Environment Interaction Reveals Altered Mammary Gland Gene Expression and Increased Tumor Growth Following Social Isolation," *Cancer Prevention Research* 2 (2009).

13. K. M. Stavraky et al., "The Effect of Psychosocial Factors on Lung Cancer Mortality at One Year," *Journal of Clinical Epidemiology* 41, no. 1 (1988); Sheldon Cohen, "Social Relationships and Susceptibility to the Common Cold," in *Emotion, Social Relationships, and Health*, ed. Carol D. Ryff and M. Burton (New York: Oxford University Press, 2001).

14. Kroenke et al., "Social Networks, Social Support." Some other studies have tested and not found a strong connection between social support and an improved survival rate after breast cancer, but most of these assessed social support in the form of a clinical intervention—people visited or provided help after the diagnosis as part of a breast cancer treatment plan—and subsequently the experimenters tested whether this (artificial social) contact had a therapeutic effect. Studies such as Kroenke et

al. are more interesting because they mimic real life by testing whether naturally occurring relationships and social networks are protective.

15. Chul-joo Lee, Stacy Wang Gray, and Nehama Lewis, "Internet Use Leads Cancer Patients to Be Active Health Care Consumers," *Patient Education and Counseling* 81, no. 1 (2010).

16. Gunther Eysenbach et al., "Health Related Virtual Communities and Electronic Support Groups: A Systematic Review of the Effects of Online Peer to Peer Interactions," *British Medical Journal* 328, no. 7449 (2004).

17. Cole et al., "Social Regulation of Gene Expression"; S. W. Cole and et al., "Transcript Origin Analysis Identifies Antigen Presenting Cells as Primary Targets of Socially Regulated Gene Expression in Leukocytes," *Proceedings of the National Academy of Sciences of the United States of America* 108 (2011).

18. Cacioppo and Patrick, *Loneliness*; M. A. Distel et al., "Familial Resemblance for Loneliness," *Behavior Genetics* 40, no. 4 (2010); John T. Cacioppo et al., "In the Eye of the Beholder: Individual Differences in Perceived Social Isolation Predict Regional Brain Activation to Social Stimuli," *Journal of Cognitive Neuroscience* 21, no. 1 (2008).

19. D. E. Stewart et al., "Attributions of Cause and Recurrence in Long-Term Breast Cancer Survivors," *Psycho-Oncology* 10, no. 2 (2001).

20. K. A. Phillips et al., "Psychosocial Factors and Survival of Young Women with Breast Cancer: A Population-Based Prospective Cohort Study," *Journal of Clinical Oncology* 26, no. 28 (2008).

21. David Kissane, "Beyond the Psychotherapy and Survival Debate: The Challenge of Social Disparity, Depression and Treatment Adherence in Psychosocial Cancer Care," *Psycho-Oncology* 18, no. 1–5 (2009); D. Kissane et al., "Effect of Cognitive-Existential Group Therapy on Survival in Early-Stage Breast Cancer," *Journal of Clinical Oncology* 22, no. 21 (2004); D. Kissane, "Letting Go of the Hope that Psycho-therapy Prolongs Cancer Survival," *Journal of Clinical Oncology* 25, no. 36 (2007).

22. The only exception to this rule, as Memorial Sloan-Kettering psychiatrist David Kissane points out, is that cancer patients with major depression

are less likely to follow their treatment plans. If you treat their depression they may live longer, because of better compliance with medical advice. See Kissane, "Beyond the Psychotherapy and Survival Debate."

23. Jan Hoffman, "Elizabeth Edwards, Through Many Eyes," *New York Times*, December 12, 2010.

24. Gail Sheehy, "Remembering Elizabeth Edwards," *wowOwow: The Women on the Web*, January 9, 2011, www.womensmedianation.com/items/view/54708; Associated Press, "Elizabeth Edwards' Cancer at a Critical Stage."

25. Stewart et al., "Attributions of Cause and Recurrence."

26. It is interesting that Sylvie attributed the arrival of breast cancer in three consecutive generations of family members to unmanaged stress instead of to the possibility that those women, including herself, were possibly carrying BRCA1, BRCA2, or a series of other genes responsible for about 5% to 10% of all breast cancers, according to the National Institute of Health's website, http://ghr.nlm.nih.gov/condition/breast-cancer.

27. Robert M. Sapolsky, *Why Zebras Don't Get Ulcers: The Acclaimed Guide to Stress, Stress-Related Diseases, and Coping*, 3rd ed. (New York: Henry Holt, 2004), 171.

28. Bert Garssen, "Psychological Factors and Cancer Development: Evidence after 30 Years of Research," *Clinical Psychological Review* 24 (2004); S. O. Dalton et al., "Mind and Cancer: Do Psychological Factors Cause Cancer?" *European Journal of Cancer* 38 (2002); Felicia D. Roberts et al., "Self-Reported Stress and Risk of Breast Cancer," *Cancer* 77, no. 6 (1996).

29. A relationship may exist between two events. And that relationship, even if it's coincidental, contributes to a feeling of control. Refraining from doing something may protect you from a known harm. But removing that one risk doesn't mean that disaster won't happen. For example, we know that drunk drivers can cause horrifying road accidents, but people who have never swallowed a drop of alcohol before getting behind the wheel may still be in a car crash. Similarly, even if we know that face-to-face social support—especially from women—can help

prevent the recurrence of breast cancer, the reverse isn't necessarily true. We can't say that the disease returned because the right support wasn't there. Nor can we say that Elizabeth Edwards's unfair share of life's worst trials, including her husband's humiliating affair, caused her cancer to metastasize.

30. M. Ewertz, "Bereavement and Breast Cancer," *British Journal of Cancer* 53 (1986).

31. In his book on stress and stress-related diseases, *Why Zebras Don't Get Ulcers*, Robert Sapolsky explains it this way: "Very high levels of glucocorticoids will suppress levels of estrogens in females and testosterone in males, and certain types of cancers are stimulated by these hormones (most notably "estrogen-sensitive" forms of breast cancer and "androgen-sensitive" prostate cancers). In these cases, lots of stress equals lots of glucocorticoids equals less estrogen or testosterone equals slower tumor growth" (162).

32. Naja Rod Nielsen et al., "Self-Reported Stress and Risk of Breast Cancer: Prospective Cohort Study," *British Medical Journal* 331, no. 7516 (2005).

33. C. Johansen and J. H. Olsen, "Psychological Stress, Cancer Incidence and Mortality from Non-malignant Diseases," *British Journal of Cancer* 75, no. 1 (1997). In this Danish study more than eleven thousand parents of children who had died of cancer were followed longitudinally. Though they suffered one of the worst trials facing any parent, they were not more likely than other parents to be diagnosed with cancer themselves.

34. Ewertz, "Bereavement and Breast Cancer"; P. Reynolds and G. A. Kaplan, "Social Connections and Risk for Cancer: Prospective Evidence from the Alameda County Study," *Journal of Behavioral Medicine* 16, no. 3 (1990).

35. Reynolds and Kaplan, "Social Connections and Risk for Cancer." The authors of this excellent study note that the cancers most commonly found in women are hormone related and that one of the major risk factors for early death is feeling socially isolated. Interestingly, social support both prompts and is prompted by hormonal activity.

36. Carol D. Ryff et al., "Elective Affinities and Uninvited Agonies"; D. Spiegel and Rachel Kimerling, "Group Psychotherapy"; and Harry T. Reis, "Relationship Experiences and Emotional Well-being," all in *Emotion, Social Relationships, and Health*, ed. Carol D. Ryff and Burton H. Singer (New York: Oxford University Press, 2001); Harry T. Reis, "The Interpersonal Context of Emotions: Gender Differences in Intimacy and Related Behaviors," in *Sex Differences and Similarities in Communication*, ed. D. J. Canary and K. Dindia (Mahwah, NJ: Erlbaum, 1998).

37. T. Seeman et al., "Social Ties and Support and Neuroendocrine Function: MacArthur Studies of Successful Aging," *Annals of Behavioral Medicine* 16 (1994); Carol D. Ryff and Burton H. Singer, "Integrating Emotion into the Study of Social Relationships and Health," in *Emotion, Social Relationships, and Health*, ed. Carol D. Ryff and Burton H. Singer (New York: Oxford University Press, 2001).

38. Carsten K. W. De Dreu, Lindred L. Greer, and et al., "The Neuropeptide Oxytocin Regulates Parochial Altruism in Intergroup Conflict among Humans," *Science* 328, no. 5984 (2010); Angela J. Grippo et al., "Oxytocin Protects against Negative Behavioral and Autonomic Consequences of Long-Term Social Isolation," *Psychoendocrinology* 34 (2009).

39. Mark Granovetter, "The Strength of Weak Ties," *American Journal of Sociology* 78 (1973).

40. Abraham Verghese, *My Own Country: A Doctor's Story* (New York: Vintage, 1994).

41. Sincere thanks go to *Globe and Mail* health reporter and Montreal bureau chief André Picard.

42. Mark Granovetter, "The Strength of Weak Ties: A Network Theory Revisited," *Sociological Theory* 1 (1983).

43. R. F. Baumeister, *Is There Anything Good About Men?* (New York: Oxford University Press, 2010); Joyce Benenson and Anna Heath, "Boys Withdraw More in One-on-One Interactions, Whereas Girls Withdraw More in Groups," *Developmental Psychology* 42, no. 2 (2006); R. F. Baumeister and Kristin Sommer, "What Do Men Want? Gender Differences and Two Spheres of Belongingness," *Psychological Bulletin*

122, no. 1 (1997); Shira Gabriel and Wendi Gardner, "Are There 'His' and 'Hers' Types of Interdependence? The Implications of Gender Differences in Collective versus Relational Interdependence for Affect, Behavior, and Cognition," *Journal of Personality and Social Psychology* 77, no. 3 (1999).

44. Baumeister, *Is There Anything Good About Men?*

45. The live interactions took place via a video feed of the experimenter, who was in the same room, in real time, as two people can't squeeze into one scanner. Elizabeth Redcay et al., "Live Face-to-Face Interaction during fMRI: A New Tool for Social Cognitive Neuroscience," *NeuroImage* 50 (2010).

46. Joshua Fogel et al., "Internet Use and Social Support in Women with Breast Cancer," *Health Psychology* 21, no. 4 (2002).

47. R. Kraut et al., "Internet Paradox: A Social Technology that Reduces Social Involvement and Psychological Well-being?" *American Psychologist* 53, no. 9 (1998); R. Kraut et al., "Internet Paradox Revisited," *Journal of Social Issues* 58, no. 1 (2002).

48. Paula Klemm and Thomas Hardie, "Depression in Internet and Face-to-Face Cancer Support Groups," *Oncology Nursing Forum* 29, no. 4 (2002); Gunther Eysenbach, "The Impact of the Internet on Cancer Outcomes," *Cancer Journal for Clinicians* 53, no. 6 (2003).

49. Norman Nie, D. Sunshine Hillygus, and Lutz Erbring, "Internet Use, Interpersonal Relations, and Sociability: A Time Diary Study," in *The Internet in Everyday Life*, ed. B. Wellman and C. Haythornthwaite (Malden, MA: Blackwell, 2002).

CHAPTER 2: IT TAKES A VILLAGE TO RAISE A CENTENARIAN

1. In *Made in America*, sociologist Claude Fischer delineates three types of places: the private, which is one's home, shared only with intimates; the public, such as main streets, department stores, and plazas; and the parochial, by which he means semi-public places implicitly reserved for group members, such as a particular bar where everybody knows your

name, or a park bench reserved for certain elderly men. He writes: "in the smallest of communities, all the space that is not private may be parochial; locals stare at strangers even on Main Street." That was my experience in Villagrande; I thought I was visiting a "public" village, but unbeknownst to me I was entering what residents considered to be a semi-private space, open primarily to locals and those with direct connections to them. Claude S. Fischer, *Made in America: A Social History of American Culture and Character* (Chicago: University of Chicago Press, 2010).

2. A sex difference in lifespan is not unique to humans. A research team led by Anne Bronikowski at Iowa State University studied how primates age around the world and discovered that the females of nearly all primate species live longer than the males. This is true of humans too, of course. The only exception to this rule in non-human primates is the muriqui monkey of Brazil. "Unlike other primates, muriqui males do not compete with each other for access to females. Instead, they cooperate with each other," explained one of the co-authors of the study, Karen Strier, an anthropologist at the University of Wisconsin. While men in central Sardinia certainly compete for the woman they most desire, as do men in all other cultures, this one non-human primate exception to the gender gap in longevity does pose a question about the life-preserving elements of cooperation within a tight social group—a feature of Sardinian society that may have developed and persisted over millennia of subsistence in an unforgiving social and geographic environment. For more details about primate lifespans, see Anne M. Bronikowski et al., "Aging in the Natural World: Comparative Data Reveal Similar Mortality Patterns across Primates," *Science* 331, no. 6022 (2011).

3. Increased male longevity in Europe, and especially France in recent years, has started to reduce the gender gap in lifespan. France Meslé, "Recent Improvements in Life Expectancy in France: Men Are Starting to Catch Up," *Population Bulletin* 61 (2006); Dr. Giovanni Pes, personal communication, January 2013.

4. Bradley J. Willcox, D. Craig Willcox, and Luigi Ferrucci, "Secrets of Healthy Aging and Longevity from Exceptional Survivors Around the Globe: Lessons from Octogenarians to Supercentenarians," *Journal of Gerontoloy* 63A, no. 11 (2008). I am grateful to Dr. Giovanni Pes, of the University of Sassari, for clarifying the current sex ratios of longevity in the Villagrande region.

5. M. Poulain et al., "Identification of a Geographic Area Characterized by Extreme Longevity in the Sardinia Island: The AKEA Study," *Experimental Gerontology* 39 (2004).

6. Robert Andrews, *The Rough Guide to Sardinia* (New York: Rough Guides, 2007); Philip Carl Salzman, *The Anthropology of Real Life: Events in Human Experience* (Prospect Heights, IL: Waveland Press, 1999).

7. In a lecture on the biology of human behavior recorded in November 2010, the brilliant Stanford biologist Robert Sapolsky explained the relationship between kin selection and altruism as follows: "When something isolates a small subsection of the population, that smaller group will become more inbred. And because then there's a high degree of relatedness, there will be more kin selection. They're all related, so they'll be more cooperative; you will fix that trait of cooperation in the group at a high rate. And then the cooperation, which is a founder-driven trait, will spread outwards. So that's how kin selection turns into reciprocal altruism. A bunch of traits that are lousy in the individual are great for the group." Robert M. Sapolsky, "Molecular Genetics II," *Human Behavioral Biology* (iTunes University, 2010). To read more about kin selection and reciprocal altruism, see Jerome H. Barkow, Leda Cosmides, and John Tooby, *The Adapted Mind: Evolutionary Pscyhology and the Generation of Culture* (New York: Oxford University Press, 1992).

8. Robert Koenig, "Sardinia's Mysterious Male Methuselahs," *Science* 291, no. 5511 (2001); Giuseppe Passarino et al., "Y Chromosome Binary Markers to Study the High Prevalence of Males in Sardinian Centenarians and the Genetic Structure of the Sardinian Population," *Human Heredity* 52 (2001). The village of Villagrande has only two founding mothers, but the number of founding mothers in the Blue

Zone region is somewhat higher (Giovanni Pes, personal communication, January 28, 2013).

9. Anne Marie Herskind et al., "The Heritability of Human Longevity: A Population-Based Study of 2872 Danish Twin Pairs Born 1870–1900," *Human Genetics* 97, no. 3 (1996).

10. Teresa Cabiddu died in January 2013, at the age of 101. Sadly, she did not live long enough to see her name and life story in print.

11. Luisa Salaris, "Sardinian Centenarians: A Lesson from the Past?" paper presented at the International Symposium on Global Longevity, Sunchang, South Korea, 2008.

12. According to Aubrey de Grey, among other prominent scientists working in the area of human aging, animal models clearly suggest that deprivation—specifically, reducing calorie intake—will reduce cell damage and, as a result, aging. "If you feed rodents (or, in fact, a wide variety of other animals) a bit less than they would like, they tend to live longer than if they have as much food as they want. This is not simply because such animals tend to overeat given the chance and become obese: animals that 'eat sensibly' and maintain a constant body weight throughout most of their lives still live less long than those given less food." Aubrey de Grey and Michael Rae, *Ending Aging: The Rejuvenation Breakthroughs that Could Reverse Human Aging in Our Lifetime* (New York: St. Martin's Press, 2007), 24. See also J. F. Trepanowski et al., "Impact of Caloric and Dietary Restriction Regimens on Markers of Health and Longevity in Humans and Animals: A Summary of Available Findings," *Nutrition Journal* 10 (2011). When I consulted Gianni Pes about this issue, he wrote: "The basic idea is that the effect of restriction is effective only in people with excess caloric intake, while in people with normal diet, restriction can cause adverse effects."

13. Lisa Barnes et al., "Effects of Early-Life Adversity on Cognitive Decline in Older African Americans and Whites," *Neurology* 79 (2012).

14. Indeed, Eva moved seven thousand miles away within a year, when she enrolled in a graduate program at the Catholic University of Leuven, in Belgium.

15. T. E. Seeman and L. F. Berkman, "Structural Characteristics of Social Networks and Their Relationship with Social Support in the Elderly: Who Provides Support," *Social Science and Medicine* 26, no. 7 (1988).

16. S. V. Subramanian, F. Elwert, and N. Christakis, "Widowhood and Mortality among the Elderly: The Modifying Role of Neighborhood Concentration of Widowed Individuals," *Social Science and Medicine* 66, no. 4 (2008). Robert Putnam, the Harvard sociologist who wrote about America's declining social capital in his book *Bowling Alone*, has shown that, in the short term, trust and reciprocity take a dive in diverse neighborhoods, as "all races tend to 'hunker down.' Trust (even of one's own race) is lower, altruism and cooperation rarer, friends fewer." Though Putnam writes that diverse communities create a more solid national identity in the long term, in the here and now there is a tradeoff between diversity and the community cohesion—and homogeneity—that promotes longevity. Robert D. Putnam, "E Pluribus Unum—Diversity and Community in the 21st Century: The 2006 Johan Skytte Prize Lecture," *Scandinavian Political Studies* 30, no. 2 (2007).

17. N. Frasure-Smith et al., "Randomized Trial of Home-Based Psychosocial Nursing: Intervention for Patients Recovering from Myocardial Infarction," *Lancet* 350 (1997); Sheldon Cohen and Denise Janicki-Deverts, "Can We Improve Our Physical Health by Altering Our Social Networks?" *Perspectives on Psychological Science* 4, no. 4 (2009).

18. I am grateful to the authors of *The Longevity Project*, Howard S. Friedman and Leslie R. Martin, who distinguish between the typical "disease and treatment" model and the more recent approach to health that focuses on health promotion, prevention, and "wellness." Rebranding the more mundane word *health* as *wellness* was indeed a stroke of genius. Here I deploy the New Age byword a little ironically, to indicate that certain practices or habits typical of a place promote "wellness" even if those practices are firmly rooted in the evolution and biology of our species.

19. Peter Crome, "Forever Young: A Cultural History of Longevity," *British Medical Journal* 328, no. 7454 (2004).

20. B. Jeune and J. Vaupel, eds., *Validation of Exceptional Longevity*, Odense Mongraphs on Population Aging, vol. 6 (Odense: Odense University Press, 1999); Poulain et al., "Identification of a geographic area"; Willcox, Willcox, and Ferrucci, "Secrets of healthy aging and longevity."

21. Mark Mackinnon, "Sad New Reality: Many Elderly Living and Dying Alone," *Globe and Mail*, October 7, 2010.

22. Resveratrol has extended the lifespan of yeasts, worms, fruit flies, and a fish with an average lifespan of two months, but it has not been shown to have a beneficial effect on mammals, including mice, rats, and humans. For evidence (based on aggregate data) on the minimal, if any, impact of diet on longevity in the Blue Zone, see Giovanni Mario Pes et al., "Lifestyle and Nutrition Related to Male Longevity in Sardinia: An Ecological Study," *Nutrition, Metabolism, and Cardiovascular Diseases* 23, no. 3 (2013).

23. Dan Buettner, *The Blue Zones: Lessons for Living Longer from the People Who've Lived the Longest* (Washington, DC: National Geographic, 2008).

24. David Snowdon, *Aging with Grace: What the Nun Study Teaches Us about Leading Longer, Healthier and More Meaningful Lives* (New York: Bantam 2001).

25. K. Lochner, "Social Capital and Neighborhood Mortality Rates in Chicago," *Social Science and Medicine* 56, no. 8 (2003).

26. Salzman, *Anthropology of Real Life*.

27. For an account of the internecine conflicts in the Nuoro region of Sardinia, read "Events on a Mediterranean Island," in Salzman, *Anthropology of Real Life*; Keith Gessen, "The Orange and the Blue: After the Revolution, the Politics of Disenchantment," *New Yorker*, March 1, 2010.

28. Jonathan Safran Foer, *Everything Is Illuminated* (New York: Houghton Mifflin, 2002).

29. J. Cacioppo and William Patrick, *Loneliness: Human Nature and the Need for Social Connection* (New York: Norton, 2008); U.S. Census Bureau Current Population Reports, *U.S. Persons Living Alone, by Sex and Age* (Washington, DC: US Census Bureau, 2010); Pew Research

Center, *Growing Old in America: Expectations vs. Reality* (Washington, DC: PRC, 2009).

30. U.K. Office for National Statistics, *Population Trends 123* (London: Palgrave Macmillan, 2006), http://www.statistics.gov.uk/cci/article.asp ?ID=2665; Statistics Canada, http://www41.statcan.gc.ca/2009/40000 /cybac40000_000-eng.htm.

31. Fischer, *Made in America*.

32. Cognitive psychologist Robin Dunbar, at the University of Oxford, and biological anthropologist Bernard Chapais, at the University of Montreal, are just two evolutionary scientists who pin the development of humans' supercharged neocortex on the need and desire to communicate with each other and to read others' intentions from observations of their behavior at close range.

33. Neenah Ellis, "The Centenarians Show," Third Coast International Audio Festival, 2011, http://thirdcoastfestival.org/library/981-re-sound-143-the-centenarians-show.

34. Also, fewer Termites lived to one hundred compared to other Americans born around 1910. According to the U.S. Social Security Administration, 0.817% (nearly 1%) of Americans born in 1910 lived until their hundredth birthday; the figure for the Termites was closer to 0.3%.

35. Joel N. Shurkin, *Terman's Kids: The Groundbreaking Study of How the Gifted Grow Up* (New York: Little, Brown, 1992).

36. Howard S. Friedman, whose book *The Longevity Project*, written with his colleague Leslie Martin, is the source of much of this information. What wasn't found in their book came from details generously provided by Friedman in email exchanges in May 2011 and December 2012, for which I am grateful. The life expectancy statistics for Americans born in 1910 derive from Social Security Administration data released in April 2011.

37. Working hard won't kill you, but working extremely long hours might well bring on a heart attack in the middle-aged (that is, people from thirty-nine to sixty-two), according to research by University College London epidemiologist Mika Kivimaki and colleagues. Those who

worked eleven hours or more a day were 66% more likely to have a heart attack, and some of those coronary events were fatal. Interestingly, those who worked ten hours or less a day were not at greater risk than those who worked far lighter schedules. Mika Kivimaki et al., "Using Additional Information on Working Hours to Predict Coronary Heart Disease," *Annals of Internal Medicine* 154, no. 7 (2011).

38. Interestingly, the 14% of Alameda County residents who didn't respond were most likely to be old, white, and male. L. F. Berkman and S. L. Syme, "Social Networks, Host Resistance, and Mortality: A Nine-Year Follow-up Study of Alameda County Residents," *American Journal of Epidemiology* 109, no. 2 (1979).

39. J. Holt-Lunstad, T. Smith, and J. B. Layton, "Social Relationships and Mortality Risk: A Meta-anyalytic Review," *PLoS Medicine* 7, no. 7 (2010). A reminder: longitudinal studies monitor what happens to large numbers of people as time progresses, in this case to see whether, subtracting things such as cigarette smoking, income, and education, people's social lives could predict how long they would live.

CHAPTER 3: A THOUSAND INVISIBLE THREADS

1. Michael Inzlicht, Alexa Tullett, and Marie Good, "The Need to Believe: A Neuroscience Account of Religion as a Motivated Process," *Religion, Brain and Behavior* 1, no. 3 (2011); M. McCullough et al., "Does Devoutness Delay Death? Psychological Investment in Religion and Its Association with Longevity in the Terman Sample," *Journal of Personality and Social Psychology* 97, no. 5 (2009); D. E. Hall, "Religious Attendance: More Cost-Effective than Lipitor?" *Journal of the American Board of Family Medicine* 19 (2006); L. H. Powell, L. Shahabi, and C. E. Thoresen, "Religion and Spirituality: Linkages to Physical Health," *American Psychologist* 58 (2003); Arthur Brooks, *Gross National Happiness* (New York: Basic Books, 2008).

2. Elizabeth Corsentino et al., "Religious Attendance Reduces Cognitive Decline among Older Women with High Levels of Depressive Symptoms," *Journal of Gerontology* 64A, no. 12 (2009).

3. Zev Chafets, "Is There a Right Way to Pray?" *New York Times Magazine*, September 20, 2009.

4. Arlie Russell Hochschild, *The Outsourced Self: Intimate Life in Market Times* (New York: Metropolitan Books, 2012).

5. Brooks, *Gross National Happiness*; Paul Bloom, "Does Religion Make You Nice? Does Atheism Make You Mean?" *Slate*, November 7, 2008, http://www.slate.com/articles/life/faithbased/2008/11/does_religion_make_you_nice.html.

6. Azim Shariff and Ara Norenzayan, "God Is Watching You: Priming God Concepts Increases Prosocial Behavior in an Anonymous Economic Game," *Psychological Science* 18, no. 9 (2007); Ara Norenzayan and Azim Shariff, "The Origin and Evolution of Religious Prosociality," *Science* 322 (2008).

7. Melissa Bateson, Daniel Nettle, and Gilbert Roberts, "Cues of Being Watched Enhance Cooperation in a Real-World Setting," *Biology Letters* 2 (2006); Terence C. Burnham and Brian Hare, "Engineering Human Cooperation," *Human Nature* 18, no. 2 (2007).

8. Jingzhi Tan and Brian Hare, "Bonobos Share with Strangers," *PLOS One* 8, no. 1 (2013).

9. Norenzayan and Shariff, "Origin and Evolution of Religious Prosociality."

10. Lionel Tiger and Michael McGuire, *God's Brain* (Amherst, NY: Prometheus, 2010).

11. Robert E. Miller, "Role of Facial Expression in 'Cooperative Avoidance Conditioning' in monkeys," *Journal of Abnormal and Social Psychology* 67, no. 1 (1963); Frans de Waal, *The Age of Empathy* (New York: Three Rivers Press, 2009), 76.

12. Nicholas Wade, "Scientist at Work—Edward O. Wilson: From Ants to Ethics: A Biologist Dreams of Unity of Knowledge," *New York Times*, May 12, 1998; Bert Hölldobler and E. O. Wilson, *The Superorganism: The Beauty, Elegance, and Strangeness of Insect Societies* (New York: Norton, 2009).

On the subject of driving on auto-pilot, I remember watching my father at the wheel of his wood-paneled station wagon as he drove along the highway on summer cross-country driving trips. His mornings began with a cigarette in one hand, an electric razor in the other; the steering wheel was controlled with the inside of his forearms. When my mother poured a cup of scalding coffee from a Thermos and handed it across the armrest, he would take it with the cigarette hand and then hold it steady between his thighs, without spilling it. Then he sipped coffee, shaved, smoked and drove a car, as if this were the most natural thing in the world.

13. With similarly wired though smaller brains than ours, the macaques acted as human stand-ins in this study. Though animal rights activists might object, electrodes are also often implanted in humans to treat epilepsy and Parkinson's disease. There may be other therapeutic applications to such basic research, including promoting mobility in amputees or those with spinal cord injuries.

14. Marco Iacoboni, *Mirroring People: The Science of Empathy and How We Connect with Others* (New York: Picador, 2008).

15. Ibid.

16. In *The Age of Empathy*, Frans de Waal points out that, remarkably, children on the autistic spectrum are immune to the yawns of others, which is just one sign that they don't perceive social signals the same way as "neurotypicals." De Waal, *Age of Empathy*.

17. Iacoboni, *Mirroring People*; Seymour M. Berger and Suzanne W. Hadley, "Some Effects of a Model's Performance on an Observer's Electromyographic Activity," *American Journal of Psychology* 88, no. 2 (1975).

18. Jared Curhan and Alex Pentland, "Thin Slices of Negotiation: Predicting Outcomes from Conversational Dynamics Within the First Five Minutes," *Journal of Applied Psychology* 92, no. 3 (2007); Alex Pentland, *Honest Signals: How They Shape Our World* (Cambridge, MA: MIT Press, 2008).

19. Shankar Vedantam, *The Hidden Brain* (New York: Spiegel & Grau, 2010).

20. I am indebted to *Philadelphia Enquirer* columnist and bird enthusiast Scott Weidensaul for the evocative phrase "silent signal of alarm," and

to my nineteen-year-old son Eric, who pointed out this book to me and knows more than I ever will about sandpipers, godwits, shanks, and phalaropes, and many other things to boot. Scott Weidensaul, *Living on the Wind: Across the Hemisphere with Migratory Birds* (New York: North Point Press, 1999), 7.

21. Michael Kesterton, "A Choir of Whales," *Globe and Mail*, August 12, 2010; Michael D. Hoffman, Newell Garfield, and Roger W. Bland, "Frequency Synchronization of Blue Whale Calls near Pioneer Seamount," *Journal of the Acoustical Society of America* 128, no. 1 (2010).

22. John Cassidy, "Rational Irrationality: The Real Reason that Capitalism Is So Crash-Prone," *New Yorker*, October 5, 2009.

23. Jamaica Kincaid, *Annie John* (New York: Farrar, Straus, and Giroux, 1983).

24. Leonard Weller and Aron Weller, "Human Menstrual Synchrony: A Critical Assessment," *Neuroscience and Biobehavioral Reviews* 17 (1993); Deborah Blum, "The Scent of Your Thoughts," *Scientific American*, October 2011; Martha K. McClintock, "Menstrual Synchrony and Suppression," *Nature* 229 (1971).

25. Geoffrey Miller, Joshua M. Tybur, and Brent D. Jordan, "Ovulatory Cycle Effects on Tip Earnings by Lap Dancers: Economic Evidence for Human Estrus," *Evolution and Human Behavior* 28 (2007).

26. Daniel S. Hamermesh, *Beauty Pays* (Princeton: Princeton University Press, 2011); Daniel S. Hamermesh and Jeff Biddle, "Beauty and the Labor Market," NBER Working Paper 4518 (Cambridge, MA: National Bureau of Economic Research, 1993); Susan Pinker, *The Sexual Paradox: Extreme Men, Gifted Women, and the Real Gender Gap* (Toronto: Random House Canada, 2008); John Marshall Townsend, *What Women Want—What Men Want* (New York: Oxford University Press, 1998).

27. Ilyana Kuziemko, "Is Having Babies Contagious? Estimating Fertility Peer Effects between Siblings," Harvard University, 2006.

28. Margaret Talbot, "Red Sex, Blue Sex: Why Do So Many Evangelical Teen-agers Become Pregnant?" *New Yorker*, November 3, 2008.

29. Ibid.; Mark Regnerus and Jeremy Uecker, *Premarital Sex in America: How Young Americans Meet, Mate, and Think about Marrying* (New York: Oxford University Press, 2011).

30. Mark Regnerus, *Forbidden Fruit: Sex and Religion in the Lives of American Teenagers* (New York: Oxford University Press, 2007); Peter Bearman and Hannah Bruckner, "The Relationship between Virginity Pledges in Adolescence and STD Acquisition in Young Adulthood," paper presented at the National STD Conference, Philadelphia, March 8–11, 2004.

31. Talbot, "Red Sex, Blue Sex"; Regnerus, *Forbidden Fruit*.

32. Nicholas A. Christakis and James Fowler, *Connected: The Surprising Power of Our Social Networks and How They Shape Our Lives* (New York: Little, Brown, 2009).

33. Robert E. Bartholomew, "Ethnocentricity and the Social Construction of 'Mass Hysteria,'" *Culture, Medicine and Psychiatry* 14, no. 4 (1990); Halley Faust and Lawrence Brilliant, "Is the Diagnosis of 'Mass Hysteria' an Excuse for Incomplete Investigation of Low-Level Environmental Contamination?" *Journal of Occupational Medicine* 23, no. 1 (1981).

CHAPTER 4: WHO'S COMING TO DINNER?

1. N. A. Christakis and J. H. Fowler, "The Spread of Obesity in a Large Social Network over 32 Years," *New England Journal of Medicine* 357, no. 4 (2007); Nicholas A. Christakis and James Fowler, *Connected: The Surprising Power of Our Social Networks and How They Shape Our Lives* (New York: Little, Brown, 2009).

2. With this finding, the Colbert-meme tester had himself become a meme. James H. Fowler, "The Colbert Bump in Campaign Donations: More Truthful than Truthy," *Political Science and Politics* 41, no. 3 (2008); Food Research and Action Center, "Overweight and Obesity in the U.S.," 2012, http://frac.org/initiatives/hunger-and-obesity/obesity-in-the-us/.

3. James H. Fowler, Jaime E. Settle, and Nicholas A. Christakis, "Correlated Genotypes in Friendship Networks," *Proceedings of the National Academy of Sciences of the United States of America* 108, no. 5 (2011).

4. Christakis and Fowler, *Connected*.

5. Justin G. Trogdon, James Nonnemaker, and Joanne Pais, "Peer Effects in Adolescent Overweight," *Journal of Health Economics* 27 (2008); Ethan Cohen-Cole and Jason M. Fletcher, "Is Obesity Contagious? Social Networks vs. Environmental Factors in the Obesity Epidemic," *Journal of Health Economics* 27 (2008); Russell Lyons, "The Spread of Evidence-Poor Medicine via Flawed Social Network Analysis," *Statisics, Politics and Policy* 2, no. 1 (2011).

6. S. J. Salvy et al., "Effects of Social Influence on Eating in Couples, Friends and Strangers," *Appetite* 49, no. 1 (2007); S. J. Salvy et al., "The Presence of Friends Increases Food Intake in Youth," *American Journal of Clinical Nutrition* 90, no. 2 (2009).

7. Natalie Munro and Leore Grosman, "Early Evidence (ca. 12,000 B.P.) for Feasting at a Burial Cave in Israel," *Proceedings of the National Academy of Sciences of the United States of America* 107, no. 35 (2010).

8. Ibid.; Heather Pringle, "Ancient Sorcerer's 'Wake' Was First Feast for the Dead?" *National Geographic Daily News*, August 30, 2010, http://news.nationalgeographic.com/news/2010/08/100830-first-feast-science-proceedings-israel-shaman-sorcerer-tortoise/.

9. Carol Vogel, "Stuff that Defines Us: The British Museum Chooses 100 Objects to Distill the History of the World," *New York Times*, October 30, 2011; Neil MacGregor, *A History of the World in 100 Objects* (London: Allen Lane, 2010).

10. J. Cacioppo and William Patrick, *Loneliness: Human Nature and the Need for Social Connection* (New York: Norton, 2008).

11. Volkhard Knigge, Rikola-Gunnar Lüttgenau, and Jens-Christian Wagner, eds., "Forced Labor: The Germans, the Forced Laborers and the War," companion volume to traveling exhibition, Jewish Museum of Berlin (Weimar: Buchenwald and Mittelbau-Dora Memorials Foundation, 2010).

12. The same forces are at work in the ugly anti-immigrant sentiment that came alive in the United States and Europe in the post-2008 financial crisis period. As people began to fear for their jobs and their pensions, hostility toward Mexicans in the U.S. and Turkish and North African

immigrants in northern Europe heated up. Chillingly, anti-Semitic incidents also increased, according to the Simon Wiesenthal Institute.

13. Jared Diamond, *The World Until Yesterday: What Can We Learn from Traditional Societies?* (New York: Penguin, 2012).

14. Isabel Wilkerson, *The Warmth of Other Suns: The Epic Story of America's Great Migration* (New York: Random House, 2010).

15. Louise Hawkley, Kipling D. Williams, and J. Cacioppo, "Responses to Ostracism across Adulthood," *Scan* 6 (2011); Tyler F. Stillman et al., "Alone and Without Purpose: Life Loses Meaning Following Social Exclusion," *Journal of Experimental Social Psychology* 45 (2009).

16. Twice as high as girls' rates, suicide rates for teenage boys have nonetheless dropped by a third since 1980, while those of girls have risen by the same proportion in Canada during that time (in the U.S. and the U.K. they'd increased for both sexes as of 2000). Robin Skinner and Steven McFaull, "Suicide among Children and Adolescents in Canada: Trends and Sex Differences, 1980–2008," *Canadian Medical Association Journal* (2012); Ingrid Peritz and Karen Howlett, "High School Taunts Push Another Teenager to Suicide," *Globe and Mail*, December 1, 2011.

17. N. I. Eisenberger, M. D. Lieberman, and K. D. Williams, "Does Rejection Hurt? An fMRI Study of Social Exclusion," *Science* 302 (2003); N. I. Eisenberger and M. D. Lieberman, "Why Rejection Hurts: A Common Neural Alarm System for Physical and Social Pain," *Trends in Cognitive Science* 8, no. 7 (2004); N. I. Eisenberger, "The Pain of Social Disconnection: Examining the Shared Neural Underpinnings of Physical and Social Pain," *Nature Reviews Neuroscience* (2012); Carrie L. Masten et al., "Neural Correlates of Social Exclusion during Adolescence: Understanding the Distress of Peer Rejection," *Scan* 4 (2009); George Slavich et al., "Neural Sensitivity to Social Rejection Is Associated with Inflammatory Responses to Social Stress," *Proceedings of the National Academy of Sciences of the United States of America* 107, no. 33 (2010).

18. Atul Gawande, "Hellhole: The United States Holds Tens of Thousands of Inmates in Long-Term Solitary Confinement. Is This Torture?" *New Yorker*, March 30, 2009.

19. Lisa Harnack et al., "Guess Who's Cooking: The Role of Men in Meal Planning, Shopping, and Preparation in US Families," *Journal of the American Dietetic Association* 98, no. 9 (1998). An alternative explanation is provided by Richard Wrangham, who argues that the advent of cooking, approximately one million years ago, was one of the catalysts that sparked sexual divisions around food (I am grateful to my brother Steve for pointing this out). Richard Wrangham, *Catching Fire: How Cooking Made Us Human* (New York: Basic Books, 2009).

20. Bernard Chapais, *Primeval Kinship: How Pair-Bonding Gave Birth to Human Society* (Cambridge, MA: Harvard University Press, 2008); Patrick Bélisle and Bernard Chapais, "Tolerated Co-feeding in Relation to Degree of Kinship in Japanese Macaques," *Behavior* 138 (2001). Details about this research project were also gleaned from Bernard Chapais (personal communication, November 11, 2011). Note also that "Hamilton's rule" is apt in this discussion about sharing and tolerated co-feeding. In 1964 William D. Hamilton came up with a theory that was the precursor of modern sociobiology. Using a mathematical formula, it predicts that animals, including humans, will help other members of their species with food, assistance, or other precious resources according to their degree of relatedness. Thus, though an altruistic gift might decrease the odds of survival and prosperity for the donor, it will increase the reproductive fitness of the recipient—one reason why gifts often flow from grandparents to grandchildren. The seniors' opportunity to reproduce may be long past, but their chance to increase the survival and reproductive odds of their children or their children's children is very much in the present. Those who are more altruistic toward closely related kin will ultimately ensure that more of their genes persist and survive. For more on Hamilton's rule, see David M. Buss, ed., *The Handbook of Evolutionary Psychology* (Hoboken, NJ: Wiley, 2005).

21. Sue C. Carter and Stephen W. Porges, "Social Bonding and Attachment," in *Encyclopedia of Behavioural Neuroscience*, vol. 3 (New York: Elsevier, 2010); S. E. Taylor, "Tend and Befriend: Biobehavioral

Bases of Affiliation under Stress," *Current Directions in Psychological Science* 15, no. 6 (2006).

22. The brain regions activated by such social behavior in women (as tested by the Prisoner's Dilemma game) include the nucleus accumbens, the caudate nucleus, the ventromedial frontal orbital cortex, and the rostral anterior cingulate cortex. James Rilling et al., "A Neural Basis for Social Cooperation," *Neuron* 35 (2002).

23. Eisenberger, Lieberman, and Williams, "Does Rejection Hurt?"

24. Manos Tsakiris, "Looking for Myself: Current Multisensory Input Alters Self-Face Recognition," *PLOS One* 3, no. 12 (2008).

25. For women's sensitivity to others' cues, see Geoffry Hall et al., "Sex Differences in Functional Activation Patterns Revealed by Increased Emotion Processing Demands," *Neuroreport* 15, no. 2 (2004); Turhan Canli and et al., "Sex Differences in the Neural Basis of Emotional Memories," *Proceedings of the National Academy of Sciences of the United States of America* 99, no. 16 (2002); R. J. Erwin et al., "Facial Emotion Discrimination," *Psychiatry Research* 42, no. 3 (1992); David C. Geary, *Male, Female: The Evolution of Human Sex Differences* (Washington, DC: American Psychological Association, 2010); M. L. Hoffman, "Sex Differences in Empathy and Related Behaviors," *Psychological Bulletin* 84, no. 712–22 (1977); M. R. Gunnar and M. Donahue, "Sex Differences in Social Responsiveness between Six and Twelve Months," *Child Development* 51 (1980); Susan Pinker, *The Sexual Paradox: Extreme Men, Gifted Women, and the Real Gender Gap* (Toronto: Random House Canada, 2008).

26. Salvy et al., "Effects of Social Influence"; Salvy et al., "The Presence of Friends."

27. Trogdon, Nonnemaker, and Pais, "Peer Effects in Adolescent Overweight." Interestingly, peers can also suppress eating in overweight teenagers, according to Sarah-Jeanne Salvy, who has shown that obese kids eat less when their normal-weight friends are around and more when they're with other overweight kids or alone. S. J. Salvy, E. Kieffer, and L. H. Epstein, "Effects of Social Context on Overweight

and Normal-Weight Children's Food Selection," *Eating Behaviors* 9, no. 2 (2008).

28. Christakis and Fowler, "The Spread of Obesity." The way wives' waistlines affect their husbands' belt size is indeed not all about who is doing the shopping and cooking, especially if you consider studies of couvade, or pregnancy-related symptoms experienced by the male partners of pregnant women. They show that somewhere between 20% and 80% of men experience some weight gain as their wife's pregnancy progresses. One hypothesis is that the more empathic the man is, the more weight he puts on.

29. Marla E. Eisenberg et al., "Correlations between Family Meals and Psychosocial Well-being among Adolescents," *Archives of Pediatric Adolescent Medicine* 158 (2004); M. E. Eisenberg et al., "Family Meals and Substance Use: Is There a Long-Term Protective Association?" *Journal of Adolescent Health* 43, no. 2 (2008); Susan K. Hamilton and Jane Hamilton Wilson, "Family Mealtimes: Worth the Effort?" *Infant, Child and Adolescent Nutrition* 1 (2009); C. Snow and D. Beals, "Mealtime Talk that Supports Literacy Development," *New Directions in Child and Adolescent Development* 111 (2006); Debra Franko et al., "What Mediates the Relationship between Family Meals and Adolescent Health Issues," *Health Psychology* 27, no. 2 (2008); D. Neumark-Sztainer et al., "Family Meals and Disordered Eating in Adolescents: Longitudinal Findings from Project EAT," *Archives of Pediatrics and Adolescent Medicine* 162, no. 1 (2008).

30. Guang Guo, Michael Roettger, and Tianji Cai, "The Integration of Genetic Propensities into Social-Control Models of Delinquency and Violence among Male Youths," *American Sociological Review* 73 (2008); Maggie Fox, "Good Parenting Overrides Bad Behavior Genes," *Globe and Mail*, July 16, 2008.

31. Stephanie Coontz, "Why Gender Equality Stalled," *New York Times*, February 17, 2013.

32. Barbara Fiese et al., "A Review of 50 Years of Research on Naturally Occurring Family Routines and Rituals," *Journal of Family Psychology* 16, no. 4 (2002).

33. Snow and Beals, "Mealtime Talk."

34. Zehava Oz Weizman and Catherine E. Snow, "Lexical Output as Related to Children's Vocabulary Acquisition: Effects of Sophisticated Exposure and Support for Meaning," *Developmental Psychology* 37, no. 2 (2001).

35. Deb Roy, "New Horizons in the Study of Child Language Acquisition," paper presented at the International Speech Communication Association Proceedings of Interspeech conference, Brighton, UK, 2009; Susan Pinker, "Someone to Watch Over Me," *Globe and Mail*, December 13, 2008; Brandon Roy, research scientist and doctoral student in the MIT media lab, email received November 21, 2011.

36. Weizman and Snow, "Lexical Output."

37. Roy, "New Horizons"; Janellen Huttenlocher et al., "Early Vocabulary Growth: Relation to Language Input and Gender," *Developmental Psychology* 27 (1991).

38. Alison Gopnik, *The Philosophical Baby: What Children's Minds Tell Us about Truth, Love, and the Meaning of Life* (New York: Farrar, Straus and Giroux, 2009).

39. In 2007 a nasty controversy arose when University of Washington developmental psychologists Frederick Zimmerman and Andrew Meltzoff, along with physician Dimitri Christakis, published an article in the *Journal of Pediatrics* showing that babies and toddlers under two who watched so-called educational videos and DVDs, such as Baby Einstein or Brainy Baby, had poor vocabulary skills on a standardized language development test. The researchers reported that for each hour of baby DVD/video watching, there was a decrease of six to eight words (out of the ninety words tested) in the baby's vocabulary—a huge effect. "Although reading every day as opposed to less often is associated with about a 7 point increase in the normed CDI score [the standardized language test used], watching one hour per day of baby DVDs/videos as opposed to none is associated with about a 17-point decrease." The authors asserted that the claims made by commercial baby DVD companies that their products boosted infants' cognitive skills were not only unsupported by

the evidence but were contradicted by their study. One consequence was that Baby Einstein, owned by the Walt Disney Company, changed its publicity and offered a refund to any consumers unhappy with its products. F. J. Zimmerman, D. A. Christakis, and Andrew Melttzoff, "Associations between Media Viewing and Language Development in Children under Age 2 Years," *Journal of Pediatrics* (2007).

40. Social and emotional development has to be tied to the word *intelligence* for it to get any respect.

41. Eisenberg et al., "Family Meals and Substance Use."

42. Neumark-Sztainer et al., "Family Meals and Disordered Eating."

43. Eisenberg et al., "Family Meals and Substance Use."

44. Eisenberg et al., "Correlations between Family Meals."

45. Family dinners early in life being linked to academic success later is an example of a positive correlation: when one factor goes up, the other one also rises. A negative correlation describes what happens when one factor rises and the other factor falls, such as more family dinners at age seven predicting fewer cigarettes smoked at age seventeen.

46. Block parties and "traveling dinners"—where neighbors transit from one house to the next for each of four courses (appetizers, soup, main course, and dessert) in order to become acquainted with each other—are supplanting the role that church, extended family, and volunteering stay-at-home mothers used to play in helping people form social bonds. See Marcus Gee, "Toronto Woman Breaks Bread with Strangers and Finds a Community," *Globe and Mail*, November 17, 2009.

47. Kelly Musick and Ann Meier, "Assessing Causality and Persistence in Associations between Family Dinners and Adolescent Well-being," *Journal of Marriage and Family* 74, no. 3 (2012); Ann Meier and Kelly Musick, "Variation in Associations between Family Dinners and Adolescent Well-being," *Journal of Marriage and Family* 76, no. 1 (2014).

48. Franko et al., "What Mediates the Relationship."

49. Snow and Beals, "Mealtime Talk"; Vibeke Aukrust and C. Snow, "Narratives and Explanations during Mealtime Conversations in Norway and the U.S.," *Language in Society* 27, no. 2 (1998).

50. Adam Gilden Tsai and Thomas A. Wadden, "Systematic Reveiw: An Evaluation of Major Commercial Weight Loss Programs in the United States," *Annals of Internal Medicine* 142, no. 1 (2005); Stanley Heshka et al., "Weight Loss with Self-Help Compared with a Structured Commercial Program: A Randomized Trial," *Journal of the American Medical Association* 289, no. 14 (2003).

51. Linda Mercandante, *Victims and Sinners* (Westminster: John Knox Press, 1996).

52. Chris Norris, "Hitting Bottom," *New York Times Magazine*, January 3, 2010.

53. Salvy et al., "The Presence of Friends"; Thomas J. Dishion, D. W. Andrew, and L. Crosby, "Antisocial Boys and Their Friends in Early Adolescence: Relationship Characteristics, Quality, and Interactional Process," *Child Development* 66 (1995); N. A. Christakis and J. H. Fowler, "The Collective Dynamics of Smoking in a Large Social Network," *New England Journal of Medicine* 358, no. 21 (2008).

54. J. Niels Rosenquist et al., "The Spread of Alcohol Consumption Behavior in a Large Social Network," *Annals of Internal Medicine* 152, no. 7 (2010).

55. Bryan Curtis, "Man-Cave Masculinity," *Slate*, October 3, 2011.

56. Daniel Okrent, *Last Call: The Rise and Fall of Prohibition* (New York: Scribner, 2010). 340–41.

CHAPTER 5: BABY CHEMISTRY

1. Sue Carter, a neuroscientist whose research revealed the powerful impact of neuropeptides such as oxytocin on pair bonding in prairie voles, has shown that oxytocin not only facilitates birth, lactation, social trust, and the formation of social bonds among mammals, but it also promotes the ability to sit still. And it's a two-way street. These activities both promote oxytocin release (and immobility) and require it. When oxytocin is given artificially, it enhances "the capacity for immobility." C. Sue Carter et al., "Consequences of Early Experiences and Exposure to Oxytocin and Vasopressin Are Sexually Dimorphic," *Developmental Neuroscience* 31 (2009).

2. Cria Perrine, "Breastfeeding Report Card—United States 2011," Centers for Disease Control and Prevention, 2011, http://www.cdc.gov /breastfeeding/pdf/2011breastfeedingreportcard.pdf.

3. Hanna Rosin, "The Case Against Breast-Feeding," *The Atlantic*, April 2009.

4. Sarah Bosely, "Six Months of Breastmilk Alone Is Too Long and Could Harm Babies, Scientists Now Say," *The Guardian*, January 14, 2011; Mary Fewtrell et al., "When to Wean? How Good Is the Evidence for Six Months of Exclusive Breastfeeding?" *British Medical Journal* 342 (2011).

5. Rosin, "The Case Against Breast-Feeding."

6. A little more than half of Canadian mothers (51%) are breastfeeding their babies exclusively at three months postpartum, and the same proportion persist with some breastfeeding at six months of age. At six months of age, the rates of any breastfeeding in the United Kingdom are half that (21%)—and closer to the American rates. Beverley Chalmers and Catherine Royale, eds., *What Mothers Say: The Canadian Maternity Experiences Survey* (Ottawa: Public Health Agency of Canada, 2009).

7. Breastfeeding has also been said to protect against obesity, asthma, diabetes, eczema, heart disease, and various cancers in babies, but the evidence for that is more controversial. And non-nutritional influences may be spinning the dice regarding the link between breastfeeding and intelligence. These days, well-educated mothers are the ones most likely to breastfeed their babies, so the cognitive boons associated with the practice may have more to do with the mother's genetic, socioeconomic, and educational background—and with the increased time and attention she gives her baby—than with the biochemical composition of breast milk per se. Geoff Der, G. David Batty, and Ian J. Deary, "Effect of Breast Feeding on Intelligence in Children: Prospective Study, Sibling Pairs Analysis and Meta-analysis," *British Medical Journal* (2006); A. Sacker et al., "Breast Feeding and Intergenerational Social Mobility: What Are the Mechanisms?" *Archives of Disease in Childhood* 98 (2013); K. Heikkila et

al., "Breast Feeding and Child Behaviour in the Millennium Cohort Study," *Archives of Disease in Childhood* 96 (2011).

8. Jill Lepore, "Baby Food: If Breast Is Best, Why Are Women Bottling Their Milk?" *New Yorker*, January 19, 2009.

9. Michael S. Kramer et al., "Breastfeeding and Child Cognitive Development: New Evidence from a Large Randomized Trial," *Archives of General Psychiatry* 65, no. 5 (2008); Michael S. Kramer et al., "Promotion of Breastfeeding Intervention Trial (PROBIT): A Randomized Trial in the Republic of Belarus," *Journal of the American Medical Association* 285, no. 4 (2001).

    Interestingly, a study published by psychologist Avshalom Caspi and his colleagues in 2007 has shown that breastfeeding only boosts intelligence in children possessing certain gene variants, providing evidence that environmental influences like breastfeeding have the effect of "switching on" certain genes—while having almost no impact on those who haven't been dealt that genetic hand. Avshalom Caspi et al., "Moderation of breastfeeding effects on the IQ by genetic variation in fatty acid metabolism," *PNAS Proceedings of the National Academy of Sciences of the United States of America* 104, no. 47 (2007).

10. Kramer mentioned one exception to his statement that there are no good data showing a cognitive effect deriving from the components of human breast milk. One study of preemies, done by Alan Lucas and his colleagues at University College London in the early nineties, found that premature babies fed banked breast milk through a gastric tube showed later cognitive gains (at ages seven to eight) compared to those who received preterm formula. The authors point out that one reason this might be true of premature infants in particular is that "they may be especially sensitive to early nutrition" compared to full-term babies, whose neurodevelopment is comparatively more mature at birth. Alan Lucas et al., "Breast Milk and Subsequent Intelligence Quotient in Children Born Preterm," *Lancet* 339 (1992).

11. Melvin Konner, *The Evolution of Childhood: Relationships, Emotion, Mind* (Cambridge, MA: Belknap Press, 2010); A. N. Meltzoff and M. K

Moore, "Imitation of Facial and Manual Gestures by Human Neonates," *Science* 198 (1997).

12. Social interaction is so critical for human development that infants placed in orphanages, where they spend hours alone in their cribs, experience developmental delays even though they are provided with other life essentials such as food, formula, and water. Over history, including most of the twentieth century, children have paid a high price for the common omission of social contact as a prerequisite for human development and survival.

13. Our primate ancestors mastered this trick too, though in reverse. By recording and playing back sound clips of different juveniles in distress, Dorothy Cheney and Robert Seyfarth, a husband-and-wife primatology team, discovered that adult female vervet monkeys and baboons can pick out their own offspring's calls from all the others (the point at which they started moving with great purpose toward the loudspeaker). Adult females not only recognized their own offspring's alarm calls but would look intently at another mother whose child's screams they'd just heard. Dorothy L. Cheney and Robert M. Seyfarth, *Baboon Metaphysics: The Evolution of a Social Mind* (Chicago: University of Chicago Press, 2007).

14. Maude Beauchemin et al., "Mother and Stranger: An Electrophysiological Study of Voice Processing in Newborns," *Cerebral Cortex* 21, no. 8 (2011); Anne McIlroy, "Infants Give Mother Tongue New Meaning," *Globe and Mail*, December 17, 2010; William Raillant-Clark, "Mom's Voice Plays Special Role in Activating Newborn's Brain," *Forum* [University of Montreal], December 16, 2010.

15. Patricia Kuhl, "Is Speech Learning 'Gated' by the Social Brain?" *Developmental Science* 10, no. 1 (2007); Michael H. Goldstein, Andrew P. King, and Meredith J. West, "Social Interaction Shapes Babbling," *Proceedings of the National Academy of Sciences of the United States of America* 100, no. 13 (2003).

16. In an amazing experiment designed to test when babies lose the ability to distinguish sounds that don't exist in their native language (e.g., the *p/b* distinctions that Spanish speakers hear but adult native English speakers

don't), Patricia Kuhl exposed nine-month-olds from English homes to someone speaking to them in Mandarin. As Perri Klass reported in her *New York Times* column, "Exposing English-language infants in Seattle to someone speaking to them in Mandarin helped those babies preserve the ability to discriminate Chinese language sounds, but when the same 'dose' of Mandarin was delivered by a television program or an audiotape, the babies learned nothing." Perri Klass, "Hearing Bilingual: How Babies Sort Out Language," *New York Times*, October 11, 2011.

Patricia Kuhl, Feng-Ming Tsao, and Huei-Mei Liu, "Foreign-language experience in infancy: Effects of short-term exposure and social interaction on phonetic learning," PNAS *Proceedings of the National Academy of Sciences of the United States of America* 100, no. 15 (2003).

17. Joni N. Saby, Andrew N. Meltzoff, and Peter J. Marshall, "Infants' Somatotopic Neural Responses to Seeing Human Actions: I've Got You Under My Skin," *PLOS One* 8, no. 10 (2013); Joni N. Saby, Peter J. Marshall, and Andrew Meltzoff, "Neural Correlates of Being Imitated: An EEG Study in Preverbal Infants," *Social Neuroscience* 7, no. 6 (2012). Thanks are due to Andrew Meltzoff for taking the time to explain his recent work and send me these studies.

18. Deborah Blum, *Love at Goon Park: Harry Harlow and the Science of Affection* (Cambridge, MA: Perseus, 2002).

19. Ibid.; Luther Emmett Holt, *The Care and Feeding of Children: A Catechism for the Use of Mothers and Children's Nurses* (New York: D. Appleton, 1907).

20. Nicholas D. Kristof, "A Poverty Solution that Starts with a Hug," *New York Times*, January 7, 2012.

21. Holt, *The Care and Feeding of Children*.

22. C. Celeste Johnston, Marsha Campbell-Yeo, and Francoise Filion, "Paternal vs Maternal Kangaroo Care for Procedural Pain in Preterm Neonates: A Randomized Crossover Trial," *Archives of Pediatric Adolescent Medicine* 165, no. 9 (2011).

23. Celeste Johnston is one of the swim-team friends first mentioned in Chapter 1 as having played a key role in Sylvie's face-to-face social

network. Like a number of female social scientists, she sustains a deep academic interest in social bonds while investing in a rich personal network of her own.

24. Kerstin Erlandsson et al., "Skin to Skin Care with the Father after Cesarean Birth and Its Effect on Newborn Crying and Prefeeding Behavior," *Birth: Issues in Perinatal Care* 34, no. 2 (2007).

25. Monica Krayneck, Mona Patterson, and Christina Westbrook, "Baby Cuddlers Make a Difference," *Journal of Obstetric, Gynecologic and Neonatal Nursing* 41, no. 1 (2012); Harvard Medical School Beth Israel Deaconess Medical Center, "NICU Programs Benefit Premature Babies and Their Parents," July 2010, http://www.bidmc.org/YourHealth/HealthNotes/ObstetricsandGynecology/HighRiskOB/NICUProgramsBenefitPrematureBabiesandTheirParents.aspx.

26. Susan Pinker, *The Sexual Paradox: Extreme Men, Gifted Women, and the Real Gender Gap* (Toronto: Random House Canada, 2008); Ruth Feldman et al., "Comparison of Skin-to-Skin (Kangaroo) and Traditional Care: Parenting Outcomes and Preterm Infant Development," *Pediatrics* 110, no. 1 (2002).

27. I am indebted to Alison Gopnik, who reminded me of the importance of alloparenting when describing the effects of touch and intimate social contact on the developing brain. Sarah Blaffer Hrdy, *Mothers and Others: The Evolutionary Origins of Mutual Understanding* (Cambridge, MA: Bellknap Press, 2009); Sarah Blaffer Hrdy, "Comes the Child Before Man: Development's Role in Producing Selectable Variation," *Evolutionary Anthropology* 21 (2012); Kristen Hawkes, "What Makes Us Human? Grandmothers and Their Consequences," *Evolutionary Anthropology* 21 (2012).

28. Evalotte Morelius, Elvar Theodorsson, and Nina Nelson, "Salivary Cortisol and Mood and Pain Profiles during Skin-to-Skin Care for an Unselected Group of Mothers and Infants in Neonatal Intensive Care," *Pediatrics* 116, no. 5 (2005); N. M. Hurst et al., "Skin-to-Skin Holding in the Neonatal Intensive Care Unit Influences Maternal Milk Volume," *Journal of Perinatology* 17, no. 3 (1997).

29. In one Israeli study that compared a group of seventy-three preemies and their mothers who practiced kangaroo care with a matched group of seventy-three preemies whose mothers did not, psychologist Ruth Feldman and her colleagues discovered that kangaroo care shortly after birth boosts the baby's cognitive development six months later. Feldman et al., "Comparison of Skin-to-Skin (Kangaroo) and Traditional Care."

30. Craig Howard Kinsley and Elizabeth Meyer, "Maternal Mentality: Pregnancy and Childbirth Shape a Woman's Mental Makeover," *Scientific American Mind*, July/August 2011; C. H. Kinsley et al., "Motherhood Induces and Maintains Behavioral and Neural Plasticity across the Lifespan in the Rat," *Archives of Sexual Behavior* 37 (2008); A. S. Fleming and M. Korsmit, "Plasticity in the Maternal Circuit: Effects of Maternal Experience on Fos-Lir in Hypothalamic, Limbic and Cortical Structures in the Postpartum Rat," *Behavioral Neuroscience* 110 (1996).

31. Pilyoung Kim et al., "The Plasticity of the Human Maternal Brain: Longitudinal Changes in Brain Anatomy during the Early Postpartum Period," *Behavioral Neuroscience* 124, no. 5 (2010).

32. Kinsley and Meyer, "Maternal Mentality"; Kim et al., "The Plasticity of the Human Maternal Brain."

33. Gloria K. Mak and Samuel Weiss, "Paternal Recognition of Adult Offspring Mediated by Newly Generated CNS Neurons," *Nature Neuroscience* 13 (2010).

34. Stephen Jay Gould, "A Biological Homage to Mickey Mouse," in *The Panda's Thumb: More Reflections in Natural History* (New York: Norton, 1980).

35. Gary Sherman, Jonathan Haidt, and J. A. Coan, "Viewing Cute Images Increases Behavioral Carefulness," *Emotion* 9, no. 2 (2009); Hiroshi Nittono et al., "The Power of Kawaii: Viewing Cute Images Promotes a Careful Behavior and Narrows Attentional Focus," *PLOS One* 7, no. 9 (2012); Gary Sherman et al., "Individual Differences in the Physical Embodiment of Care: Prosocially Oriented Women Respond to Cuteness by Becoming More Physically Careful," *Emotion* 13, no. 1 (2013).

36. S. Henkel, M. Heistermann, and J. Fischer, "Infants as Costly Social Tools in Male Barbary Macaque Networks," *Animal Behaviour* 79, no. 6 (2010); Michael Kesterton, "Sensitive, Huggy Guys," *Globe and Mail*, April 23, 2010; Brian Mossop, "The Brains of Our Fathers: Does Parenting Rewire Dads?" *Scientific American Mind*, July/August, 2011.

37. Konner, *The Evolution of Childhood*, 432.

38. Joan B. Silk et al., "The Benefits of Social Capital: Close Social Bonds among Female Baboons Enhance Offspring Survival," *Proceedings of the Royal Society Biological Sciences* 2009, no. 276 (2009); J. B. Silk, D. S. Alberts, and J. Altmann, "Social Bonds of Female Baboons Enhance Infant Survival," *Science* 302 (2003); Cheney and Seyfarth, *Baboon Metaphysics*.

39. Leslie A. Pray, "Epigenetics: Genome, Meet Your Environment," *The Scientist*, July 4, 2004.

40. L. H. Lumey, "Decreased Birthweights in Infants after Maternal in Utero Exposure to the Dutch Famine of 1944–1945," *Paediatric and Perinatal Epidemiology* 6, no. 2 (1992); Bastiaan Heijmans et al., "Persistent Epigenetic Differences Associated with Prenatal Exposure to Famine in Humans," *Proceedings of the National Academy of Sciences of the United States of America* 105, no. 44 (2008).

41. G. Kaati, L. O. Bygren, and S. Edvinsson, "Cardiovascular and Diabetes Mortality Determined by Nutrition during Parents' and Grandparents' Slow Growth Period," *European Journal of Human Genetics* 10, no. 11 (2002); Marcus Pembrey et al., "Sex-Specific, Male-Line Transgenerational Responses in Humans," *European Journal of Human Genetics* 14 (2006).

42. Ian C. G. Weaver et al., "Epigenetic Programming by Maternal Behavior," *Nature Neuroscience* 7, no. 8 (2004); Michael J. Meaney, "Maternal Care, Gene Expression, and the Transmission of Individual Differences in Stress Reactivity across Generations," *Annual Review of Neuroscience* 24 (2001).

43. Blum, *Love at Goon Park*, 177.

44. Francesca Cirulli et al., "Early Life Stress as a Risk Factor for Mental Health: Role of Neurotrophins from Rodents to Non-human Primates," *Neuroscience and Biobehavioral Reviews* 33 (2009).

45. Claudia Fahlke et al., "Rearing Experiences and Stress-Induced Plasma Cortisol as Early Risk Factors for Excessive Alcohol Consumption in Nonhuman Primates," *Alcoholims: Clinical and Experimental Research* 24, no. 5 (2000).

CHAPTER 6: DIGITAL NATIVES

1. Ruth Hubbell McKey and et al., "The Impact of Head Start on Children, Families and Communities: Final Report of the Head Start Evaluation, Synthesis and Utilization Project," in *Head Start Evaluation, Synthesis and Utilization Project* (Washington, DC: US Government Printing Office, 1985); Valerie E. Lee et al., "Arc Head Start Effects Sustained? A Longitudinal Follow-up Comparison of Disadvantaged Children Attending Head Start, No Preschool, and Other Preschool Programs," *Child Development* 61, no. 2 (1990). The Lee et al. study does show long-term effects of preschool experience in general, but children attending Head Start interventions showed no long-term advantages over other kids from similar backgrounds in other preschool programs.

2. Alan Mendelsohn et al., "The Impact of a Clinic Based Literacy Intervention on Language Development in Inner-City Preschool Children," *Pediatrics* 107, no. 1 (2001); P. E. Klass, R. Needlman, and Barry Zuckerman, "The Developing Brain and Early Learning," *Archives of Disease in Childhood* 88 (2003); N. Golova et al., "Literacy Promotion for Hispanic Families in a Primary Care Setting: A Randomized Controlled Trial," *Pediatrics* 103 (1998); Barry Zuckerman, "Promoting Early Literacy in Pediatric Practice: Twenty Years of Reach Out and Read," *Pediatrics* 124, no. 6 (2009).

3. C. E. Huebner and A. N. Meltzoff, "Intervention to Change Parent–Child Reading Style: A Comparison of Instructional Methods," *Journal of Applied Developmental Psychology* 26, no. 3 (2005).

4. V. J. Rideout, Ulla G. Foehr, and Donald F. Roberts, *Generation M2: Media in the Lives of 8- to 18-Year-Olds*, (Menlo Park, CA: Henry J. Kaiser Family Foundation, 2010); Matt Richtel, "Wasting Time Is the New Divide in the Digital Era," *New York Times*, May 29, 2012.

5. These children lived in a downtrodden part of Chicago where only 16% of the elementary school population had met the local low-ball *No Child Left Behind* standards. Dan Hurley, "Can You Build a Better Brain? A New Working Memory Game Has Revived the Tantalizing Notion that People Can Make Themselves Smarter," *New York Times Magazine*, April, 22, 2012.

6. Zuckerman, "Promoting Early Literacy."

7. B. E. Hamilton, J. A. Martin, and S. J. Ventura, "Births: Preliminary Data for 2010," *National Vital Statistics Reports* 60, no. 2 (2011).

8. B. E. Hamilton, J. A. Martin, and S. J. Ventura, "Births: Preliminary Data for 2009," *National Vital Statistics Reports* 60, no. 1 (2010): 4, table 3.

9. United Nations Department of Economic and Social Affairs, Population Division, "Age Specific Fertility Rates by Major Area, Region and Country (Births per 1000 Women): Estimates 1995–2010," *World Population Prospects: The 2010 Revision* (2011).

10. Marco Francesconi, *Adult Outcomes for Children of Teenage Mothers* (Bonn: Institute for the Study of Labor, 2007); United Nations, "Age Specific Fertility Rates."

11. Lisa Belkin, "So, Like You Want Your Kids to Speak, Like Properly?" *Huffington Post*, http://www.huffingtonpost.com/lisa-belkin/teen -speech-patterns_b_1307114.html?view=print&comm_ref=false.

12. Rideout, Foehr, and Roberts, *Generation M2*; Lydia Plowman, J. McPake, and C. Stephen, "The Technologisation of Childhood? Young Children and Technology in the Home," *Children and Society* 24, no. 1 (2010); E. De Decker et al., "Influencing Factors of Screen Time in Preschool Children: An Exploration of Parents' Perceptions Through Focus Groups in Six European Countries," *Obesity Reviews* 13, no. 1 (2012); Aric Sigman, "Time for a View on Screen Time," *Archives of Disease in Childhood* 97, no. 11 (2012).

13. V. J. Rideout, Ulla G. Foehr, and Donald F. Roberts, *Generation M2: Media in the Lives of 8–18 Year-Olds* (Menlo Park, CA: Henry J. Kaiser Family Foundation, 2010).

14. Suzy Tomopoulos et al., "Infant Media Exposure and Toddler Development," *Archives of Pediatric Adolescent Medicine* 164, no. 12 (2010); Alan Mendelsohn et al., "Infant Television and Video Exposure Associated with Limited Parent–Child Verbal Interactions in Low Socioeconomic Status Households," *Archives of Pediatric Adolescent Medicine* 162, no. 5 (2008).

15. Annette Lareau, *Unequal Childhoods: Class, Race and Family Life*, 2nd ed. (Berkeley: University of California Press, 2011).

16. Elizabeth Vandewater, David Bickham, and June Lee, "Time Well Spent? Relating Television Use to Children's Free-Time Activities," *Pediatrics* 117, no. 2 (2006); Mendelsohn et al., "Infant Television and Video Exposure"; Tomopoulos et al., "Infant Media Exposure."

17. Kevin Hartnett, "The Perils of Parenting Style," *Pennsylvania Gazette*, September/October 2011; David Brooks, *The Social Animal: The Hidden Sources of Love, Character, and Achievement* (New York: Random House, 2012).

18. Brooks, *The Social Animal*.

19. Hartnett, "The Perils of Parenting Style"; Lareau, *Unequal Childhoods*.

20. De Decker et al., "Influencing Factors of Screen Time."

21. B. Hart and T. R. Risley, *Meaningful Differences in the Everyday Experiences of Young American Children* (Baltimore: Brookes, 1995); Lareau, *Unequal Childhoods*; Brooks, *The Social Animal*.

22. Hilary Stout, "Hi, Grandma! (Pocket Zoo on Hold)," *New York Times*, October 17, 2010.

23. Carly Shuler, "Kids and Apps: The Pass-Back Effect Marches Forward" [blog], Joan Ganz Cooney Center, April 2010, http://www .joanganzcooneycenter.org/2010/06/02/kids-apps-the-pass-back-effect -marches-forward/; Aaron Smith, "Smartphone Ownership 2013 Update," Pew Internet and American Life Project, June 5, 2013; Joanna Brenner, "Pew Internet: Mobile," Pew Internet and American Life

Project, September 18, 2013, http://www.pewinternet.org/Commentary/2012/February/Pew-Internet-Mobile.aspx.

24. F. J. Zimmerman, D. A. Christakis, and A. N. Meltzoff, "Television and DVD/Video Viewing in Children Younger than 2 Years," *Archives of Pediatric Adolescent Medicine* 161 (2007); De Decker et al., "Influencing factors of screen time"; Plowman, McPake, and Stephen, "The Technologisation of Childhood?"; Lydia Plowman, J. McPake, and C. Stephen, "Just Picking It Up? Young Children Learning with Technology at Home," *Cambridge Journal of Education* 38, no. 3 (2008).

25. Carly Shuler, "iLearn II: An Analysis of the Education Category on Apple's App Store." (New York: Joan Ganz Cooney Center, 2012).

26. A. N. Meltzoff et al., "Foundations for a New Science of Learning," *Science* 325 (2009).

27. Ari Brown, "Media Use by Children Younger than 2 Years," *Pediatrics* 128, no. 5 (2011); D. A. Christakis, "The Effects of Infant Media Usage: What Do We Know and What Should We Learn?" *Acta Paediatrica* 98 (2009); Zimmerman, Christakis, and Meltzoff, "Television and DVD/Video Viewing"; V. J. Rideout and E. Hamel, *The Media Family: Electronic Media in the Lives of Infants, Toddlers, Preschoolers, and Their Parents* (Menlo Park, CA: Henry J. Kaiser Family Foundation, 2006); Pooja S. Tandon et al., "Preschoolers' Total Daily Screen Time at Home and by Type of Child Care," *Pediatrics* 124, no. 6 (2009); Susan Lamontagne, Rakesh Singh, and Craig Palosky, "Daily Media Use among Children and Teens Up Dramatically from Five Years Ago," Henry J. Kaiser Family Foundation (website), January 2010.

28. Kamila B. Mistry et al., "Children's Television Exposure and Behavioral and Social Outcomes at 5.5 Years: Does Timing of Exposure Matter?" *Pediatrics* 120, no. 4 (2007).

29. The only factor the team did not control for was genes. Interestingly, lots of television- and video-watching also takes place in child care—especially home daycare centers, according to two huge, well-executed studies. This is an especially pernicious practice given that most parents are under the impression that while they are at work, their child is

being stimulated by age-appropriate supervised play with peers of the same age. This is not necessarily the case. Though children in organized day centers had lower rates of screen time (3.2 hours) than those staying with parents at home (4.4 hours), children in home-based day-care centers had the highest rates of television and video watching of all (5.5 hours). Tandon et al., "Preschoolers' Total Daily Screen Time'" D. A. Christakis, F. J. Zimmerman, and M. Garrison, "Television Viewing in Child Care Programs: A National Survey," *Community Report* 19 (2006).

30. L. S. Pagani et al., "Prospective Associations between Early Childhood Television Exposure and Academic, Psychosocial, and Physical Well-being by Middle Childhood," *Archives of Pediatrics and Adolescent Medicine* 164, no. 5 (2010); Sylvain-Jacques Desjardins, "Toddlers and TV: Early Exposure Has Negative and Long-Term Impact," *Forum* (University of Montreal), May 3, 2010.

31. David Biello, "Fact or Fiction: Archimedes Coined the Term Eureka in the Bath," *Scientific American*, December 8, 2006.

32. Steven Pinker, *The Language Instinct* (New York: William Morrow, 1994).

33. D. A. Christakis et al., "Audible Television and Decreased Adult Words, Infant Vocalizations, and Conversational Turns: A Population Based Study," *Archives of Pediatric Adolescent Medicine* 163, no. 6 (2009).

34. F. J. Zimmerman and D. A. Christakis, "Children's Television Viewing and Cognitive Outcomes," *Archives of Pediatrics and Adolescent Medicine* 159, no. 7 (2005): Tomopolous et al., "Infant Media Exposure"; D. L. Linebarger and D. Walker, "Infants' and Toddlers' Television Viewing and Language Outcomes," *American Behavioral Scientist* 48, no. 5 (2005); Mendelsohn et al., "Infant Television and Video Exposure."

35. P. Greenfield et al., "The Program-Length Commercial: A Study of the Effects of Television/Toy Tie-Ins on Imaginative Play," *Psychology and Marketing* 7, no. 4 (1990); J. T. Piotrowski, N. Jennings, and D. L. Linebarger, "Extending the Lessons of Educational Television with Young American Children," *Journal of Children and Media* 7, no. 2 (2013).

36. Dina L. G. Borzekowski and J. E. Macha, "The Role of Kilimani Sesame in the Healthy Development of Tanzanian Preschool Children," *Journal of Applied Developmental Psychology* 31, no. 4 (2010); D. L. Linebarger and K. McMenamin, *Evaluation of the Between the Lions Mississippi Literacy Initiative, 2008-2009* (Philadelphia: Annenberg School of Communication, University of Pennsylvania, 2010); Piotrowski, Jennings, and Linebarger, "Extending the Lessons of Educational Television"; M. B. Robb, R.A. Richert, and E. Wartella, "Just a Talking Book? Word Learning from Watching Baby Videos," *British Journal of Developmental Psychology* 27 (2009).

37. D. L. Linebarger and Sarah E. Vaala, "Screen Media and Language Development in Infants and Toddlers: An Ecological Perspective," *Developmental Review* 30 (2010); D. R. Anderson and T. A. Pempek, "Television and Very Young Children," *American Behavioral Scientist* 48, no. 5 (2005); Robb, Richert, and Wartella, "Just a Talking Book?"; Christakis, "The Effects of Infant Media Usage"; Brown, "Media Use by Children"; Katherine Nelson, "Structure and Strategy in Learning to Talk," *Monographs in Social Research in Child Development* 38, no. 1/2 (1973).

38. Tamar Lewin, "No Einstein in Your Crib? Get a Refund," *New York Times*, October 23, 2009; Josh Golin, "These Apps Will Not Educate Your Baby," *Huffington Post*, August 13, 2013; Federal Trade Commission v. Your Baby Can LLC, et al., 3:12 CV 02114 DMS BGS, United States District Court, Southern District of California (2013).

39. Plowman, McPake, and Stephen, "The Technologisation of Childhood?"; Rideout and Hamel, *The Media Family*.

40. Christakis, "The Effects of Infant Media Usage."

41. D. A. Christakis et al., "Early Television Exposure and Subsequent Attentional Problems in Children," *Pediatrics* 113, no. 4 (2004). This is a large, well-executed study of about 1,300 children surveyed from infancy to age seven as part of the National Longitudinal Survey of Youth. But as this is an observational, not an experimental, study, we still can't tell whether children who watch more television as

preschoolers later develop difficulties with sustaining their attention, or whether children who already find it difficult to concentrate and sit still may find it especially appealing to sit in front of a screen with rapidly changing video images. I suspect the two are intertwined, and probably compounded by the fact that ADHD is often hereditary. A parent with ADHD may be less likely than a parent without this syndrome to set limits for a restless child. Sigman, "Time for a View on Screen Time."

42. Angeline Lillard and Jennifer Peterson, "The Immediate Impact of Different Types of Television on Young Children's Executive Function," *Pediatrics* 128, no. 4 (2011).

43. C. Fitzpatrick, L. S. Pagani, and T. A. Barnett, "Early Exposure to Media Violence and Later Child Adjustment," *Journal of Developmental and Behavioral Pediatrics* 33, no. 4 (2012); Kimberly Schonert-Reichl et al., *Middle Childhood Inside and Out: The Psychological and Social World of Children 9–12* (Vancouver: University of British Columbia and United Way of the Lower Mainland, 2007).

44. Adam Gorlick, "Media Multitaskers Pay Mental Price," *Stanford University News*, August 24, 2009; Eyal Ophir, Clifford Nass, and Anthony D. Wagner, "Cognitive Control in Media Multitaskers," *Proceedings of the National Academy of Sciences of the United States of America* 106, no. 37 (2009).

45. Roy Pea et al., "Media Use, Face-to-Face Communication, Media Multitasking and Social Well-being among 8- to 12-Year-Old Girls," *Developmental Psychology* 48, no. 2 (2012); Rideout, Foehr, and Roberts, *Generation M2*.

46. Sam Anderson, "The Hyperaddictive, Time-Sucking, Relationship-Busting, Mind-Crushing Power and Allure of Silly Digital Games," *New York Times Magazine*, April 8, 2012.

47. The more sinister posts feature photos of girls taken when they were too drunk to know that some high-school boys had raped them and texted photos of their "conquest" or posted them on social networking sites. Dennis Cauchon, William Cummings, and John Bacon, "Ohio High

School Football Team Players Guilty in Rape Case," *USA Today*, March 17, 2013.

48. N. I. Eisenberger, M. D. Lieberman, and K. D. Williams, "Does Rejection Hurt? An fMRI Study of Social Exclusion," *Science* 302 (2003); N. I. Eisenberger and M. D. Lieberman, "Why Rejection Hurts: A Common Neural Alarm System for Physical and Social Pain," *Trends in Cognitive Science* 8, no. 7 (2004); David C. Geary, *The Origin of Mind: Evolution of Brain, Cognition and General Intelligence* (Washington, DC: American Psychological Association, 2005).

49. Carrie L. Masten et al., "Neural Correlates of Social Exclusion during Adolescence: Understanding the Distress of Peer Rejection," *Scan* 4 (2009).

50. Michael Tomasello, *Origins of Human Communication* (Cambridge, MA: MIT Press, 2008); Alex Pentland, "To Signal Is Human: Real-Time Data Mining Unmasks the Power of Imitation, Kith and Charisma in Our Face to Face Social Networks," *American Scientist* 98 (2010).

51. Pentland, "To Signal Is Human"; Alex Pentland, *Honest Signals: How They Shape Our World* (Cambridge, MA: MIT Press, 2008).

52. Leslie Seltzer, Toni Ziegler, and Seth Pollak, "Social Vocalizations Can Release Oxytocin in Humans," *Proceedings of the Royal Society B* 277 (2010); Sue C. Carter and Stephen W. Porges, "Social Bonding and Attachment," in *Encyclopedia of Behavioural Neuroscience*, vol. 3 (New York: Elsevier, 2010).

53. Leslie Seltzer et al., "Instant Messages vs. Speech: Hormones and Why We Still Need to Hear Each Other," *Evolution and Human Behavior* 33 (2012). Given that Amanda Lenhart, from the Pew Center, has shown that teens communicate more through texts than through any other medium, including in-person socializing, it is important to convey that texts don't always do the trick. Amanda Lenhart, *Teens, Smartphones & Texting* (Washington, DC: Pew Internet and American Life Project, 2012).

54. Ted Ruffman et al., "What Mothers Say and What They Do: The Relation between Parenting, Theory of Mind, Language and Conflict/Cooperation," *British Journal of Developmental Psychology* 24 (2006).

55. Barbara Schneider and L. J. Waite, eds., *Being Together, Working Apart* (Cambridge: Cambridge University Press, 2005).

56. B. Campos et al., "Opportunity for Interaction? A Naturalistic Observation Study of Dual-Earner Families after Work and School," *Journal of Family Psychology* 23, no. 6 (2009).

CHAPTER 7: TEENS AND SCREENS

1. Matt Richtel, "Growing Up Digital, Wired for Distraction," *New York Times*, November 21, 2010.

2. Amanda Lenhart, *Teens, Smartphones & Texting* (Washington, DC: Pew Internet and American Life Project, 2012); Nielsen Company, "U.S. Teen Mobile Report Calling Yesterday, Texting Today, Using Apps Tomorrow," Nielsen Newswire, October 14, 2010, http://blog.nielsen .com/nielsenwire/online_mobile/u s-tcen-mobile-report-calling -yesterday-texting-today-using-apps-tomorrow/.

3. Jack P. Shonkoff and Deborah A. Phillips, eds., *From Neurons to Neighborhoods: The Science of Early Childhood Development* (Washington, DC: National Academy of Sciences, 2000).

4. Lee Rainie and Barry Wellman, *Networked: The New Social Operating System* (Cambridge, MA: MIT Press, 2012); Clay Shirky, *Here Comes Everybody* (London: Allen Lane, 2008).

5. Elizabeth K. Englander, "Research Findings: MARC 2011 Survey Grades 3–12," *MARC Research Reports* 2 (2011); Amanda Lenhart, "Teens, Stranger Contact and Cyberbullying," Pew Internet and American Life Project, April 30, 2008, http://cyber.law.harvard.edu/sites/cyber.law.harvard.edu /files/Pew%20Internet%20teens.pdf.

6. Sameer Hinduja and Justin Patchin, "Bullying, Cyberbullying, and Suicide," *Archives of Suicide Research* 14, no. 3 (2010).

7. Lenhart, *Teens, Smartphones & Texting*.

8. Sindy R. Sumter et al., "Developmental Trajectories of Peer Victimization: Off-Line and Online Experiences during Adolescence," *Journal of Adolescent Health* 50, no. 6 (2012).

9. Dan Hruschka, *Friendship: Development, Ecology, and Evolution of a*

Relationship (Berkeley: University of California Press, 2010).

10. Sameer Hinduja and Justin Patchin, "Cyberbullying: An Exploratory Analysis of Factors Related to Offending and Victimization," *Deviant Behavior* 29 (2008).

11. Shari Kessel Schneider et al., "Cyberbullying, School Bullying, and Psychological Distress: A Regional Census of High School Students," *American Journal of Public Health* 102, no. 1 (2012); Jing Wang, Ronald J. Iannotti, and Tonja Nansel, "School Bullying among Adolescents in the United States: Physical, Verbal, Relational, and Cyber," *Journal of Adolescent Health* 45, no. 4 (2009).

12. David C. Geary, Benjamin Wingard, and Bo Winegard, "Reflections on the Evolution of Human Sex Differences: Social Selection and the Evolution of Competition among Women," in *Evolutionary Perspectives on Human Sexual Psychology and Behavior*, ed. V. A. Weekes-Shackelford and T. K. Shackelford (New York: Springer, 2014).

13. Wang, Iannotti, and Nansel, "School Bullying"; Joyce Benenson et al., "Under Threat of Exclusion, Females Exclude More than Males," *Psychological Science* 22, no. 4 (2011); Geary, Wingard, and Winegard, "Reflections on the Evolution of Human Sex Differences"; David C. Geary, *Male, Female: The Evolution of Human Sex Differences* (Washington, DC: American Psychological Association, 2010); Eleanor Maccoby and Carol Jacklin, *The Psychology of Sex Differences* (Stanford, CA: Stanford University Press, 1974); Susan Pinker, *The Sexual Paradox: Extreme Men, Gifted Women, and the Real Gender Gap* (Toronto: Random House Canada, 2008); Joyce Benenson et al., "Human Sexual Differences in the Use of Social Ostracism as a Competitive Tactic," *International Journal of Primatology* 29 (2008).

14. Catherine Sebastian et al., "Social Brain Development and the Affective Consequences of Ostracism in Adolescence," *Brain and Cognition* 72 (2010).

15. Dorothy L. Cheney and Robert M. Seyfarth, *Baboon Metaphysics: The Evolution of a Social Mind* (Chicago: University of Chicago Press, 2007).

16. Linda Mealey, *Sex Differences: Developmental and Evolutionary Strategies* (San Diego, CA: Academic Press, 2000); Pinker, *The Sexual Paradox*.

17. Cheney and Seyfarth, *Baboon Metaphysics*. Thanks go to my son Carl for pointing out the interesting parallel between threat grunts and Facebook comments.

18. Jaana Juvonen and Elisheva Gross, "Extending the School Grounds? Bullying Experiences in Cyberspace," *Journal of School Health* 78, no. 9 (2008).

19. Jing Wang, Tonja Nansel, and Ronald J. Iannotti, "Cyber and Traditional Bullying: Diffferential Association with Depression," *Journal of Adolescent Health* 48, no. 4 (2011).

20. According to researchers Sameer Hinduja and Justin Patchin, the bully's most common online offense was "Posted something online about another person to make others laugh," while the victim's most common humiliating experience was "Received an upsetting email from someone you know." These seem fairly common and anodyne online experiences, yet shockingly, 20% of those teens who sent or received such messages started to think about suicide. Hinduja and Patchin, "Bullying, Cyberbullying, and Suicide."

21. Frank Bruni, "Of Love and Fungus," *New York Times*, July 21, 2013.

22. R. Kraut et al., "Internet Paradox: A Social Technology that Reduces Social Involvement and Psychological Well-being?" *American Psychologist* 53, no. 9 (1998).

23. Patti M. Valkenburg and Jochen Peter, "Online Communication and Adolescent Well-being: Testing the Stimulation versus the Displacement Hypothesis," *Journal of Computer Mediated Communication* 12 (2007); "Preadolescents' and Adolescents' Online Communication and Their Closeness to Friends," *Developmental Psychology* 43, no. 2 (2007); "Social Consequences of the Internet for Adolescents: A Decade of Research," *Current Directions in Psychological Science* 18, no. 1 (2009); R. Kraut et al., "Internet Paradox Revisited," *Journal of Social Issues* 58, no. 1 (2002).

24. Valkenburg and Peter, "Social Consequences of the Internet"; "Preadolescents' and Adolescents' Online Communication."

25. The wall as a device to create romantic and narrative tension was used not only by Ovid but also by Shakespeare in A *Midsummer Night's Dream* and *Romeo and Juliet*, Jonathan Safran Foer in *Everything Is Illuminated*, and Nick Hornby in *Juliet, Naked*—the latter was one of the first novelists to use email missives to convey the false intimacy created by online romantic exchanges.

26. A. Sharabi and M. Margalit, "The Mediating Role of Internet Connection, Virtual Friends, and Mood in Predicting Loneliness among Students with and without Learning Disabilities in Different Educational Environments," *Journal of Learning Disabilities* 44, no. 3 (2010); M. Hu, "Will Online Chat Help Alleviate Mood Loneliness?" *CyberPsychology & Behavior* 12 (2009); Kraut et al., "Internet Paradox"; Kraut et al., "Internet Paradox Revisited"; Elisheva Gross, Jaana Juvonen, and Shelly Gable, "Internet Use and Well-being in Adolescence," *Journal of Social Issues* 58, no. 1 (2002).

27. Regina van den Eijnden et al., "Online Communication, Compulsive Internet Use, and Psychosocial Well-being among Adolescents: A Longitudinal Study," *Developmental Psychology* 44, no. 3 (2008); E. B. Weiser, "The Functions of Internet Use and Their Social and Psychological Consequences," *CyberPsychology & Behavior* 4 (2001); M. L. Ybarra, C. Alexander, and K. J. Mitchell, "Depressive Symptomatology, Youth Internet Use, and Online Interactions: A National Survey," *Journal of Adolescent Health* 36, no. 1 (2005).

28. Sharabi and Margalit, "The Mediating Role of Internet Connection"; Junghyun Kim, Robert LaRose, and Wei Peng, "Loneliness as the Cause and the Effect of Problematic Internet Use: The Relationship between Internet Use and Psychological Well-being," *CyberPsychology & Behavior* 12, no. 4 (2009); P. E. Klass, "Fixated by Screens, But Seemingly Nothing Else," *New York Times*, May 9, 2011.

29. Klass, "Fixated by Screens."

30. M. De Choudhury et al., "Predicting Depression via Social Media,"

paper presented at the 7th International AAAI Conference on Weblogs and Social Media, Boston, MA, July 2013.

31. M. A. Moreno et al., "Feeling Bad on Facebook: Depression Disclosures by College Students on a Social Networking Site," *Depression and Anxiety* 28, no. 6 (2011); De Choudhury et al., "Predicting Depression"; M. A. Moreno et al., "A Pilot Evaluation of Associations between Displayed Depression References on Facebook and Self-Reported Depression Using a Clinical Scale," *Journal of Behavioral Health Services and Research* 39, no. 3 (2011).

32. Sherry Turkle, "The Flight from Conversation," *New York Times*, April 22, 2012; *Alone Together: Why We Expect More from Technology and Less from Each Other* (New York: Basic Books, 2011).

33. Arthur Levine and Diane R. Dean, *Generation on a Tightrope: A Portrait of Today's College Student* (San Francisco: Jossey Bass, 2012).

34. Carlo Rotella, "No Child Left Untableted," *New York Times Magazine*, September 15, 2013.

35. Mark Warschauer and Morgan Ames, "Can One Laptop Per Child Save the World's Poor?," *Journal of International Affairs* 64, no. 1 (2010).

36. Ibid.; Nicholas Negroponte, "No Lap Un-topped: The Bottom Up Revolution that Could Re-define Global IT Culture," NetEvents Global Press Summit, Hong Kong, 2006; Seymour Papert, "Digital Development: How the $100 Laptop Could Change Education," USINFO Webchat.

37. Warschauer and Ames, "Can One Laptop Per Child Save the World's Poor?"; Mark Warschauer and Tina Matuchniak, "New Technology and Digital Worlds: Analyzing Evidence of Equity in Access, Use, and Outcomes," *Review of Research in Education* 34, no. 1 (2010).

38. Jeff Patzer, "Are Laptops the Most Important Thing?" [blog], 2010.

39. All figures from the OLPC website.

40. J. Hourcade et al., "Early OLPC Experiences in a Rural Uruguayan School," in *Mobile Technology for Children: Designing for Interaction and Learning*, ed. A. Druin (Boston: Morgan Kaufmann, 2009); Pierre Varly, "Evaluations in One Laptop Per Child: What For? What Has

Been Done, What Could Be Done?" in *Varlyproject: A Blog on Education in Developing Countries,* October 16, 2010.

41. US Department of Labor, Bureau of International Labor Affairs, *U.S. Department of Labor's 2010 Findings on the Worst Forms of Child Labor* (Washington, DC: ILAB, 2011); Varly, "Evaluations in One Laptop Per Child."

42. Varly, "Evaluations in One Laptop Per Child."

43. Philip Elliott, "Study: US Education Spending Tops Global List," *Huffington Post,* June 25, 2013.

44. Geoffrey York, "Congo's Malaria Surge Confounds Medical World," *Globe and Mail,* May 18, 2012.

45. Daniel T. Willingham, *When Can You Trust the Experts? How to Tell Good Science from Bad in Education* (San Francisco: Jossey-Bass, 2012).

46. F. A. Inan et al., "Pattern of Classroom Activities during Students' Use of Computers: Relations between Instructional Strategies and Computer Applications," *Teaching and Teacher Education* 26 (2010); C. V. Baussell, "Tracking U.S. Trends," *Education Week* 27, no. 30 (2008); Matt Richtel, "In Classroom of the Future, Stagnant Scores," *New York Times,* September 3, 2011; Rotella, "No Child Left Untableted."

47. Willingham, *When Can You Trust the Experts?*; Tad Simons, "England's Experience with Whiteboards Is Instructive for the Rest of Us," *Training,* January 11, 2005.

48. Luke Hopewell, "Budget 2012: OLPC Gets Cash, Praises Govt," *ZD Net,* May 9, 2012.

49. Tom Vanderbilt, "The Call of the Future," *Wilson Quarterly,* Spring 2012, http://www.wilsonquarterly.com/essays/call-future.

50. Jacob L. Vigdor and Helen F. Ladd, "Scaling the Digital Divide: Home Computer Technology and Student Achievement," NBER Working Paper 16078 (Cambridge, MA: National Bureau of Economic Research, 2010).

51. Bryan Goodwin, "One-to-One Laptop Programs Are No Silver Bullet," *Educational Leadership* 68, no. 5 (2011); Larissa Campuzano et al.,

Effectiveness of Reading and Mathematics Software Products: Findings from Two Student Cohorts (Washington, DC: National Center for Education Evaluation and Regional Assistance, 2009); Richtel, "In Classroom of the Future"; D. L. Lowther et al., *Freedom to Learn Program: Michigan 2005–2006 Evaluation Report* (Memphis, TN: Center for Research in Educational Policy, 2007); K. Shapley et al., *Evaluation of the Texas Technology Immersion Pilot: Final Outcomes for a Four-Year Study (2004–2008)* (Austin: Texas Center for Educational Research, 2009).

52. Julia Gillen et al., "A 'Learning Revolution?' Investigating Pedagogic Practice Around Interactive Whiteboards in British Primary Classrooms," *Learning, Media, and Technology* 32, no. 3 (2007).

53. S. Higgins, G. Beauchamp, and D. Miller, "Reviewing the Literature on Interactive Whiteboards," *Learning, Media, and Technology* 32, no. 3 (2007).

54. Goodwin, "One-to-One Laptop Programs"; Lowther et al., *Freedom to Learn Program*.

55. Though the students with laptops scored slightly higher in math, their writing skills were weaker and their reading skills the same as those of students without laptops in the classroom. Shapley et al., *Evaluation of the Texas Technology Immersion Pilot*.

56. Of ten reading and math programs tested on ten thousand American schoolchildren, the only one that showed statistically significant positive effects was Leap Track, a fourth-grade reading instructional package. This huge study, sponsored by the National Center for Education Evaluation, compared ten software products to see if they improved students' academic performance over two years. Four hundred and twenty-eight volunteer teachers from 132 schools were randomly assigned either to a technologically enhanced classroom or to one that was not. The students involved were tested at the beginning of the school year and at the end. In the interim, classroom observations at three points during the year, class marks from the kids' files, and teacher questionnaires supplemented the formal testing. In short, there were

gobs of data on the effectiveness of reading and math software products at every point in the academic year. After one year there were no differences in the performance of students randomly assigned to laptop classrooms versus those in regular classes. After a second year of using them, might the teachers have had more experience with the software and thus have been able to help the students learn more? Sadly, no. This study showed that, compared to teens in traditional classrooms, there were no differences in the students' reading scores, and their math skills were even worse than those of kids taught without educational software. The results were controversial, especially for software companies. Only one out of the ten software suites had a positive and statistically significant effect on reading or math skills. Of the nine remaining products, five had negative effects on academic performance and four had positive but statistically insignificant effects. Campuzano et al., *Effectiveness of Reading and Mathematics Software Products.*

57. Shapley et al., *Evaluation of the Texas Technology Immersion Pilot*; Wesley A. Austin and Michael W. Totaro, "Gender Differences in the Effects of Internet Usage on High School Absenteeism," *Journal of Socio-Economics* 40 (2011).

58. Inan et al., "Pattern of Classroom Activities"; S. M. Ross et al., "Using Classroom Observations as a Research and Formative Evaluation Tool in Educational Reform: The School Observation Measure," in *Observational Research in U.S. Classrooms: New Approaches for Understanding Cultural and Linguistic Diversity*, ed. H. C. Waxman (Cape Town: Cambridge University Press, 2004).

59. David L. Silvernail et al., *A Middle School One-to-One Laptop Program: The Maine Experience* (Gorham, ME: Maine Education Policy Research Institute, 2011).

60. Higgins, Beauchamp, and Miller, "Reviewing the Literature"; Tim Rudd, "Interactive Whiteboards in the Classroom" (Bristol, UK: Futurelab, 2007).

61. Raj Chetty, John N. Friedman, and Jonah Rockoff, "The Long-Term Impacts of Teachers: Teacher Value-Added and Student Outcomes in

Adulthood," NBER Working Paper 17699 (Cambridge, MA: National Bureau of Economic Research, 2012).

62. William L. Sanders and Sandra P. Horn, "Research Findings from the Tennessee Value-Added Assessment System (TVAAS) Database: Implications for Educational Evaluation and Research," *Journal of Personnel Evaluation in Education* 12, no. 3 (1998); William L. Sanders and June C. Rivers, "Cumulative and Residual Effects of Teachers on Future Student Academic Achievement" (Knoxville: University of Tennessee Value-Added Research and Assessment Center, 1996); Steven G. Rivkin, Eric A. Hanushek, and John F. Kain, "Teachers, Schools, and Academic Achievement," *Econometrica* 73, no. 2 (2005); Elizabeth Green, "Can Good Teaching Be Learned?" *New York Times Magazine*, March 7, 2010; M. Brendgen et al., "Gene–Environment Processes Linking Aggression, Peer Victimization, and the Teacher–Child Relationship," *Child Development* 82, no. 6 (2011); Doug Lemov, *Teach Like a Champion: 49 Techniques that Put Students on the Path to College* (San Francisco: Jossey-Bass, 2010).

63. Randy Yerrick, "How Notebook Computers, Digital Media and Probeware Can Transform Science Learning in the Classroom," *Contemporary Issues in Technology and Science Teacher Education* 9, no. 3 (2009).

64. Shapley et al., *Evaluation of the Texas Technology Immersion Pilot*; Silvernail et al., *A Middle School One-to-One Laptop Program*; Rudd, "Interactive Whiteboards"; B. Somekh and H. Haldane, "How Can Interactive Whiteboards Contribute to Pedagogic Change?", paper presented at Imagining the Future for ICT and Education, Alesund, Norway, 2006.

65. Shapley et al., *Evaluation of the Texas Technology Immersion Pilot*; Silvernail et al., *A Middle School One-to-One Laptop Program*. The fact that self-esteem is a standalone benefit that doesn't make you good at much else has been demonstrated in a comprehensive and fairly stunning review article by Roy Baumeister. R. F. Baumeister et al., "Does High Self-Esteem Cause Better Performance, Interpersonal Success,

Happiness, or Healthier Lifestyles?" *Psychological Science in the Public Interest* 4, no. 1 (2003).

66. Dawn Walton, "Drug-Free Distractions for Kids with Cancer," *Globe and Mail*, June 7, 2012.

67. Edward Swing et al., "Television and Video Game Exposure and the Development of Attention Problems," *Pediatrics* 126, no. 2 (2010); Markus Dworak et al., "Impact of Singular Excessive Computer Game and Television Exposure on Sleep Patterns and Memory Performance of School Aged Children," *Pediatrics* 120, no. 5 (2007).

68. Yan Zhou et al., "Gray Matter Abnormalities in Internet Addiction: A Voxel-Based Morphometry Study," *European Journal of Radiology* 79, no. 1 (2011); Fuchun Lin et al., "Abnormal White Matter Integrity in Adolescents with Internet Addiction Disorder: A Tract-Based Spatial Statistics Study," *PLOS One* 7, no. 1 (2012).

69. Jeremy Laurance, "Addicted: Scientists Show How Internet Dependency Alters the Human Brain," *The Independent*, January 12, 2012; Michael Kesterton, "Gamer Lives in Cafe," *Globe and Mail*, April 5, 2013.

70. One study that compared ADHD kids with a control group found that non-ADHD kids were more negatively affected by screen time. Excessive time spent watching television or on electronic media affected the cognitive processing and attention skills of the healthy kids, whereas the screen time had negligible effects on the ADHD kids. Ignacio David Acevedo-Polakovich et al., "Disentagling the Relation between Television Viewing and Cognitive Processes in Children with Attention-Deficit-Hyperactivity Disorder and Comparison Children," *Archives of Pediatric Adolescent Medicine* 160 (2006).

CHAPTER 8: GOING TO THE CHAPEL

1. Ninety-three percent of Americans state that having a happy marriage is one of their top objectives, while the number one aspiration of high-school seniors is "having a good marriage and family life." Linda J. Waite and Maggie Gallagher, *The Case for Marriage* (New York: Broadway Books, 2000).

2. In the National Survey of Health and Social Life, which describes the romantic and sexual lives of 3,432 randomly selected American adults, about 68% of married couples met their spouses after being introduced by people they knew, while 60% met them in face-to-face social environments such as school, church, or social clubs. More recently, the 2005 Pew Internet Study found that 72% of married couples or those in a committed relationship had met their partners in "real world" settings such as work or school or through family and friends. Only 3% had met their partners online, though that figure may have increased somewhat since then. N. A. Christakis and J. H. Fowler, *Connected: The Surprising Power of Our Social Networks and How They Shape Our Lives* (New York: Little, Brown, 2009); E. O. Laumann, *The Social Organization of Sexuality: Sexual Practices in the United States* (Chicago: University of Chicago Press, 1994); Eli J. Finkel et al., "Online Dating: A Critical Analysis from the Perspective of Psychological Science," *Psychological Science* 13, no. 1 (2012); M. Madden and Amanda Lenhart, *Online Dating* (Washington, DC: Pew Internet and American Life Project, 2006).

3. Chris M. Wilson and Andrew J. Oswald, *How Does Marriage Affect Physical and Psychological Health? A Survey of the Longitudinal Evidence* (Bonn: Institute for the Study of Labor, 2005).

4. Steven Stack and Ross Eshleman, "Marital Status and Happiness: A 17-Nation Study," *Journal of Marriage and Family*, 60, no. 2 (May 1998).

5. Two enterprising British economists, Chris Wilson and Andrew Oswald, who surveyed all the longitudinal studies on marriage completed as of the mid 2000s, baldly summarized the terrain: "Intriguingly, unlike marriage, cohabiting produces few benefits." Wilson and Oswald, *How Does Marriage Affect Physical and Psychological Health?*

6. Wendy D. Manning and Jessica Cohen, "Premarital Cohabitation and Marital Dissolution: An Examination of Recent Marriages," *Journal of Marriage and Family* 74, no. 2 (2012).

7. Robin Marantz Henig and Samantha Henig, *Twentysomething: Why Do Young Adults Seem Stuck?* (New York: Hudson Street Press, 2012).

8. Beatrice Gottlieb, *The Family in the Western World from the Black*

Death to the Industrial Age (New York: Oxford University Press, 1993), quoted in Stephanie Coontz, *Marriage, a History: How Love Conquered Marriage* (New York: Penguin, 2005); Gottlieb, *The Family in the Western World*, chap. 9, "From Yoke Mates to Soul Mates."

9. Matt Ridley, *The Rational Optimist: How Prosperity Evolves* (New York: Harper, 2010); Şevket Pamuk and Jan-Luiten van Zanden, "Standards of Living," in *The Cambridge Economic History of Modern Europe*, ed. Stephen Broadberry and Kevin H. O'Rourke, Vol. 1, *1700–1870* (Cambridge: Cambridge University Press, 2010).

10. Christakis and Fowler, *Connected*; Tara Parker-Pope, "Is Marriage Good for Your Health?" *New York Times*, April, 14, 2010; Waite and Gallagher, *The Case for Marriage*; Tara Parker-Pope, *For Better: The Science of a Good Marriage* (New York: Dutton, 2010). By the early nineteenth century it was well known from hospital statistics that most inpatients were single (George Weisz, McGill Faculty of Medicine medical historian, personal communication, July 6, 2012).

11. Christakis and Fowler, *Connected*; Frans Van Poppel and Inez Joung, "Long-Term Trends in Marital Status Mortality Differences in the Netherlands, 1850–1970," *Journal of Biosocial Sciences* 33 (2001); Mark Regnerus, "Say Yes. What Are You Waiting For?" *New York Times*, April 26, 2009; L. J. Waite, Y. Luo, and A. C. Lewin, "Marital Happiness and Marital Stability: Consequences for Psychological Well-being," *Social Science Research* 38, no. 1 (2009); Waite and Gallagher, *The Case for Marriage*; Parker-Pope, *For Better*; J. K. Kiecolt-Glaser et al., "Marital Quality, Marital Disruption, and Immune Function," *Psychosomatic Medicine* 49, no. 1 (1987); Stack and Eshleman, "Marital Status and Happiness."

12. Ami Sedghi and Simon Rogers, "Divorce Rates Data, 1858 to Now: How Has It Changed?," *The Guardian Datablog*, February 6, 2014, http://www.theguardian.com/news/datablog/2010/jan/28/divorce-rates -marriage-ons; Institute of Marriage and Family Canada, "Canadian Divorce," November 15, 2010, http://imfcanada.org/fact-sheet/canadian -divorce; United States Census Bureau, "Number, Timing, and Duration

of Marriages and Divorces: 2009," May 2011, http://www.census.gov /prod/2011pubs/p70-125.pdf.

13. Coontz, *Marriage, a History*.

14. Kay S. Hymowitz, "American Caste: Family Breakdown Is Limiting Mobility and Increasing Inequality," *City Journal* 22, no. 2 (2012).

15. Catherine E. Ross, John Mirowsky, and Karen Goldsteen, "The Impact of the Family on Health: The Decade in Review," *Journal of Marriage and Family* 52 (1990).

16. **Viruses:** Sheldon Cohen, "Social Relationships and Health," *American Psychologist* (2004). **Chronic illness:** L. F. Berkman, "The Role of Social Relations in Health Promotion," *Psychosomatic Medicine* 57, no. 3 (1995). **Cancer, heart attacks and surgery:** J. K. Kiecolt-Glaser and Tamara L. Newton, "Marriage and Health: His and Hers," *Psychological Bulletin* 127, no. 4 (2001); Kathleen King and Harry T. Reis, "Marriage and Long-Term Survival after Coronary Artery Bypass Grafting," *Health Psychology* 31, no. 1 (2012). **Dying after cancer surgery:** James Goodwin et al., "The Effect of Marital Status on Stage, Treatment, and Survival of Cancer Patients," *Journal of the American Medical Association* 258 (1987). **Cancer and suicide:** Waite and Gallagher, *The Case for Marriage*; V. L. Ernster et al., "Cancer Incidence by Marital Status," *Journal of the National Cancer Institute* 63 (1979); J. S. House, K. R. Landis, and D. Umberson, "Social Relationships and Health," *Science* 241, no. 4865 (1988); J. K. Kiecolt-Glaser and R. Glaser, "Psychological Influences on Immunity," *Psychosomatics* 27, no. 9 (1986); Jack C. Smith, James A. Mercy, and Judith M. Conn, "Marital Status and the Risk of Suicide," *American Journal of Public Health* 78 (1988); Emile Durkheim, *Suicide: A Study in Sociology* (New York: Free Press, 1951). **Crime and jail:** R. J. Sampson, J. H. Laub, and C. Wimer, "Does Marriage Reduce Crime? A Counterfactual Approach to Within-Individual Causal Effects," *Criminology* 44, no. 3 (2006).

17. Yin Bun Cheung, "Marital Status and Mortality in British Women: A Longitudinal Study," *International Journal of Epidemiology* 29 (2000); Lamberto Manzoli et al., "Marital Status and Mortality in the Elderly:

A Systematic Review and Meta-analysis," *Social Science and Medicine* 64 (2007); P. Hajdu, M. Mckee, and F. Bojan, "Changes in Premature Mortality Differentials by Marital Status in Hungary and England," *European Journal of Public Health* 5, no. 4 (1995).

18. Waite and Gallagher, *The Case for Marriage*; World Health Organization, "Maternity Mortality Ratio (per 100,000 Live Births)," http://www.who.int/healthinfo/statistics/indmaternalmortality/en/index.html; Yuanreng Hu and Noreen Goldman, "Mortality Differentials by Marital Status: An International Comparison," *Demography* 27, no. 2 (1990). The Canadian statistics are also from census data.

19. Julianne Holt-Lunstad, W. Birmingham, and Brandon Jones, "Is There Something Unique about Marriage? The Relative Impact of Marital Status, Relationship Quality and Network Social Support on Ambulatory Blood Pressure and Mental Health," *Annals of Behavioral Medicine* 35 (2008).

20. W. Troxel et al., "Marital Happiness and Sleep Disturbances in a Multi-ethnic Sample of Middle Aged Women," *Behavioral Sleep Medicine* 7, no. 1 (2009); W. Troxel et al., "Attachment Anxiety, Relationship Context, and Sleep in Women with Recurrent Major Depression," *Psychosomatic Medicine* 69 (2007).

21. Kiecolt-Glaser and Newton, "Marriage and Health"; Berkman, "The Role of Social Relations."

22. Robert A. Carels, A. Sherwood, and J. Blumenthal, "Psychosocial Influences on Blood Pressure during Daily Life," *International Journal of Psychophysiology* 28 (1998).

23. Ibid.; Holt-Lunstad, Birmingham, and Jones, "Is There Something Unique about Marriage?"; J. Holt-Lunstad, Brandon Jones, and W. Birmingham, "The Influence of Close Relationships on Nocturnal Blood Pressure Dipping," *International Journal of Psychophysiology* 71 (2008).

24. K. Appelberg et al., "Interpersonal Conflict as a Predictor of Work Disability: A Follow-up Study of 15,348 Finnish Employees," *Journal of*

Psychosomatic Research 40 (1996); K. Orth-Gomer et al., "Marital Stress Worsens Progrnosis in Women with Coronary Heart Disease: The Stockholm Female Coronary Risk Study," *Journal of the American Medical Association* 284, no. 23 (2000).

25. Vicki Helgeson, "The Effects of Masculinity and Social Support on Recovery from Myocardial Infarction," *Psychosomatic Medicine* 53 (1991).

26. Ibid.; J. H. Hibbard and C. R. Pope, "The Quality of Social Roles as Predictors of Morbidity and Mortality," *Social Science and Medicine* 36, no. 3 (1993).

27. J. K. Kiecolt-Glaser et al., "Marital Stress: Immunologic, Neuroendocrine, and Autonomic Correlates," *Annals of the New York Academy of Sciences* 840 (2006).

28. A telephone survey conducted by Mental Health America in 2008 found that men are more likely than women to turn to their spouse for emotional support, while women are most likely to turn to other family members. Mental Health America, *Social Connectedness and Health*, May 2008.

29. J. B. Silk et al., "Strong and Consistent Social Bonds Enhance the Longevity of Female Baboons," *Current Biology* 20 (2010); J. B. Silk, D. S. Alberts, and J. Altmann, "Social Bonds of Female Baboons Enhance Infant Survival," *Science* 302 (2003); Dorothy L. Cheney and Robert M. Seyfarth, *Baboon Metaphysics: The Evolution of a Social Mind* (Chicago: University of Chicago Press, 2007); Joan B. Silk et al., "The Benefits of Social Capital: Close Social Bonds among Female Baboons Enhance Offspring Survival," *Proceedings of the Royal Society Biological Sciences* 2009, no. 276 (2009); Robert M. Seyfarth and Dorothy L. Cheney, "The Evolutionary Origins of Friendship," *Annual Review of Psychology* 63 (2012).

30. Silk et al., "Strong and Consistent Social Bonds"; Natalie Angier, "The Spirit of Sisterhood Is in the Air and on the Air," *New York Times*, April 23, 2012.

31. Angier, "The Spirit of Sisterhood."

32. J. Lehmann, K. Andrews, and R. I. M. Dunbar, "Social Networks and Social Complexity in Female-Bonded Primates," in *Social Brain, Distributed Mind*, ed. R. I. M. Dunbar, C. Gamble, and J.A. Gowlett (Oxford: Oxford University Press, 2010); R. M. Wittig et al., "Focused Grooming Networks and Stress Alleviation in Wild Female Baboons," *Hormones and Behaviour* 54 (2008).

33. When I asked Janice Kiecolt-Glaser what might motivate people to participate in such an invasive, time-consuming experiment, she replied that each couple was paid $1,000 for two hospital stays and daily follow-up visits to examine their blisters and draw blood for hormone analysis. It was the couple's responsibility to make those appointments (Janice Kiecolt-Glaser, personal communication, August 5, 2012).

34. S. Carrère and J. M. Gottman, "Predicting Divorce among Newlyweds from the First Three Minutes of a Marital Conflict Discussion," *Family Process* 38, no. 3 (1999); Parker-Pope, *For Better*.

35. J. K. Kiecolt-Glaser et al., "Hostile Marital Interactions, Proinflammatory Cytokine Production, and Wound Healing," *Archives of General Psychiatry* 62, no. 12 (2005).

36. Ibid.; Lisa M. Christian et al., "Psychological Influences on Neuroendocrine and Immune Outcomes," in *Handbook of Neuroscience for the Behavioral Sciences*, ed. Gary G. Berntson and J. Cacioppo (Hoboken, NJ: Wiley, 2009).

37. W. Marcenes and A. Sheiham, "The Relationship between Marital Quality and Oral Health Status," *Psychology and Health* 11 (1996); Kiecolt-Glaser and Newton, "Marriage and Health"; A. J. Zautra et al., "An Examination of Individual Differences in the Relationship between Interpersonal Stress and Disease Activity among Women with Rheumatoid Arthritis," *Arthritis Care and Research* 11 (1998); S. M. Greene and W. A. Griffin, "Effects of Marital Quality on signs of Parkinson's Disease during Patient–Spouse Interaction," *Psychiatry* 61, no. 35–45 (1998).

38. Sarah L. Master et al., "A Picture's Worth: Partner Photographs Reduce Experimentally Induced Pain," *Psychological Science* 20, no. 11 (2009);

Simo Saarijarvi, Ulla Rytokoski, and Sirkka-Liisa Karppi, "Marital Satisfaction and Distress in Chronic Low-Back Pain Patients and Their Spouses," *Clinical Journal of Pain* 6, no. 2 (1990).

39. J. K. Kiecolt-Glaser, Jean-Philippe Gouin, and Liisa Hantsoo, "Close Relationships, Inflammation, and Health," *Neuroscience and Biobehavioral Reviews* 35 (2010).

40. O. Manor and Z. Eisenbach, "Mortality after Spousal Loss: Are There Socio-demographic Differences?," *Social Science and Medicine* 56, no. 2 (2003); J. R. Moon et al., "Widowhood and Mortality: A Meta-analysis," *PLOS One* 6, no. 8 (2011); F. Elwert and N. A. Christakis, "Wives and Ex-wives: A New Test for Homogamy Bias in the Widowhood Effect," *Demography* 45, no. 4 (2008).

41. Amazingly, one study has found that married people tend to use higher-quality hospitals than those who've been widowed. They are more likely to be seen at teaching hospitals and to have shorter lengths of stay as inpatients, because their spouses act as their advocates and decision-makers as opposed to simply being health-care assistants. T. J. Iwashyna and N. A. Christakis, "Marriage, Widowhood, and Health-Care Use," *Social Science and Medicing* 57, no. 11 (2003).

42. Moon et al., "Widowhood and Mortality."

43. F. Elwert and N. A. Christakis, "The Effect of Widowhood on Mortality by the Causes of Death of Both Spouses," *American Journal of Public Health* 98, no. 11 (2008); Manor and Eisenbach, "Mortality after Spousal Loss."

44. The impact of stress and distress on cardiovascular functioning is well known, but one study led by Robert Carels specifically documents my father-in-law's experience: an emotional trauma had deregulated the rhythm of his heartbeat. Robert A. Carels, Holly Cacciapaglia, et al., "The Association between Emotional Upset and Cardiac Arrhythmia during Daily Life," *Journal of Consulting and Clinical Psychology* 71, no. 3 (2003).

45. Charlie's real recovery began when he joined a men's aqua-fitness class at the YMHA one year after his wife's death. The class gave his day structure, and the friends he met there—who all went out for

lunch after their swim class—gradually replaced the social network he had lost when his wife died. The exercise was good for his broken heart too.

46. House, Landis, and Umberson, "Social Relationships and Health"; L. F. Berkman and S. L. Syme, "Social Networks, Host Resistance, and Mortality: A Nine-Year Follow-up Study of Alameda County Residents," *American Journal of Epidemiology* 109, no. 2 (1979)"; L. F. Berkman, "Social Epidemiology: Social Determinants of Health in the United States: Are We Losing Ground?," *Annual Review of Public Health* 30 (2009); K. Orth-Gomer, A. Rosengren, and L. Wilhelmsen, "Lack of Social Support and Incidence of Coronary Heart Disease in Middle-Aged Swedish Men," *Psychosomatic Medicine* 55, no. 1 (1993).

47. Alain de Botton, *Religion for Atheists* (Toronto: McClelland & Stewart, 2012).

48. Bert Hölldobler and E. O. Wilson, *The Superorganism: The Beauty, Elegance, and Strangeness of Insect Societies* (New York: Norton, 2009).

49. Nicholas Wade, *The Faith Instinct* (New York: Penguin, 2009); David Sloan Wilson, *Darwin's Cathedral: Evolution, Religion, and the Nature of Society* (Chicago: University of Chicago Press, 2002); David Eagleman, "The Moral of the Story: Make-Believe Is More than Fun and Games," *New York Times Book Review*, August 5, 2012. The wonderful phrase "the smartest, boldest, best guys that ever were" is Jonathan Gottschall's, excerpted from the book that David Eagleman was reviewing: Jonathan Gottschall, *The Storytelling Animal: Why Stories Make Us Human* (New York: Houghton Mifflin, 2012).

   To read more about why humans evolved to have religious beliefs and rituals, see *Darwin's Cathedral*, by evolutionary biologist David Sloan Wilson, and *The Faith Instinct*, by Nicholas Wade.

50. Andrew Newberg and Mark Robert Waldman, *How God Changes Your Brain: Breakthrough Findings from a Leading Neuroscientist* (New York: Ballantine Books, 2010).

51. Michael Inzlicht et al., "Neural Markers of Religious Conviction," *Psychological Science* 29, no. 3 (2009).

52. N. I. Eisenberger, M. D. Lieberman, and K. D. Williams, "Does Rejection Hurt? An fMRI Study of Social Exclusion," *Science* 302 (2003); N. I. Eisenberger and M. D. Lieberman, "Why Rejection Hurts: A Common Neural Alarm System for Physical and Social Pain," *Trends in Cognitive Science* 8, no. 7 (2004); Inzlicht et al., "Neural markers"; Andreas Bartels and Semir Zeki, "The Neural Correlates of Maternal and Romantic Love," *Neuroimage* 21 (2004).

53. R. F. Baumeister and M.R. Leary, "The Need to Belong: Desire for Interpersonal Attachments as a Fundamental Human Motivation," *Psychological Bulletin* 117 (1995); R. F. Baumeister and Michael McKenzie, "Believing, Belonging, Meaning, and Religious Coping," *Religion, Brain and Behavior* 1, no. 3 (2011); Jonathan Haidt, *The Righteous Mind: Why Good People Are Divided by Politics and Religion* (New York: Pantheon, 2012).

54. Michael Inzlicht, Alexa Tullett, and Marie Good, "The Need to Believe: A Neuroscience Account of Religion as a Motivated Process," *Religion, Brain and Behavior* 1, no. 3 (2011); D. E. Hall, "Religious Attendance: More Cost-Effective than Lipitor?" *Journal of the American Board of Family Medicine* 19 (2006).

55. Wilson, *Darwin's Cathedral*.

56. Haidt, *The Righteous Mind*.

57. Steven Morris, "Second Life Affair Leads to Real Life Divorce," *The Guardian*, November 13, 2008; Sarah Boesveld, "No Online Sex Please, We're British," *Globe and Mail*, November 15, 2008.

58. Michael Winerip, "His 50 First Dates," *New York Times*, July 5, 2009.

59. Finkel et al., "Online Dating"; C. L. Toma, J. T. Hancock, and N. B. Ellison, "Separating Fact from Fiction: An Examination of Deceptive Self-Presentation on Online Dating Profiles," *Personality and Social Psychology Bulletin* 34 (2008).

60. I borrowed the example about wine from an interview with Dan Ariely: "Online dating sites assume that people are easy to describe on searchable attributes. They think that we're like digital cameras, that you can describe somebody by their height and weight and political affiliation and so on. But it turns out people are much more like wine. That when

you taste the wine, you could describe it, but it's not a very useful description. But you know if you like it or you don't. And it's the complexity and the completeness of the experience that tells you if you like a person or not. And this breaking into attributes turns out not to be very informative." Dan Hirschman, interview with Dan Ariely," "Big Think's Guide to 21st Century Dating," 2010, http://www.bigthink.com.

61. Paul W. Eastwick, Eli J. Finkel, and Alice H. Eagly, "When and Why Do Ideal Partner Preferences Affect the Process of Initiating and Maintaining Romantic Relationships?" *Journal of Personality and Social Psychology* 101, no. 5 (2011); Paul W. Eastwick and Eli J. Finkel, "Sex Differences in Mate Preferences Revisited: Do People Know What They Initially Desire in a Romantic Partner?" *Journal of Personality and Social Psychology* 94 (2008).

62. For more on why we're so bad at predicting what will make us happy, read Harvard's Dan Gilbert: Daniel Gilbert, *Stumbling on Happiness* (New York: Knopf, 2006).

63. Finkel et al., "Online Dating: A critical analysis from the perspective of psychological science."

64. Matching personality traits do not predict the longevity of a relationship, according to a meta-analysis of 313 studies: R. Matthew Montoya, Robert S. Horton, and Jeffrey Kirchner, "Is Actual Similarity Necessary for Attraction? A Meta-analysis of Actual and Perceived Similarity," *Journal of Social and Personal Relationships* 25, no. 6 (2008).

65. The following assertion appeared on eHarmony's website in August 2012: "Our compatibility matching models are based on 35 years of clinical experience and rigorous scientific research into which characteristics between spouses are consistently associated with the most successful relationships." Yet their matching system—which is proprietary—has neither been shared with social scientists nor tested, and no evidence is provided to substantiate such claims.

66. Bradley M. Okdie et al., "Getting to Know You: Face-to-Face versus Online Interactions," *Computers in Human Behavior* 27, no. 1 (2011); Harry T. Reis et al., "Familiarity Does Indeed Promote Attraction

in Live Interaction," *Journal of Personality and Social Psychology* 101, no. 3 (2011).

67. How and where you meet your mate matters, too. Couples who meet through people they know or through their community activities are more likely to feel buttressed by social support, and this may affect the longevity of their relationship. Couples who meet through the Internet, or other anonymous arenas, tend to feel less social support for their unions. There was a class difference; meeting through strong, face-to-face ties was more common among the middle-class, whereas meeting in anonymous cyber-settings or bars was more common among the working class. Sharon Sassler and Amanda Jayne Miller, "The Ecology of Relationships: Meeting Locations and Cohabitors' Relationship Perceptions. *Journal of Social and Personal Relationships* 31, no 2 (2014).

68. Read Tim Kreider's "True Stories: Getting Offline" at http://www.nerve.com/love-sex/true-stories/true-stories-getting-offline, to get a feeling for online dating. His charming, self-deprecatory essay is also quoted in Finkel et al., "Online Dating."

69. Michael Kesterton, "His and Hers Faces," *Globe and Mail*, April 24, 2012.

70. Montoya, Horton, and Kirchner, "Is Actual Similarity Necessary for Attraction?"; Marian Morry, M. Kito, and I. Ortiz, "The Attraction-Similarity Model and Dating Couples: Projection, Perceived Similarity, and Psychological Benefits," *Personal Relationships* 18 (2011).

71. Xun (Irene) Huang, et al., "Going My Way? The Benefits of Travelling in the Same Direction," *Journal of Experimental Social Psychology* 48 (2012).

CHAPTER 9: WHEN MONEY REALLY TALKS

1. Anne Sutherland, "Bad Luck Brought the Victims of Earl Jones Together, and Together They Have Effected Change on How White-Collar Criminals Are Dealt With," *West Island Gazette*, July 7, 2010.

2. Martin Patriquin, "'We Trusted Him,'" *Macleans*, July 29, 2009.

3. Earl Jones was released from detention after serving four years of his sentence, in March 2014, just as this book was going to press.

4. Paul Delean, "Did West Islander Pull a Madoff?," *Montreal Gazette*, July 11, 2009.

5. Tu Thanh Ha and Les Perreaux, "How Earl Jones Found His Clients," *Globe and Mail*, July 27, 2009.

6. Nicole E. Ruedy et al., "The Cheater's High: The Unexpected Affective Benefits of Unethical Behavior," paper presented at annual meeting of the Academy of Management, Boston, 2012.

7. Drake Bennett, "Confidence Game: How Imposters Like Clark Rockefeller Capture Our Trust Instantly," *Boston Globe*, August 17, 2008.

8. Edward O. Wilson, "Kin selection as the Key to Altruism: Its Rise and Fall," *Social Research* 72, no. 1 (2005); Steven Pinker, *The Better Angels of Our Nature* (New York: Viking, 2011).

9. Jerome H. Barkow, Leda Cosmides, and John Tooby, *The Adapted Mind: Evolutionary Pscyhology and the Generation of Culture* (New York: Oxford University Press, 1992); Frans de Waal, *The Age of Empathy* (New York: Three Rivers Press, 2009); M. J. O'Riain and J. U. M. Jarvis, "Colony Member Recognition and Xenophobia in the Naked Mole-Rat," *Animal Behaviour* 53 (1997).

10. Bernard Chapais, *Primeval Kinship: How Pair-Bonding Gave Birth to Human Society* (Cambridge, MA: Harvard University Press, 2008); Patrick Bélisle and Bernard Chapais, "Tolerated Co-feeding in Relation to Degree of Kinship in Japanese Macaques," *Behavior* 138 (2001).

11. Dorothy L. Cheney and Robert M. Seyfarth, *Baboon Metaphysics: The Evolution of a Social Mind* (Chicago: University of Chicago Press, 2007).

12. David C. Geary, *The Origin of Mind: Evolution of Brain, Cognition and General Intelligence* (Washington, DC: American Psychological Association, 2005); D. E. Brown, *Human Universals* (Philadelphia: Temple University Press, 1991).

13. Iris Bohnet et al., "Betrayal Aversion: Evidence from Brazil, China, Oman, Switzerland, Turkey and the United States," *American Economic Review* 98, no. 1 (2008).

14. William P. Barrett, "An Affinity for Fraud," *Forbes*, June 1, 2007.

15. Jen Cutts, "Hezbollah Embarrasssed by Fraudster," *Maclean's*, October 5, 2009.

16. J. Willis and Alexander Todorov, "First Impressions: Making Up Your Mind after 100 ms Exposure to a Face," *Psychological Science* 17 (2006).

17. Alexander Todorov et al., "Inferences of Competence from Faces Predict Election Outcomes," *Science* 308 (2005).

18. Daniel Kahneman, *Thinking Fast and Slow* (Toronto: Doubleday Canada, 2011).

19. Alexander Todorov, "Evaluating Faces on Trustworthiness," *Annals of the New York Academy of Sciences* 1124 (2008); Andrew Engell, James Haxby, and Alexander Todorov, "Implicit Trustworthiness Decisions: Automatic Coding of Face Propertics in the Human Amygdala," *Journal of Cognitive Neuroscience* 19, no. 9 (2007).

20. Willis and Todorov, "First Impressions"; Allan Mazur, Julie Mazur, and Caroline Keating, "Military Rank Attainment of a West Point Class: Effects of Cadets' Physical Features," *American Journal of Sociology* 90, no. 1 (1984).

21. Daniel S. Hamermesh and Jeff Biddle, "Beauty and the Labor Market," NBER Working Paper 4518 (Cambridge, MA: National Bureau of Economic Research, 1993); Barry Harper, "Beauty, Stature and the Labour Market: A British Cohort Study," *Oxford Bulletin of Economics and Statistics* 62 (2008); Todorov, "Evaluating Faces"; Todorov et al., "Inferences of Competence."

22. Nikolaas Oosterhof and Alexander Todorov, "The Functional Basis of Face Evaluation," *Proceedings of the National Academy of Sciences of the United States of America* 105, no. 32 (2008).

23. R. Adolphs, D. Tranel, and A. R. Damasio, "The Human Amygdala in Social Judgment," *Nature* 393 (1998); Todorov, "Evaluating Faces."

24. Todorov, "Evaluating Faces"; C. F. Bond and M. Robinson, "The Evolution of Deception," *Journal of Nonverbal Behavior* 12 (1988).

25. Nalini Ambady and Robert Rosenthal, "Thin Slices of Expressive

Behavior as Predictors of Interpersonal Consequences," *Psychological Bulletin* 111, no. 2 (1992).

26. Robert B. Cialdini, *Influence: Science and Practice* (Needham Heights, MA: Allyn and Bacon, 2001).

27. Dan Ariely, *The (Honest) Truth about Dishonesty* (New York: Harper Collins, 2012).

28. Ibid.; Francesca Gino, Shahar Ayal, and Dan Ariely, "Contagion and Differentiation in Unethical Behavior: The Effect of One Bad Apple on the Barrel," *Psychological Science* (2009).

29. Rebecca Nash, Martin Bouchard, and Aili Malm, "ERON Mortgage Corporation: Diffusion of Fraud Through Social Networks," paper presented at Third Annual Illicit Networks Workshop, Montreal, 2011.

30. R. F. Baumeister, *Is There Anything Good About Men?* (New York: Oxford University Press, 2010); Louann Brizendine, *The Female Brain* (New York: Morgan Road Books, 2006); S. E. Taylor, "Tend and Befriend: Biobehavioral Bases of Affiliation under Stress," *Current Directions in Psychological Science* 15, no. 6 (2006); David C. Geary, *Male, Female: The Evolution of Human Sex Differences* (Washington, DC: American Psychological Association, 2010); D. C. Geary et al., "Evolution and Development of Boys' Social Behavior," *Developmental Review* 23 (2003); Susan Pinker, *The Sexual Paradox: Extreme Men, Gifted Women, and the Real Gender Gap* (Toronto: Random House Canada, 2008); Eleanor Maccoby, "Gender and Relationships: A Developmental Account," *American Psychologist* 45 (1990); Jeffrey Zaslow, *The Girls from Ames* (New York: Gotham Books, 2009).

31. Deborah Tannen, *You Just Don't Understand: Women and Men in Conversation* (New York: Quill, 2001).

32. Vasyl Palchykov et al., "Sex Differences in Intimate Relationships," *Scientific Reports* 2 (2012).

33. David Geary, private communication, Heidelberg, 2010.

34. Geary, *Male, Female*; Jonathan Haidt, *The Righteous Mind: Why Good People Are Divided by Politics and Religion* (New York: Pantheon, 2012).

35. Historical statistics from R. I. M. Dunbar, *How Many Friends Does One Person Need? Dunbar's Number and Other Evolutionary Quirks* (London: Faber, 2010); Canadian Armed Forces statistics courtesy of Ethan Kraus; co-working sites: Diane Jermyn, "200 Office-Mates, One Copier: It's All about Sharing," *Globe and Mail*, November 3, 2010; Susan Pinker, "Social Links Essential for Good Work," *Globe and Mail*, November 15, 2010; Masters swim team size: Jennifer Levett, personal communication, April 24, 2013.

36. In his Connected Lives study, Canadian sociologist and pioneering network scientist Barry Wellman showed that there are no "close ties maintained solely via the internet; all meet in person at least once in a while." While Wellman would not be likely to agree that there are biologically set limits to the number of relationships one can sustain in the Internet age, his notion of a relationship is very different than Dunbar's. "People you never see or never really talk to" would not be included in your intimate social network, according to a lecture Dunbar gave at Oxford in 2011. Contrast that with Wellman's view, that "it takes little work to keep large numbers of hardly known (or long-lost) ties on your 'friend' list. While many are weak ties at the moment, they can be called upon when needed." Lee Rainie and Barry Wellman, *Networked: The New Social Operating System* (Cambridge, MA: MIT Press, 2012). My view is that those weak ties might provide the name of a good restaurant in their hometown if you're visiting, and might return an email. But regular lifts to chemotherapy, or a hot meal at their house when you need it? Probably not.

37. Sam G. B. Roberts and R. I. M. Dunbar, "The Costs of Family and Friends: An 18-Month Longitudinal Study of Relationship Maintenance and Decay," *Evolution and Human Behavior* 32 (2011).

38. R. I. M. Dunbar, "You've Got to Have (150) Friends," *New York Times*, December 25, 2010.

39. R. I. M. Dunbar, "Neocortex Size as a Constraint on Group Size in Primates," *Journal of Human Evolution* 20 (1992).

40. Dunbar, *How Many Friends*.

41. Thomas Pollet, Sam G. B. Roberts, and R. I. M. Dunbar, "Use of Social Network Sites and Instant Messaging Does Not Lead to Increased Offline Social Network Size, or to Emotionally Closer Relationships with Offline Network Members," *CyberPsychology, Behavior and Social Networking* 14, no. 4 (2011).

42. Roberts and Dunbar, "The Costs of Family and Friends"; Gerald Mollenhorst, "Networks in Context: How Meeting Opportunities Affect Personal Relationships," unpublished paper, University of Utrecht, 2009); Gerald Mollenhorst, Beate Volker, and Henk Flap, "Social Contexts and Personal Relationships: The Effect of Meeting Opportunities on Similarity for Relationships of Different Strength," *Social Networks* 30, no. 1 (2008).

43. William Taylor, "Your Call Should Be Important to Us, But It's Not," *New York Times*, February 26, 2006.

44. Daniel Kahneman et al., "A Survey Method for Characterizing Daily Life Experience: The Day Reconstruction Method," *Science* 306, no. 5702 (2004).

45. Kahneman, *Thinking Fast and Slow*.

46. Tony Hsieh, *Delivering Happiness: A Path to Profits, Passion and Purpose* (New York: Grand Central, 2010).

47. Alexandra Jacobs, "Happy Feet," *New Yorker*, September 14, 2009.

48. Zeynep Ton, "Why 'Good Jobs' Are Good for Retailers," *Harvard Business Review* 90, no. 1/2 (2012).

49. James Surowiecki, "The More the Merrier," *New Yorker*, March 26, 2012.

50. Charles Duhigg, "What Does Your Credit-Card Company Know about You?" *New York Times Magazine*, May 17, 2009.

51. Alex Pentland, "To Signal Is Human: Real-Time Data Mining Unmasks the Power of Imitation, Kith and Charisma in Our Face to Face Social Networks," *American Scientist* 98 (2010).

52. Sinan Aral, Erik Brynjolfsson, and M. Van Alstyne, "Productivity Effects of Information Diffusion in Networks," *Proceedings of the 28th Annual International Conference on Information Systems*, Montreal,

2007; Sinan Aral and M. Van Alstyne, "Networks, Information and Social Capital," paper presented at the International Conference on Network Science, New York, 2007.

53. Lynn Wu et al., "Mining Face-to-Face Interaction Networks Using Sociometric Badges: Predicting Productivity in an IT Configuration Task," *Proceedings of the 29th International Conference on Information Systems, Paris, 2008* (ICIS: 2009); Mark Granovetter, "The Strength of Weak Ties: A Network Theory Revisited," *Sociological Theory* 1 (1983).

54. Daniel Olguín Olguín, Peter A. Gloor, and Alex Pentland, "Capturing Individual and Group Behavior with Wearable Sensors," paper presented at the Association for the Advancement of Artificial Intelligence Spring Symposium, Palo Alto, CA, March 2009; Pentland, "To Signal Is Human"; Alex Pentland, *Honest Signals: How They Shape Our World* (Cambridge, MA: MIT Press, 2008).

55. Alex Pentland, "The New Science of Building Teams," *Harvard Business Review* 90, no. 4 (2012).

56. Michael Kosfeld et al., "Oxytocin Increases Trust in Humans," *Nature* 435, no. 2 (2005).

57. Gert-Jan Pepping and Erik Timmermans, "Oxytocin and the Biopsychology of Performance," *Scientific World Journal* (2012); M. W. Kraus, C. Huang, and D. Keltner, "Tactile Communication, Cooperation, and Performance: An Ethological Study of the NBA," *Emotion* 10, no. 5 (2010).

58. Susan Pinker, "The Chemical that Fosters Team Loyalty," *Globe and Mail*, January 24, 2011; Carsten K. W. De Dreu, Lindred L. Greer, and et al., "The Neuropeptide Oxytocin Regulates Parochial Altruism in Intergroup Conflict among Humans," *Science* 328, no. 5984 (2010).

CONCLUSION: CREATING THE VILLAGE EFFECT

1. *Mayberry R.F.D.* was an American television series about an idealized, fictional rural community that aired in the early seventies. R.F.D. stands for "Rural Free Delivery," which is a quaint reference to the mail

delivery system in American rural communities during the early-to-mid twentieth century.

2. Cohousing residents own their own houses or condos and don't pool their income.

3. Diane Margolis and David Entin, "Report on Survey of Cohousing Communities 2011," Cohousing Association of the United States, 2011, http://www.cohousing.org/.

4. Matt Ridley, "Human Evolution Isn't What It Used to Be," *Wall Street Journal*, May 26, 2012.

5. Christopher Lasch, *The True and Only Heaven: Progress and Its Critics* (New York: Norton, 1991).

6. D. G. Blanchflower and Andrew J. Oswald, "Well-being over Time in Britain and the USA," *Journal of Public Economics* 88 (2004); Betsey Stevenson and Justin Wolfers, "The Paradox of Declining Female Happiness," *American Economic Journal: Economic Policy* 1, no. 2 (2009); Cari Nierenberg, "Happiness Declining among Twitter Users: A Review of Billions of Tweets Shows a Drop in Global Happiness," WebMD, 2011, http://www.webmd.com/balance/news/20111222/study-happiness-has-declined-among-twitter-users-recent-years.

7. Michael Argyle, "Causes and Correlates of Happiness," in *Well-being: The Foundations of Hedonic Psychology*, ed. Daniel Kahneman, Ed Diener, and Norbert Schwarz (New York: Russell Sage Foundation, 2003); R. F. Baumeister and M.R. Leary, "The Need to Belong: Desire for Interpersonal Attachments as a Fundamental Human Motivation," *Psychological Bulletin* 117 (1995); David G. Myers, "Close Relationships and Quality of Life," in *Well-being*, ed. Kahneman, Diener, and Schwarz.

8. For more about the characteristics of "third places," see Ray Oldenburg, *The Great Good Place: Cafes, Coffee Shops, Community Centers, Beauty Parlors, General Stores, Bars, Hangouts, and How They Get You Through the Day* (New York: Paragon, 1989); Ray Oldenburg, *Celebrating the Third Place: Inspiring Stories about the "Great Good Places" at the Heart of Our Communities* (New York: Marlowe, 2000). Thanks are due to my brother Steve for introducing me to the term *meatspace*.

9. Kyungjoon Lee et al., "Does Collocation Inform the Impact of Collaboration?" *PLOS One* 5, no. 12 (2010); Jonah Lehrer, "Groupthink: The Brainstorming Myth," *New Yorker,* January 30, 2012; Greg Lindsay, "Engineering Serendipity," *New York Times,* April 7, 2013; Michelle Young, "Googleplex, Mountain View: Designing Interior Spaces at an Urban Scale," Untapped Cities, January 2, 2012, http://untappedcities. com/2012/01/02/googleplex-mountainview-designing-interior-spaces -at-an-urban-scale/; Paul Goldberger, "Exclusive Preview: Google's New Built from Scratch Googleplex," *Vanity Fair,* February 22, 2013. Another social scientist who has written persuasively about physical proximity as a catalyst for ideas and economic growth is Edward Glaeser, who writes: "The most important communications still take place in person, and electronic access is no substitute for being at the geographic center of an intellectual movement." Edward Glaeser, *Triumph of the City* (New York: Penguin, 2011).

10. Sheldon Cohen, "Social Relationships and Susceptibility to the Common Cold," in *Emotion, Social Relationships, and Health,* ed. Carol D. Ryff and M. Burton (New York: Oxford University Press, 2001); Sheldon Cohen and Denise Janicki-Deverts, "Can We Improve Our Physical Health by Altering Our Social Networks?" *Perspectives on Psychological Science* 4, no. 4 (2009).

11. Cohen and Janicki-Deverts, "Can We Improve Our Physical Health"; L. F. Berkman, "Tracking Social and Biological Experiences: The Social Etiology of Cardiovascular Disease," *Circulation* 111, no. 23 (2005); L. F. Berkman et al., "From Social Integration to Health: Durkheim in the New Millennium," *Social Science and Medicine* 51, no. 6 (2000); T. E. Seeman, "Social Ties and Health: The Benefits of Social Integration," *Annals of Epidemiology* 6, no. 5 (1996); T. Seeman, "How Do Others Get under Our Skin? Social Relationships and Health," in *Emotion, Social Relationships and Health,* ed. Carol D. Ryff and Burton H. Singer (New York: Oxford University Press, 2001).

12. R. J. Sampson, "When Disaster Strikes, It's Survival of the Sociable," *New Scientist,* May 17, 2013; Eric Klinenberg, *Heat Wave: A Social Autopsy of*

Disaster in Chicago (Chicago: University of Chicago Press, 2002); Daniel P. Aldrich, "The Power of People: Social Capital's Role in Recovery from the 1995 Kobe Earthquake," *Natural Hazards* 56 (2011).

13. K. M. Stavraky et al., "The Effect of Psychosocial Factors on Lung Cancer Mortality at One Year," *Journal of Clinical Epidemiology* 41, no. 1 (1988); Cohen, "Social Relationships and Susceptibility to the Common Cold."

14. V.P. Goby, "Personality and Online/Offline Choices," *CyberPsychology and Behavior* 9 (2006); Q. Tian, "Social Anxiety, Motivation, Self-Disclosure, and Computer-Mediated Friendship," *Communication Research* 40, no. 2 (2013).

15. Micah O. Mazurek, "Social Media Use among Adults with Autism Spectrum Disorders," *Computers in Human Behavior* 29 (2013).

16. Human Resources and Skills Development Canada, "Indicators of Well-being in Canada: School Drop-Outs," Employment and Social Development Canada, 2013, http://www4.hrsdc.gc.ca/.3ndic.1t.4r@-eng.jsp?iid=32; Patrice de Broucker, *Without a Paddle: What to Do about Canada's Young Dropouts* (Ottawa: Canadian Policy Research Networks, 2005).

17. Sarah-Maude Lefebvre, "Quebec Hides Dropout Numbers," Canoe.ca, 2012, http://cnews.canoe.ca/CNEWS/Canada/2012/02/20/19402596.html.

18. Kate Hammer, "Winning Back Dropouts with a Simple Call," *Globe and Mail*, May 31, 2012.

19. UNICEF, "Basic Education and Gender Equality: The Big Picture," February 6, 2014, http://www.unicef.org/education/index_bigpicture.html.

20. Dana Burde and Leigh Linden, "The Effect of Village-Based Schools: Evidence from a Randomized Controlled Trial in Afghanistan," NBER Working Paper 18039 (Cambridge, MA: National Bureau of Economic Research, 2012); Dana Burde and Leigh Linden, "Bringing Education to Afghan Girls: A Randomized Controlled Trial of Village-Based Schools," *Applied Economics* 5, no. 3 (2013).

21. Though I review the evidence in more detail in Chapters 6 and 7, a comparison of effects for two meta-analyses—the first of interactive book reading to stimulate literacy, the second on literacy and academic outcomes from nine one-to-one laptop programs—showed effect sizes (*d*) ranging from 0.36 to 0.72 in the interaction study and 0.17 to 0.28 in the laptop study. Suzanne Mol, Adriana G. Bus, and Maria T. de Jong, "Interactive Book Reading in Early Education: A Tool to Stimulate Print Knowledge as Well as Oral Language," *Review of Educational Research* 79, no. 2 (2009); Binbin Zheng and Mark Warschauer, "Teaching and Learning in One-to-One Laptop Environments: A Research Synthesis," paper presented at annual meeting of the American Educational Research Association, San Francisco, 2013.

    For more evidence on the benefits of parent and teacher training, see Alan Mendelsohn et al., "The Impact of a Clinic Based Literacy Intervention on Language Development in Inner-City Preschool Children," *Pediatrics* 107, no. 1 (2001); Alan Mendelsohn et al., "Do Verbal Interactions with Infants during Electronic Media Exposure Mitigate Adverse Impacts on Their Language Development as Toddlers?" *Infant and Child Development* 19 (2010); Alan Mendelsohn et al., "Primary Care Strategies for Promoting Parent–Child Interactions and School Readiness in At-Risk Families," *Archives of Pediatric Adolescent Medicine* 165, no. 1 (2011).

22. Raj Chetty, John N. Friedman, and Jonah Rockoff, "The Long-Term Impacts of Teachers: Teacher Value-Added and Student Outcomes in Adulthood," NBER Working Paper 17699 (Cambridge, MA: National Bureau of Economic Research, 2012).

23. There are a few exceptions. A laptop program designed to improve the writing skills of a thousand fifth-graders in Colorado made no difference to the group as a whole: after a year of a one-to-one laptop program taught by trained teachers, the students' writing skills were the same as they would have been without the digital technology. But when black and Hispanic students were separated out of the mix, the researchers saw some slight gains for that group. Zheng and

Warschauer, "Teaching and Learning in One-to-One Laptop Environments."

24. Ibid.; Mark Warschauer, *Learning in the Cloud* (New York: Teacher's College Press, 2011).

25. Adele Diamond and Kathleen Lee, "Interventions Shown to Aid Executive Function Development in Children 4 to 12 Years Old," *Science* 333 (2011).

26. Barack Obama, *The Audacity of Hope* (New York: Vintage, 2006).

27. Chetty, Friedman, and Rockoff, "The Long-Term Impacts of Teachers."

28. Nicholas D. Kristof, "How Mrs. Grady Transformed Olly Neal," *New York Times*, January 22, 2012.

29. Robert D. Putnam, "Requiem for the American Dream? Unequal Opportunity in America," lecture presented at the Aspen Ideas Festival, Aspen, CO, June 29, 2012; David Brooks, "The Opportunity Gap," *New York Times*, July 9, 2012; Margaret Wente, "The Long Climb from Inequality," *Globe and Mail*, July 14, 2012; Sean F. Reardon, "No Rich Child Left Behind," *New York Times*, April 28, 2013; Sean F. Riordan, "The Widening Academic Achievement Gap between the Rich and the Poor: New Evidence and Possible Explanations," in *Whither Opportunity? Rising Inequality and the Uncertain Life Chances of Low-Income Children*, ed. R. Murnane and G. Duncan (New York: Russell Sage Foundation, 2011).

30. Rachelle DeJong, "Why Do Students Drop Out of MOOCs?" Minding the Campus, November 10, 2013, http://www.mindingthecampus.com/originals/2013/11/why_do_students_drop_out_of_mo.html; Ezekiel J. Emanuel, "Online Education: MOOCs Taken by Educated Few," *Nature* 503, no. 342 (2013).

31. Matt Richtel, "A Silicon Valley School that Doesn't Compute," *New York Times*, October 22, 2011.

32. Jacob L. Vigdor and Helen F. Ladd, "Scaling the Digital Divide: Home Computer Technology and Student Achievement," NBER Working Paper 16078 (Cambridge, MA: National Bureau of Economic Research, 2010).

33. Warschauer, *Learning in the Cloud*, 96–97.

34. United States Census Bureau. "State and County Quick Facts: Miami-Dade County, Florida," 2012, http://quickfacts.census.gov/qfd/states/12/12086.html (accessed June 1, 2013).

35. Kwame Anthony Appiah, "The Art of Social Change," *New York Times*, October 22, 2010; Kwame Anthony Appiah, *The Honor Code: How Moral Revolutions Happen* (New York: Norton, 2010).

36. During a field trial lasting ten years, women visiting new mothers in rural India reduced infant deaths by 70% (in comparison with matched control villages). Abhay T. Bang et al., "Neonatal and Infant Mortality in the Ten Years (1993 to 2003) of the Gadchiroli Field Trial: Effect of Home-Based Neonatal Care," *Journal of Perinatology* 25, no. S1 (2005): S92–S107. In Youndé, Cameroon, women belonging to voluntary associations called *tontines*—which are social networks of a sort—are more likely to use condoms and encourage their use among their close friends. T. W. Valente et al., "Social Network Associations with Contraceptive Use among Cameroonian Women in Voluntary Associations," *Social Science and Medicine* 45, no. 5 (1997); Ann Swidler, "Responding to AIDS in Sub-Saharan Africa," in *Successful Societies: How Institutions and Culture Affect Health*, ed. Peter Hall and Michèle Lamont (New York: Cambridge University Press, 2009).

37. A small but clever study shows that people who are accompanied by a friend estimate a hill to be less steep compared to people assessing the same terrain who are alone. S. Schnall et al., "Social Support and the Perception of Geographical Slant," *Journal of Experimental Social Psychology* 44, no. 5 (2008); Catherine T. Shea, Erin K. Davisson, and Grainne Fitzsiomons, "Riding Other People's Coattails: Individuals with Low Self-Control Value Self-Control in Other People," *Psychological Science* 24, no. 5 (2013).

Image and Figure Credits

p. 5 Photograph courtesy of the author

p. 15 Author's sociogram by Yanick Charette

p. 21 Photograph of YMCA Masters' team at Canadian National Championships courtesy of Robin Berlyn

p. 28 Isolated and group-living rats from Figure B, in Martha K. McClintock, Suzanne D. Conzen, Sarah Gehlert, et al., 2005. "Mammary Cancer and Social Interactions: Identifying Multiple Environments that Regulate Gene Expression Throughout the Life Span," *Journals of Gerontology* Series B, 60B, p. 36. Reprinted with the permission of Sarah Gehlert.

p. 36 Sylvie La Fontaine's sociogram by Yanick Charette

p. 41 John McColgan's sociogram by Yanick Charette

p. 49 Bronzetti from left to right: Traveller with staff, and praying woman: reprinted with the permission of Scala/White Images/Art Resource, NY. Priest with conical hat, photograph by Gianni Dagli Orti, reprinted with the permission of The Art Archive at Art Resource

p. 54 Photograph courtesy of the author

p. 69 Graph adapted from Figure 6, in Julianne Holt-Lunstad, Timothy Smith, and J. Bradley Layton, 2010. "Social Relationships and Mortality Risk: A Meta-analytic Review," *PLoS Medicine*, 7 (7), p. 14. Reprinted with the permission of Julianne Holt-Lunstad.

p. 70 Photograph courtesy of Giovanni Pes

p. 78 Photograph of "Tuke" at Kibale Park courtesy of Jessica Hartel

p. 96 John McColgan's second degree sociogram by Yanick Charette

p. 104 "Figure of the Week," Amstettner Anzeiger, April 18, 1943. From the University of Vienna Library. In Volkhard Knigge et al, *Forced*

Labor: The Germans, The Forced Laborers, and the War. Weimar 2010. Reprinted with the permission of the Jewish Museum of Berlin

p. 110 Photograph courtesy of Jennifer Levett

p. 133 'Imitation of facial and manual gestures by human neonates.' From A. N. Meltzoff & M. K. Moore, *Science*, 1977. Reprinted with the permission of Andrew Meltzoff and The American Association for the Advancement of Science.

p. 145 Photograph courtesy of the author.

p. 172 "She thinks it's a touchscreen," Copyright Emily Flake, reprinted with the permission of The New Yorker Collection/The Cartoon Bank.

p. 178 Photograph courtesy of Daniel Olguín Olguín, who is pictured wearing the sociometric badge.

p. 240 Images of Amy Taylor, David Pollard and their avatars reprinted with the permission of SWNS.

p. 261 Facial array adapted from Figure 3, in Alexander Todorov and Nikolaas N. Oosterhof, 2011. "Modeling Social Perception in Faces." *IEEE Signal Processing Magazine*, p.121. Reprinted with the permission of Alexander Todorov

p. 262 Photograph of Salah Ezzedine reprinted with the permission of the European Pressphoto Agency. Photograph of Earl Jones courtesy of Ginny Nelles